"Engaging, suspenseful, and often heartbreaking... This stirring account is a testimony to [Vogel's] continuing work as a strong advocate for America's farmers."　　　　　　　　　　　　　　　　　　　　　*—Booklist*

"An enjoyable true-life legal drama on par with *Erin Brockovich*."
　　　　　　　　　　　　　　　　　　　　　　　　—Library Journal

"Vogel is a gifted writer, weaving history, politics and vivid descriptions of the people and landscape with personal challenges... *The Farmer's Lawyer* will leave readers inspired as she details their fight for truth, justice and family farms in the 1980s."　　　　　　　　　　　　　　　*—Shelf Awareness*

"An engrossing legal saga."　　　　　　　　　　*—Publishers Weekly*

"Essential reading for any ag lawyer, farmer, lender or anyone who has anything to do with agriculture."　　　　　　　　　　*—Des Moines Register*

"Remarkable... An advocate's tale of fighting callous bureaucrats and cold-hearted prosecutors, while struggling to keep the lights on in her own home."
　　　　　　　　　　　　　　　—The Christian Science Monitor

"This is my kind of story—the young, inexperienced lawyer facing big odds. It's remarkably well told and heartfelt. I really enjoyed it."　　*—John Grisham*

"*The Farmer's Lawyer*, both an exquisitely written American saga and a trove of lived research, might serve as the definitive document of the 1980s farm crisis that in some ways never ended. Sarah Vogel's heroic battle on behalf of family farmers was historic—and has never been more relevant."
　　　　　　　　　　　　　　—Sarah Smarsh, author of Heartland

"Riveting. [*The Farmer's Lawyer*'s] characters amount to a new pantheon of heroes—author Sarah Vogel as well as the white and Native American farmers

whose dogged righteousness prevails and inspires. I am humbled, heartened, and moved."   —Elizabeth Fenn, Pulitzer Prize–winning author of
Encounters at the Heart of the World

"Sarah Vogel's passion to save the family farm comes through in *The Farmer's Lawyer*, which is not only a genuine and brilliant story, but a necessary one."
                    —Stephanie Land, author of *Maid*

"Sarah Vogel is a tireless advocate, and *The Farmer's Lawyer* is a powerful account about her never-ending pursuit of justice."
                    —Dan Barber, author of *The Third Plate*

"The struggle for justice for farmers is as old as the American story. No one has written a braver or better chapter than Sarah Vogel. She recounts it here, with all the historical perspective, legal genius, and righteous passion that made her the great champion of the women and men who work the land."
        —John Nichols, author of *The Fight for the Soul of the Democratic Party*

"A fascinating political history about farming in America, a gripping personal story about one person battling a vast, unjust system, and a clear-eyed investigation of the discriminatory systems and policies that drove so many family farmers out of business."   —Megan Kimble, author of *Unprocessed*

"The most important book about the practical issues farmers face that I have ever read."

                    —Dr. Frederick L. Kirschenmann, distinguished fellow
                    for the Leopold Center for Sustainable Agriculture
                    and president of the board of directors, Stone Barns

The Farmer's Lawyer

THE NORTH DAKOTA NINE AND THE FIGHT TO SAVE THE FAMILY FARM

SARAH VOGEL

BLOOMSBURY PUBLISHING

NEW YORK • LONDON • OXFORD • NEW DELHI • SYDNEY

BLOOMSBURY PUBLISHING
Bloomsbury Publishing Inc.
1385 Broadway, New York, NY 10018, USA

BLOOMSBURY, BLOOMSBURY PUBLISHING, and the Diana logo are trademarks
of Bloomsbury Publishing Plc

First published in the United States 2021
This paperback edition published 2023

Although this is a work of nonfiction, the author has used pseudonyms for certain individuals to
protect their privacy. She has used original documents (such as court transcripts and letters)
when available, and otherwise has reconstructed dialogue to the best of her recollection.

Bloomsbury Publishing Plc does not have any control over, or responsibility for, any third-party
websites referred to or in this book. All internet addresses given in this book were correct at the
time of going to press. The author and publisher regret any inconvenience caused if addresses
have changed or sites have ceased to exist, but can accept no responsibility for any such changes.

ISBN: HB: 978-1-63557-526-2; PB: 978-1-63973-192-3; EBOOK: 978-1-63557-525-5

LIBRARY OF CONGRESS CATALOGING-IN-PUBLICATION DATA IS AVAILABLE

2 4 6 8 10 9 7 5 3 1

Typeset by Westchester Publishing Services
Printed and bound in the U.S.A.

To find out more about our authors and books visit www.bloomsbury.com and sign up
for our newsletters.

Bloomsbury books may be purchased for business or promotional use. For information on
bulk purchases please contact Macmillan Corporate and Premium Sales Department at
specialmarkets@macmillan.com.

This book is dedicated to the farmers of America,
the ones who feed us all.

The great cities rest upon our broad and fertile prairies.
Burn down your cities and leave our farms, and your cities will
spring up again as if by magic; but destroy our farms and the grass
will grow in the streets of every city in the country.

—WILLIAM JENNINGS BRYAN, FROM A SPEECH DELIVERED
AT THE 1896 DEMOCRATIC NATIONAL CONVENTION

No cracked earth, no blistering sun, no burning wind, no grasshoppers,
are a permanent match for the indomitable American farmers and
stockmen and their wives and children who have carried on through
desperate days and inspire us with their self-reliance, their tenacity and
their courage. It was their fathers' task to make homes; it is their task to
keep those homes; it is our task to help them with their fight.

—PRESIDENT FRANKLIN DELANO ROOSEVELT,
SEPTEMBER 6, 1936, FIRESIDE CHAT

CONTENTS

CAST OF CHARACTERS

* Indicates lead plaintiffs in *Coleman v. Block*, also known as the North Dakota Nine
** Indicates defendants in *Coleman v. Block*

THE FARMERS

North Dakota farmers

Dwight Coleman*—cattle and grain (Dunseith, ND)

Lester and Sharon Crows Heart*—beef cattle and grain (Fort Berthold Indian Reservation, ND)

Russel and Anna Mae Folmer*—grain, beef cattle, dairy (Wing, ND)

George and June Hatfield*—dairy and grain (Ellendale, ND)

Don and Diane McCabe*—dairy (Dickey, ND)

Richard and Marlene DeLare—beef cattle and grain (Minot, ND)

Chuck Perry—dairy (New Salem, ND)

Montana farmers

Tom and Anna Nichols—hog farmers (Wolf Point, MT)

Ralph and Kay Clark—ranchers (Jordan, MT)

THE LAWYERS

Sarah Vogel—the farmer's lawyer and the author

Robert Vogel—the author's father, former U.S. Attorney and North Dakota Supreme Court Justice

Allan Kanner—class action expert for *Coleman*, then based in Philadelphia
Burt Neuborne—National Litigation Director for the ACLU in New York City
Dale Reesman—from tiny law firm in rural Boonville, MO

THE GOVERNMENT

Ronald Reagan—President of the United States
David Stockman—Director of the Office of Management and Budget
John Block**—Secretary of Agriculture
Charles Shuman**—National Administrator of Farmers Home Administration
Ralph Leet**—Director of North Dakota Farmers Home Administration
Rodney Webb—U.S. Attorney for the State of North Dakota
Gary Annear—Assistant U.S. Attorney representing USDA in *Coleman v. Block*
Arthur Goldberg—Attorney, Department of Justice, Civil Division

THE JUDGE

Bruce M. Van Sickle—U.S. District Court Judge based in Bismarck, ND

FOREWORD BY WILLIE NELSON

One thing I love about being "on the road again" is the chance I have to travel the highways and back roads of this country. On those trips, I meet good people in cities and small towns who share their stories with me. Across the heartland, during the early 1980s, I learned of a problem so important to me that I've stayed involved in the fight for family farmers ever since. During that time, family farmers were losing their farms—and with them, their homes— at an alarming rate. Some farmers took their lives in the face of the possibility of losing their livelihoods, their identities. Hundreds of thousands of farm families were pushed from the land in just a matter of years. Agricultural legacies passed down through generations were dashed to pieces with the strike of a gavel in courthouses and at farm auctions across the heartland.

To me, it wasn't just a disaster for those folks directly affected. It was a deep crisis of identity for our country. Just who were we to allow this to happen? How could we stand by while families suffered terrible losses—of their liveli- hoods, their land, their homes, their pasts, and their futures? And what larger suffering would this crisis bring to our landscape, our rural communities, our democracy . . . our entire country? I didn't know the answers, but I knew that it was important to ask the questions.

In September of 1985, John Mellencamp, Neil Young, and I came forward in the only way we knew: to organize a concert for family farmers. We called on the help of our friends, and more than eighty artists played for family farmers at Farm Aid on September 22. Neil, John, and I didn't know at the time that we were starting an organization; we merely planned to raise awareness about the problem and money to help fix it. As artists, we did what we could, using music to help in some way—lending our microphones, our stages, our platforms. I believe that every one of us—no matter how big or small our voice—has that power. You don't need to know everything to stand up and say, "Hey, this isn't right." This just might be the greatest superpower—and responsibility—we each have.

This standing up to say, "This isn't right!" is just what Sarah Vogel did in the 1980s, though in her case, she had the expertise to do something very specific about it. To me, Sarah is one of the heroes of the farm movement. It took guts to stand up to our government and put her own personal security on the line. It took brilliance, too, and she used hers to find a winning legal strategy that changed the course of history. We thank Sarah for that, and for her commitment to advocating for family farmers to this day, including working tirelessly to make sure that all family farmers receive equitable and fair treatment from the U.S. Department of Agriculture.

Though our careers couldn't be more different, Sarah and I are cut from a similar cloth. We were both raised with a deep respect for agriculture and the people who do it. Drawing on those strong roots, when she was called upon to make many sacrifices to stand up for farm families, she did it faithfully. The results of her effort can still be seen today in the thousands of farm families who were able to stay on the land thanks to her landmark class action lawsuit on behalf of family farmers against the most formidable opponent: the U.S. government.

The Farmer's Lawyer tells a story that is every bit as gripping as a good old-fashioned Western film—a genre I know a thing or two about. It takes place in the West, specifically in North Dakota, a state notable for its historic support of its agricultural producers and populist politics. It teaches us about our history, illuminating the plot at the top levels of government to drive out independent family producers and corporatize our agricultural system. It reflects our current politics, mirroring today's relentless and singular focus by many on Capitol Hill to slash government spending at the expense of people's survival. Sarah and her farmer clients, the North Dakota Nine, are the good guys going up against the bad guys, who can be traced from the local Farmers Home Administration office right up to the highest Reagan administration officials in the White House. Like the cowboys who were my childhood heroes, Sarah lives the ideals that I hold dear: you live your life with loyalty, you fight for the right side, and you protect your own. This is a true underdog story, thankfully—for farmers and all of us—with a perfect Hollywood ending.

The Farmer's Lawyer is a compelling personal story, in addition to being an important history lesson. But even more crucially, it's a warning to help us head off the next possible farm crisis. From her place as legal expert, farm advocate, and rural community member, Sarah shares the challenges that farmers continue to face, including a changing climate and the ever-increasing power of corporate consolidation. While the farm crisis of the 1980s has ended, in part thanks to the work of the farmer's lawyer, Sarah Vogel, it is no easier to be a farmer in our country. In fact, it's likely even more difficult today. But as the climate rapidly changes and food production faces extreme swings, we need people who are farmers and stewards of the land if we're going to have the means of production for food that sustains us and our soil, water, and climate.

The work of Farm Aid and of the greater family farm movement of which we're part is to inspire a new generation of farmers and farm advocates who stand and say, "We're still not treating our farmers right!" I'm grateful for this important book for its inspiring call to action to each of us to do what we can to strengthen family farmers and stand up for the kind of agriculture that delivers good, healthful food, strong rural communities, and the clean soil, water, and air that helps to mitigate climate change and contribute to the health and well-being of us all. And I'm grateful to you, reader, for picking up this book to learn about a hero I'm proud to consider a friend and some of the brave farmers who fought for their livelihoods and a better future for us all.

PREFACE

The Farmer's Lawyer is a memoir of a lawsuit I brought against the federal government during a period now known as the 1980s farm crisis. During those hard times, I drew inspiration from lawyers and political leaders who helped farmers survive the Great Depression of the 1930s.

Most Americans learned about the Great Depression in school, and many have read *The Grapes of Wrath*, but few people realize the savior of the Joad family was a little-known federal agency called the Resettlement Administration. Almost no Americans know that this same federal agency, under less compassionate management, played a significant role, fifty years later, in the 1980s farm crisis, which was characterized by farm foreclosures, farmer protests, and a devastating increase in farmer suicide. Unless you have seen the movie *Country*, or watched a Farm Aid concert, you might not even know that there *was* an '80s farm crisis.

But it did happen. I lived through it. And I fear we are in another farm crisis today, caused by years of farmers growing crops and raising livestock below their cost of production, exacerbated by natural disasters and the Covid-19 pandemic.

We can all picture a quintessential "family farm": the red barn, the white frame house with potted geraniums on the front porch, cows and horses grazing on meadows, and tidy green fields stretching out from the homestead. For generations, farms like these—middle-sized farms operated and owned by real people, not corporations—have been disappearing.

The number of American farms peaked in 1935 at six million; between 1935 and 2012, we lost four million farms.[1] The hardest-hit category of farmers has been the midsize family-owned-and-run farms. The largest farms have grown larger; 75 percent of all agriculture sales now come from just 5 percent of operations.[2] Very small farmers can survive with off-farm income, but full-time, middle-sized family farmers—the historic backbone of rural America—are in danger of extinction.

They have been operating at a loss for years. And then it got worse: a disastrous trade war with China, severe weather, continued exploitation by agribusinesses, topped off by the Covid-19 pandemic. Corporate agriculture can afford lawyers and lobbyists to protect them, while family farmers are forced to either give up voluntarily, or be pushed out involuntarily.

Of course, the ongoing loss of family farm agriculture doesn't affect only farmers. It hurts the people and economies in rural communities across America.

I never thought that our present farm crisis would come as soon as the 2020s. There was a fifty-year gap between the 1930s and 1980s farm crises, but this one is occurring on a faster trajectory. Further, it seems likely that the farm crisis of the 2020s might be worse than its predecessors because it will coexist and overlap with climate change, hunger and food insecurity, unemployment, multiple federal, state, and local budget shortfalls, a "red state" and "blue state" political divide, and the economic and social aftershocks of the terrible worldwide Covid-19 pandemic.

I can't fathom how we solve any of these crises without ensuring that our historic system of family farm agriculture endures and thrives. We have to develop solutions "from the ground up." If there is a cataclysmic decline in family farm agriculture in the United States, it will have a devastating ripple effect and hamper recovery in every part of the economy. This dire prophecy should not be dismissed out of hand, as were Cassandra's predictions in Greek mythology.

This memoir tells the story of ordinary citizens who stuck together to fight for a moral economy and fair treatment from their government. I hope it will inspire readers who are working to remedy injustice and disparities in their own lives and communities.

PROLOGUE: THE CALL

In the summer of 1983, I was thirty-seven years old, the single mother of a young son, working to win the case of my life. All over the country, farmers were in crisis, drowning in debt, on the verge of losing everything. My phone never stopped ringing. I had seen a man who'd been farming for thirty years break down and cry helplessly in my office. I had watched younger men choke up over the death of their dreams. For two hours, a mother of seven wept silently while her husband haltingly explained their troubles. These farmers' bank accounts had been frozen, their income seized, leaving nothing to pay the doctor or the electricity bill. I had witnessed too many good, brave people who believed in hard work and sacrifice brought to their knees by an agency of the federal government.

They called me the farmer's lawyer.

For a year, I had been working on a class action lawsuit with nine named plaintiffs on behalf of eighty-four hundred family farmers in North Dakota who had borrowed from the Farmers Home Administration, an agency of the U.S. Department of Agriculture. Many of these farmers were being threatened with the loss of their homes and livelihoods. I'd decided on a class action lawsuit because my nine lead plaintiffs were getting beaten up by the government, and they represented thousands more who were suffering similar fates.

I had never wanted to be a trial lawyer—I was too shy. I was a "writing" lawyer. I loved the grunt work of legal research. I loved developing my theories and putting my arguments down on paper. I spent long days and nights at the library, researching laws that had been passed in the 1930s to protect farmers during the Great Depression.

On a Sunday night in the middle of September, after we had our mac and cheese, I brought my four-year-old son, Andrew, back to the office with me, as I did many nights. Andrew was an adorable blond, blue-eyed kid, smart and imaginative. He was convinced he had magical powers and I tended to agree. Andrew's favorite thing to do was to "write" like his mom, and he set himself up with pens, pencils, and crayons, occasionally showing me the "words" that wavered across scrap paper, calendars, and occasionally the documents on my desk. While he did his work, I did mine. When Andrew's bedtime approached, I set up a little nest with a quilt and his blankie under my desk. The desk was wonderful, solid oak with drawers on either side. It had been built by a grateful farmer client who couldn't afford to pay me.

Most of my clients couldn't pay me. During the two years I'd been working for broke farmers, I'd racked up $50,000 in personal debt. I lost my house and Andrew and I had to move into my parents' basement. I abandoned my private practice to work out of my father's law office.

I was up against a huge federal agency that was represented by the nation's biggest law firm: the Department of Justice. Department of Justice lawyers didn't like to lose—and they were used to getting their way. They were a tough and relentless adversary. I knew I could never outmuscle them. The only way to win was to outwork them.

I'd spent weeks writing two huge legal briefs, arguing why FmHA's ruthless practice of denying farm families funds for food, electricity, feed for their animals, and other essential living and operating expenses deprived farmers of their due process rights under the U.S. Constitution. Our final hearing was scheduled for September 20, less than forty-eight hours away.

Despite it all, I felt buoyed with confidence, as I mentally rehearsed the oral argument I would make in front of the judge in two days. The hardest part of the case was behind me.

Late on Monday afternoon, I was going through a few last-minute edits before I got on the road when the phone rang. One of the secretaries told me it was Lynn Boughey, the judge's law clerk. That was strange. It was unusual for court personnel to call lawyers.

"Hi, Lynn," I said. "How are you?" Feeling guilty that I hadn't gotten my brief to the judge earlier, I said I'd have copies to give him in person the next morning.

"That's not why I'm calling," he said. "I wanted to find out which witnesses you were bringing to the trial tomorrow."

Witnesses to the trial tomorrow? That couldn't be right. Just a few months earlier, I had sat in a conference room where the assistant U.S. attorney for USDA, Gary Annear, and I had agreed to wrap up the case without witnesses, relying on paperwork and one final hearing.

"Witnesses?" I asked. I heard my voice come out faint as a child's.

"Yes, witnesses." Lynn proceeded to list those Annear planned to bring. They were names I knew all too well. I'd deposed them all: the state director of Farmers Home, who signed off on all the loan accelerations, like the one sent to my client Dwight Coleman in mid-December that demanded full payment of more than $300,000 on Christmas Eve. And the district director who said my middle-aged client Russel Folmer had failed to operate his farm "in a husband-like manner" when he'd been farming successfully since he was sixteen years old. As Lynn read the names of the government witnesses, I began to shake.

I took a couple of deep breaths. "I'll be bringing my clients as witnesses," I said. "See you tomorrow."

Not only had I never done a trial in my life—I'd never even attended one. My only experience in court was standing in front of a judge in a courtroom and saying things like "As I stated in my brief on page two . . ." At law school, I'd done moot court as an extracurricular and I remember hearing a loud *bang bang bang* while I was making my oral argument in front of the student judges. The sound was my trembling hands gripping the edges of the lectern and rattling it against the floor. I got an F in my civil procedure class because NYU was shut down during antiwar protests and I thought I didn't have to study for final exams.

I had to find a trial lawyer immediately. But first I needed to find a babysitter for what could be a multiday trial. I called my mom to see if she could watch Andrew—not just overnight, but for several days.

"Sure," she said. "Happy for the company."

Relieved, I turned to my next challenge: finding a trial lawyer.

My father was the obvious choice. He was reputed to be the best trial lawyer in North Dakota. He'd done hundreds of trials and even taught trial advocacy at the University of North Dakota. But there was a problem: my dad hadn't been involved in the nitty-gritty of the case. He supported me by paying my salary, and worrying about me, and occasionally answering questions about federal court procedures, but he didn't know the details of this case enough to take the lead on this trial.

I immediately ran across the hall. "Dad, Annear pulled a fast one. It's going to be a real trial tomorrow, can you at least come with me?"

But it was impossible. He had to be in court in Fargo.

I spun around and went back to my desk to call for help. First I tried my co-counsel Burt Neuborne, the litigation director at the ACLU, in New York City. I told the secretary who answered the phone that it was urgent.

"Burt!" I said. "You have to help. There's a trial tomorrow and I just learned that Annear is bringing witnesses. Can you come?"

Oh, how Burt wanted to help me, but he couldn't. He said he had another case in court tomorrow and that I should try calling Allan.

Allan Kanner was my class action expert from Philadelphia. He was only twenty-seven years old, but he had already won a huge victory for the Three Mile Island disaster victims and was a sought-after expert on class actions.

"For sure!" Allan said he would help me. He said he'd grab a cab to the airport and catch the next flight to Bismarck.

Next, I needed witnesses. I called my clients in order of distance from their farms to Bismarck. First, Dwight Coleman, who lived near the Canadian border, almost two hundred miles north of the courthouse. Dwight had no phone of his own, but I reached his mother at the hardware store in Dunseith just before closing time. I told her, "Dwight needs to be in Bismarck tonight. We have a trial tomorrow. It might last for days." I told her he could stay at my sister's house and gave the address. "Tell him to wear his good clothes."

I called Don and Diane McCabe, though I didn't have high hopes they would make it. They still had cows, and cows needed to be milked twice a day or else there was a danger of mastitis and infection. And they had little kids. Did they even have gas money?

"Hello?" Diane answered.

"It's Sarah. I just found out we have a trial tomorrow. I know it's late notice, but do you think you could come to Bismarck?" I asked.

"Oh, Sarah, I don't think we can make it," Diane said. "It's supposed to rain and Don has to get the hay up. If we don't, it will rot."

"I understand."

"Hang in there," Diane said. "Sometimes there's light at the end of the tunnel."

Lester and Sharon Crows Heart couldn't come either. Because Farmers Home had seized all their farming income and made them sell their cattle, Lester had taken a job at the gas plant in Beulah and couldn't get off work.

I called George and June Hatfield and Russel and Anna Mae Folmer. They said they would be there bright and early. In the morning, I would have to somehow prepare my clients to be witnesses, though all I could think to do was have them reread their own affidavits and get ready for questions from Annear insinuating that their farm troubles were the result of their "bad management" after Farmers Home had done everything to help them.

My phone rang. It was Allan.

"There aren't any connections that will get me to Bismarck in time," he said.

I slumped in my chair, utterly deflated. "What should I do?" I asked.

Allan paused for a few seconds.

"I've always had good luck calling the other side's witnesses first," he said. "It throws the lawyer for the other side off their stride. They frigging hate it! Why don't you try that?"

I closed my eyes. I knew exactly who I would call as my first witness: the self-righteous North Dakota state director of Farmers Home.

I went outside, into the gap between our office building and the small art gallery next door. Though the wind was cold and biting, I managed to light a cigarette. I stood there, puffing furiously and shivering, mentally preparing for my first trial.

PART I   The Sowing

CHAPTER 1

The Platform

My life began with an eighty-mile trip along a two-lane highway. My parents, Bob and Elsa, and my two-year-old sister, Mary, were in the car. It was perfectly sensible to leave a couple of days in advance of my anticipated due date; after all, it was May, and who knew what the weather might be like when my mother's contractions started.

North Dakota is as far inland as it is possible to be in the United States. From Fargo, North Dakota's biggest city, on the eastern edge of the state, a crow must fly east 1,210 miles to reach the Statue of Liberty. From its western edge, near the incongruously named town of Beach, the crow would need to fly 1,012 miles west to reach the cliffs of the Pacific Ocean.

North Dakota is not just in the middle of the United States—it is the center of the North American continent. There is a famous (to North Dakotans at least) fifteen-foot rock obelisk in front of a gas station in Rugby, North Dakota, with an engraved sign boldly proclaiming GEOGRAPHIC CENTER OF NORTH AMERICA.

A continental divide dissects North Dakota, separating two immense watersheds. From the northeastern side of the state, water flows north to the Arctic Ocean Watershed, but from the rest of North Dakota, water flows south to the Gulf of Mexico Watershed. North Dakotans like to brag about their state (the World's Biggest Holstein Cow, the World's Biggest Walleye Fish, the World's

Biggest Buffalo), but this continental divide is featureless. It would be unknown except for the big federal sign on Interstate 94 that announces YOU ARE NOW CROSSING THE CONTINENTAL DIVIDE, in the middle of a vast area of almost flat prairie. Most travelers probably take this as a weird North Dakota joke, like the highway billboards in the 1980s that read WELCOME TO NORTH DAKOTA / MOUNTAIN REMOVAL PROJECT COMPLETED.

North Dakota has the population of a medium-sized city. In 2019, the state was home to an estimated 762,000 people.[1] One of North Dakota's most famous expatriates, the journalist Eric Sevareid, called North Dakota "a large, rectangular blank spot in the nation's mind."[2]

Any North Dakotan traveling out of state who says that he or she is from North Dakota will almost invariably hear, "Oh, I've been to Mount Rushmore! It's wonderful!" When the North Dakotan patiently replies, "Actually, Mount Rushmore is in *South* Dakota," an awkward silence ensues while the new acquaintance searches for something, anything, to say about North Dakota.

In North Dakota, a "city" is any settlement of more than two hundred people. Garrison, where I lived until second grade, was a big city with about nineteen hundred people.[3] It served the surrounding countryside with grain elevators, farm supply stores, stockyard, banks, and a single lawyer—my father.

North Dakota's economy depends on agriculture. The motto on the North Dakota coat of arms is "Strength from the Soil." I was raised on the near-religious dogma that the way of life exemplified by family farming was the basis of American culture and the very foundation of our democracy. But we Vogels weren't farmers anymore. As far as I knew, the last time my relatives had farmed was back in Norway. I grew up as a town kid in a farm state.

When my parents moved to Garrison on August 26, 1943, it was big news in the local paper: GARRISON HAS AN ATTORNEY. ROBERT VOGEL MOVES HERE. (The paper made no mention of Elsa Vogel's arrival.)

My dad had large, luminous brown eyes and a high forehead. As an admiring child, I felt that his forehead meant he had a bigger brain than other people. He was five feet ten in shoes, but his hands looked as if they belonged to a giant. When he picked up a pen, his fingers were so big that the pen looked like a miniature pen. I have inherited those hands; I call them "Norwegian milker's hands."

My mother almost never spoke of her childhood in Dawson, a small town in Minnesota, but from stray comments over the years, we pieced together that her father had been a talented carpenter and a superb violinist, but her mother had died young and the kids had scattered far and wide. When she reached the big city of Minneapolis, she transformed herself from Elsie Myrtle Mork into Elsa Marie Mork. Elsa Marie suited her; she had vivid blue eyes and thick red "Viking" hair that in later years she dyed a dull brown (she said redheads suffered discrimination among Norwegians, as they were supposedly ill-tempered).

In Garrison, my parents first lived in a second-floor apartment above my father's office. Mary was born in May 1944 and I was born in May 1946. My given name was Sarah May Vogel, but everyone called me Sally. By then my father had bought a little frame house on a bare plot of land about three blocks from the city center. He busily planted trees around the perimeter of the lot to try to break the constant wind and provide shade.

When my mother came to North Dakota, I think she missed trees the most. Minnesota is full of natural forests and is the land of ten thousand lakes. But the Great Plains are mostly treeless. Apart from the river bottomlands and a few areas like the Turtle Mountains, almost every tree in North Dakota has been planted and nurtured by a human hand. The trees march in stiff rows called shelter belts up and down the borders of fields, and cemeteries always have pines guarding the graves of ancestors whose descendants left for more hospitable places. Most of these trees were planted in the 1930s by the Civilian Conservation Corps or the Works Progress Administration to prevent another Dust Bowl. Trees are precious. North Dakota has a law that if anyone purposefully damages a tree on another person's property, that person is subject to a lawsuit and the victim can recover treble damages.

Living in Garrison provided great professional and political opportunities for my father, and he was busy morning to night. Garrison may have been lonely and isolating for my mother, but it was idyllic for us kids. From a very young age we could go downtown to wander the aisles of the five-and-ten-cent store. We could leave town altogether and go to the prairie (a few short blocks away), where we'd lie down on the slope of a hill, our bodies cushioned by soft scented grasses, and gaze at the ocean-blue sky that rose so vastly above us. We watched fat white cumulus clouds float at tremendous speed from one end of the sky to the other, calling out, "There's a dragon!"

"I see a camel!"

"A boat."

When my brother Frank was born in June 1949, Mary and I took him with us to the prairie in a little red wagon. Our long summer days (at midsummer, the sun does not set until after ten) were punctuated only by mothers calling their children to come home to eat. In the daytime, we watched dragonflies. At night, we tried to catch the fireflies that lit up the yard. We never wore sunscreen. There were no televisions, but there was a bookmobile.

When my father read to us from Kipling's *Just So Stories*, *Winnie-the-Pooh*, or other classic tales that we already knew by heart, Mary, Frank, and I would sit as close to him as possible.

"Winnie-the-Pooh suddenly felt . . ."

"Eleven o'clockish!" we all chimed in. We were not a physically demonstrative family, and reading was perhaps the only Nordic way to touch, be close, and be together.

For recreation, we'd drive to the edge of town to watch the railroad train coming in with a huge plume of smoke and the deafening shriek of a train whistle as the conductor saw us kids standing by the parked car. Sometimes we drove down a long gravel road that disappeared into a great gray lake with bobbing debris on its surface and muddy shores.

"Daddy, why does the road go into the water?" I asked.

"It's because of the dam. The river has been stopped and it's making a lake."

My father stared into the distance, while we kids tried and failed to make stones skip on the choppy surface. I was too young to understand the engineering of the dam, but I would later learn how the new lake flooded the fertile land our Native American neighbors had been farming for centuries.

We kids often went on road trips with my father to political meetings and conventions. These trips were my education on North Dakota. As a kid, I became suddenly and violently motion sick if I read so much as one line of a book, magazine, or comic, or even "Mars Bar" on a candy label. Everyone in my family was terrified to sit near me, so I was given the privileged front passenger seat next to the open window. My father would fight the boredom of these long drives by talking to me about all aspects of North Dakota history, geography, sociology, and politics.

To my father, the landscape was never boring. In the spring, we watched as a farmer on a tractor plowed a field, leaving furrows of black ground behind him. Flocks of pure-white gulls swooped and dived behind the plow in search of whatever it was that was being uncovered. It seemed to me that the gulls were dancing in joy at the beauties of spring after a long, hard winter. As the crops grew in the rich black soil, the fields would gradually be touched by pale green, and then overnight it seemed everything was bursting with life. As the days grew longer, the wheat fields gradually turned from vivid green to a gorgeous gold. When the winds sweep over those fields, the heads of the wheat dip and rise in patterns exactly like waves on a lake: the "amber waves" of "America the Beautiful." Even from the ground level of a speeding car, the mix of crops (wheat, oats, flax, corn, barley) in tidy square fields looked like a patchwork quilt.

My father—like all North Dakotans—believed that a healthy family farm economy was central to every aspect of life in North Dakota. Farmers were the reason for the towns; they were the reason for the farm-to-market highways; they were the reason why we had electricity everywhere in the state; they were the most valued citizens of North Dakota.

He told the dramatic story of how the railroads and the Minneapolis grain dealers had used devious marketing techniques to steal from hardworking, honest North Dakota farmers until the farmers rose in rebellion in 1917 and, in the most fascinating but little-known political revolution in America's history, formed their own political party, the Nonpartisan League. He assured me that I had been a member of the Nonpartisan League since the day of my birth.

"Remember this: You are Sally Vogel, and all Vogels are proud Nonpartisan Leaguers!"

He inoculated me against what enemies of the League might say by telling me that the League's political enemies who had captured the state's major newspapers, the Fargo *Forum* and the *Bismarck Tribune*, routinely lied about the League. He also told me how most North Dakota history books were slanted and didn't cover the "real" history of the League and its role within the State of North Dakota.

In 1954, after eleven years as a country lawyer in Garrison, my father was appointed by President Eisenhower to be the top federal legal officer in North Dakota: the U.S. attorney. We moved to Fargo.

With all of us in school, my mother hoped for more freedom, but my youngest brother, Bobby, was born with spina bifida and many other serious health problems. He was often in the hospital and required much care, and my mother's chance for freedom from home responsibilities slipped away. My father was now an important political figure in North Dakota, and if his wife worked, it would have given the appearance that he couldn't support his family. As a self-centered child, I viewed my mother's loneliness and isolation with insufficient sympathy.

In a Nordic family one did not dwell on feelings or express emotion. Great unhappiness was expressed by utter silence. I focused on Bobby, sensing that my mother's blue moods left a hole in his life. My role as Bobby's friend, playmate, and big sister, as he encountered many physical and social challenges from the outside world, combined with the Nonpartisan League credo to stick up for the little guy, coalesced into a vow that when I grew up I'd do something to help people like Bobby—people with challenges, who had been ill-treated by society.

THE NONPARTISAN LEAGUE was founded in 1915 by a charismatic socialist named Arthur C. Townley and several other disaffected North Dakota farmers who were all tired of being exploited by the grain millers and railroads headquartered in Minneapolis/St. Paul.

North Dakota's climate was perfectly suited to growing spring wheat, used primarily for bread, and durum wheat, used primarily for pasta. By the 1930s, North Dakota grew 85 percent of the durum wheat grown in the United States.[4] Their grain was in high demand, but for years, the evidence had been accumulating that North Dakota farmers—despite their hard work and sacrifice—were not in control of their own destiny. Farmers were incensed to learn that Minnesota grain buyers were systemically cheating them. The grain barons did this by operating what farmers sarcastically called "grain hospitals," at which North Dakota wheat graded and purchased as No. 3 or No. 4 grade wheat would be converted magically into No. 1 and No. 2 grade wheat as soon as it reached Minneapolis, thus generating a profit for the grain dealer that should have gone to the farmer.[5]

The railroads also cheated North Dakota farmers, by charging freight rates that were much higher for North Dakota wheat than for other freight.[6] As one of the League founders, Albert E. Bowen, said, "There are only two ways of making a living in North Dakota. One way is to dig the wealth out of the ground. The other way is to dig it out of the hide of the fellow who digs it out of the ground."[7]

The League said it would establish a state system of uniform and honest grain grading at the point of sale in North Dakota, plus state-owned grain elevators, flour mills, packing plants, and other businesses that would be set up to compete in the marketplace by paying farmers fair prices.

Most farmers in North Dakota lived on credit: they borrowed money for operating costs (seed, fuel, equipment) and paid it back at harvest. Many of them had real estate mortgages. While other businesses were charged 6 percent interest at most, farm real estate loans averaged 8 percent and were as high as 12 percent in western North Dakota. Some bankers and machinery dealers even charged as much as 25 or 50 percent interest, in anticipation of real or imagined risks. Farmers who objected were blacklisted.[8] The League promised it would set up rural credit banks that would lend money at cost to farmers.

The NPL did not want to be a separate political party. Instead, it said it would support any candidate who backed its platform, which addressed the main economic complaints of North Dakota farmers.

Townley noticed that farmers always ask "What does it cost?" when they buy farm supplies but ask "What will you pay?" when they sell. In a 1917 speech, he said,

> I never saw but one man that dared to say that he had anything to say about the price he got for what he raised. One time a great tall Scandinavian got up and said, "I had something to say about the price that I sold a steer for." I said: "Brother, by golly, you are the first man that I ever saw that he had anything to say about the price he sold a steer for." I said: "What did you say about the price of this steer?"
>
> He got up, towering above the audience, and he looked them over, and said: "There are so many ladies and children here that I don't like to repeat what I said about the price of that steer."[9]

The NPL platform offered a brand-new system of state socialism (run by elected politicians) blended with private capitalism that would help the struggling farmers and workers of North Dakota. To spread the word and grow their membership, League leaders used modern technology (airplanes, Ford Model T's), home correspondence courses, and their own newspaper, the *Nonpartisan League Leader*, which was spiced up with biting political cartoons.

Townley hired John M. Baer, an engineer, postmaster, and farmer, to be the *Leader*'s cartoonist. The recurring characters in his astute, satirical cartoons included "Big Biz," a scowling portly man in a three-piece suit smoking a cigar, and "Hiram Rube," a tall, wholesome farmer dressed in work clothes who bore a remarkable resemblance to Uncle Sam. (His name was a tongue-in-cheek contraction of "Hi, I'm a rube," playing off the farmers' belief that they were unfairly condescended to by bankers and politicians.) In one cartoon, Hiram carries a large bag of "liberty seeds" over his shoulder and sows "Democracy" across a plowed field with the American flag as a backdrop. An ominous black crow labeled "Old Gang" sits on the dirt in the foreground waiting to peck up the seeds.[10]

A 1916 John Baer cartoon, "Hands Off!," shows the hand of the "Big (Biz) Five" ("Railroads," "Money Trust," "Grain Combine," "Implement Trust," and "Packing Trust") looming over an isolated farmer. But the Big Biz Five is held back by another hand: "N. Dak. Farmers Strength Combined."

The *Leader* worked to mobilize and educate its membership, and in the 1918 election, the League swept into total power. The NPL dominated the state legislature and promptly put their "Industrial Program" into effect with a state-owned mill and elevator and a state-owned bank that provided real estate loans for farmers.

Because the League believed in the equality of women in farm families, its leaders made women's suffrage part of their platform and gave women the right to vote in North Dakota for county, city, township, and presidential elections. The League's first two legislative sessions also put limits on child labor, empowered labor unions, established the nation's first workers' compensation program, and provided state hail insurance.

The NPL model of grassroots politics and support of a platform, not a party, rapidly spread, with A. C. Townley at the helm. At its peak, the National Nonpartisan League had more than a quarter of a million dues-paying members in thirteen states and two Canadian provinces.[11]

During World War I, the food supply in Europe was sharply cut. To meet wartime demand, the U.S. government stepped in with policies that led American farmers to vastly increase their output of food. When Herbert Hoover, who was food administrator at the time, set the price of wheat at $2.20 a bushel, farmers increased wheat acreage by nearly 40 percent and output by almost 50 percent.[12] Wheat at $2.20 ($44.53 in 2020 dollars) was like catnip to the farmers of North Dakota. They borrowed heavily to buy and plow grasslands to grow more and more wheat. To farm all this land, many of them borrowed even more to buy gas-powered farm equipment. Farmers received draft deferments because their labor supported the war effort. The message was to produce enough to feed the world.

In 1915, North Dakota raised the staggering total of 151 million bushels of wheat,[13] a quantity unmatched until World War II.[14] Though drought and a wheat disease called black rust blasted the yield in 1916 and 1918 to a quarter or a third of the peak 1915 yield, the farmers kept expanding to feed the war machine, especially once the United States finally entered the fight in 1917.

But the good years for farmers came to an abrupt halt when the house of cards built upon the foundation of huge wartime demand began to collapse after Armistice Day in 1918. While the rest of the country enjoyed the Roaring Twenties, the seeds of the Great Depression were being sown in North Dakota. Farmers who had bought on credit during the war found themselves heavily in debt at a time when the cost of living was rising, markets were shrinking, and prices were falling.[15] Wartime price supports had ended and mechanization had increased agricultural production past the capacity of the market to consume it. Rather than enjoying a guaranteed $2.20 per bushel, the market delivered only 97 cents a bushel in the twenties.

Farmers' income was inadequate to pay the principal and interest on the farm debt they'd accumulated by expanding to support the war effort. As total land values plummeted from $1.5 billion in 1920 to $688 million in 1935,[16] many farmers owed more than their land was worth. Between 1921, when the price of wheat began to drop, and 1929, when the national depression was recognized, North Dakota had already lost many farms to foreclosure.[17]

Growing up in the 1950s, we were still surrounded by painful reminders of the 1930s. On many drives across the countryside, my father would point out abandoned farmsteads with derelict barns, the paint long gone and the trees scraggly. The empty, abandoned farmsteads seemed to be as ubiquitous as the cozy occupied farmsteads.

A farm family in western North Dakota, photographed by Russell Lee, August 1937.

A few times, we left the highways and drove down an overgrown trail to one of those lonely farmsteads. The front door would be half open, swinging on rusty hinges. The bright sunshine came though broken windows, dust motes dancing in the hushed air. On the main floor, there usually was a small living room and a big kitchen with old-fashioned appliances (no electric poles led to these farms). Sometimes there would be a framed Bible verse on the wall, or a schoolbook on the floor.

Once, when we saw the thickness of the walls of the house we were standing in, we realized it was built of squares of sod cut from the prairie. My father told us that sod houses were common when North Dakota was settled but almost all of them were long gone.

My mother quietly added, "These houses were hard to keep clean."

We didn't speak out loud in these abandoned houses, but only whispered: sadness and broken dreams were palpable.

My father said, "It was those years, the bad years, that the farmers really needed the Nonpartisan League."

IN 1932, NORTH Dakota was in desperate shape. Thousands of farmers were facing foreclosure and eviction.[18] Though violence was feared across the Midwest, North Dakota farmers expressed most of their frustration and rage at the ballot box, beginning with the June primary. The right of citizens to adopt laws directly—called the initiated measure—was a power given to voters by the Nonpartisan League in 1917. By collecting thousands of signatures, a suite of initiated measures was on the June 29, 1932, ballot. One of these measures, the anti-corporate farming law, would shape the character of North Dakota for decades to come.

By a vote of 114,496 to 85,932, North Dakota voters prohibited corporations from owning farmland and from engaging in the business of farming and ranching.[19] This prevented corporations from buying land from desperate family farmers and gleaning profits from tenant farmers. However, the law did permit cooperatives composed of "actual farmers, residing on farms or depending principally on farming for their livelihood" to acquire farmland and engage in cooperative farming and ranching.[20] Corporations were given ten years to divest themselves of land by selling to a family farmer.[21] Corporate farmers weren't welcome in North Dakota, and nearly a hundred years later, corporate farming is still severely restricted.

Encouraged by NPL leaders such as Bill Lemke, who gave ninety-nine speeches for Franklin Delano Roosevelt, the Republican voters of North Dakota in 1932 overwhelmingly chose Roosevelt (with 178,350 votes) over Hoover (71,772 votes). The voters' shift to the Democratic column for FDR was a cataclysmic change. Nonetheless, they also voted for the entire ticket of NPLers who were running in the Republican column. In a historic move, the state House of Representatives elected its only female member, NPLer Minnie D. Craig, to be Speaker—the first female Speaker of a state House of Representatives in U.S. history.

North Dakotans elected William "Wild Bill" Langer governor. My grandfather Frank Vogel was credited with managing Langer's successful campaign.

In his first speech to the legislature, Governor Langer said, "There can be no return to prosperity in North Dakota that does not begin with the farmer."[22]

These farmers may have been cold and hungry, uncertain of how they would make it through the winter and unable to see when their luck might turn and yield a bumper crop and better prices at market so that they could repay their debts. But it wasn't too late for them—as long as they could keep their land. Because of the NPL, North Dakota had one of the strongest responses to the onslaught of farm foreclosures in the country.[23]

Beginning in 1932, farmers upset by low prices had decided that they would take a "holiday" from farming. The bold purpose of the national Farmers' Holiday Association was

> To prevent foreclosure, and any attempt to dispossess those against whom foreclosures are pending if started; and to retire to our farms, and there barricade ourselves to see the battle through until we either see cost of production or relief from the unjust and unfair conditions existing at present, and we hereby state our intention to pay no existing debts, except for taxes and the necessities of life, unless satisfactory reductions are made on such debts.[24]

The North Dakota branch of the Holiday Association formed "committees of defense" in every one of the fifty-three counties in the state. North Dakota membership in the Holiday Association was 46,000 in late 1932, and at its peak in 1934, it had 70,000 farmer members.[25] If a farmer was threatened with a foreclosure, nearby members were called out to protect one of their own from homelessness and loss of livelihood.

The Holiday Association in North Dakota disavowed violence. But it was perfectly comfortable with the type of advantageous negotiating position that could arise if several hundred farmers appeared at a foreclosure sale and, while glaring at the sheriff or auctioneer, demanded that the sheriff or auctioneer cease the sale.

If a sale proceeded, the committee of defense submitted bids for a penny, nickel, or dime while the rest of the crowd at the auction stood by without bidding. If the penny auction went forward, the purchased property would be given back to the original owner. If the auction was canceled because the sellers didn't want pennies, nickels, or dimes, the committee visited the lender the next day to explain the futility of an auction while suggesting ways to compromise or restructure the debt (a practice that would be resurrected fifty years later as part of the farm advocacy movement).

In Wells County, six hundred farmers showed up after a farmer was evicted and his belongings were put outside, exposed to the elements. The farmers compelled the sheriff to put the household goods back inside and reassemble the kitchen stove, and they made the banker sweep the floors.[26]

The Farmers' Holiday Association was accused of being a communist organization. But its president, attorney and former North Dakota lieutenant governor Usher L. Burdick, explained that the organization only sought to save the economy from complete breakdown. He argued that the "existing government was created by the people and they can change it if a majority of the people want it altered," and he worked hand in hand with newly elected Governor Langer.[27]

The most dramatic and radical development of the 1933 battle against farm foreclosures was a moratorium proclamation, written by Burdick and signed, on March 4, 1933, by Langer. It came to be known as the Langer foreclosure moratorium.

Since the economic conditions in North Dakota were such "that many of our citizens are threatened through real and personal property mortgage foreclosure and execution sales with the loss of their homes and of their livestock and farm machinery necessary for the pursuit of their usual occupation," the proclamation called for a temporary suspension of foreclosures until "the crisis has subsided."

The proclamation said that property rights and civic peace were supported by the moratorium: "Forced sales of homes and of personal property needed for farming purposes can only lead to disorder and disrespect for laws affording no adequate protection to debtors in such an emergency," the moratorium said.[28]

> THEREFORE, I, William Langer, as Governor of the State of North Dakota, under authority in me vested by law, do hereby proclaim and declare that hereafter, and until this proclamation is by me revoked, no mortgage foreclosure or execution sale of livestock and other personal property used by an actual farmer of this State in the operation of his farm . . . shall be held . . .
>
> The general purpose and object of this proclamation is to preserve the homes of citizens in this State and retain them in a position of status quo until a change in the financial conditions shall release our people from a helpless situation.

While most sheriffs were sympathetic to the proclamation, they were faced with a conflict between their obligation to carry forward previously ordered sales and Langer's directive. Langer promised to protect them. A sheriff's liability for failing to sell property was suspended if the failure was due to "an act of war," so Langer called out the National Guard to create the necessary act of war.[29]

Between April 15 and June 21, 1933, Langer called out the National Guard thirty times to stop foreclosure sales. Any debtor threatened with foreclosure or eviction could contact the local Farmers' Holiday committee of defense, which would alert Burdick, or Langer directly.

Despite being almost identical in square miles, North Dakota had twelve thousand fewer foreclosures during that time than South Dakota.[30]

The end game of Governor Langer and the Farmers' Holiday Association was to keep a thumb in the dike of foreclosures until the provisions of the Farm Relief Bill, then wending its way through Congress, could take effect. This law poured new money to lenders if they agreed to refinance farm loans and reduce the interest rate on existing loans.

The Farm Relief Bill,[31] signed by FDR on May 12, 1933, was likely more successful in the long run, but the Langer foreclosure moratorium was successful in the short term. All across the state, farmers said, "Langer saved our farm." Langer was either a hero or a villain, depending on whom you asked, but people were never neutral about him. In my family, he was a complete hero, and we were proud that my grandfather Frank Vogel was his most trusted adviser. In 1932 my grandfather had been the chief strategist and parliamentarian in nominating Wild Bill to the governorship. Langer had subsequently appointed him to be highway commissioner, tax commissioner, and manager of the state-owned Bank of North Dakota.

I often joked that I grew up in the NPL religion and Langer was our god.

As a young girl growing up in a League family, I absorbed the lessons of the 1930s from my father. I believed that during terrible economic times, foreclosures of farmers were unjust and unfair. I believed that the Farmers' Holiday Association, the masses of angry farmers, and the politicians who stuck up for them like my grandfather, Langer, and Burdick were on the right side. I believed that lenders who cracked down on farmers during tough times were on the wrong side.

CHAPTER 2

The First Farmer

Although I would eventually represent more than 240,000 farmers in *Coleman v. Block*, my lawsuit might never have been filed if not for my first farmer client. His name was Charles Perry, but everybody knew him as Chuck.

We met when I was sixteen. The summer of 1962 was a campaign summer and my father was running for U.S. Congress. Mary and I were working at a publishing house run by our dad's political allies. Our job was operating a state-of-the-art machine that could automatically type a letter. All we had to do was input the name, address, and salutation.

One day, when I had completed my stack of letters, Chuck (whose job involved moving rolls of paper) came over to me at the robo-typewriter. Chuck was a handsome, friendly, blue-eyed, six-foot-something guy with tousled blond hair and a guileless face. His eye contact was eerily hypnotic. He offered to give me a ride home after work, and he wrapped me in a magic veil of flattery and praise. I floated into the house and immediately told Mary about this wonderful boy who really, really, really liked me.

My sister listened and then dryly said she had received the same pitch the day before.

"Don't trust him," she said.

Despite her warning, I went on a date with him. I told him I'd be in big trouble if I got home after curfew, but he wanted to park (which in the '60s meant making out).

By the time I got home, I was late and past curfew. Chuck told me not to worry and proceeded to confidently lie to my father: a flat tire, emergency repairs, it couldn't be helped, but *Hey, aren't you running for Congress? My father is a Democratic Nonpartisan Leaguer and is for you!* All with direct eye contact.

My dad, a suspicious father of two teenaged girls, and someone who had put people in the federal penitentiary for lying when he was U.S. attorney, was not only convinced of the truth of what Chuck was saying, but even impressed. When I went on dates with boys with ducktails who idled their hot rods in the driveway, he'd ask, "Whatever happened to that nice young man Chuck Perry?"

"He moved on, Dad," I snapped. The truth was Chuck never called me for a second date, but I was relieved. Anyone who could lie like that was not to be trusted.

Just a few years later, I met my husband, James, my sophomore year at the University of North Dakota. He'd just gotten back from a trip to an Israeli kibbutz and stood out as gloriously tan compared to the pale North Dakotans. He was a doctoral candidate in psychology and could quote Camus and French poetry. I thought James was brilliant and far more mature than any of the other boys I'd dated. We got married five months after we met. I was nineteen; he was twenty-four. He washed out of his grad school program at UND soon thereafter. The first plane ride I ever took was with James a year later, when we moved to New York City so I could go to law school at NYU. James was admitted to the philosophy master's program at the New School for Social Research.

It used to be a rather sad joke that North Dakota's greatest export was its young people—but it was true. I was eager to find out if I could be a success in some place where I would not be known as Bob Vogel's daughter or Frank Vogel's granddaughter. I had several options for law school, but I picked a place as dissimilar to North Dakota as possible: Greenwich Village.

I was unprepared for the crowds in New York City, but aside from the noises, the smells, and the often spoiled food in the grocery stores (James and I found New York City ground beef to be inedible), I fell in love with the city. I loved the way New Yorkers pronounced "coffee." I even loved how quarrelsome New

Yorkers were, in comparison to taciturn North Dakotans. A North Dakotan wouldn't argue; he might just leave the room and never speak to the person who had offended him ever again. A Norwegian feud could go on for decades.

James never left my side. Our amusements as students on a budget were limited, but I never tired of sitting on a bench in Washington Square watching the crazy pageant of the Village pass by.

Of the 260 first-year law students at NYU, thirty-seven were women. We were told on admittance that we were the largest group of women law students accepted into any law school in the history of the United States. A significant number of the women in the class of 1967 had enrolled in law school for a specific purpose: to vindicate women's civil rights and liberties. They had spent years working in the civil rights movement in the South or in the Peace Corps, where their male colleagues tried to shuffle the highly educated women to clerical tasks. This disparate treatment motivated them to go to law school, and upon graduation, they intended to use their degrees to ensure other women didn't suffer the same treatment. I found them inspirational and courageous. They became my friends and role models.

My favorite class was my second-year constitutional law class, taught by Norman Dorsen. Professor Dorsen was a brilliant teacher and brilliant lawyer. He demonstrated that the Constitution was a living document that affected the lives of real people.

In 1967, Professor Dorsen had changed U.S. law in the case of *In re Gault*. The case involved Gerald Gault, who at age fourteen was given a seven-year sentence for a lewd prank phone call. He wasn't allowed to see his parents or a lawyer. If he had been an adult, he would have received—at most—a sixty-day sentence. Professor Dorsen took his case all the way to the U.S. Supreme Court, which ruled 8 to 1 in Jerry Gault's favor, establishing, for juveniles who were accused of a crime, the right to a lawyer, the right to avoid self-incrimination, written notice of the charges, the right to have witnesses, and the right to cross-examine the witnesses. Hearing Professor Dorsen talk about this case, and the many other cases on which he was working with the ACLU and other organizations, was more than inspiring. It made it seem possible that someone—even someone like me—could use the Constitution to fight injustice and make the world a better place.

My first job after graduation was in an all-women legal department at the New York City Department of Consumer Affairs. From there, I was recruited for other legal positions (one in a big bank, another at a Fortune 500 company), always with more responsibilities and higher pay, while James remained a philosophy graduate student, which began to cause tension between us. I hoped to take time off to have a baby, but James hadn't found full-time employment. He was supportive of my career—but when was he going to start his own?

In 1977, we moved to Washington, D.C., for my new job at the Federal Trade Commission, as the program director for the newly passed Equal Credit Opportunity Act. The ECOA (pronounced "ee-*ko*-ah" or by its initials) prohibited business and consumer credit discrimination based on race, color, religion, national origin, sex, marital status, or age. Enforcing the new ECOA was the perfect job for an NPLer. At twenty-nine, I had ten full- and part-time attorneys working under me to enforce the ECOA and also raise public awareness about the new law.

The Equal Credit Opportunity Act required creditors to give specific reasons for turning applicants down. It protected low-income people by requiring creditors to consider the value of food stamps and welfare payments, and it protected divorced moms by requiring alimony and child support to be counted as income on credit applications. One of the key features of the ECOA was that at the bottom of every credit rejection notice, the creditor had to put the specific reason for denial and the federal agency to whom the applicant could complain if she (and most of our complaints came from women) suspected discrimination.

The complaints flooded in. In 1976, there were two thousand. Two years later, there were eleven thousand. We developed a computer system for sorting, and when we found a pattern of complaints, we sent subpoenas to the creditor for their records. When we caught a bad actor, we had to get approval from a majority of the five FTC commissioners, and then we had to persuade the lawyers at the Department of Justice to serve a complaint against the creditor. Whenever my team and I made it to this phase, it felt like we were facing a second wave of discrimination: the DOJ lawyers (all white men) didn't seem to care that Black neighborhoods were being redlined, that waitresses were being told only "waiters" could get credit cards, that single women weren't "creditworthy." *Were the lawyers at Justice just lazy?* I wondered. *Or did they really see nothing wrong with the discrimination we'd found?* It took as much effort to get the DOJ lawyers to agree to sue as it took the Federal Trade Commission lawyers to develop the whole case.

It was a happy day when we forced the lawyers at the Department of Justice to sue Montgomery Ward for redlining Black neighborhoods. Ward settled almost immediately and agreed to pay $175,000 in a civil penalty (the highest ever collected by the FTC at the time) and to stop using zip codes as a credit scoring factor.

The Equal Credit Opportunity Act radically changed the way that most creditors treated borrowers other than white men. The Federal Trade Commission publicized ECOA violations by creditors, and creditors quickly found discrimination was bad for business.

I loved going to work. Our office was filled with crusading young lawyers who wanted to fix the ills of corporate America, and I kept getting raises and promotions. James and I bought a condo across the river in Virginia, in a development of curving streets lined with brick duplexes that had been upgraded from their World War II origins, with new kitchens, cute little backyards, tennis courts, and a pool. It had two bedrooms—one for us and one for the baby I hoped we'd have when the time was right.

But the right time never came. I was absorbed in work, and the more I advanced in my career, the more remote James became. He was supposed to be the brilliant one, yet he had spent the past ten years in graduate school and working at unskilled jobs. We were drifting apart, and when I realized I was pregnant, it came as a big surprise to both of us.

I desperately wanted the baby, but I wasn't sure if I wanted to stay married. Divorce seemed out of the question. No Vogel had ever gotten a divorce. I started seeing a marriage counselor on my own (after one session, my husband refused to come with me). James thought our relationship would improve if we separated. He said he'd stay with a guy friend; I found out later he'd moved in with a woman he met at his job reading to the blind at the library.

"You can't tell anyone we're separated," he warned me. "It won't help us get back together if everyone's gossiping."

Pregnant and alone in the condo we'd bought, I became increasingly isolated and unhappy. I threw myself even harder into my work. Then one day I got a phone call.

"Hello, Sally? It's Chuck Perry."

I hadn't thought of him in years. While I'd been building my career on the East Coast, Chuck had been working on political campaigns. He harbored ambitions for a future as a Democratic–Nonpartisan Leaguer and figured he'd be more attractive to voters if he were a farmer. He started to tell me about his new organic farming venture and bold plans.

"I'm in D.C. for just a few days," he said. "Would love to see you."

He was either flirting with me or trying to get me to introduce him to my D.C. connections, or both. I was still married to James and hoped we would reconcile. Chuck was married too. I remembered Mary's warning: *Don't trust him.* I told Chuck I was too busy to get together.

AT WORK, WE'D started getting a slew of complaints about an agency of USDA I'd never heard of before called the Farmers Home Administration (FmHA, pronounced by its initials). The letters we got were unreal. Black people said they were rejected for home and farm loans before they'd even turned in their applications; single women of childbearing age were told they were ineligible for home loans because they might get pregnant and have to quit their jobs; divorced women were told they were ineligible; working women whose salaries supported the mortgage payments were told they didn't qualify because additional costs would be required so they could hire men to make home repairs.

The fact that we had received so many complaints about Farmers Home at our office was also incredible. Instead of following the ECOA requirements to include the Federal Trade Commission's address at the bottom of their rejection letters, Farmers Home put its own address. Yet many applicants who'd been denied credit managed to figure out that they should write to us at the FTC. I think it was because our ECOA credit practices program was so often in the news for bringing big credit discrimination cases.

We received many complaints about many different creditors, but I decided to target FmHA because of their application form. The signature line said "farmer" and "wife." I'd never forgotten the sharp sense of injustice I felt when a credit card I applied for based on my salary was issued in James's name, even though he was unemployed, or the employment discrimination I'd suffered in my job search right out of law school. One big firm told me to my face, "Sorry, we don't hire women." Others wouldn't even interview women. When I read the FmHA application form, all I could think was, *How blatant is this!*

I opened an investigation and sent a letter to the top administrator at Farmers Home, summarizing the complaints we'd received and listing the various ways it was in violation of the Equal Credit Opportunity Act. The letter gave the agency the option of correcting those violations before we took enforcement action. In my experience, once we caught a creditor red-handed, it usually agreed to follow the law. We were confident FmHA would do the same.

We were wrong.

The high-ranking administrator I'd contacted shuffled me over to lower-ranking staff, who dodged our demands for change in their application forms and outreach for months. The defense was that Farmers Home was exempt from the ECOA because it operated a "supervised credit" program under their own laws passed by Congress. They thought they were special.

Frankly, I didn't care whether Farmers Home's "supervised credit" programs had been created by God Almighty. I simply wanted FmHA to stop illegally discriminating against women and racial minorities.

I soon viewed Farmers Home as the worst, most discriminatory creditor of all the hundreds of creditors we regulated at the Federal Trade Commission.

If I had known at the time about the agency's origin story in the midst of the Great Depression, I would have been even more outraged by how they were trying to illegally circumvent offering credit to the borrowers who needed their help the most.

ON APRIL 30, 1935, Franklin Delano Roosevelt signed an executive order implementing the Emergency Relief Appropriation Act of 1935. It was the largest single appropriation ever made by the federal government, and a massive amount of money was authorized for "rural rehabilitation and relief in stricken agricultural areas."[1] This executive order created the Resettlement Administration, which would become the Farmers Home Administration decades later.[2]

The brand-new Resettlement Administration was intended to help resettle destitute families from rural and urban areas, construct model suburban communities (the model community program was a favorite of Eleanor Roosevelt), and make grants and loans to help small farmers purchase land, machinery, and livestock. From the beginning, it had "an astonishing diversity of projects, programs and problems," writes the historian Sidney Baldwin.[3]

FDR put Undersecretary of Agriculture Rexford G. Tugwell in charge. He was a charismatic agriculture economist from Columbia University who was eager to boldly experiment. Tugwell was close to FDR and was one of the original brain trust advisers on the New Deal, along with Harry Hopkins. In April 1935, FDR entrusted Tugwell with running huge relief programs, ranging from migrant labor camps and fighting soil and seacoast erosion to rural and urban resettlement projects and farm debt adjustment.[4] Tugwell later called this array of duties a compilation of "everybody else's headaches."[5]

Tugwell quickly built a staff for his new agency. On May 1, 1935, the Resettlement Administration had twelve employees. By the end of the year, it employed 16,386 people.[6]

One of Tugwell's assistants, Lewis Hewes, described those early months during which their work became their life:

> We held fingers in dikes of improvisation against bureaucratic tidal waves; rushed fireman-like from one catastrophic threat to another; frantically recruited unknowns, then flung them unprepared into well-paid positions . . . Cash grants were poured into the parched northern and southern Great Plains; ill-nourished, apathetic sharecroppers and cotton tenants from the Atlantic seaboard to Texas began to eat regularly; food and medical care went to thousands of wandering families in Arizona and California. But Tugwell took no pride in conducting a first-aid program; our real job was to cure the deeper malady.[7]

This deeper malady was "human erosion." In a radio address in December 1935, Tugwell spoke of a farmer he called Homer Grant, as an example of how the Resettlement Administration could work to end human erosion.[8]

Homer had a small farm where he raised corn and hogs. He'd hoped to send his children to college someday, "but farm prices fell disastrously," Tugwell said, and when Homer went to the bank it was "not to deposit money but to withdraw his savings." Soon his account was emptied and the mortgage holder began prodding him for overdue payments. "You know the rest of his familiar story. It has been reenacted in hundreds of thousands of farm homes in the United States. His resources became completely exhausted and he had to ask for public relief."

Working with a county rehabilitation agent, Homer received a $600 loan, with which he was able to buy livestock, tools, fertilizer, and seed. "Resettlement gave him a chance to get back on his feet," Tugwell continued. "A good farmer has been saved to continue the efficient cultivation of his own farm by a small loan which will be repaid to the government."[9]

Sidney Baldwin writes that during the Roosevelt era, the Resettlement Administration represented a "historic attempt . . . to exploit the promise, the power, and the possibilities of politics in securing salvation from the human suffering, social injustice, and economic waste of chronic poverty."[10]

Tugwell was an iconoclast, a brilliant innovator, and a strong administrator, and he inspired his staff. Of his agency's broad and urgent mandate, some in Washington said that "no one but Tugwell would have had the courage or foolhardiness to assume such a burden."[11]

At Columbia, Tugwell had co-authored a popular economics textbook. His co-author, Roy Stryker, had selected the illustrations for the text. Now Tugwell recruited Stryker to work with him at the new agency to gather visual evidence that would help the public understand and support what they were doing. Tugwell coached Stryker on the kind of photographs he wanted: "Roy, a man may have holes in his shoes, and you may see the holes when you take the pictures. But maybe your sense of the human being will teach you there's a lot more to the man than the holes in his shoes, and you ought to try to get that idea across."[12]

Unbeknownst to Stryker or Tugwell, the photographer Dorothea Lange was already working for the Resettlement Administration because it had absorbed the Division of Rural Rehabilitation of the California State Emergency Relief Administration (SERA).[13] Lange had been hired at SERA at the insistence of Paul Taylor, a Berkeley professor and a noted expert on poverty and migration of farm laborers. When asked if he needed field workers for his research, he said "Yes, I need a photographer."

There was no vacancy for a photographer, but a young man working for SERA put his own job on the line when he lied and put Lange down as a clerk typist. He also covered her photography expenses by calling them "clerical supplies."[14]

Rexford G. Tugwell talking to farmers, 1936.

Taylor and Lange began to go up and down California, where they documented masses of migratory workers flooding into the state. They prepared a report that included fifty-seven of Lange's photographs, proposing that California use SERA funds to set up migrant camps. The report was successful: after reading it, the division chief recommended that $100,000 be allocated to the camps in California.[15] Another request, for the Federal Emergency Relief Administration to reallocate to California $20,000 not being used in Washington, was also approved, and it was this money that built two camps at Marysville and Arvin, the first federal public housing in the United States.[16]

In *The Grapes of Wrath*, the fictional Weedpatch Camp is based on the actual Arvin Sanitary Camp, which provided safety, refuge, and hope to Dust Bowl refugees like the Joad family. The camp's administrator, Tom Collins, shared detailed notes of life at the camp with John Steinbeck, and the novel is dedicated to "Tom who lived it."

North Dakota farmers waiting for federal grants at the Resettlement
Administration Office, photographed by Arthur Rothstein, July 1936.

The restoration of dignity that Ma Joad feels on her first morning at the
Weedpatch Camp, after she's able to hospitably give a cup of coffee to Jim
Rawley, is palpable in her speech to Rose of Sharon:

> "An' now I ain't ashamed. These folks is our folks—is our folks. An' that
> manager, he come an' set an' drank coffee, an' he says, 'Mrs. Joad' this, an
> 'Mrs. Joad' that—an' 'How you getting' on, Mrs. Joad?'" She stopped
> and sighed. "Why, I feel like people again."[17]

The young man who had lied to get Lange hired, Lewis Hewes, became
Tugwell's assistant, and he shared Taylor and Lange's reports with Stryker and
Tugwell. They were enthusiastic about the photographs and soon, Taylor and
Lange (who were falling in love) were working in Nevada, Utah, New Mexico,
and Arizona, too.

President Roosevelt visited nine states on drought tours, stopping twice in North Dakota. Back in Washington, on September 6, 1936, he delivered his eighth fireside chat on the subject of farmers and laborers, vividly conveying the devastating effects of drought on land, livestock, and family farmers: "I talked with families who had lost their wheat crop, lost their corn crop, lost their livestock, lost the water in their well, lost their garden and come through to the end of the summer without one dollar of cash resources, facing a winter without feed or food—facing a planting season without seed to put in the ground . . .

"Yet I would not have you think for a single minute that there is permanent disaster in these drought regions," he said. "No cracked earth, no blistering sun, no burning wind, no grasshoppers, are a permanent match for the indomitable American farmers and stockmen and their wives and children who have carried on through desperate days and inspire us with their self-reliance, their tenacity and their courage. It was their fathers' task to make homes; it is their task to keep those homes; it is our task to help them with their fight."

FDR in Bismarck on a drought tour, 1936.

When we think of the Great Depression, many of us recall "Migrant Mother," Lange's portrait of Florence Owens Thompson, a thirty-two-year-old Native American migrant farm worker and mother of seven. The photographs that Lange and the other Resettlement Administration photographers captured remain vivid reminders of this period of "cracked earth" in American history, when many farmers were forced to migrate with their families while others, "without one dollar of cash resources," as Roosevelt said, stayed put and fought to save the family farm.

When FDR ran for reelection, a major part of his platform was support for the family farm. In Omaha, Nebraska, during a farm state tour, he gave a speech called "The American Farmer Living on His Own Land Remains Our Ideal of Self-Reliance and of Spiritual Balance," in which he declared, "We cannot, as a Nation, be content until we have reached the ultimate objective of every farm family owning its own farm."[18]

But what was a "family farm"? In his history of the Resettlement Administration, Baldwin refers to a definition from a 1949 USDA report:

> a farm on which the operator, devoting substantially full time to the farming operations, with the help of other members of his family and without more than a moderate amount of outside labor, can make a satisfactory living and maintain the farm plant.[19]

Even today, USDA's farm loan regulations restrict farm ownership loans to family-sized farm operators.[20]

Part of the hardship of the 1930s was the devastation caused by bank failures: banks could not collect from farmers who could not pay, and this tipped banks into insolvency. Family farmers and farm tenants needed access to low-cost credit, and banks wouldn't touch them. USDA came to the rescue.

The Bankhead-Jones Farm Tenant Act created powers for USDA to institute a new program of supervised farm ownership loans. These loans, with forty-year terms at 3 percent interest, were made to farm tenants and sharecroppers for the purpose of buying land, seed, feed, and fuel and were intended to lift qualified farm tenants into ownership status.

As successful as the Resettlement Administration was at providing rural relief (it lent hundreds of millions of dollars to impoverished farmers with a remarkably low default rate), Tugwell soon became the most controversial member of FDR's circle (conservatives called him Rexford the Red), and he resigned at the end of 1936. The secretary of agriculture, Henry Wallace, took over, and the Resettlement Administration was rebranded as the Farm Security Administration. It had new leadership, but its focus on helping those who were down and out stayed intact.

By 1941, the Farm Security Administration had 2,270 county offices, serving eight hundred thousand family clients in forty-eight states plus Puerto Rico and Hawaii.[21] The farm ownership loans were made on the condition that the new farmer would follow a carefully designed Farm and Home Plan, based upon the guidance of the rural rehabilitation supervisor and the home management supervisor. The home management supervisors were women with home economics training, typically with a college degree, who worked with the farmer's wife and the home.[22] Her counterpart, the rural rehabilitation supervisor, concentrated on the farm and the husband's work. The home management supervisors "spent considerable time in intimate conversation with the client farm wife in her kitchen, discussing food preparation, raising children and problems with her farmer husband."[23]

Eventually, the rural rehabilitation supervisors were renamed county supervisors, and the contracts of the home management supervisors weren't renewed (none had civil service protection).

I remember looking at FmHA's Farm and Home Plan at the Federal Trade Commission and wondering why FmHA was requesting data on the size of the borrower's planned garden, how many eggs, chickens, and canned vegetables and fruits the family planned to raise for themselves, and the estimated cash value of those products.

The Farm and Home Plan also had a checklist to ask borrowers if they had running water, refrigerator, washing machine, telephone, sewing machine, full bath, home freezer, dryer, television set, and water heater. On page 3, it asked for planned expenses in the categories of household operating, food including lunches, clothing and personal care, health, house repair and sanitation, school, church and recreation, personal insurance, transportation, and furniture. *Why,* I thought, *would a lender care if the family gave money to their church?*

What I didn't realize was that these questions weren't designed to be intrusive, or to ferret out wasteful spending, but rather to help county supervisors help a farm family to become happier, healthier, and more self-sufficient at home.

The Farm and Home Plan was a ghostly reminder of the social workers and idealists who worked with families like the Joads during the bitter years Woody Guthrie sang about in "Dust Bowl Blues" and "This Land Is Your Land":

> In the shadow of the steeple I saw my people,
> By the relief office I seen my people[24]

In 1962, the Museum of Modern Art showed an exhibit of photographs taken by the Resettlement Administration photographers. In his introduction to the exhibit, Tugwell wrote that the Great Depression "can never happen again to so many in the same ways—partly because we have these reminders of what happened when we turned our backs on fellow citizens and allowed them to be ravaged."[25]

It can never happen again. Ever the idealist, he was wrong.

I WAS FIVE months pregnant on the day of my showdown with the Farmers Home Administration. I brought four other lawyers from the Federal Trade Commission with me.

My team had reviewed hundreds of complaints of FmHA. I'd sent lawyer and paralegal teams to visit county offices in Texas, Florida, and Georgia, where they interviewed employees and came back shocked at what they'd heard. We'd pored through volumes of FmHA regulations and procedures. We'd talked to public interest groups who cared about fair housing and to legal services offices that had had run-ins with the agency. We knew of four Equal Credit Opportunity Act lawsuits that had already been filed against USDA by private attorneys—a victim of credit discrimination had the right to sue for damages in federal court.

Our case was rock solid. We were going to give them one last chance to follow the law before we handed the case over to the Department of Justice.

We all sat at a huge conference table. David Larson, the chief of Records, Forms and Communication Management, had thirteen FmHA employees with him; all were white, and just one was a woman. The men all wore the FmHA uniform: flimsy white shirts and polyester sport coats. The woman was dressed like a mouse, all in gray.

I opened with an exhaustive list of the ECOA violations we'd uncovered in our investigation. Larson responded for FmHA. To me he seemed insulting and condescending as he insisted the forms and regulations we criticized were fine because they had been reviewed by Congress.

"Do you understand that the Federal Trade Commission has the authority to fine your agency ten thousand dollars a day for every violation of the law?" I asked him.

"You're being too fussy," Mr. Larson said.

No matter what I said, it was clear they had no intention of changing. I stood to leave.

"Honey," he said, looking at my maternity smock, "I don't know why you bother with this in your condition."

I looked at him.

I said not a word.

But I thought, *You will be very sorry you called me honey.*

ANDREW WAS BORN in October, and I came back from my brief maternity leave in November to present our Farmers Home credit discrimination case to the commissioners at the FTC who would decide whether to bring the lawsuit to the Department of Justice. Andrew was sleeping soundly in his blue corduroy baby sling, and I gently handed him off to a female colleague while I made my pitch to the commission.

Ultimately, the Federal Trade Commission never sued Farmers Home, and I will never know why.

Perhaps it was because Congress was threatening to put the FTC on half pay due to its enforcement of too many trade rules and antitrust cases. Perhaps it was because the Democratic commissioners believed it was awkward to sue Jimmy Carter's administration for race and sex discrimination with an election year coming up. Maybe they foresaw that the Department of Justice wouldn't sue one federal agency on behalf of another. Or maybe the FTC commissioners believed that USDA was finally going to start complying with the requirements of the ECOA—four years after the act was passed by Congress—because they'd made the small gesture of using the terms "borrower" and "co-borrower" on their forms, rather than "farmer" and "wife."

My status as "wife" was also over. After Andrew was born, all became clear. I found out about James's liaison and he promised to end it with Patricia, but then I found a Christmas gift in the trunk of the car addressed "To Dearest Patricia, With All My Love."

I changed the locks in our house and hired a full-time nanny. Now I had to pay for a divorce lawyer in addition to childcare.

My childhood friend Sara Garland, who worked for Senator Quentin Burdick, told me the Treasury Department was looking for a special assistant to the secretary of the Treasury for consumer affairs.[26] The duties of the job were advising the secretary on how to protect consumers who dealt with the many divisions of the Treasury (IRS, Customs, Savings Bonds). It sounded fascinating, and the pay was much better than my salary at the FTC. I applied with a glowing recommendation from Senator Burdick and was careful not to mention that I was the single mother of a small child. The fact that the FTC hadn't taken action against Farmers Home also made me less attached to staying.

When I found out I got the job at Treasury, it seemed my life after separation was finally starting to turn around. Then I got the phone call that would change the trajectory of my life.

"Sally Vogel, it's Chuck Perry. How the heck are ya? Listen, I'm calling because I'm in town looking for a lawyer and you're the smartest girl I know. Farmers Home is trying to shut me down. They're out to foreclose on me. You know anything about them?"

He asked if I could meet him at a bar so he could tell me the whole story, and this time, I said yes.

Here was a farmer fresh from North Dakota who was battling the same government agency that had stonewalled me.

That summer, I went out with Chuck and introduced him to my D.C. social circle. He wore blue jeans, plaid shirts, cowboy boots, and a red cap with white polka dots. Sometimes he really put on the dog and wore bib overalls. He could dance a mean two-step. He charmed my girlfriends by describing the blue skies and prairie flowers back home. He deemed his farm sacred because it contained a rare turtle effigy, a stone arrangement in the shape of a turtle placed by Native Americans, on the top of a butte overlooking the Heart River Valley.

Depending on the audience, Chuck had two versions of why he was facing foreclosure. When speaking to idealistic hippies, Chuck claimed that big agribusiness and chemical companies were working behind the scenes to crush an environmental leader like Chuck, to prevent him from inspiring other farmers to become organic.

If he was speaking to bureaucrats or lawyers, Chuck said that the foreclosure was being masterminded by unnamed politicians who hated him for working on the campaign of a third-party candidate for Senate that split the North Dakota vote between a longtime Republican incumbent and a well-liked Democrat challenger, handing the election to the incumbent.

Both versions resonated with me, but the political conspiracy theory seemed more plausible. The first time he'd applied for an FmHA loan, it was swiftly rejected: not enough experience. When Chuck applied again, he was found to be eligible and got $150,000 in USDA loans in 1975, as well as a first mortgage worth about $50,000 from the Bank of North Dakota. Chuck would later tell the press that the loan was given because of "political connections."[27]

But getting a loan wasn't enough. Chuck also had to comply with the loan conditions—and he didn't.

In 1979, USDA started foreclosure on him for falling behind on payments. In fact, he wasn't delinquent on the loans, but he had breached the loan agreement by selling his cows (which were collateral purchased with FmHA funds) and applying the proceeds to various bills he owed around town. This breach is called "conversion" and ordinarily results in criminal (not civil) charges.

Chuck, however, was convinced that the foreclosure was instigated by unknown persons to destroy his future as a potential North Dakota politician. He also saw himself as persecuted by FmHA because he didn't fit their idea of a farmer. My immediate reaction to his impassioned story of unjust treatment was: *Of course FmHA would do something like that!*

Outraged on his behalf, dazzled by his charisma, and basking in his attention, I accepted Chuck's story at face value and said I would try to help him. He told me he needed help getting his files from FmHA through the Freedom of Information Act. He believed that when he got the information, he would be able to defend himself, and he was certain he would recover damages because of the illegal way he had been treated.

I introduced Chuck to a highly regarded litigator, the husband of a Federal Trade Commission co-worker, who agreed to work on his FOIA request pro bono. By October 1979, the lawyer had gotten USDA to hand over four hundred pages of documents, and Chuck spread them all over my Arlington condo, poring over the records for proof of the conspiracy. Every page triggered memories. He loved to talk about himself, and he elaborated on the circumstances of each event of his brief farming career: dealing with a veterinarian, quarreling with the county supervisor at FmHA, getting bids for a better milking system, buying the cows, selling the cows, selling the milk.

I often interrupted for an explanation of farm lending and agriculture terms: *What does the county committee do? What do you use an operating loan for? What do you mean by "parity"?*

Chuck subscribed to a newspaper that was all about parity, which, to farmers, was the holy grail of agriculture policy.[28] The word "parity" is derived from the Latin *paritas*, from *par*, meaning "equal." Parity is how USDA measures the prices farmers receive for their crops, compared to the cost of the supplies it takes to produce those crops, based on the prosperous farming years of 1910 to 1914,[29] when prices were stable and there was an equilibrium between the purchasing power of rural and urban Americans.

"If costs are going way up for farmers and the prices farmers are getting are going way down, those are conditions beyond the farmer's control," Chuck explained to me. There was a farmer activist movement growing called the American Agriculture Movement (AAM). Of course I knew them from the tractors they'd driven from across the United States to the Capitol in 1978 and 1979, but I didn't know they cared about parity.

Even though I was not Chuck's attorney, I instinctively began to act as one. I focused on the documents and the legal principles, as I'd been taught in law school and in all the jobs I'd had over the past decade. I'd worked on consumer credit and home loans; I told myself that farm loans just had an extra set of zeros.

I've always enjoyed legal research and tracking obscure regulatory trails to find a clear answer. It became clear to both me and Chuck that records were missing. We worked together on a draft document for his lawyer to use to persuade the court that FmHA was lying. There had to be more records.

Farmers Home "discovered" 160 more pages, and the trial court declared the case finished. Still believing the records on the conspiracy were hidden, Chuck filed a reply, and a few more records surfaced. But there was no evidence of conspiracy in those pages either. The trial judge ultimately dismissed the case and denied Chuck's request for damages. Chuck appealed, with me as his lawyer, but we lost at the D.C. Circuit Court.[30]

I was so wrapped up with the FOIA case and my day job that I was oblivious to the larger warning signs in the countryside.

IN THE EARLY 1970s, some believed the United States was entering a golden age of agriculture, like the decade leading up to the First World War.[31] From 1971 to 1973, American farmers sold massive quantities of wheat, corn, and other commodities to Russia, which faced extreme food shortages caused by years of crop failures. As a result of market demand, the price of wheat rose 195 percent between 1972 and 1973; the price of corn rose 133 percent; the price of soybeans rose 133 percent.[32] The average price of a bushel of #1 dark northern spring wheat in North Dakota jumped from $1.32 a bushel in 1971 to $4.41 in 1974.[33] National net farm income in 1973 was $29.9 billion, a record that was not to be matched—even with inflationary dollars—for many years.[34]

As farmers invested in more land, the average farmland value per acre across the United States rose by huge amounts. In North Dakota, the average value of land and buildings per acre rose by more than 400 percent in the 1970s, from $94 an acre in 1970 to $195 in 1975 to $300 in 1978 and to $399 in 1980. In Minnesota, where there was more cropland, the rise was even more extreme, jumping from $226 an acre in 1970 to $1,061 in 1980.[35]

But the equity created by rising land values was ephemeral, because the exceptional prices created by Russian demand did not last. In response to high grain and corn prices, multinational corporations with no loyalty to American farmers invested in South America, making it possible for Brazilian and Argentinian farmers to compete in the world market. With more competition, wheat and corn prices for U.S. farmers plummeted.[36]

Rising land values meant American farmers were still rich on paper, but they couldn't pay the interest and the principal on the debts once prices for their crops dropped. A large gap grew between the value of their crops and the cost of staying in business. They were sinking and they knew it. They needed better prices, but instead they got more credit.

Recognizing the cliff they were about to fall over, in 1977, a group of farmers met in Colorado to organize the American Agriculture Movement (AAM), and it grew rapidly in membership and activism. In 1978, they made plans to bring their tractors to Washington and pressure President Carter and Congress to restore parity to the marketplace. My investigation of FmHA focused mostly on sex and race discrimination in loans for houses; I was unaware of the growing farm distress.

Like the loan programs of FmHA, the concept of parity arose out of the Great Depression and the efforts of farm state politicians like the Nonpartisan Leaguers.

During the 1920s, parity of farm income compared to city dwellers was a goal for many of the Nonpartisan Leaguers in Congress. North Dakota senator Lynn Frazier, for example, proposed a bill that would have guaranteed prices at the cost of production, plus a fair profit.[37] Leaguers also supported the McNary-Haugen Farm Relief Act, which would have provided government subsidies to farmers, by buying surplus crops at prewar prices and storing or exporting them. The bill was passed by Congress three times but was vetoed twice by Coolidge and once by Hoover.

Then, during Roosevelt's first hundred days, the Parity Program (as the McNary-Haugen law became known) was included, along with the Farm Relief Bill and a panoply of other programs, in the Agricultural Adjustment Act of 1933. The AAA allowed USDA to regulate farm production in order to balance supply and demand, to prevent surpluses that cause prices to drop. It also created a national grain reserve to prevent prices from skyrocketing in times of drought or other national disasters.

The AAA also created the Commodity Credit Corporation.[38] Whenever the price of goods fell below the cost of production, the CCC could lend money to farmers. These price support loans allowed farmers to avoid selling their crops at a loss; instead, they could pledge their crops, receive a loan to pay urgent bills, and wait for the prices to rise. When prices rose to a fair level, farmers sold their grain on the market, and repaid the CCC with interest.

By reducing surpluses of crops and livestock and providing price support loans to farmers so they had more flexibility in terms of when they sold their products, FDR and Congress set out to improve prices and reach parity, which would level the economic playing field for farmers. And it worked. Thanks in part to the parity programs, farm income in 1935 was 50 percent higher than farm income in 1932.[39]

Parity may have been good for family farmers, but it did not benefit the corporations that fed off the farm economy. It didn't provide the grain traders with cheap taxpayer-subsidized grains for export; it didn't push farmers to supercharge the productivity of their land with excessive amounts of high-priced fertilizer; it didn't encourage farmers to get bigger and bigger to compensate for a tiny rate of return per acre.

In the decades that followed, the parity program was under constant attack by corporate lobbyists for being a "socialist" program standing in the way of "modernizing" agriculture. The stability of farming in the 1940s created the impression that the programs—and the supply management theories on which they were based—were no longer needed. And as the key components of a functional parity program were removed from federal laws by politicians swayed by these lobbyists, there was a gradual loss of family farmers who lived on the land.[40] According to the U.S. Agriculture Census, farm population across the United States dropped by nearly 30 percent between 1950 and 1960 and another 26 percent between 1960 and 1970.[41]

By the end of 1977, the price for corn, wheat, and barley was only 64 percent of parity and on a downward trajectory. To stay afloat, farmers borrowed against the value of their land to put in the crop. But at the end of the season, the market was glutted when every farmer put their crop up for sale at the same time (loans came due at the end of December), and prices often weren't high enough to pay the loan plus interest. Their operating loans were rolled into their real estate loans, year after year. Many of these farmers borrowed from FmHA.

As the American Agriculture Movement began to organize in 1977, the "parity" they sought was a return to prices from the golden years of the early seventies.

When the AAM farmer activists showed up in Washington in 1978, they met with key members of Congress to draft a bill that would restore flexible parity to the marketplace. Amazingly, it passed the Senate, was amended by the House, and was sent to conference committee, where it was expected to pass.

But the Carter administration fought hard against the bill, believing that it would cause consumer prices to rise and it would be too costly for the taxpayers. As a compromise, Congress offered to fill the gap between the low prices and high cost of production with easy credit, provided largely by the Farmers Home Administration.

But more credit and easier repayment terms had not been a goal of the American Agriculture Movement; they wanted better prices.

The Agricultural Credit Act of 1978 authorized $4 billion in economic emergency loans. On August 4, President Carter proclaimed, "The act I am signing today will give many farmers an opportunity to refinance the debts they incurred during the past period of low prices; for some this will mean the difference between staying in farming and being driven out."

Buried within this law was a small section that gave farmers who borrowed from Farmers Home the right to apply for deferral when they were temporarily unable to pay due to circumstances beyond their control. It was codified as 7 USC 1981a, and though few paid attention to it at the time, this section would become central to the Farmers Home appeals cases I would soon take on.

Members of the AAM believed the failure of their parity bill was a congressional sellout to corporate interests, and when they returned, they were no longer Midwestern nice, politely lobbying at the Capitol. This time, one of the leaders was an aggressive farmer from Georgia, Tommy Kersey, who was angry over the betrayal he believed had occurred the year before.[42] The AAM parked nine hundred tractors on the National Mall in February 1979.

"Washington did not open its doors," historians of the movement later wrote. In fact, "AAM found most legislators unavailable except for the briefest discussions. No ranking administration officials made protesters feel at home. In retaliation, many farmers became belligerent and threatening, which further isolated them from their targets. By midwinter, with most television networks and newspapers criticizing their personal behavior and ignoring their political complaints, most AAM protesters left town despite their earlier threats to stay until spring."[43]

By February 1979, the American Agriculture Movement was "everyone's subject of criticism; and it had lost even more supporters from its own ranks. Its behavior was labeled a disgrace by the media, Congress, USDA, other agricultural groups, consumer groups, and many who had helped found it."[44] As the farmers hung out together on the Mall, they ramped up their resentments and amped up their outrage, but they did a poor job communicating with the ordinary working people in Washington whose lives they were affecting—like my own.

In 1978, I'd barely noticed the tractorcade, and I was vaguely supportive of AAM. In 1979, I did notice them, and this time I wasn't so supportive. Because hundreds of tractors blocked the streets used by commuters driving in from

Virginia, my carpool was forced to take elaborate detours through clogged streets to get to the Federal Trade Commission. Our half-hour commute doubled. I was in the throes of my separation from James and the single mom of a nursing infant. I wanted to keep my workday commute as short as possible in order to spend more time at home.

The outward appearance of these AAM farmers, in their winter uniform of brown quilted Carhartt onesies, their billed caps with earflaps to keep out the bitter wind, reminded me of the friendly farmers I'd seen back in North Dakota coming to town for supplies. But back home, they didn't block the streets or prevent people from getting to work. When I was growing up, North Dakota farmers didn't scream or carry signs. But one of the hand-painted "Deere John" signs I saw on the Mall read: WE'VE RAISED TOO MUCH CORN / AND NOT ENOUGH HELL.[45]

MY MEMORIES OF North Dakota, with its small farms dotting the landscape, were still distinct, but I didn't realize that the family-sized farms I remembered were on the cusp of huge changes.

Had I been paying closer attention, I would have seen the beginnings of industrial farming by huge corporations building supply chains aimed at market domination. Corporate lawyers at seed and pesticide companies like Monsanto were beginning to plot how to patent seeds and draft contracts that would prohibit farmers from the practice of saving seeds for the next season that farmers had been using since time immemorial.

In 1969, in North Carolina, a farmer named Wendell Murphy incorporated himself as Murphy Family Farms, Inc., and began to experiment with having his neighbors raise his hogs pursuant to contracts written by his lawyers and presented on a "take it or leave it basis." He copied the contract farming method from corporations that were raising poultry.[46] These contracts put much of the risk on the farmer growing the hogs or the chickens and gave the bulk of the profit to the corporation that wrote the contracts.

Another big change came when the 1978 Agricultural Credit Act allowed larger loans, variable interest rates, and new ways of appraising the values of farmland. As a result, bigger farms that were not even close to meeting the family-sized limitations that had governed FmHA since Tugwell set up these programs in the 1930s got huge FmHA loans. A *60 Minutes* exposé, "The Grapes of Wealth," uncovered four loans totaling $23 million that had been made to multimillionaires in one of the richest counties of California.[47] One loan was for a "tennis ranch" and one was for a racehorse breeding stable. One borrower drove a Rolls Royce. All owned luxury homes and had other businesses and properties. Some of these extravagant loans soon went into default, which caused a loss of goodwill and bad press for FmHA's traditional loan programs.[48]

The historic middle-sized and family farm sector of the agriculture economy was beginning to hollow out. The number of farms in America peaked around six million in 1935. By the late 1970s, two million of those farms were gone.[49] Smaller farms could be supported by off-farm income; bigger farms could survive by producing massive quantities, albeit at lower per-bushel or per-animal values. But middle-sized family farmers—the backbone of American agriculture—were being squeezed by new economic trends, in addition to the pressures caused by trade wars, droughts, and the like. These pressures on middle-sized farms caused them to close at a rate of more than 10 percent every five years, while the large and mega-farms grew steadily.[50] And the message that came from many economists and USDA officials was "get big or get out."

The American Agriculture Movement blamed Carter for fighting the 1978 parity bill, and Carter became even more unpopular after he declared an embargo on sales of 17 million metric tons of wheat to the Soviet Union on January 4, 1980, in retaliation for the Soviet invasion of Afghanistan. Farmers across the country recoiled at the implications of using food as a weapon and the loss of a major wheat buyer.

Within days of the embargo, the Carter administration put in place numerous programs to ameliorate the impact on U.S. farmers (such as permitting the Commodity Credit Corporation to purchase grain for food assistance, and establishing incentives for farmers to participate in farmer-owned grain reserves). The price of wheat and other crops fell for several days but then picked up and remained stable, or even increased, during 1980, with a year high of $5.41 a bushel.

But the Republican Party smelled blood in the water. Their platform proclaimed that there was a "crisis in agriculture" and the Republican Party would bring back profits to farmers.

At the Treasury Department, I thought President Carter would survive. How could farmers support a California movie star over a Georgia peanut farmer?

But farmers pulled the lever for Reagan, just as they had done for FDR. Back in North Dakota, the vote was 193,695 for Ronald Reagan, 79,189 for Jimmy Carter, and 23,640 for independent John Anderson.

These farmers could not have known that Reagan would choose a thirty-five-year-old budget director who advocated "liberating" the farmers from USDA price supports and supply management.

CHAPTER 3

Cottonwood Haven

Accepting the Treasury job meant giving up my civil service protection. At Treasury, I was a political appointee with top secret clearance, and I could be fired at will. I wasn't worried, though. Within my bubble of liberal friends and colleagues, we were sure that Carter would be reelected, and our certainty increased when the Republicans nominated Ronald Reagan.

But as the summer turned to fall and the election approached, I began to get glimmers that Carter might not win. The conversations in the hushed, carpeted meeting rooms on the executive floor of the Treasury Department showed an undercurrent of deep concern about the deficit, the economy, Main Street, Wall Street, the price of gasoline, stagflation. My main project was preparing regulations to require the Bureau of Alcohol, Tobacco and Firearms to put fetal alcohol warning labels on liquor, beer, and wine bottles. Carter operatives feared he'd lose California unless the fetal alcohol warnings were dropped. I was bitter over this, thinking of all the babies that would be born with lifelong disabilities because their mothers didn't understand the danger of drinking while pregnant.

"I'm sorry," the secretary told me. "Your warning label regulations were stopped by the White House."

On election night, I was standing in a long line of tired voters when the word came that Reagan had won. Smarting over the fetal alcohol warning label, I voted for Anderson.

I knew enough about Reagan's bitter hatred of legal services offices and his bias toward corporations to know that he'd never renew Carter's executive order on which my Treasury job rested. For several days after the election, my co-workers wandered the halls of the Treasury Department, describing their job searches. They asked me what I'd do but I had no idea. I knew I could get another Fortune 500 corporation or big bank job as a shill—at an even higher salary than I'd earned at the Treasury Department—but that was repugnant to me. I longed for a "real" job representing "real" people and began to dream of going back to North Dakota. On paper, my job at Treasury entailed protecting hundreds of thousands of people, but none of them came to my office or told me about their lives. I longed for a job in which I could represent the good guys against the big corporations and federal government, just as the Nonpartisan League had done in the early days of North Dakota.

Then Chuck's pro bono FOIA lawyer was offered a job with the Reagan administration. The appeal was pending and I naively said I could take it over, not realizing that I'd first need to quit working for the federal government. When I figured that out, it seemed preordained. I submitted my resignation to the deputy secretary.

My financial troubles began as soon as I quit. December 13, 1980, was my last paycheck. For years, I had disregarded the advice and example of my father, who had been a teenager in the 1930s. He was horrified by debt and allergic to interest payments. I thought that was old-fashioned. I had credit cards from fancy department stores and I used them liberally to upgrade my wardrobe (scruffy was fine for the FTC, but not for the hallowed halls of the Treasury Department). I had a credit card from Amoco, and another from a hardware chain. I'd even charged the baby crib. I used credit cards for lunches out and then paid only the minimum, and the balances grew. James was paying $200 a month in child support, but I was making the mortgage and car payments on my own. Money seemed to fly out the door. I hadn't been without work for years, and I rapidly chewed through my minimal savings, my vacation pay lump sum, and my retirement account.

Chuck saw my newfound availability as an opportunity for me to do additional volunteer legal work for him. He had been sued for foreclosure in July 1979,[1] and a Bismarck lawyer, who had also fallen for Chuck's razzle-dazzle, had filed a counterclaim against FmHA seeking millions of dollars in damages for "violating" his rights. Suddenly I was flying back and forth to North Dakota to help with the case.

On those trips, I was rediscovering the beauty, peace, and stability of my home state. I drove on old Highway 10, a little-used two-lane blacktop that meandered past little towns where the only activity seemed to be running late for church. I had the feeling of riding ocean swells as I drove up hills and down valleys with hawks overhead amid pure and utter quiet. Back in Bismarck, I saw two young boys riding bikes with their fishing poles attached— clearly headed to an afternoon of adventure on the banks of the Missouri River. No babysitters. No parents hovering. No fear. I knew that on the East Coast, Andrew would never have the kinds of adventures these kids took as a matter of course. Adventures that I had enjoyed while growing up in a small town.

Moving back to North Dakota began to seem more and more appealing. I sent my résumé to a few law firms in Bismarck and Mandan but didn't hear back. (Consumer protection experience was not an asset when everyone knew everyone.) One lawyer offered me a job doing his spillover divorce cases, but I couldn't bear the idea of doing that after going through it myself. I was unemployable, but I didn't realize it.

Chuck suggested I set up my own law office specializing in farmers, and he would send me clients—clients like him, with cases worth "millions."

My sister, Mary, heard about a house on the Missouri River, and the next time I was in town, we went to see it. It was on a half acre of land next to the river, with huge cottonwood trees and a chorus of birdsong. It was only three miles from downtown Bismarck. The house was in foreclosure. I loved it so much that I barely noticed that there was no kitchen sink, refrigerator, stove, or counters, or that the stairs to the second floor and the loft balcony lacked a railing. I didn't think about how I would mow the lawn in the summer, nor how I would extricate myself in the winter when the snow drifted across the long driveway. It seemed irrelevant that I didn't have a job, or that my condo hadn't sold, or that I hadn't been admitted to the North Dakota bar.

I told James that I wanted to move to North Dakota and when I did he could stop paying child support and spend the money instead on traveling to and from North Dakota. He jumped at the offer.

On August 4, I put $1,000 down on my dream house. The asking price was $81,200, which I thought was a bargain. I based my mortgage application on my résumé and projected income from my projected law practice. I also scraped by on the last name of Vogel—daughter of Robert and Elsa, grand-daughter of Frank and Luella.

Then I flew back to Washington and put my Virginia condo up for sale by owner. I hired a painter to touch up the rooms, hung new wall-paper in the bathrooms, and had the windows replaced. Chuck said he would stay in Virginia to sell my condo, then pack a U-Haul van and bring all my possessions to North Dakota. I assumed the sale would be swift: the comparable condos were all briskly selling for $100,000. Andrew and I flew back to Bismarck, taking a photo in an airport photo booth to memorialize the trip.

But Chuck didn't keep his promise. His fight against FmHA was featured on the front page of the *Minneapolis Tribune* (BRASH NORTH DAKOTA FARMER BATTLES BUREAUCRACY). With copies in hand to lend credibility to his conspiracy story, he began a coast-to-coast odyssey telling farmers and journalists (and single women) about his mission, his cause, and his brand-new organization, the Farmers and Ranchers Protective League (obviously a nod to the Nonpartisan League) in which farmers should "invest." The League would have ample resources to do battle with the Farmers Home Administration, he said. He used the money farmers gave him to go to the next state, where he spent it on lunches, dinners, motels, car rentals, and recruitment of more investors.

I started to get a sketch of his travels from the charges on my credit card (that I'd given him for the U-Haul expenses) and the phone calls I received from farmers.

"Chuck Perry said you could help me," they all said.

IN OCTOBER, ANDREW turned three, and we moved into the house on the Missouri River. While we waited for Chuck to deliver our belongings from the condo back in Virginia, we collected a weird assemblage of furniture, dishes, and toys from friends and family. In the living room, which was wrapped with windows on three sides, we had a card table for eating, folding chairs, and some lawn furniture that overlooked the views of the cottonwood trees and river. The centerpiece of the room was a woodstove, faced by a relic: my parents' Scandinavian-style couch, upholstered in the same scratchy brown fabric I remembered from high school. On cold days, I built a fire, and a fan high up on the knotty pine ceiling sent wafts of warm air to heat the whole house. There was something comforting about the wood heat, and even when the weather was at its most bitter, I rarely used the backup furnace.

I had been so taken by the river setting and the views that I hadn't noticed until we moved in that the kitchen was unfinished, with raw plywood for countertops. At least there was a sink with running water. I borrowed a refrigerator from my brother-in-law and bought a hot plate and an electric frying pan on which I cooked almost all of our meals.

Living on the river immediately felt right. All day and night, the big cottonwood trees that grew on the riverbanks played their song. Cottonwood leaves spin and dance in even a slight breeze, and as thousands of leaves touch each other in this dance, they whisper a rustling sound that is much like the sound of waves receding from a sandy shore. Because the wind is almost constant, the song of the cottonwoods lasted until the last of their leaves turned yellow and fell in the late fall. After years of living surrounded by concrete, I relished the nature, and Andrew's imagination flourished as he made playgrounds from the woodpile and imaginary forts in the tall weeds. (We had no lawn mower.) On warm days, when I needed a break from paperwork, I carried Andrew piggyback and waded through shallow water to our own private sandbar.

My sister, Mary—a teacher with two kids of her own—provided us with tons of toys and books and games for Andrew. The theory was that Andrew would quietly play while I worked in a main floor bedroom that I'd converted to an office, with a desk made of a door stacked on plywood sawhorses. It didn't quite happen that way.

My work was Andrew's enemy, and he had various means to distract me from it. I don't remember him screaming, crying, or being angry. Instead, his toolkit included showing me his artwork, sharing his discoveries ("Look at the gun I made!" while brandishing sticks that he had laboriously bound together), putting a book in front of me and asking me to read to him (I was never able to resist that request), or asking surprisingly insightful questions such as "Why do leaves turn yellow?"

For a three-year-old, Andrew had a remarkable capacity for mimicry. "This is you, Mom," he'd say with a beaming smile, before crookedly staggering toward the kitchen coffee maker, like a drunk, eyes almost closed, with one hand waving an empty coffee cup with dregs from the night before. His impersonation of my morning routine was very funny, but this depiction of my condition most mornings reflected a growing problem. During the day, I was mostly "Mom" to Andrew, but after he went to sleep, I was working late into the night. As Chuck floated from coast to coast, talking up the Farmers and Ranchers Protective League, he was giving out my phone number. And I was being drawn into a maelstrom of legal troubles and traumas. It seemed that everyone who called me was in crisis.

WHEN TOM NICHOLS, a hog farmer out of Wolf Point, Montana, called me, I scribbled pages of notes on a yellow legal pad as Tom described his troubles: *Just had appeal with state. It was a joke. Decision maker not there. County supervisor shows stupidity. Their minds are made up.*

Tom said that the hearing officer acted more like a prosecutor than a neutral appeals judge. "I'm thirty years old, six foot six, two hundred fifty pounds," Tom told me. "I was tempted to club them."

Having lost his appeal at the state level, Tom asked if I'd represent him for his national appeal.

"Sure," I said, "but you'll have to come to Bismarck." I also told Tom that he and his wife, Anna, would have to bring sleeping bags, as I had no furniture in the guest room.

Tom was one of many farmers and ranchers who were starting to hear about my work through word of mouth. "There's a woman lawyer who will represent farmers fighting FmHA for free," the rumor went. That rumor happened to be true.

I believed that the federal government would pay my legal fees, not the farmers, because in October 1981, the same month I moved into my house on the river, the Equal Access to Justice Act went into effect. The premise of EAJA ("*ee*-ja") was that if a citizen or small business sued the United States (or was sued by the United States), and the citizen or small business won, then the government should pay that citizen's or small business's legal fees, because the citizen or small business was doing the public a service by correcting wrongful government action. When I read about EAJA and the liberal estimate of attorneys' fees that were expected to be awarded (Congress estimated it would be $367 million over a three-year period[2]), it seemed that EAJA had been ready-made for farmers like Tom and Anna who were fighting FmHA with the help of lawyers like me.

I'm not sure how Tom and Anna Nichols found my house at the end of a long driveway hidden by trees and covered by snow on a dark afternoon in December, but they did. When I went to the door to welcome them, the first thing I noticed was their size. They were both encased in layers of tan insulated Carhartt coveralls, the winter uniform of all Western farmers and ranchers. Over their Carhartts, Tom and Anna wore fur-trimmed Army surplus green parkas. The heating system in their truck had been on the blink during their seven-hour drive on icy roads from their farm outside Wolf Point, Montana.

Tom was tall and wide-shouldered, with a serious expression on his face that softened into a warm smile once he felt he could trust me. Anna, at five foot ten, seemed petite beside Tom. She was blonde, blue-eyed, and apple-cheeked, wholesome and pretty. Neither of them had an ounce of pretension. Both Anna and Tom had grown up as hardworking kids on hardscrabble farms in Roosevelt County. They were still newlyweds, having married only two years before the sky started to fall on their dreams. They even had a brand-new house at their farmstead (financed by FmHA). Their future should have been bright, but instead they were facing ruin and homelessness.

Before the Nicholses' arrival, Andrew and I removed his toys and collection of sticks he used for *Star Wars* battles from the spare room across from my office. Tom and Anna unrolled the twin mattresses they'd brought, along with warm blankets and quilts, sheets, and pillows.

I showed them where the bread, peanut butter, mac and cheese, canned soups, and yogurt were, but Tom and Anna viewed the condition of my kitchen as tragic.

"What in the world is yogurt?" Tom asked. They'd never heard of yogurt (which I'd discovered in New York at Greek grocery stores), and they'd never met a vegetarian before.

The Nicholses were "preppers." They were prepared for being snowed in on their farm for weeks at a time—the nearest grocery store was miles from their farm, a serious expedition even in good weather. They went back out to the truck and began to haul in big coolers of supplies, including boxes of eggs from hens they'd raised themselves. There were canned and frozen vegetables from their garden, and breads and pies baked by Anna, and home-butchered meats. They had no cash to speak of (they'd borrowed gas money to get to Bismarck), but Anna bustled into the kitchen and made a hearty dinner for all of us, to Andrew's great delight.

Within a day or two, I was no longer a vegetarian.

TOM AND ANNA Nichols were tough people from the toughest part of a tough state.

Eastern Montana is quite unlike the landscapes featured in Montana tourism brochures. The region is miles and miles of emptiness, with a narrow strip of road bisecting the earth and disappearing at the horizon. When I saw Tom and Anna's part of Montana for the first time the following summer, I could not believe how bucolic, green, and settled North Dakota looked in comparison. If the Civilian Conservation Corps had tried to grow trees in eastern Montana after the Dust Bowl of the 1930s, they hadn't been successful.

The Nicholses came from a different world than I did. We spoke different languages. While they'd been learning about agriculture and self-reliance since they were young children, I'd been studying political science, history, and English, and my family got all our food from the grocery store. I knew more about conditions for farmers during the 1930s than I did about what farmers were facing in the early '80s. I understood nothing about Tom's passion: raising hogs. Over the ensuing days, he painstakingly taught me what I needed to know for the national appeal brief.

Tom and his father believed that hogs would provide steady cash income for their small farm, and they began with two sows and a boar. They planned how they would make the most of what they had in terms of land, buildings, and crops in order to run a diversified hog operation. Tom went to college to study agri-science, taking classes in crops and soil and swine production, and after graduating with his associate degree, he visited a large Cargill plant, and he studied how to grow and market hogs. Tom studied until he knew to the penny and the pound what the hogs would weigh, what they would be worth, how he would hedge against price fluctuations, and how he'd manage risk.

Tom was only twenty-four years old when he lost his father in 1976. He bought his dad's farm, 320 acres, from the estate and, with little thought or fanfare, assumed the balance of his father's loan from FmHA.

Two years later, Tom had made huge progress due to hard work, extreme frugality, and a full-time job working for the Agricultural Soil and Conservation Service (ASCS), a sister USDA agency that managed the farm programs. He married Anna in 1979.

The couple built up their farm and hog stock in a short amount of time. By January 1981, they had a group of hogs worth $13,500 ready to market, when the worst blizzard of the century hit Roosevelt County. It lasted seven days. The drifts were fifteen feet high and covered the buildings in which the hogs were housed. The hog housing became a death trap. Tom tried to carry the hogs through the blizzard to another building, but even for huge, strong Tom, carrying a 250-pound hog that was frantic with fear and confusion through a raging snowstorm was too much. Tom couldn't save them. Too many hogs perished, and as a result, the Nicholses couldn't make their scheduled January 1981 payment to FmHA.

The huge piles of snow at last began to melt in May. That spring, Tom had the heartbreaking task of digging his hogs out of the dwindling snowdrifts so he could bury them.

In the 1930s, President Roosevelt and Rexford Tugwell had established the Resettlement Administration to help struggling farmers like Tom and Anna through precisely this kind of natural disaster. And FmHA should have done so for the Nicholses in 1981.

By the early 1980s, the scope of FmHA's original mission of providing loans and grants to depression-stricken low-income farmers had vastly expanded, making FmHA the lead rural development agency in the United States. And it was huge. By 1979, FmHA had 7,895 full-time employees working out of two thousand county, district, and state offices throughout the United States and in Puerto Rico, the Virgin Islands, and other territories.[3]

Farm loans were still the agency's bread and butter, but it also supported rural communities through housing loans to low-income and disabled residents, loans for building community health facilities such as hospitals and nursing homes, funds for safe drinking water and waste disposal, and thousands of guaranteed loans to help start rural businesses.[4] Between 1935 and 1979, FmHA had helped to repopulate small towns across America and provide better living conditions for millions of people. By 1979, FmHA had lent and granted a total of $73.1 billion since its inception.[5]

FmHA's farm programs were remarkably successful. These farm loans were limited to the bottom tier of farmers—farmers who could not qualify for credit from private lenders—and yet the losses were minuscule. Losses on farm loans accounted for less than 1 percent of the principal advanced.[6] As land values rose, especially in the late '70s, the "average" U.S. farmer saw the value of their farmland skyrocket from $73,000 in 1970 to $227,400 in 1979. The balance sheets of farmers with FmHA loans improved along with those of all other farmers. But this precipitous rise in land values also made it harder for a young farm family to get started. And this is where FmHA came to the rescue with its panoply of services and loan programs aimed at helping farmers just starting out. By 1979, an average borrower with an FmHA farm ownership loan was only thirty-seven years old, while the average U.S. farmer was forty-nine.[7] Tom and Anna were younger than average, but their drive to succeed and prosper and their youthful energy made them likely to succeed—if given a fair chance.

As the volume of loans skyrocketed in the late 1970s (45 percent of all loans made by FmHA since 1933 were made in 1977, 1978, and 1979),[8] the agency's staffing stagnated. In 1970, FmHA had 7,638 employees to supervise $2.4 billion in loans and grants; in 1979, it had 7,895 employees and $14.6 billion in loans and grants.[9] The staffing had gone up a minuscule 3.4 percent, while the dollar value of loan and grant volume went up 508 percent.

By 1980, farm loan supervision had mostly been reduced to two tasks: developing a farm plan at the beginning of the year, and an annual on-farm review of collateral (to ensure all machinery and cattle were accounted for). However, the elaborate array of FmHA regulations and procedures continued to assume that the county supervisor (a paternalistic role that originated during the agency's

beginning in the Great Depression) was deeply connected to the farming operation, and he (they were almost always men) was a friendly, helpful adviser
deeply committed to the success of the farm family. Because of this assumption,
the county supervisor exercised broad powers over management of the farm and
the farmers' finances—powers that had no parallel in private commercial
lending.

As a beginning farmer in the late '70s, Tom went to FmHA in order to get
low-cost credit on generous terms. But within just a couple of years, he would
learn that he and Anna were entangled in a powerful bureaucracy suffering from
massive mismanagement and subject to the whims of the top officials in
Washington, D.C. When times were hard, the county supervisor's deep and
intrusive involvement in the day-to-day operation of the farm, including control
over the family's checkbook, could go very wrong indeed.

Tom and Anna's farm was in Roosevelt County, a sparsely populated area of
2,073 square miles (about half the size of Connecticut). In the 1970 census it
had about ten thousand people. The county seat of Roosevelt County was Wolf
Point, a small town located within the Fort Peck Indian Reservation.

Between 1976, when Tom assumed his father's FmHA loan and started to
farm on his own, and July 1979, the FmHA office in Wolf Point hired and then
lost seven different county supervisors. Perhaps Wolf Point was too remote,
with too few amenities. Perhaps it was too cold in the winter and too hot in the
summer. Or perhaps it had too many Native Americans for the comfort of
the white county supervisors. Then, in July 1979, Clifford Harvey arrived. Tom
later heard he'd been transferred out of three prior FmHA offices. But at Wolf
Point, Harvey at last had total job security. No other FmHA employee in the
entire state of Montana was willing to work there.[10]

As county supervisors cycled through the revolving door of the Wolf Point
FmHA office, Tom kept raising hogs. Sometimes he would get his farm plan
approved by one county supervisor, only to have it revoked by the next. Loans
that should have been made in the spring were made in the fall. Or a loan was
approved to buy pigs, but no provision was made in the farm plan to feed those
pigs. While most of FmHA's thousands of county offices operated smoothly
with long-term employees who lived in the communities they served, the Wolf
Point office was a mess due to constant turnover. When Harvey arrived, the
mismanagement got even worse.

Harvey scheduled, then missed (or canceled) county committee meetings at which the Nicholses loans were to be discussed. He had them prepare five different farm plans for 1980 before agreeing to sign.

In 1981, they agreed on a farm plan that authorized the Nicholses to buy sixty bred gilts in March. (I had to ask Tom about gilts. He told me a gilt was a female pig that has not yet given birth to a litter. A *bred* gilt had already been impregnated.) According to the plan, the bred gilts would have piglets and the piglets would be ready to sell in July. At that point, Tom and Anna could make their loan payments to FmHA.

But Harvey didn't release money to buy the bred gilts in March.

"Instead, he made us wait until May, and by then there were no bred gilts available," Tom told me. "So we bought ninety *unbred* gilts and they didn't come until late June." Tom and Anna had to breed these ninety gilts themselves, and the delay disrupted their time line for feeding and raising the offspring. July came and went without having pigs ready to go to market.

Many farmers had been delinquent from time to time over the half century since Rexford Tugwell and his band of idealistic social workers had started the Resettlement Administration. The mere fact of being delinquent was not that important. Rather, the county supervisor and the farmers would look at *why* the loan was delinquent and fashion solutions so that the farm could become more productive or profitable in the future. Sometimes the loan was rewritten to fold the overdue payment into the balance of a new loan. Other times, it was simply carried as delinquent until the next crop came in. This tolerant and humane system worked well for decades.

With their delinquencies accumulating, Tom and Anna asked to meet with Harvey's boss, the district director, in order to explain their concerns about the shoddy way the Wolf Point office was being run and to present ideas on how they could catch up on the overdue payments.

The district director invited Harvey to the meeting. Instead of taking the Nicholses' suggestions and comments to heart, Harvey seemed irate over the Nicholses' insubordination. Less than three weeks later, Harvey sent a letter demanding that the Nicholses "voluntarily liquidate" their farm, their machinery, and their livestock.

This seemed like a crazy suggestion to Tom and Anna. They had just gotten their buildings, their hogs, and their new home all set. *Why quit now?*

They went to see Harvey in person and he laid out the deal: If Tom and Anna agreed to immediately list their farm, livestock, and equipment for sale, Harvey would release money from the farm's checking account to feed the pigs and pay for other farm and living expenses until the farm sold. But if they refused to sell out, there would be no money released whatsoever for feed for the animals, for electricity, for insurance, or for anything else. This seizure was against the agency's own regulations, but Harvey claimed that he was just "protecting the government's interest."

When farmers went to borrow money from FmHA, they pledged collateral—property that they owned or would own or that would be generated by their labor—to guarantee the loan in a security agreement (for non real estate) or a mortgage (for real estate). A farmer like Tom had a chattel security agreement, which meant that FmHA would lend him money for hogs but the agency also had a financial stake in those hogs, so when they were sold at market, a two-party check would be issued in the farmer's name and the lender's.

Tom and Anna refused to capitulate to Harvey's demands and found a banker who would lend them money. Even though it would have cost FmHA nothing, Harvey refused to sign off on the necessary collateral in order for the Nicholses to secure a private loan, and soon Harvey put a draft of a formal acceleration notice and intention to foreclose in front of the state director, who believed Harvey's version of the facts and signed it. When Tom and Anna opened the certified letter from the state FmHA office, they felt like they'd been clobbered with a bat.

They found a young, sympathetic attorney named Mark Parker in Billings, three hundred miles away, to help them. Aided by Tom's research and his own, Parker concluded that Harvey was violating FmHa's regulations. He scheduled a meeting with Harvey in Wolf Point and hired a private plane to take him there. But Harvey canceled the meeting while Parker was on the plane. It was a costly, wasted trip.

Parker wrote a letter of complaint to the state director about Harvey's conduct, only to have Harvey retaliate by filing a disciplinary complaint against Parker with the Montana Bar Association. The disciplinary complaint was absolutely meritless, but it threw Parker's senior partners at the Billings law firm into a tizzy. Parker wrote a sorrowful letter to the Nicholses saying that his partners said he wouldn't be able to help them any further unless they could pay him—too much time was being spent defending the disciplinary complaint.

Without funds to pay for Parker's legal services, Tom and Anna represented themselves at their state appeal hearing on September 4, 1981, an all-day affair before a district director. Ominously, the state director who had signed Harvey's recommendation to accelerate the loan payments and then to foreclose was sitting in as an "observer." The Nicholses were prepared to confront Harvey with carefully prepared questions and detailed information about their farm operation, but Harvey—the key witness against them—was a no-show. (He was "away at a training.")

During the hearing, the district director, who was supposed to be neutral, was, according to Tom, unprepared, argumentative, and completely on Harvey's side. And, as Tom wryly observed to me, Harvey's boss, the state director, was in the room watching how the hearing went. Since the state director was the one who officially made the decision to foreclose, it was obvious to Tom that the district director wasn't about to disagree with his boss.

Throughout the day, Tom rebutted every false allegation about his farming operations and corrected the false information Harvey had presented to justify the foreclosure. Tom and Anna's efforts were fruitless. FmHA was a hierarchical organization and the Nicholses were not part of it.

A few weeks later, the decision came. It wasn't even signed by the hearing officer, as it should have been. It was signed by the state director, and it said, "Your accounts are being accelerated because of your failure to meet scheduled payments and to keep your accounts current. Your indebtedness has reached the point that there is no possible chance for success in the proposed operation. In order to protect the security interests of the Government, the decision to accelerate your loan accounts is being upheld."

After they lost their state appeal, Tom called me.

CHAPTER 4

Cut, Slash, Chop

What the Nicholses didn't realize in the fall of 1981 was that they were caught, along with thousands of farmers nationwide, in a machine built to meet "delinquency reduction goals" in order to dramatically reduce government spending. The mastermind of the budget cuts was David Stockman, the thirty-five-year old whom President Reagan had chosen to be the director of the Office of Management and Budget.

David Stockman was a self-described "farm boy" from Michigan. Growing up, he was active in the Future Farmers of America and learned "the truths of Christianity and Republicanism" from his grandfather.[1] Ambitious and competitive, David raced his brothers to see who could get the most work done, later bragging that he always won even when his brothers teamed up against him. He was the first in his family to attend college, and there he was briefly seduced by liberal politics. "Like many in my generation," he writes in his book *The Triumph of Politics*, "I took up Marxism and America-hating ... slowly I discovered that the left was inherently totalitarian." He quickly recovered and reclaimed "the virtues of unfettered capitalism."[2]

Stockman began his career on Capitol Hill as a staffer for an Illinois congressman. In Washington, the more he learned about government programs and regulations, the more he found "waste, excess, and injustice."[3] He gained political power when he was elected to Congress in 1977 as a representative of

Michigan and focused his sights on the arcane arena of the federal budget, believing that the founding principle of the American economy was capitalism and that politicians were destroying the economy by turning government "into a lavish giveaway auction."[4]

In the months leading up to the 1980 election, Stockman helped Reagan practice his debating skills by assuming the persona of Jimmy Carter. The Reagan circle was impressed by his detailed understanding of the federal budget. One day after the election, he got the call: "Dave, I've been thinking about how to get even with you for that thrashing you gave me in the debate rehearsals," President-elect Reagan said. "So I'm going to send you to OMB."[5]

At the Office of Management and Budget, Stockman had enormous power to implement a plan he called the Grand Doctrine that would save the economy by dismantling vast segments of the federal budget.[6] By the end of the fiscal year in 1980, the federal deficit was $74 billion, roughly equivalent to $232 billion in 2020.[7] "To keep the budget solvent," Stockman explains, "required draconian reductions on the expenditure side—a substantial and politically painful shrinkage of the American welfare state."[8] His Grand Doctrine meant "abruptly severing the umbilical cords of dependency that ran from Washington to every nook and corner of the nation" and would require the "ruthless dispensation of short-run pain" to every corner of the federal budget—farm programs, food stamps, school lunch subsidies, legal services—in the name of long-run gain to the economy. He felt it was essential to get the government out of areas it didn't belong in. Ominously for American farmers, Stockman wanted "complete elimination of subsidies to farmers and businesses."[9] He said farmers who relied on FDR-era farm programs were enjoying "a way of life based on organized larceny."[10]

The American Agriculture Movement farmers who had abandoned Jimmy Carter and supported Ronald Reagan would soon discover that they'd made a terrible mistake.

On February 16, 1981, Stockman's youthful face appeared on the cover of *Newsweek*, hovering above a towering stack of paperback budget books. Behind him—like a halo—is a circular seal that says OFFICE OF THE PRESIDENT. On the left side of his calm and eager face, in vivid yellow, are the words CUT, SLASH, CHOP.

As a former member of Congress, he knew that "dismantling" USDA's elaborate network of loans, price supports, and supply management wouldn't be easy. But if he could pull it off, "the liberation of American agriculture from the whole rot of USDA subsidies and price supports . . . would free the labor and capital trapped in inefficient, surplus farm output for redeployment to productive, profitable uses elsewhere in the national economy."[11] In reality, "freeing" labor from farms meant farmers would lose farms that might have been in their families for generations. "Trapped capital" was a poor choice of words to depict the harsh effect of erasing the life savings of farmers who for decades had prudently reinvested profits back into land and machinery. "Redeployment" of labor meant farm families would stop being self-employed and swell the ranks of Americans already unemployed.[12]

Stockman called his plans "gospel," as in "We had to go out and sell that gospel. Make it sound good—because it was good."[13] He planned to attack each government program separately, thereby preventing a coalition from having sufficient strength to push back: "Divide and Conquer." He condensed the entire budget process into six weeks.[14]

In March 1981, the *New York Times* profiled Stockman as THE PRESIDENT'S CUTTING EDGE of tax cuts and "trickle-down" economics, intended to reduce the national deficit.

In his fervor to cut government spending, Stockman ignored the benefits brought to the countryside by programs such as those offered by Farmers Home. Growing up, he'd heard his father and grandfather criticize FDR's programs as wasteful and unnecessary: "good farmers" didn't need any help from the government; hard work and frugality yielded prosperity. In Washington, Stockman had come to believe that special interest groups (the National Education Association, the Wheat Growers Association, school lunch administrators, mortgage bankers) had taken over the reins of government and would soon bankrupt the United States.[15]

Stockman believed that "the good society . . . was best served by a smaller, less activist state and by a more dynamic, productive and fluid marketplace."[16] "Unfettered capitalism" was the solution for everyone, whether you were a wheat farmer or schoolteacher.

Most farmers, farm organizations, ag economists, historians, and members of Congress would not have agreed with Stockman's gospel that USDA subsidies and price supports were "rot." These loan and supply management programs were valuable parts of national policy for domestic tranquility, affordable food, and a strong national defense. While Stockman exempted defense programs from the budget ax, he did not exempt USDA, even though USDA had representatives embedded in ninety U.S. embassies throughout the world. Food trade and food aid are integral components of U.S. national defense and foreign policy. Napoleon Bonaparte said, "An army marches on its stomach," and World War II demonstrated the value of U.S. agriculture not only to the United States but to its allies. (It is also significant that USDA was founded in wartime by President Lincoln.) Hundreds of thousands of farmers nationwide had made long-term business plans based on federal commitments that Stockman deemed to be dispensable.

But Stockman couldn't execute his plans for USDA programs alone. Every good villain needs henchmen, and at USDA, Stockman's henchmen were Secretary of Agriculture John Block and National Administrator of Farmers Home Administration Charles W. Shuman. Both were from Illinois, where they had been active in the Republican Party and in the Illinois branch of the American Farm Bureau, a conservative national farm organization that tended to attract Republican members. The AFB believed in limiting the role of government in agriculture and farm lending.

Shuman's father, Charles B. Shuman, had been the national president of the American Farm Bureau, where he had preached that "government subsidies were morally and economically wrong because they oppose 'the pattern of God's plan.'"[17]

In his new office at USDA, Charles W. Shuman put up a framed copy of a *Time* magazine cover from 1965, with a portrait of his father, captioned THE MAN WHO WANTS THE GOVERNMENT TO GET OFF THE FARM.[18] The elder Shuman is wearing a collared white dress shirt without a tie—not the attire of a working farmer. Behind him is an expanse of farmland, wheat on the left and corn on the right. Dark gray storm clouds threaten the sky above. In North Dakota, such clouds would cause farmers to turn away from the painter and his easel, wondering, *Will these clouds bring down hail to flatten the crop? Do these threatening skies presage an early blizzard? If so, will I be able to collect from federal crop insurance or get a disaster loan if I can't harvest?* But Shuman's confident gaze betrays no fear of those storm clouds.

Empowered by the near-religious fervor of Stockman's Grand Doctrine and emboldened by Secretary Block and the American Farm Bureau philosophy of reducing government involvement in agriculture, Charles W. was in a prime position to implement his father's vision for getting the federal government off the farm. As national director of FmHA, Shuman was in charge. The fates of thousands of farmers were in his hands.

Every year, FmHA typically had a certain number of delinquencies, that is, loans on which the borrower was late or overdue on payments. These delinquencies often correlated with various weather patterns and other farming situations. In 1976—a very good year—7 percent of farm ownership loans were delinquent and 21 percent of farm operating loans were delinquent.[19] In 1980, the delinquencies rose slightly. In 1982, ominously, delinquency rates rose once more, to 14 percent of farm ownership loans and 26 percent of farm operating loans. The massive Economic Emergency Loan Program, passed by Congress in the last days of the Carter administration, had given risky loans to bigger farmers, and those delinquencies skyrocketed, reaching 40 percent by 1983.[20]

On August 25, 1981, just a few weeks after he assumed his position as national administrator of FmHA, Shuman sent out Administrative Notice 580 to all state directors of the Farmers Home Administration. Each state director was a political appointee, meaning the Carter Democrats had now all been replaced by Reagan Republicans.

Administrative Notice 580 was a two-page document that was benignly captioned "Servicing and Supervision of Loans" and read, "Attached are delinquency goals for your State for the major farm loan programs. We believe these figures are attainable with sufficient effort at all levels within FmHA."

Each state director received a list of delinquent loans, by type, for their state, and a "goal" for reducing those delinquencies by March 31, 1982. Shuman set a goal of 23 percent, on average, for each state office of FmHA to reduce the delinquent loans on their books. I believed each of these delinquent accounts belonged to a family farmer who had most likely fallen behind on their payments due to hard times. It was hard to see how the farmers who were already suffering from low prices, high production costs, drought, and other disasters could cure the delinquencies from their sparse 1981 crop before March 31, 1982. In March in North Dakota, and many other states, the snow is still on the ground. There was no way farmers could grow another crop or raise more livestock to sell in time to meet that deadline. They were already with the lender of last resort.

If a state FmHA office couldn't meet their 23 percent reduction goal, future funding for rural housing and farm loans was in jeopardy. District directors were put on notice by Shuman that their merit pay bonuses depended on how well they met the new quota. Shuman wrote, "I anticipate reducing loan funds allocated to those states whose delinquency is higher than deemed appropriate."

With low crop and livestock prices, combined with high interest rates and catastrophic weather, state directors across the United States quickly realized that the only way to "reduce delinquencies" was to foreclose on delinquent farmers, sell the farmland, cattle, and machinery and thereby convert delinquent loans to "current" or "paid" loans. Better yet, they could "persuade" the farmers to quit "voluntarily." And "voluntary liquidations" were far easier to execute than going through the hassle and delays of a foreclosure or court action.

Farmers Home officials sought to keep Administrative Notice 580 confidential, but dogged journalists got copies, and soon these copies were shared among farm advocates and organizations. I got a copy from a journalist friend with connections to the state FmHA office, and when I read it, I was appalled.

In my opinion, AN 580 triggered the '80s farm crisis in the same way the stock market crash in 1929 triggered the Great Depression. It threw oil on a fire that was already burning. Administrative Notice 580 came to be known as the Foreclosure Quota Memo.

EVEN BEFORE TOM and Anna lost their state appeal in September 1981, FmHA had frozen the money in their supervised bank account. Harvey now had total control over the Nicholses' farm checkbook. Without money to buy feed, the Nicholses, in desperation, turned their starving pigs loose to graze on their drought-stricken wheat fields. Some of the pigs escaped through the fence into a neighbor's field.

Harvey now threatened Tom and Anna that he would charge them with the crime of "cruelty to animals," even as Tom's neighbors wrote letters in his defense.[21]

You didn't need a law degree to understand injustice. Farmers like Tom and Anna felt it acutely.

Anna played with Andrew to keep him occupied while Tom and I spent days working on the brief for the national appeal. For each instance of unfair treatment that Tom relayed to me, I was dead certain I would find a violation of a regulation in my hardcover copy of the Code of Federal Regulations, or in the United States Code provisions that I'd copied at a nickel a page at the North Dakota Supreme Court law library.

"Look," I'd say. "This section of 7 CFR says that Harvey had the authority to lend you the money for feed for the pigs. And here it says the farm plan should have been followed by the county supervisor, which means Harvey violated the farm plan by refusing to finance the sixty bred gilts. FmHA should have revised the farm plan when you had to buy the ninety unbred gilts."

According to the regulations, FmHA was supposed to treat family living and farm operating expenses as top priority—before any income was applied to the loan balance. The Roosevelt County FmHA staff flatly disregarded this regulation.

Not only had they disregarded the regulations—they had also violated the law.

I handed Tom a copy of the 1978 deferral law. The Nicholses had heard about this law, through news stories, but hadn't actually read it. Slowly, in a quiet voice, Tom began to read to Anna, "the Secretary may permit, at the request of the borrower, the deferral of principal and interest . . . and may forgo foreclosure . . . upon a showing by the borrower that due to circumstances beyond the borrower's control, the borrower is temporarily unable to continue making payments . . . That's us." Tom looked up at me. "We should have been offered the chance to apply for a deferral," he said.

"Absolutely," I said.

I was incensed by FmHA's failure to follow the deferral law. I'd been raised to believe that federal officials were a cut above everybody else and had to meet the highest standards of conduct. The concept of federal officials simply blowing off a federal law was wildly divergent from my upbringing, not to mention what I'd learned in law school. What I didn't know at the time was that the interpretation of the phrase "may permit" would be hotly contested in the legal battles to follow.

To the Nicholses, however, the worst part was not failing to follow the deferral law but failing to allow them to feed their hogs. I'd been raised by a lawyer; they'd been raised by farmers who, for generations, had entwined their work with their faith. Proverbs 12:10 says, "The righteous care for the needs of their

Sarah and Tom Nichols at a 1982 hearing. © Grey Villet

animals." Months later, it still cut Tom and Anna to the quick to remember the hungry animals that relied on them for food they were unable to provide because of Harvey's actions. These pigs weren't "units" of a market economy; they were living, breathing, suffering animals for which Tom and Anna were responsible.

My fifty-six-page brief for the Nicholses' national appeal was a detailed deconstruction of all the errors made by the staff of the Wolf Point FmHA office in administering the loans, with another long section about FmHA's violations of the appeal regulations at the hearing. I argued that the Nicholses qualified for deferral relief because of blizzards, droughts, and other circumstances beyond their control, and demonstrated that they'd never been offered a deferral by FmHA. Citing the Fifth Amendment to the U.S. Constitution, I argued that Harvey's use of nasty tactics to force Tom and Anna to quit had violated principles of constitutional due process. The freezing of their income without a prior due process hearing violated both FmHA's own rules and the Constitution. Their state appeal hearing was also riddled with flagrant due process flaws—for example, Harvey, the main witness against the Nichols, didn't show up at the September hearing to be cross-examined.

On December 14, 1981, I express mailed the brief with all of its attachments, weighing two pounds, to the office of Charles W. Shuman.

BY THE END of 1981, true to the promise of the aggressive Foreclosure Quota Memo, FmHA had commenced 2,395 foreclosures and sent out 13,318 acceleration letters, demanding that farmers pay their delinquent loans in full or prepare to face foreclosure.[22]

I pictured these families, some with little children and dairy cows named Suzy and Sweetheart. These were families with hayfields and croplands named after the original settlers (the Carlson quarter, Schmidt's pasture). These were families with memberships in churches and social groups (Sons of Norway, the Bohemian Hall). These families were the "real" people I had longed to work for when I felt isolated in my office in the Treasury Department. They were so much more than stats on a memo.

Losing a home is traumatic. Losing a farm is even more so. For family farmers, everything was at stake: their livelihood, their heritage, their standing in the community, their school, their church, their legacy, their identity.

As soon as I had a copy of the delinquency quota memo in hand, I had to show it to my dad, who'd been a U.S. attorney in the 1950s and early '60s. During that time, he had received only three foreclosure requests from FmHA.

"Only three?" I asked. "In eight years?"

"Maybe four. Three or four."

None had been for nonpayment.

"Something must be wrong," I said. It seemed unbelievable. How could thousands of farmers be heading to foreclosure in just one year? Farmers were more productive and efficient than they had been in the 1950s and '60s. It couldn't be their fault.

Farm advocates across the country were as appalled as I was. National news stories appeared about the "foreclosure quotas." And the government officials behind the quotas claimed there was no such thing. USDA Undersecretary for Small Community and Rural Development Frank W. Naylor Jr. told an AP reporter, "We are not out on a massive foreclosure policy." He was more concerned about "the rumor mill" about "an alleged plan to foreclose on the bottom 25 percent of our portfolio."[23] Secretary of Agriculture John Block insisted that Farmers Home was being lenient with farmers, going the extra mile to help them "through these cloudy times," at the same time that FmHA employees who worked for him were sending thousands of acceleration letters to farmers all over the country.[24] USDA's statements were carefully crafted to ameliorate the public outcry and to defuse the political power that farm state representatives had in Congress. It didn't work.

USDA denied that there was a loan crackdown, but these denials weren't credible to Congress. Instead, members of Congress listened to their constituents. On December 11, 1981, the U.S. Senate passed Senate Resolution 257, urging FmHA to use—to the maximum extent possible—the "ample authority" provided by Congress to "extend the term of, defer the repayment of, or refinance the unpaid balance of" FmHA loans.[25] But the Reagan administration, fueled by the certainty of David Stockman that farmers needed to be "weaned" from cheap credit like a calf from a cow, stuck to their quotas. USDA now was ignoring not only the law, but also a congressional resolution.

In North Dakota, Stockman and Shuman's willing henchman was Ralph Leet, a career FmHA employee. In an interview with the *Bismarck Tribune* in April 1981, soon after he became state director, Leet said that he believed the agency had been "too lax" in handing out money. As a result, foreclosures were needed because of "overly liberal past practices."[26] Leet proudly spoke of his self-reliant homesteading Norwegian ancestors and said that his father didn't rely on credit (indeed, he said that his father thought that use of credit was a "sin"). What Leet didn't mention was that his homesteading forebears had not really done it on their own: they had received homestead land just north of Devils Lake.

Leet's unsympathetic position was that foreclosure was good, even for the farmers about to lose their livelihoods: "By foreclosing when it becomes obvious that a loan will not be repaid . . . a loan recipient may be able to walk away with enough money to make a new start. If, though, a person is allowed to slide too long, he or she may end up with nothing."[27]

I WAS SLIDING down to nothing, too, right alongside my clients. I was very busy building a law practice for farmers who couldn't afford my fees. My dad tried to help by sending news articles and relevant cases. But he also hinted that

Andrew and I could move up to Grand Forks and there would be a position waiting for me at his law firm: steady paycheck, health insurance. I could give up all the stress that came along with my private practice.

"I can't, Dad," I told him.

"Just think about it, Sally."

"And anyway I know I'm going to get a big fee soon." I fantasized about the hours I would submit once I won the Nicholses' national appeal. Under the Equal Access to Justice Act, my payday would be $10,000.

By the end of 1981, my financial situation had gone from dire to dreadful. I'd never had trouble paying bills before, and I was deeply ashamed of my situation. When James and I divorced, the settlement said that I'd be responsible for all of the condo payments. The live-in nanny I'd hired to care for Andrew while I worked full time at Treasury seemed an essential expense, even though the cost far exceeded the child support I received. Other expenses (taxes, water bills, condo fees) added up, and before I knew it, I was making only monthly minimum payments on all my credit cards.

With the best of intentions in launching my private law practice, I got telephone and electrical service and bought office supplies and a typewriter. Now I was getting bills from both North Dakota and from Washington. My father lent me a car when I moved because I'd left my own car behind, parked in front of the condo. This was yet another valuable possession Chuck was supposed to deliver. Instead, the Civil Service Credit Union sent a letter to say they would repossess my car if I didn't catch up with my payments. I couldn't.

I went to sleep every night worrying about money and woke each morning to the same anxieties.

I now owed over $100,000 on the condo. I'd assumed it would sell easily, as the condo was nice and within easy commuting distance to Washington. Naively, I had trusted Chuck to handle the sale, but it became clear that he wasn't showing the house, much less packing it up to bring my furniture to North Dakota, as I got calls from farmers all over the country who'd encountered Chuck: *Hi, this is Jack Townsend from Maine, Chuck Perry was just here and he said you could help me . . . Hello, this is Joe Jackson from Pennsylvania . . . Hello, Sarah, you don't know me, but I'm Charles Hewitt from Wyoming, and Chuck Perry says . . .*

I found a real estate agent who did his best to show the condo during midday because the electricity had been turned off—I'd failed to honor a payment plan Chuck had negotiated but not told me about. In Bismarck, the pre-foreclosure notice on the condo's second mortgage arrived. *Dear Ms. Vogel, In compliance with the requirements contained in your Note, dated July 13, 1981, please be advised that your loan is hereby declared in default.*

I should have simply left North Dakota, gone to Virginia, and taken care of matters there, but I didn't even see that as an option.

I developed the ability to ignore troubles, specifically those troubles that came in the form of bills from back east. I was in North Dakota now. My immediate needs were to put gas in the car I'd borrowed from my father and pay the phone bill. Work was my escape from worry.

That winter, there were occasional days of vivid white snow, blue skies, and optimism when a few hundred dollars of fees came in. But the predominant view from the picture windows was of cold gray skies. The river views weren't as pretty when it was covered with jagged ice. The charm of the rural country setting of our house had drawbacks in the winter; the biggest was how to get out of a long driveway after it snowed. I found a friendly hippie who lived in a rainbow-hued trailer a short way down the river, who plowed us out when Andrew and I were snowed in.

Andrew and I spent Christmas in Grand Forks, where my father not so subtly tried to dissuade me from practicing law by myself but also gave me the keys to the law school library, where I could continue my research on due process that I intended to use against FmHA. I was very grateful that my Christmas present from my parents was money. When we got home, even Andrew's small Christmas checks for college from his grandparents were cashed for food. College was a long way away. We had to eat every day.

CHAPTER 5

The Starve Out

After I turned off the lamps in my cluttered office, I would stoke the wood-stove to keep the heat up during the night and then put on my coat, hat, and gloves and go out on the deck to smoke. The cigarettes were my secret relief from anxiety.

On clear nights, especially if it was very cold, often well below zero, the stars seemed impossibly bright, with the Milky Way a bright ribbon across the navy-blue sky. I'd missed those stars in D.C. and New York City, where I went months without seeing any stars at all. When there was a full moon, the moon and its reflection off the snow were so bright it seemed like daytime.

I didn't just smoke late at night. During the day, when tension would rack me, or if I couldn't think straight, I would sneak out back behind the house, or go into the garage, to smoke. The worry that dogged my days and kept me from sleeping at night were assuaged by nicotine—or so I believed.

I was often lonely. I didn't go out to socialize, to attend church, or even to go to bars. I'd always had co-workers, who often were also my friends, and working alone was new to me. I'd sometimes call Norma, my best friend in New York, and say, "It's twenty-seven degrees below zero and fantastically beautiful! Come visit!" This, as it turned out, was a poor way to encourage visitors from the East Coast.

. . .

WHILE I MAY not have had much of a social life, or any law partners with whom I could share the work, I still had allies who were of immeasurable support to me.

The biggest difference between the East Coast and North Dakota was actually not the weather, but the role of politicians in our lives. Politics in North Dakota was face-to-face, not driven by data, polls, or artificial "name recognition" advertising. In terms of population, North Dakota was the size of a medium-sized East Coast city, but we had two senators and one congressman. Most citizens of North Dakota had met, worked with, and felt comfortable with all three. We knew them by their first names.

Farmers in North Dakota had been working with their elected leaders for decades. They thought nothing of writing letters asking for guidance, information, or help from politicians—regardless of whether they had voted for or against that politician—and they typically received letters or phone calls back containing meaningful advice.

Wild Bill Langer, my family's hero, was known for going above and beyond in his constituent services. As an undergrad at the University of North Dakota, I'd reviewed boxes of Governor Langer's correspondence files, and I saw that almost every letter was answered within one or two days, and the answers were substantive:

I've written to the head of the purchasing division of the state hospital to find out why he did not accept your bid for flour. If you were the low bidder, he should have done so.

I've called out the National Guard to stop the foreclosure sale that you told me about.

As soon as I moved back, I reconnected with local Democratic–Nonpartisan League politicians. It was like a family reunion. I knew Senator Quentin Burdick (whose father, Usher, had been the head of the Farmers' Holiday Association in the '30s) because my friend Sara Garland worked for him. I knew Congressman Byron Dorgan, who was friendly and a fearless farmer advocate. I knew Tax Commissioner Kent Conrad, whose parents and grandparents had been political allies of my father and grandfather. They referred farmer clients to me and I called on them when I needed help. We all had to work together, especially as the parallels to the Dirty Thirties became more and more clear.

On March 28, 1982, the *New York Times*'s front page headline read U.S. FARMERS SAID TO FACE WORST YEAR SINCE 1930'S.[1] Farmers across the country were suffering the catastrophic effects of a "cost-price squeeze": it cost more and more for farmers to produce their crops and raise their livestock, and the prices they were getting at market were lower than the cost of production. Despite bland assurances from USDA that the farmers would be "fine," there was growing consensus that the farm economy was crashing. The delinquencies at FmHA had now reached 58 percent, "the highest in memory," according to the *Times*. The article quotes Stanley Weston, director of information at Farmers Home:

> "I've never met a farmer who hadn't just had a bad year," said Weston . . . commenting on how farmers love to complain. "But I've been in this business for 25 years and what I'm picking up now is really scary."

Congressman Dorgan sent a couple of dairy farmers my way in March 1982 because they, like so many others, were facing FmHA's harsh collection methods. Don and Diane McCabe were from Dickey, a tiny town in LaMoure County, 140 miles southeast of Bismarck. Everybody knew everybody in Dickey. LaMoure County was not a county that people moved to.

"If you don't get along with everybody, you don't speak to anybody" is how Diane described it.

They arrived at my house at midday, as all dairy farmers did. I hadn't yet graduated from my crash course in farming, but even I knew that dairy cows had to be milked morning and night, 365 days a year. The McCabes couldn't leave the farm until after the morning milking, and they had to be home and in their milking clothes by late afternoon.

Don and Diane had never been to the state capital before, and they'd likely never met a lawyer until that day. They arrived nicely dressed in their town clothes. They were guileless, trusting people. Unlike some of the other gargantuan farmers I'd met, Don was slim and of medium height. Diane was petite and pretty, with dark hair. I offered them folding chairs and we got to work.

"Do you want to start?" Diane asked.

"You go on, honey," Don said.

Though she'd grown up on a dairy farm, Diane had never dreamed she'd become a dairy farmer herself. As a kid, she and her brother had milked thirty-eight cows a day, by hand. "I was so happy to get off that place," she said. (Diane and her siblings had been worked to the bone even as young children.) But when her dad called and asked if she and Don would come home from Fargo and help out, they couldn't say no. Don yearned to live in the country and work with animals. Diane gave in on the condition that she would not live in the same house as her harsh taskmaster father.

In 1977, Don and Diane bought a 320-acre dairy farm in tiny LaMoure County with a $154,600 emergency loan from FmHA. The McCabes were among the many farmers who received emergency loan funding during the Carter years. And USDA wasn't alone in pouring more credit out to farmers. In 1977, total farm debt outstanding was $118,936,000, and it rose precipitously to $195,422,000 by 1981.[2] Prices in the marketplace weren't keeping pace with the ever-increasing costs of farmers. Farmers filled the difference between what they earned and what they spent with credit. Land values had been steadily rising for decades; it seemed like a safe bet for the lenders and the farmers.

"We just wanted to get off on our own," Diane said. They borrowed additional money for operating expenses such as seed, fertilizer, and feed. Don and Diane scrupulously followed the instructions of their county supervisor, but early on, FmHA wouldn't lend them money for a simple pole barn to shelter their cows, and one night, in the winter of 1977, seven of their cows froze to death.

"When *one* dies, it hurts," Diane said.

"They were my buddies," Don said.

Then came the natural disasters: hail in '78 and drought in '79 and '80. This affected their ability to grow enough feed for their herd, and they started to fall behind on their scheduled loan payments.

These loan payments were calculated based on a certain number of cows producing milk. They started with fifty-two cows, which Don knew by name. "Absolutely I can tell one from another," he said. "None of them alike."

"They won't go in for milking until he calls their name," Diane added.

But as cows grow older and their teeth wear out, they eat less and produce less milk. These older cows need to be "culled" (sold into the slaughter market) and periodically replaced with new cows. The McCabes told me that, inexplicably, the FmHA county director would not let them buy replacement cows, nor let them keep heifer (female) calves to raise to milking age. Now they only had twenty-seven cows, and they simply couldn't produce enough milk to pay their debt. FmHA demanded (as most lenders did) a milk assignment. Similar to wage garnishment, a milk assignment required the McCabes to repay their loans with a set amount from the money they earned from the dairy where they sold the milk. In a salaried job, a creditor can take no more than 25 percent of an employee's disposable income when garnishing wages. There was no such cap on FmHA. They were taking 50 percent of the McCabes' dairy income. What was left over for the McCabes after FmHA took its payment was barely enough for them to buy feed or pay for the electricity for milking, let alone cover their living expenses.

"Do you know that the number one priority for farm income is supposed to be family living expenses?" I asked.

"They never told us that," Diane said.

It was obvious that Don and Diane were both farmers. But when they went in to meet with their supervisor at the FmHA office, Diane was ignored. "We go in there and basically they talk to Don. Like I'm not in the room."

Even with all the financial stress, the McCabes knew that if they could just restore the number of cows in their herd and provide better feed and supplements to their cows, they could work their way out of hard times. But their application for an operating loan for 1982 was rejected by FmHA. That meant no money for feed or replacement cows. It would be better, according to the FmHA staff, if they quit farming altogether.

In desperation, they went to a LaMoure County bank to get a loan—that also needed to be repaid, of course. As a result, there were now two milk assignments of their dairy income: 50 percent to FmHA and 50 percent to the bank. There was nothing left for the McCabes to live on.

Don and Diane had two little kids, Shawn and Tiffany. Even if they sold their remaining cows, their equipment, and their land, the market was so depressed that the funds generated wouldn't pay FmHA off in full. Would their debt follow them and their children? they asked me.

I was enraged by how they'd been treated. Even I could see how stupid it was not to let dairy farmers replace aging dairy cows.

"Did they tell you that you had a right to appeal when they rejected your operating loan application?"

"No," Don said.

"How about when your cattle died? Or after the drought? Did they tell you that you had a right to apply for a deferral?"

"No."

"They didn't tell you about your rights?"

Don paused. He looked at Diane, who shook her head. "I didn't know I had any rights," he said.

"We just do what they tell us because they're FmHA's cows," Diane said.

"No, they're not, Diane!" I yelled. Her face went pale. "Those are *your* cows!" I took a deep breath and explained the security interest. "When you signed the paperwork, it said that Farmers Home has a security interest in your cows, which you pledge as collateral for the loan. It just means if you go into default and there's a sale of those cows, FmHA gets the proceeds, up to the value of their security interest."

"We figured that was their cattle," Don said.

"We didn't know if we could eat a pea out of the garden," Diane joked, relieved that she wasn't in trouble.

Even with all the cardboard boxes and piles of paper in my office, I knew exactly where my Code of Federal Regulations was, and I showed them the specific regulations that affected their loans and how FmHA had violated their rights. Diane asked how she could get her own copy of the CFR. (I didn't realize it at the time, but this simple purchase of a volume of the Code of Federal Regulations would launch Diane's subsequent career as a farm credit activist.)

I told them about their right to appeal and their right to apply for a deferral under the deferral law passed by Congress. And I told Don and Diane that there were thousands of farmers, all over the country, who were in a similar boat.

"You mean I'm not the only one?" Don asked.

They were not alone, and they were not at fault. I saw a visible lifting of shame as I insisted that their inability to pay was "due to circumstances beyond their control"—just as the deferral law said.

Our meeting gave the McCabes spirit and hope. They went back to the FmHA office, where they were told if they "left quietly" and sold their land to a neighbor or conveyed their farm to FmHA, and took their cows to an auction barn, and moved away, FmHA would let them off the hook of any debt that exceeded the value of the sales. *Oh*, the county supervisor added, the McCabes would also need to pay them $500 in cash. Don thought it might have been a demand for a bribe. I told them no, it was more likely a debt settlement.

"Get them to put it in writing," I told Don over the phone.

Soon I heard back: no one at the county office would put the terms of the debt settlement in writing.

"The man says that we have to accept it based on his verbal offer. We have to trust him," Don said.

But the trust Don and Diane had in FmHA had vanished. They wanted to keep farming and they wanted to be treated fairly by the rules.

From that point forward, FmHA refused to release any cash to the McCabes, refused all loans, and started the internal process to accelerate the debts they owed. The McCabes now had cows but no way to feed them. The couple scrambled: they got hay in exchange for work they did for neighbors and they cut additional hay from grass growing in ditches. The family went without, but the cows at least had feed.

I didn't even try sending a bill (or I didn't have the time to write one), but the McCabes somehow managed to send me $100 with a handwritten note from Diane, on a small green piece of paper, that said:

> I realize it isn't that much, but it's all we can afford right now. Just want to send along a thank-you for the help you've given us and all the advice. I'm sure it seems like all your efforts just don't get rewarded, but we're going to do all we can to remedy that. Sarah, can you please send us some sort of statement of what we owe you. Will try to send more soon.
>   God bless you Sarah and thanks a lot,
>   Don and Diane McCabe

Faced with their courage, I couldn't quit either.

AFTER SHUMAN DISPATCHED his Foreclosure Quota Memo, I found that Farmers Home rarely followed the regulation that said family living expenses were the first priority. This was brought home to me when I got a call from a farmer in Oliver County. I'd been helping him get his files to help prepare for an appeal but he called one night with a new crisis.

His voice shook as he described what he'd learned that day: his check for health insurance had bounced. When he called to find out why, he was told that his supervised bank account was empty. All of the funds had been removed by

FmHA. His wife was in a precarious pregnancy and would need specialized medical care at the birth. He had only a day or two before the insurance would lapse. He had six kids, and one of them had medical issues.

The next day, I called the Oliver County office. They brushed me off, so I called Congressman Dorgan's office and he sent an aide down the hall to the state FmHA office and that aide sweet-talked them into telling the county office to release part of the income from a crop sale to the family so they could pay the premium. That particular crisis was, at least temporarily, averted.

On another night I'll never forget, I received a collect call from Mary Lacina, a friend of the McCabes who farmed with her husband, Jim, south of Jamestown. The couple had what looked like a prosperous farm: good land, nice home and farm buildings, well-kept machinery. Their crops and calves were being produced at the anticipated volumes. The wrinkle was that the prices for their crops and calves were lower than the cost of production. They were losing money despite their "success."

The Lacinas were among the hundreds of farmers in North Dakota selected by FmHA for "elimination" of their delinquent loans. Their loans had been accelerated, which meant the full balance was due imminently. They had already let their health insurance lapse. Mary sounded at the edge of panic. In the background, I could hear a child wailing. The child was ill, Mary said, and she had gone to a doctor's office in the nearest town for medicine. Without insurance, the doctor insisted on payment up front, but the supervised bank account had been emptied.

That night, I had no legal magic remedy to offer Mary or the sick child.

I thought of the welfare recipients I'd worked with as a volunteer with the ACLU during my last year at NYU. There was a case, *Goldberg v. Kelly*, argued in the U.S. Supreme Court in October 1969, involving the due process rights of poor mothers who received Aid to Families with Dependent Children (AFDC). They sued John Kelly, the administrator of the New York City welfare programs. The plaintiffs were suspected of welfare fraud and had their benefits suspended without being given a chance to tell their side of the story. They were not even told the reasons why welfare officials believed they had committed fraud.

These mothers' benefits, for essential items like rent and groceries, were suspended as soon as they were accused of the fraud, but they were not offered a hearing at which they could defend themselves and learn the reasons behind

Sarah Vogel at her river house in 1982. © Grey Villet

the cutoff until months *after* the benefits had been revoked. Worse, when they finally did get a hearing, the hearing officer was not a neutral party but an employee of the same office that wanted to take away their benefits.

New York City argued that their hearing process was good enough and complied with the Constitution. The lawyers for the plaintiffs disagreed. They argued that taking away these benefits was a denial of due process protections guaranteed by the U.S. Constitution.

In my favorite constitutional law class, Professor Dorsen taught us that the right to "due process of law" was put into effect by the Fifth Amendment, which said, "No person shall be . . . deprived of life, liberty, or property, without due process of law," and by the Fourteenth Amendment, which said, "nor shall any State deprive any person of life, liberty or property, without due process of law." In due process litigation, one of the biggest issues is defining what is "property," and the *Goldberg* case addressed the question of whether welfare benefits were "property" under the protection of the Fifth and Fourteenth amendments.

The plaintiffs' lawyers argued that the welfare recipients were entitled to a "pretermination" hearing that met constitutional muster *before* their benefits were cut off. The city argued that welfare benefits belonged to the state, which had the right to expend them as needed, that the welfare recipients had a "mere expectancy" that the benefits would be continued, and that a hearing offered after the benefits were cut off was hunky-dory.

The *Goldberg* decision, issued March 23, 1970, settled that argument. The Supreme Court said these welfare recipients were entitled to due process and a fair hearing *before* the very means of their survival could be taken away.

Throughout the city, the lawyers representing the poor mothers and children (and they were almost all mothers and children) immediately went into action gathering information for the fair hearings that the Supreme Court now required. They reached out to the NYU Law School's ACLU chapter, to which I belonged. At an evening meeting in the basement of the law school, excited legal services lawyers asked us to help gather evidence. We were thrilled to be given a chance to put the Constitution into practice.

That night, we learned that a *Goldberg* fair hearing was a hearing that occurred *before* essential benefits were taken away—not after. And the hearing itself had to meet certain conditions of fairness: The recipient was entitled to adequate notice of the date of the hearing and of detailed reasons for the proposed termination. The recipient should be given the opportunity to defend herself.

I was given the name and address of a woman in the Bronx, a borough I had been to only once before—in a car. My memory of the client meeting has been eclipsed by what I saw on the street as soon as I got out of the subway.

The Bronx looked like pictures of London after the Blitz. Falling-down buildings, boarded-up windows, broken windows, trash everywhere. I wasn't prepared for the scale of devastation I witnessed. The Bronx didn't even seem occupied. It appeared even the trees were dead.

As I walked down the broken sidewalk toward the street and building where my client lived, I saw a Pieta of Poverty that made the dry words of the *Goldberg v. Kelly* decision come to tragic life. A young Black woman holding a small child was sitting on a stoop with her head down, weeping, hopeless. On the sidewalk next to her was a small chaotic pile of once precious possessions (a mattress, bedding, chairs, clothes, pots and pans). This "trash" on the sidewalk had once furnished a home for her and her child. The image was burned into me.

This poor woman did not receive a fair hearing. She lost the very means of her survival. A hearing in two weeks or two months could never restore her life. Never could I have imagined that the plight of these single Black mothers would provide me with the inspiration to develop a legal theory that would protect North Dakotan family farmers a decade later.

CHAPTER 6

A Little Bit of Nothing

North Dakotans keep their eyes on the receding snowbanks for the first true sign of spring: the "prairie crocus," or pasque flower. When it emerges from a tangle of dun-colored prairie grasses, it's a sign that the earth is still alive and will grow green again. Throughout the day, the pale lilac to vivid purple flowers slowly move in an arc from horizon to horizon as each flower greets the sunrise and watches the sun set. God designed the flower to capture every beam of sunshine. Its leaves and petals are covered with fine threadlike hairs to maximize exposure to warmth.

The spring of 1982 was my first spring in North Dakota since 1967, and just as my parents had taken me to see the first crocuses in the prairie outside Garrison, I took Andrew to see the crocuses along the bluffs above the Missouri River valley. Every south-facing hillside was dotted with patches of lilac. Just seeing the prairie crocuses emerge from a mat of dried prairie grasses brought joy and hope to people who had endured a long hard winter. Native Americans believed that its song encouraged other plants to awaken.

But as the earth sprang to life with hope, the crisis for farmers was only growing worse. That spring, as Shuman's deadline for meeting delinquency reduction quotas came and went, ninety-six farm auctions took place[1] in the single richest and most fertile stretch of farmland in the United States: the Red River Valley of North Dakota and Minnesota. The *Bismarck Tribune* reported fifty-four bankruptcies in North Dakota, Minnesota, and South Dakota in just the first six months of 1982, compared to nineteen in the entire prior year.[2] When the Agriculture Council of America held a twelve-hour open conference call, four thousand farmers called in. Thirty-two percent said the farm conditions were the "worst ever"; 30 percent said they were "bad"; 14 percent said they did not expect to survive in farming and ranching.[3] At farm crisis rallies in the South, white farmers protested alongside Black farmers. (The Black farmers, who had been fighting FmHA for years, probably welcomed the help.) USDA insisted that the problems were minimal, but its protestations were less credible by the day.

For the first time since 1954, the overall value of farmland had declined in the United States, due to high interest rates and a squeeze on farm profits.[4] Farmland appraisals typically changed very little from year to year because they were based on the average of several years of comparable sales. But that changed on May 10, 1982, when Charles W. Shuman, the national administrator of FmHA, issued Administrative Notice 695, which said, "Market values of farm real estate has changed drastically in some areas during recent months... *Comparable property sales occurring over 12 months before the appraisal is prepared should not be used*" (emphasis added).

The same order applied to machinery and livestock appraisals. Not only were farmers earning less, the value of what they owned was precipitously dropping. And, because FmHA had so many loans and was acquiring so much property through "voluntary" liquidation, FmHA's land and collateral devaluations influenced other lenders to also focus on recent depressed prices.

Secretary of Agriculture John Block wrote an editorial in the South Dakota Farmers Union newspaper, shilling "good news": a short wheat crop in Russia and the Falklands War between Argentina and Great Britain both spelled opportunity for American farmers. In general, bad news elsewhere (crop failure, drought, floods) is good news for scarce markets. At a meeting in Georgia, farmers presented him with a roll of auction bills tied with a black ribbon.

BACK IN BISMARCK, I felt I was always behind, never getting enough done.

I'd done all that work on Tom Nichols's national appeal thinking I'd get paid through the Equal Access to Justice Act if we won. And we did win—sort of. In my appeal brief to FmHA, I'd pointed out a number of flaws with the decision, one of which was that it wasn't even written by the district director, the purported "judge" who presided over the Nicholses' hearing. Rather, the state director—whose decision we were appealing—upheld his own decision.

The general counsel of USDA called this a "procedural irregularity." And what a procedural irregularity it was! Imagine if a prosecutor lost a criminal trial and then pushed the judge off the bench, stole his robe, threw the robe on over his suit, and sat on the bench to bang the gavel and yell, "A win for the prosecution!"

It wasn't the decision we'd hoped for, in which the national director would rule in Tom's favor and demand the local Montana office make things right, but at least we won. So what if we won on a "procedural irregularity"? So what if the general counsel had thrown in the gratuitous statement "This does not mean the decision to accelerate was incorrect"? We still won. Within days, I sent in a motion for an award of $10,000 in attorney's fees under EAJA, reflecting many weeks of work at $75 an hour.

I received a curt reply saying that FmHA did not consider the EAJA to apply to its administrative appeal system. Game, set for FmHA.

My whole strategy for getting paid for my FmHA appeals was shot to hell. If I wanted to be paid on any FmHA appeal that I won, I'd have to sue FmHA in federal court and win and then go back to the agency. That could take many years. If I spent all my time trying to collect legal fees, I'd have no time to work on my cases.

And now FmHA was after the Nicholses with even greater ferocity. The state director wrote to Tom saying that if he did not turn in a new farm plan "based on his current situation" by April 7, 1982, the acceleration would be reinstated.

After eight and a half months of having his income frozen, plus ever-accumulating interest on his loans, Tom's financial situation was even worse than it had been the year before. Tom wrote back: "First, you *annihilate* my operation and then you ask me to submit a plan based on my *current* situation?"

I sent a sharp letter to Shuman, cc'ing the Office of General Counsel and the Montana State Office, to say Shuman had a regulatory obligation to review the merits of appeals like Tom and Anna's, but it was fruitless. A new acceleration notice dated April 12, 1982, was issued with the same reasons as the acceleration notice dated July 29, 1981, affording them the "opportunity" to go through the appeal charade again. Game, set, match for FmHA.

Tom was tenacious and a brilliant problem solver, and I always admired him for refusing to be cowed by any bureaucracy. He sent in a FOIA (*"foy*-yah") request for a complete set of all the bulletins, instructions, and other rules that governed FmHA employees and comprised FmHA "policy" but weren't published in the *Federal Register* or in the Code of Federal Regulations.

The FOIA office of USDA in Washington replied that if Tom wanted them, he'd have to pay $2,408 in cash, up front.

I knew these nasty gambits only worked while we were in FmHA's arena. We needed to get out of FmHA's arena. I just didn't yet see how.

Fueled by outrage, my energy was high, but my funds were running critically short. Financially, I was in the same boat as most of my clients. I received checks only sporadically, for $200, $100, or $50, never the full value of my time. Often I was too busy (or disorganized) to send bills at all. Some of my clients were able to borrow money from relatives, but most had no resources whatsoever. Deeply ashamed of their inability to pay me, they brought me homemade bread, frozen farm-processed meat (I had abandoned vegetarianism when Tom and Anna came to stay), and jars of home-preserved tomatoes. One farmer went fishing and had exceptional success. He gutted and scaled the fish and prepared packets of fish fillets, which he froze and brought to me in a cooler. Several farmers drained gas from their on-farm gasoline tanks (farmers did not like to drive thirty miles to town to refill a gas tank, so it was common for them to have bulk tanks on their farmsteads) and brought five or ten gallons to Bismarck. (My car was almost always on empty, and the brakes were giving out too.)

But I couldn't pay my mounting bills with home preserves. I tried to get my clients to call me so the charge would go on their phone bill, but all too often I was out of the office and I had no choice but to call them back. My March phone bill was $449. On top of all my expenses in North Dakota (office supplies, phone, utilities, Andrew's pediatrician), unpaid utility bills and department store credit card statements kept coming from D.C.

By April 21, I was eight months overdue on my Virginia condo payments and I was served with a "Warrant in Debt" by the sheriff. I drafted a rather optimistic form letter I could send to my many creditors, to whom I owed hundreds, if not thousands, of dollars. "To Whom It May Concern," it said:

I have enclosed a token check for $5.00. I'm sorry for the delay in making prompt payments in the past. I have been making progress in the new law firm and expect I will be able to make regular monthly payments in the future.

On April 27, the South Dakota Farmers Union flew me to a farm crisis meeting in Pierre (pronounced "Peer"). The organizers intended to bring farmers and ranchers together to see what common action could be taken to prevent foreclosure. I was there to instruct farmers on how to get their files from FmHA. I told them they had rights, including the right to appeal, and that there was a law that said that farmers could apply for a deferral if they could not pay due to circumstances beyond their control. But there were right-wing tax protesters in the audience who used the platform to broadcast some more radical solutions.

One man said that Americans were subsidizing Satan by paying federal income taxes. "There's no way a Christian can sign, file, and pay an income tax," he told the room.

Another activist claimed that paper money was worthless because it was no longer backed by silver or gold (FDR had severed the connection between the dollar and gold in 1933 in order to pump more money into the economy). Paper money was just "Rockefeller toilet paper" and it was time for farmers to seek criminal charges against the government officials running lending programs like FmHA's because they were perpetuating an unconstitutional currency system.

In the parking lot, one of the cars had a bumper sticker that said HAVE YOU TOLD A BUREAUCRAT TO GO TO HELL TODAY?[5]

That night, the president of the SDFU asked if I would help a couple of farmers named Eugene and Linda Myran appeal their loan acceleration in a few days. The Farmers Union would send a plane for me, and the Myrans somehow found (or borrowed) a little money to pay me for my time.

I met the Myrans in a motel room the night before the hearing. They were excellent farmers, hard workers, and strong Farmers Union members. Eugene had lost half of one arm in 1968, but this hardly affected his farming. "I think I got more than one arm," he told me, gesturing at his stump. "It comes in handy for some things that you can't do with a regular arm."

On May 5, at eight thirty A.M., the hearing began in a small, dim conference room with tan walls and fluorescent lights overhead. For two and a half hours, the Myrans described the drought, livestock disease, and grasshoppers that had devastated their farm in the summer of 1981.

"One hundred percent disaster," Eugene said. "We didn't have any snow. It warmed up early in the spring and the alfalfa come along eight, ten inches high and then it froze and by the time a guy cut it and let it dry down and put it up you had nothing—a little bit of nothing." He was as succinct and plainspoken as Pa Joad in *The Grapes of Wrath*.

Farmers Home made their case that the Myrans were simply bad managers.

Despite losing 60 percent of their crop to drought and selling cattle at a loss, they had managed to pay almost $200,000 to FmHA on December 10, 1981. While they were still $79,981 delinquent, they had obviously done well in spite of the disasters they'd faced.

According to regulations, FmHA employees reviewing a delinquent loan were first supposed to determine *why* the loan was delinquent. They were then supposed to meet with the farmer to offer advice and set up a plan of action.

On the Myrans' record, the reason for delinquency was given as "tough deal." The space for improvement was left blank. The Myrans' "farm plan" laid out their options: if there was no "voluntary" sale in 1982, there would be a foreclosure in 1983.

"Were you ever offered a deferral?" I asked Eugene and Linda.

"No," they said.

I handed a copy of the 1978 deferral law to their county supervisor. "Were you ever advised that farmer borrowers are eligible for deferrals under the law?" I asked.

He was familiar with deferrals only for rural housing loans, not for farm loans.

I started to read aloud from the law, but the district director interrupted me to say these quotes were from the housing section of the law.

"No, they're not," I said. I introduced the law as an exhibit.

Although I was frustrated, I can't say I was surprised by these employees' willful ignorance. They had been trained to follow the policies set forth in bulletins sent out by the national office. They weren't trained to think for themselves; they were trained to be good soldiers and obey orders.

I made a final argument for why the foreclosure was improper and the acceleration should be reversed. The county supervisor justified his decision for recommending the foreclosure. The hearing was over by eleven.

I had done the best I could, but we still lost. I would go on to lose nearly every single appeal hearing I did in front of FmHA.

One minute after the Myran hearing adjourned, at twelve oh one P.M. eastern time, my Virginia condo was sold in a trustee's sale on the front steps of the Arlington County courthouse by a law firm called Perry, Perry & Perry.

PART II

The Growing

CHAPTER 7

The Organizers

On May 7, 1982, I opened a letter from my father that said "Aren't you practicing law without a license? I can't sleep at night worrying about you committing malpractice. Come to Grand Forks, and work here, if necessary." At the end, he did not sign it "Love, Dad." He didn't sign it at all. I flushed with shame. I did not disagree with him. I intended to get licensed but I was always too busy. I had no money for the hefty bar license fee. I rationalized that if I did only the kinds of work that a nonlawyer could do, like an FmHA appeal, I was within the guidelines. (I was wrong.) I didn't write back to my father.

I kept thinking that something was bound to break soon. My friends at Congressman Dorgan's office told me that many members of Congress were doing their utmost to get USDA to back off on their campaign to "eliminate" delinquent loans by pressuring farmers to "voluntarily liquidate." I knew that complaints had been filed in Georgia and Kansas to compel USDA to provide farmers with the right to apply for deferrals. This was the same argument I'd used in hearings like the Myrans', and if either the Georgia or Kansas case won, I believed the legal principles would apply to FmHA borrowers in North Dakota. FmHA offices nationwide were supposed to follow identical rules.

One glorious day that spring, Andrew was outside playing "war" with sticks from the woodpile while I was on the phone with a distraught farmer. The doorbell rang.

"Are you Sarah Vogel?" I didn't know the man on my doorstep.

"Yes?"

He handed me a stiff envelope and asked for a signature. As he drove away, I tore open the envelope: "Notice Before Foreclosure." The mortgage on my Bismarck house had been accelerated and I had thirty days to pay the full balance of $80,000 or face foreclosure.

I went to the living room, sat down on one of the hand-me-down chairs facing the big picture window, and cried. I loved living on the river, surrounded by the song of the cottonwoods. I'd been there for only eight months. Where would Andrew and I go? My only realistic option was to quit private practice, move to Grand Forks, and concede that I couldn't keep doing farmer cases. My father believed that lawyers should spend 10 percent of their time on pro bono cases; I knew he'd never tolerate my practice, which was (unintentionally) 90 percent pro bono. The guilt was searing. All of the farmers who were relying on me would be lost if I left.

My whole body ached. After a few minutes, I felt Andrew's warm little hands on my face, brushing away my tears. "Mama, what's wrong?" His big blue eyes were wide with worry.

"I'm all right," I said. "It's okay."

"Don't cry," Andrew pleaded. "I'll help you!" He climbed into my lap and threw his arms around my neck. I resolved to never again be that weak in front of him; it was my Scarlett O'Hara moment.

"Let's go down to the river!" I said.

We splashed through the shallows toward our favorite sandbar and played until we grew hungry. Then we headed back inside. The sunshine and fresh air had calmed my panic, and when I picked up the notice that I'd dropped on the floor, this time I read it as a lawyer would. I realized that the lawyers that prepared the notice hadn't followed the 1933 law[1] adopted by the Nonpartisan League that gave debtors the right to cure the default (pay the amount owed) before a loan could be accelerated and before a foreclosure action could be filed. My notice of acceleration was as illegal as the notices that FmHA was giving to all my farm clients.

Yes, I was delinquent on my mortgage payments, but I was confident that the notice of acceleration was void. I could stall—which for the moment was enough.

. . .

MARK RITCHIE WAS a policy analyst at the Minnesota Department of Agriculture and a farm organizer who modeled his work on the "old-timers" of the 1930s like William Langer, Usher Burdick, and the Farmers' Holiday Association. The first time I ever went to Mark's house in St. Paul, he introduced me to his special guest: ninety-year-old Clarence Sharp, a progressive activist who'd worked under A. C. Townley, founder of the Nonpartisan League, before joining the Communist Party in the 1930s and leading penny auctions against farm foreclosures in South Dakota.[2]

Clarence remembered my grandfather Frank well. "He knew everybody," he said. "He could always get a crowd—even on short notice."

Mark Ritchie started organizing meetings to bring organizers from Clarence's era and younger farm advocates together to map strategy, share information, and lend support. I didn't have anyone to talk to in North Dakota other than my clients, who just didn't have the big picture—they were trying to feed their animals and children and keep the electricity on. The folks at Mark's meetings saw the big picture, and they could inspire and educate many hundreds of others. They came from Nebraska, Iowa, Minnesota, and Illinois.

Over coffee and caramel rolls at a meeting in Minnesota, I met Annette Higby and Gene Severens from the Center for Rural Affairs, who were working on a plain-language guide for farmers on FmHA programs and remedies. I met Dave Ostendorf and Danny Levitas, who were working at the Midwestern office of Rural America, a liberal rural advocacy group, in Iowa. Dave was a United Church of Christ minister and a skilled organizer. Danny was Dave's intern, and the youngest among us, but we soon realized he was the sharpest tack in the box. He'd grown up in New York City, the son of an editor at the *New York Times*, and had amazing writing and speaking skills. He'd rebelled as a teenager by leaving New York City and attending the School of Natural Resources at the University of Michigan. After college, he moved to rural Iowa to intern at an organic dairy farm and to work as an organizer with Rural America and the Progressive Prairie Alliance. These rural organizations drew inspiration from the NPL and the Farmers' Holiday Association, and they showed the movie *Northern Lights*, a 1978 film dramatizing the origins of the NPL, at many of their meetings.

The meetings of our ragtag group of farm advocates moved around from state to state. I was the only North Dakotan who attended, and I could afford only the time and gas money to get to Minnesota, not to the other states. The six-hour drive from Bismarck to St. Paul was a long and lonely one, and sometimes I'd mentally rehearse my farewell speech, which went something like, "I'm worn out, broke, and tired. I don't have a salary. I have a little kid who needs a roof over his head. I can't do it anymore. I'm here because I thought I owed it to you to tell you in person."

But by the end of the meeting, Mark or Danny or Dave would have helped me see a light at the end of the tunnel. I'd have learned about some accomplishment in Iowa, or been informed of a hearing at which members of Congress excoriated Secretary Block. We fancied ourselves a "movement," like the civil rights movement or the fight for women's suffrage.[3] And we were. When I left those meetings, I felt inspired, renewed, and hopeful.

The small group of people Mark brought together were like slender fibers woven together into a strong rope. A particular fiber separated from the others can easily be snapped, but when all of the fibers are united, woven back and forth and working together, they are impervious to snapping. The young activists were scattered in small Midwestern towns all over, but woven together, we were a force to be reckoned with.

From his little basement office in the Minnesota Department of Agriculture, Mark gathered and shared information from every corner of the United States and the world. Among the many farm organizations Mark worked with were Black farmer organizations such as the Federation of Southern Cooperatives and the Sharecroppers Union. In early 1982, Mark told many of us about a lawsuit that had been filed in Georgia, called *Curry v. Block*. The plaintiffs represented a class of Georgia farmers whose FmHA loans "have been foreclosed, are in foreclosure, are threatened with foreclosure, or shall be foreclosed upon or threatened with foreclosure." The plaintiffs alleged that USDA had violated the law by not properly implementing 7 USC Section 1981a, which gave borrowers the right to apply for deferral.

Curry v. Block was brought by a Georgia Legal Services lawyer named Martha Miller. Initially, I was jealous of Martha. I wished I had a salary and the support of an employer who paid the rent and the phone bills!

But I was also amazed that Georgia Legal Services could do such a case, because I'd unsuccessfully tried to get Legal Services of North Dakota to help me and they couldn't. Eligibility was based on *gross* assets, not net assets. Even a small farmer had tens of thousands of dollars in assets. None of my clients would be eligible for legal services. How had Martha found farmers who met the eligibility standards for legal services? They must be very poor sharecroppers or have tiny farms, I thought. On top of that, President Reagan hated legal services lawyers from his time as California governor,[4] and David Stockman wanted to cut, slash, and chop legal services from the federal budget. Congress prevented the elimination of legal services to the poor, but under Reagan, legal services lawyers were essentially barred from doing any kind of "public interest" litigation and prohibited from starting class actions. Many decades later, I learned that Martha Miller felt so strongly about doing the case for Remur Curry and other Georgia farmers that she'd quit her Legal Services job to take the case to court as an attorney in private practice.

Curry was heard before the chief judge of the Georgia District Courts, Judge Anthony A. Alaimo. He was a Republican who was appointed by President Richard Nixon. In Georgia, Judge Alaimo was famous for having been a prisoner of war during World War II and for requiring major reforms of Georgia's unconstitutional and cruel incarceration practices.

In the early 1950s, when he was having a hard time supporting his family as a lawyer, he spent two years working on his wife's family farm in Ohio. Alaimo's biographer, Vincent Coppola, tells a story from that time:

> Tony was out in the stubbled fields harvesting the last of the corn crop when the corn picker on his tractor broke down . . . "I was down there on the ground trying to fix one of the gathering chains on the damn thing," he recalled. "I spent four hours working on it and just about froze to death. Finally, I said, 'Hell, I'm going back to practice law.'"[5]

It is lucky for farmers that he did.

It was also lucky that the *Curry* case had been filed in Georgia, because Martha Miller and Judge Alaimo knew something that I didn't know, which was that USDA had settled a case, *Williams v. Butz*,[6] in federal court in Georgia in October 1977, involving a law that was almost identical to the deferral law. In the *Williams* case, the secretary of agriculture under Carter agreed that USDA would provide personal notice to people who were in default on their FmHA home loans of their right to apply for deferrals.

But under President Reagan, Stockman put unrelenting pressure on USDA to make collection of overdue debts a top priority, and USDA adamantly refused to acknowledge that farmers had any right to apply for deferrals.

That is where matters stood before Secretary Block and FmHA Administrator Shuman were hauled into Judge Alaimo's courtroom. The balance of power between farmers and USDA irrevocably changed on June 11, 1982, when Judge Alaimo issued his ruling in *Curry v. Block*.

Mark Ritchie called me on the phone. "It's a win! Alaimo ruled in favor of the farmers!" he said. I had to wait anxiously for my copy to arrive in the mail before I could read the full decision.

When I finally had the opportunity to see the decision for myself, I was white-hot with optimism about what this could mean for farmers in the Midwest.

In his twenty-six-page decision, Judge Alaimo refused to look at the deferral law in isolation, and instead said it was necessary for the court to review "the history of federal involvement in agriculture credit through 1978, beginning with the Homestead Act of 1863," which he said was "designed to provide farming opportunities for small-scale, family farmers." FmHA's loan programs were "spawned in the Depression years . . . [and] the object of the legislation is to aid the 'underprivileged' farmer, and is therefore a form of social welfare legislation."[7]

Judge Alaimo had a personal understanding of the Great Depression. He was born in Sicily, and shortly thereafter, his nearly illiterate parents fled for better opportunity. During the Depression years, the Alaimo family lived in a third-floor tenement in a blue-collar town in upstate New York. It was a dire struggle to feed and clothe themselves. Judge Alaimo's father, a bricklayer who had become a citizen in 1928, had been forced to "stand in line at the welfare office." As a boy, Judge Alaimo "would register a similar shame" when he was no longer able to collect a bucket of fresh milk from a farm two miles away because the farmer "cut off the family's credit."[8]

The legal issue at stake in *Curry v. Block* was the interpretation of the 1978 deferral law, which included the phrase "the Secretary may permit, at the request of the borrower, the deferral of principal and interest . . ." USDA argued that the word "may" meant they could do it or not do it, at their discretion. But Judge Alaimo disagreed. In this context, he argued that "may" meant "shall."[9]

Any discretion enjoyed by FmHA extended only to whether the qualifications for deferral were met.

Judge Alaimo forbade USDA to foreclose on farmers with delinquent farm program loans in Georgia until the regulations giving farmers the right to apply for deferral were in full force and effect.

FmHA was a national program, and its regulations applied uniformly throughout the United States. If USDA had to implement the deferral law through regulations, then those regulations—I hoped—would protect farmers all over the country, not only in Georgia.

Had Ralph Leet heard about the Curry *decision yet?* I wondered. *Would the national office of FmHA tell him to follow the regulations for North Dakota borrowers?*

On July 2, I received the answer to my questions.

Dear Ms. Vogel:
This is in response to your June 30 inquiry regarding the Georgia court decision.

We have been advised that decision prohibits foreclosures for the time being only in that State. It does not apply to other states.

Sincerely,
Ralph H. Leet
State Director

As USDA appealed Judge Alaimo's ruling to the Fifth Circuit, copycat cases were being hastily filed all over the country. The Center for Rural Affairs issued a warning: *Curry v. Block* had been carefully prepared by Martha Miller, and rushing into court without similar preparation was a huge risk. The warning was not well heeded. Federal judges in Wisconsin, South Carolina, Alabama, and Arkansas disagreed with Judge Alaimo.[10] Farmers were still losing.

If I was going to bring anything like a *Curry* case in North Dakota, I knew I'd have to prepare thoroughly. USDA had Department of Justice lawyers to defend them. I'd dealt with DOJ lawyers during my time at the FTC, and while I didn't like them, I respected them. They had the advantage of sharing expertise with thousands of other lawyers across government agencies throughout the country. To have even a chance at winning, I'd have to be much smarter, and much more relentless.

I drove into town to my home away from home, the Supreme Court law library. As Bob Vogel's daughter, I benefited from the goodwill he had built up with the staff there during his years on the North Dakota Supreme Court. The law librarians directed me to an entire shelf of books on Rule 23, the section of the Federal Rules of Civil Procedure that covered class actions.

According to Rule 23, in order to sue as a class, you had to meet certain prerequisites. The first of these was that the class had to be so numerous that it was impractical to list the names of all the plaintiffs. I thought, *I've got that covered!* The second requirement was that there had to be "questions of law or fact common to the class." No problem: all FmHA loans were governed by identical laws, regulations, administrative announcements, and forms. The third prerequisite was that "the claims and defenses of the representative parties had to be typical" of other members of the class. So many farmers told me of similar stories of mistreatment by FmHA that this typicality seemed easy to meet. The fourth and final requirement was that the "representative parties will fairly and adequately protect the interests of the class." This was vague, but I'd figure it out later.

The idea that I might bring my own class action on behalf of North Dakota farmers became more and more real, and I described what I was learning to Don and Diane McCabe the next time I visited their small farmhouse. They'd received notice on May 6 that their loans had been accelerated and they had to pay $231,547.66 in unpaid principal plus $30,314.05 in interest by June 4 or FmHA would foreclose on their farm. They'd failed "to liquidate voluntarily." There was no mention of their right to apply for deferral. A partial payment would not suffice. The notice, signed by Ralph Leet, said that if "you submit to the United States any payment insufficient to pay the entire indebtedness ... such payments WILL NOT CANCEL the effects of such notice." But the notice also gave the McCabes the "opportunity" to have a hearing before the foreclosure took place, so that's what we were preparing for.

At the kitchen table, we planned how we'd defend their case on appeal. One of the reasons for the acceleration was that "dairy production has been very poor," but the McCabes explained that it was the lack of nutritional supplements and not being allowed to purchase the proper quality of feed that was the problem with their dairy production—not the care that they gave the cows.

They agreed to get a local dairy expert to write an affidavit to that effect. Even with a strong defense, I anticipated losing the state appeal and having to carry it through to a national appeal. I mentally calculated $3,000 in legal fees I would likely never see.

"I can't keep doing this," I said.

"We know how busy you are, Sarah," Diane said.

"We sure appreciate the help," Don said.

I lit a cigarette. Andrew was outside, playing tag with Tiffany and Shawn. "No, I mean one at a time. One appeal at a time." It was like pushing a boulder up a mountain. I was only one person. Even if I was doing ten FmHA appeals at a time, that was nothing. There were hundreds of farmers in North Dakota alone being pressured by FmHA to "leave quietly" when they fell behind on payments.

"I want to do a class action like they did in Georgia," I said. "But I can't do it without any funding. I just don't see how."

"Well, why don't we put an ad in the paper?" Diane asked.

"You get five hundred farmers with Farmers Home to give ten dollars and a hundred farmers to give fifty—" Don added.

"And twenty to give a hundred, that's twelve thousand dollars," said Diane, who, like all farmers, could swiftly calculate numbers in her head. "How much do you need, Sarah?"

"Wait," I said, "the farmers who *haven't* borrowed from Farmers Home need to give, too." The land values were already starting to tip downward, and I figured that the value of farmland would fall rapidly if FmHA forced large numbers of FmHA borrowers to put farmland on the market in a short span of time. Then, their wealthier neighbors would watch their own equity vanish. Back in the 1930s, farmland prices had collapsed when the number of foreclosures rose. Further, legal scholars estimated that a foreclosure sale brought—at most—50 percent of the actual value of the land. Having many foreclosure sales would inevitably depress farmland values, and land values would inevitably spiral down, and down, and down. I believed that at least some of the farmers who weren't in any trouble with FmHA would find it worth their while to kick in a modest amount, say a thousand dollars each, to support a lawsuit that would prevent a crash in land values.

"We'll run it in the *Green Sheet*, honey," Don said to Diane. The *Farm Forum Green Sheet* covered agriculture news, agriculture prices, farm auctions, ads for chemicals and machinery, and other topics of interest to farmers. Farmers throughout North Dakota read every issue cover to cover.

Our ad ran right alongside the auction notices:

> FmHA Borrowers: Are you having trouble with the FmHA? So are we. Let's work together. Georgia FmHA borrowers stopped foreclosures. Call us!

CHAPTER 8

Problem Case

In western North Dakota, summertime rodeos were as ubiquitous as wintertime basketball tournaments. Mandan's motto was "Where the West Begins," and the Mandan Rodeo Days had taken place every Fourth of July since 1879. It was a three-day extravaganza of parades, street dances, street food with a North Dakota flavor (fleischkuekle, kuchen, and desserts containing rhubarb sold as fundraisers by various clubs), local bands playing country music, and steel barrels of beer, pumped under pressure into plastic cups.

I hadn't been in Mandan on a Fourth of July weekend since I moved out east, so on July 4, Andrew and I made a day of it. We watched the parade in the morning and Andrew was thrilled ("Mom, people are throwing candy at me!"). Late in the afternoon, we were in the first traffic jam I'd ever seen in North Dakota, with a mile-long line of trucks and cars trying to get into the rodeo grounds. Eventually, we were waved over to a parking spot in a pasture and walked to the arena under the shade of rustling cottonwoods. Finding a seat on the bottom tier of vast wooden bleachers, we joined a happy throng of about a thousand people (a huge crowd by North Dakota standards).

It seemed that everyone but Andrew and me was wearing full Western regalia: boots, tight Wrangler jeans, colorful cotton shirts with pearl snaps. I decided the cowboys must be very secure in their masculinity if they wore pink and purple flowered shirts. There were many Native Americans in the bleachers cheering on their relatives who were competing. I was to learn later, when I did legal work for the North Dakota Rodeo Association, that rodeo was one area of North Dakota life that was fully integrated; indeed, rodeo might have been the only integrated North Dakota activity. In rodeo, success was measured only by the seconds a man could stay on a bull or took to rope a steer or a woman could race around barrels on a fast horse. In rodeo, the color of the contestant's skin didn't matter.

Many men and women who strolled back and forth on the boardwalk in front of the grandstand wore huge belt buckles that marked their rodeo achievements. I liked the idea of belt buckles. How nice it would be if I, as a lawyer, could walk into a courtroom with a big belt buckle marking my career highlights, such as making the Montgomery Ward Company stop using zip codes to redline Black neighborhoods. But no, I just got a signed settlement agreement.

The highlight of the rodeo for me was the Grand Entry of gloriously dressed, sparkly-hatted, perfectly coiffed young women. They were called Rodeo Royalty—girls and young women who had been crowned rodeo queens and princesses in smaller rodeos throughout the state or region. The titles weren't awarded for their beauty (though they all were beautiful), but rather for their horse skills. As the crowd watched, hushed, these queens and princesses loped into the arena on beautifully trained horses, with perfectly erect posture, holding the horse's reins in one gloved hand and a large flagpole with a fluttering flag from their state or Canadian province in the other as a tinny loudspeaker blared "God Bless America." Finally, the riders lined up in perfect order, and Miss Mandan Rodeo 1982 cantered in wide circles around the arena, with her hair flowing from under her glitzy cowboy hat (with a tiara in place of a hatband), while the entire audience stood for the Pledge of Allegiance.

The rodeo events followed in rapid succession. Some were only for women, others only for men. They included saddle and bareback bronc riding, barrel racing, team roping, steer wrestling, and the highlight (always last), bull riding. The slanting sun gradually set over the colorful arena, with an added glow caused by the dust of the horses and cattle, and then bright arena spotlights came on.

I knew that many people out east believed rodeos were a form of animal cruelty, but I wondered how many of them had ever been to a rodeo. The animals at the Mandan Rodeo appeared to have the better part of the bargain;

the humans were the ones in danger. I watched cowboys get hurled through the air by bucking horses or almost trampled by bulls. It was only the skill of the pickup men and rodeo clowns that kept the contestants from being grievously injured. Pickup men galloped alongside a bucking horse and plucked cowboys off the saddle, if the cowboy had survived the requisite seconds to finish the ride. Rodeo clowns were elite athletes who dressed up in goofy outfits to distract the bulls from goring or trampling the cowboy the bull had just thrown off his back.

Throughout the rodeo, the announcer sat perched in a high wooden structure at the head of the arena. He kept up a steady patter, announcing contestants and the times of their various rides (often measured in seconds), giving praise or pity ("Whatta ride that was!" or "Better luck next time, cowboy"). The bulls and the bucking horses were introduced by name too; a separate scoring system kept track of their successes.

Whenever the action in the arena lagged, the rodeo announcer made jokes, often using a rodeo clown as a foil. I was dismayed that the jokes that seemed to get the most laughs were lawyer jokes:

ANNOUNCER: How many lawyers does it take to change a lightbulb?
CLOWN: How many can you afford?
ANNOUNCER: What do you call five hundred lawyers at the bottom of the ocean?
CLOWN: A good start!
ANNOUNCER: You know how cold it got last winter?
CLOWN: No, I don't.
ANNOUNCER: It was so cold my lawyer's hands were in his own pockets.[1]

Years later, at a rodeo in Minot, I saw a stunt where a rodeo clown wearing a gray business suit and carrying a briefcase dashed out of a cattle chute. He was chased down by a mounted cowboy lazily twirling a lariat. When the cowboy eventually roped the "lawyer," the crowd cheered!

It was apparent to me that it would be lawyers and judges who would help many of the people at the rodeo survive the dark days ahead. I also hoped that the crowd's laughter at lawyer jokes was not aimed at women lawyers, who were as scarce as hen's teeth in rural areas of North Dakota.

I was used to sex discrimination in law, but I was not used to its absence. Graduates of NYU Law School were blessed with a great placement service, but we women learned pretty quickly that many law firms had policies against hiring women. One huge firm told me during an interview, "Sorry, we don't hire women lawyers." Another said, "While we sometimes hire women in the Trusts and Estates department, because women are naturally good at dealing with widows and children, I see you haven't taken advanced classes in trusts and estates. Sorry!" Like a Midwestern "schmuck" (a New York City word I'd learned that year), I politely said, "Well, thank you anyway." But inside I was fuming.

In North Dakota, being a woman lawyer was an advantage. When I met a farmer face-to-face, he or she didn't think of me as a lawyer but rather as a person who knew about FmHA and was on their side.

Meanwhile, I still hadn't been admitted to the bar. One day I answered the phone and it was the North Dakota Supreme Court's clerk of court, who was also in charge of admissions to practice law.

"I hear you're back in North Dakota, Sally," she said cheerfully. She was a friend of my dad's. "But seems you aren't licensed yet?"

Shamefully, I explained that I didn't have the money for the application fee.

"The character review process can take months, so why don't I get that started for you, and you can pay the fee later."

I thanked her profusely and then called Diane McCabe to find out how much money we'd raised. After the requisite weather chitchat, I anxiously asked, "How is the money coming in from the ad?"

"We got one check for ten dollars," Diane said. She sounded optimistic, as if this were only the beginning of more checks to come.

Bitterly, I thought of Chuck Perry. Under the guise of the Farmers and Ranchers Protective League, he was traveling from coast to coast, raising money for a massive lawsuit that he promised would net millions in damages from FmHA. Chuck kept giving out my phone number, saying I was affiliated with the League. When his referrals called, I was always sick to hear they'd kicked in what little they had to Chuck's cause. The cause was a scam. When I was naive and smitten enough to believe Chuck's tall tales, I'd spent many late nights doing legal research to see if there was any way to sue for damages. But it was a dead end. As a government agency, FmHA had "sovereign immunity," a legacy of the English common law doctrine that the king can do no wrong. None of the folks Chuck swindled would ever see a dime. If I was going to bring a class action similar to *Curry v. Block*, it would be a lawsuit to force FmHA to follow the law. There would be no financial damages for the class.

How come Chuck is so much better at fundraising than I am? I fumed. *Oh, because he's a con artist.*

On July 7, my phone rang early in the morning. I suspected the call was from a dairy farmer, as they tended to call early.

"Is this Sarah Vogel? I've heard that you work with farmers, is that right?"

His name was Russel Folmer, and he farmed near Wing. He'd seen our ad and then checked my reputation with one of his neighbors.

"Randy lives near me and he says you're okay," Russel said. Among laconic North Dakota farmers, saying someone is "okay" is equivalent to saying that they are wonderful and can be trusted. On the other hand, "Oh, I don't really know" would be equivalent to a blackball for bad character. I was absurdly pleased by Randy's glowing reference. Russel continued, "I'd like to meet with you as soon as possible."

I was in my home office, surrounded by unanswered mail, unpaid bills, stacks of papers from other clients, and messy yellow legal pad drafts of the class action complaint I worked on late at night. I already owed so many people so much work. "Could we get together in a couple weeks?" I asked.

"I don't have that much time," Russel said. There was something in his voice, the plea of a proud, self-reliant man who had come to the end of his rope, that made me say yes and ask for directions to his farmstead.

The day was sunny, with bright blue skies and white puffy clouds—a beautiful day to drive. I left the interstate after twenty-five miles and headed north on Highway 14, a little two-lane road that stretched like a black ribbon between vivid green pastures and fields of nodding sunflowers. It was a Grant Wood painting. Interspersed among the fields and pastures were small bodies of water called sloughs.

As a child, my father had often said, "Sally, look over at that slough and all the ducks that are on it." Sometimes we'd pull our car over and tiptoe to the edge of a slough and pick a bouquet of cattails. If you broke a cattail in two, the inside was filled with soft downy white fibers that Native Americans used for insulation in bedding and pillows and medicinal purposes.

As we drove along Highway 14, Andrew and I were in the Prairie Pothole Region, an area that swings from Canada through the middle of North Dakota and through the eastern half of South Dakota. From the ground, it's hard to tell how large it is, but from an airplane it's impossible to miss, with its thousands of vivid blue sloughs surrounded by deep green or yellow circles. In drought years, the border is black earth.

Russel had told me to watch my odometer, and that at mile 18 after leaving the interstate, I should look for a big slough on the right followed by a white mailbox and a driveway leading back about a quarter mile to a farmstead surrounded by trees. If I saw a second large slough right after the mailbox, I should turn around. I'd found that farmers never put their names on mailboxes. (After all, what would be the point? Everyone in the neighborhood knew where everybody else lived.)

As I drove up the Folmers' driveway, I said, "Look, Andrew!" We didn't have time to stop and pick cattail bouquets, but I could show him the flocks of ducks and red-winged blackbirds swooping above the sloughs on either side of the driveway. The most striking features of the Folmers' farm were the huge rows of trees and shrubs that sheltered the farmstead from hot summer winds and from freezing winter blasts. The shelter belt stretched off as far as the eye could see along the borders of the fields. When Andrew and I got out of the car, we could hear the birdsongs coming from those trees.

Based on the size and condition of their farmstead, the Folmers appeared prosperous. Their big red barn seemed freshly painted. They had shiny metal Quonset sheds for machinery storage. The three white houses on the property weren't big, but they had large, freshly mowed lawns and flowerbeds. "Look, Mom, swings!" Andrew called out.

We met Russel and his wife on their stoop. Russel was in his midfifties and heavyset with a receding hairline. His wife, Anna Mae, was striking, her hair elegantly coifed in the style of a fifties beauty queen. In dark blue Wranglers and a floral blouse, she looked like Elizabeth Taylor starring in a Western.

"We've never met a lawyer before," she said.

They offered to give me a brief tour of the place while Andrew played on the swing set.

Russel had started farming when he was fourteen. At the beginning, the farm was just bare ground and a three-room shack he moved into with Anna

Mae when they married. They raised five children in that shack and didn't build a "real" house until 1970, when their youngest was eight years old. Over the years, they'd invested over $250,000 in their farm, planted many thousands of trees, built barns, including a modern dairy barn, and put up fences. In addition to their original house, there were two more, where their married children lived. Russel and Anna Mae were fighting not only for themselves but for the future of their family.

They explained their roles to me. Russel took care of the machinery, the crops, the beef cattle, haying in the summer and plowing in the winter. Anna Mae took complete care of the dairy cows, in big boots and coveralls and a scarf over her pretty hair. I knew that dairying could be difficult and dirty and I was fixated on her appearance: How did she remain so pretty, so poised, so lovely while taking care of so many cows?

Before we sat down at the kitchen table to work, Anna Mae put out a fresh pot of coffee and a plate of cookies. In addition to running the dairy, I had to assume she also took care of the house, volunteered at the church, grew a garden, and cooked all the family meals. This demarcation in gender-based duties was almost universal in the countryside of North Dakota. Anna Mae followed in the tradition of many generations of farm women who earned money (sometimes the only money earned by the family) by selling their milk, cream, butter, chickens, and eggs to customers in town for cash. In the settler days, women farmers called cash that they earned from those sales their "pin money."[2]

"So," I said. "Let's start from the beginning. When did you first borrow from Farmers Home?"

The Folmers had gotten loans from Farmers Home when they were just starting out in the 1950s. For decades, they had the same county supervisor, George Weber, who became not only a mentor but a good friend. The Folmers were able to pay off their FmHA loans in full in the early 1970s.

"Free and clear!" Russel said. The Folmers were telling me a success story. Russel was a leader in his community and had served as director of the local township board for eighteen years. He'd also been chairman of the Republican Party for Burleigh County, which was a big deal—Burleigh County included Bismarck, the state capital.

"What happened next? After you were 'free and clear'?" I asked.

"We went back to Farmers Home to borrow money to modernize the dairy," Anna Mae said. "That was in 1978. And then we had three straight years of drought."

"In '79, I didn't even take the combine out of the shed," Russel said.

During the drought years, they became delinquent on their loans to FmHA, to the Bank of Steele, and to the Bank of North Dakota, which had a mortgage on some of their land. Their income was also adversely affected by the cost-price squeeze that plagued all farmers in the late '70s and early '80s.

Although they were falling behind, they still had plenty of equity, and their machinery, their livestock, and their land were set up for success.

But then George Weber, their friend and ally at the Burleigh County FmHA office, retired. Across the United States, many county supervisors like Weber, who had been working at FmHA for decades, were now eligible to retire, and they were replaced by eager go-getters who didn't understand or respect the agency's Depression-era origins. In Burleigh County, the new county supervisor was named Jim Well, and he arrived in March 1982, right around Shuman's deadline for the first delinquency reduction goals. Within a month, Well had reviewed the Folmers' entire file and accused the Folmers of "conversion" by failing to turn over money from cattle sales to FmHA. After scaring the Folmers with threats of jail (conversion is a felony) and loss of their entire farm, he told them the only way they could keep their land was if they sold fifty dairy cows.

Well and others like him believed that forcing farmers to quit when times were hard was actually good for them because by quickly selling out, the Folmers would be able to preserve some of their equity for a fresh start elsewhere. This paternalistic view was anathema to farmers like Russel. At fifty-six, he didn't want to start anew. He wanted to keep farming where his roots were as deep as the roots of the trees he had planted decades earlier.

I couldn't help but reflect on the irony that the Folmers had almost certainly voted for Reagan, who, by appointing Stockman as head of OMB, had set off the chain of events that brought us together at this kitchen table.

Well's accusation of conversion bewildered the Folmers, because they had done everything by the book according to County Supervisor Weber. Milk prices were low, so Russel decided that selling the dairy cows was a good business idea anyway, but he adamantly refused to sell the cows on Well's tight schedule. In March, the cows were skinny and producing well under their potential after having been cooped up in the barn since January.

"They're like people," Anna Mae said. "They need sun and fresh air."

Russel flatly told Well he'd sell the cows on his own time frame, and for months he stuck to his guns. When the dairy cows were healthy, and the market was strong, Russel sold fifty-one of them at auction on June 22 for a good price.

And then, even though they'd done what County Supervisor Well had pressured them to do, on June 30, 1982, Well signed a Real Estate Problem Case for the Folmers and issued a notice of acceleration.

IN THE LATE 1970s, farmers like the Folmers didn't think they had to worry. They'd been making money for decades. And if you didn't make money one year, so what? Your lender would give you an operating loan to carry you over for the next season, and if the next season didn't work as well as expected, he'd helpfully roll it over into a new note and secure it against the value of your real estate. Good times! Economists saw only rosy scenarios. The cautions of the 1930s (*Don't borrow unless you have to, don't count on a good year, have savings, conserve, spend as little as possible, don't buy new equipment, fix what's broken*) were disregarded. The older generation's cautionary tales about the dangers of debt, failed banks, and the seizure of bank accounts due to "bank holidays" were drowned out by the chorus of positive and progressive farmers whose worldview was framed by their experience in the 1940s, '50s, '60s, and '70s.

In 1980, Dr. Neil Harl, an Iowa lawyer and economist, published a multivolume series on agriculture law that included absolutely nothing on defending a farm foreclosure. To be fair, there was no need for such a chapter at that time. Foreclosures were so rare as to be almost unheard of. If there was a foreclosure, it was caused by mental illness, an intrafamily feud, or failure to pay taxes by self-styled patriots who disavowed any obligation to the federal or state government. Lawyers knew how to get loan paperwork in order, but they had never defended a foreclosure.

The farmers who borrowed from FmHA knew all about farming and machinery, crops and livestock, but they knew little to nothing about the clauses in their loan paperwork that would apply when things went from bad to worse.

When farmers went to their local county FmHA office to take out loans, they likely didn't read the fine print on the promissory note.

Tom and Anna Nichols signed. Don and Diane McCabe signed. Eugene and Linda Myran signed. And Russel and Anna Mae Folmer signed. Thousands of farmers all over the United States signed promissory notes to the Farmers Home Administration. And buried within the fine print of that promissory note was a very important clause, known in lending and real estate circles as an "acceleration clause." It allowed the lender to speed up the schedule of payments that would otherwise be payable over a span of time and make the remaining interest and principal payments "immediately due and payable" if the borrower was overdue or had violated any terms of the agreement. Russel and Anna Mae Folmer were $17,000 delinquent on their loans, and that gave FmHA the right to declare all of their debt "immediately due." They now owed $268,395 unpaid principal and $29,997.35 unpaid interest. It was due now.

Below the clause, the promissory note read, "This note shall be subject to the present regulations of the Farmers Home Administration and to its future regulations not inconsistent with the express provisions hereof."

These "present regulations" were 764 pages long.

Russel handed me the notice of acceleration and I read the reasons given, which included failure to pay loans on time, failure to pay real estate taxes, "failure to operate farm in husbandlike manner" (this was like a knife in Russel's heart), and, of course, failure to liquidate "voluntarily."

"But our crops this year look very good," Russel said. "And we have eighty beef cows ready for market."

"With less dairy cows, we have extra hay. We can sell it!" Anna Mae added.

I was amazed at how optimistic they still were. They were convinced that they could work their way out of their present trouble. And I agreed with them. Their situation was far superior to that of any other farmer couple I was working with.

"I will help you fight this," I said. I explained how: First I'd write a letter demanding that FmHA send them all of their records. As soon as they received them, they'd have to drop everything and call me, so we could use every day we had between then and their appeal hearing to study them. We'd request a hearing date as late as possible, to give us more time to prepare our defense.

"I never knew what they were writing about us when we came into the office," Russel said. "They would never let me read the notes."

"You have the right to see everything," I said. There wasn't time to explain everything I'd learned during Chuck Perry's Freedom of Information Act case in D.C. Only a year before, I'd believed all of Chuck's promises. Now I knew the truth: He wasn't a real farmer like Russel Folmer. He was on the run, living off the generosity of broke and desperate people while he avoided paying his child support debts in the state of North Dakota.

"Before you go," Russel said, "I want to show you something."

I followed him to the living room, which was filled with comfortable furniture, pictures of all the kids at their high school graduations, and a small TV. He took a large, framed photograph off the wall and handed it to me. It was a color aerial photograph (very rare and expensive in those days) of the Folmer farmstead. The buildings I'd seen from the ground were there, but the stars of the photograph were the trees—rows and rows of trees.

"I won the Burleigh County Soil Conservation Award for my tree planting and for the way I farm and treat the soil," Russel said quietly. Unshed tears welled in his eyes, and I pretended not to notice.

"I see," I said. I was grateful that Russel had shared his highest farming honor with me.

On the ride home, Andrew fell asleep in the backseat and I fell into a meditative trance along the empty expanse of Highway 14, imagining that someday the hardworking Folmers might get to tell their story to a judge.

CHAPTER 9

The Farmer's Lawyer

I n June 1982, the National Farmers Union published a fifty-page booklet titled *Depression in Rural America*.[1] The frontispiece of the report quoted from a famous Williams Jennings Bryan speech from 1896:

> The great cities rest upon our broad and fertile prairies. Burn down your cities and leave our farms, and your cities will spring up again as if by magic; but destroy our farms and the grass will grow in the streets of every city in the country.

The NFU had held nine field hearings in March and April at which hundreds of farmers and ranchers and scores of bankers, feed dealers, insurance agents, politicians, and pastors testified. The authors of the report concluded agriculture was in a depression that would soon spread to the nation as a whole. The booklet's stark table of contents included these captions: "Tight Credit," "Declining Net Income," "Threatened Rural Communities," and "Destroying a Way of Life." *The Depression Report*, as it came to be known, said that even the American Bankers Association was alarmed.[2] Interest rates were between 15 percent and 21 percent.[3] One farmer in Kansas brought his tax returns to the hearing and said, "In 1981, my interest payments exceeded my 1978 gross income."[4]

I read the report cover to cover. It was excellent, but I was dismayed to discover that there were no references to legal solutions. No mention of the

Curry case, no mention of the deferral law, no mention of state laws that could be used to help farmers.

The report focused its pleas on Congress, asking for a wave of *credit* to provide immediate relief: "We fully recognize that agriculture cannot borrow itself into prosperity. However, without the immediate infusion of additional farm credit resources at affordable interest rates, thousands of family-sized farm units will be liquidated." The National Farmers Union also asked Congress to "forcefully and independently . . . establish an immediate end to foreclosures or forced liquidations of family-sized farm units by federal agencies . . ."[5] I thought that asking Congress to stop foreclosures wouldn't work. Congress had been futilely pressuring FmHA to implement the right to apply for deferrals since at least 1981. I thought it was time to focus on the judicial branch.

My farmer clients were flat broke, but what about farm organizations? After reading *The Depression Report*, I thought that perhaps organizations like the National Farmers Union could also support litigation.

I told my father about this idea, and he said his friend Stanley Moore might be able to help. Moore was the longtime president of the North Dakota Farmers Union. He and my father had been political allies for decades on issues such as North Dakota's anti-corporate farming law, which the NDFU fervently supported. Since its founding in 1927, the NDFU had been in bitter competition with the North Dakota Farm Bureau, the right-leaning, corporate-farm oriented farm organization that worked to nullify the anti-corporate farming law and other policy objectives of the NDFU.

In 1982, the North Dakota Farmers Union was big and successful, with forty thousand members. It had a shiny new office building in Jamestown with a huge parking lot and lovely landscaping. On a Sunday afternoon, Andrew and I were met at the door by President Moore's policy assistant, Karl, who courteously greeted Andrew as though he were a visiting dignitary. We walked down a long hallway with polished floors and framed photographs of beautiful farm scenes on the walls.

Mr. Moore's office was huge, with a bank of windows overlooking bright flowerbeds, a golden oak desk undisturbed by papers, and a large conference table with room to seat a board of twelve, where we three adults sat down to talk. They didn't seem bothered by the fact that this business meeting had been arranged for a Sunday, with a four-year-old as one of the meeting participants.

As soon as we sat down, I launched into my vision for a legal defense fund that would help farmers fight foreclosure. "There are more lawyers working for creditors than for farmers," I said. "I was just at a legal seminar in Grand Forks about debt collection remedies where one of the seminars was titled 'So You Can't Collect the Debt, You Can Still Send the Debtor to Prison.'"

Mr. Moore raised his eyebrows.

"Farmers Home is terrifying families and starving them off their farms. These are *your* members. We need to put together a legal defense or else there's going to be more and more foreclosures and land values are going to plummet, just like they did in the thirties. Did you know twenty-six thousand farmers went under in the Midwest between 1977 and 1980? And it's only getting worse. Last year land values dropped for the first time in thirty years. But I have a plan. There was a case in Georgia that forced Farmers Home to follow the deferral law, and I want to do the same thing in North Dakota. It's urgent." I was so focused on my pitch that I lost track of Andrew's whereabouts. "There's so much legal work to do, so much more we can to do defend farmers. Think of it as an investment in your members. I'm asking for a hundred thousand dollars to start."

Mr. Moore and Karl looked startled, but they weren't looking at me. Their gaze was fixed on Andrew, who was now stark naked but for a white towel tied around his neck. With his arms raised in a V for victory, he ran across the room and began jumping on the couch, shouting, "I'm Superman! I'm Superman!"

I kept talking as Karl patiently rose from his chair to retrieve Andrew's clothes and get him dressed. "There are other lawsuits I'm trying to develop, too," I said. "If we can force compliance with the Equal Access to Justice Act, then farmers could recover legal fees when they win their foreclosure appeals—"

"I'm sorry, Sarah," Mr. Moore said. "But I think you should raise all this with the National Farmers Union. They have more resources."

I tried the National Farmers Union, but all their resources were committed to getting Congress to provide relief.

I then called Mark Ritchie, who was connected to every development in the unfolding agriculture crisis.

"Hey, do you know of any foundations that give money for lawsuits?" I asked.

"No, but I'll find out," he said.

Within a few days, Mark called back. "There are a lot of foundations, but it looks like none of them will give grants for litigation. I did find one in Chicago called the J. Roderick MacArthur Foundation. The founder is a bit of a radical. He has funded a couple of prison and civil rights lawsuits."[6]

I put together a funding proposal for what the McCabes and I were calling the Family Farm Foreclosure Legal Assistance Project. Our goal, I wrote, was "to help keep family farms in business by compelling FmHA to meet its *existing* statutory and regulatory duties by means of lawsuits and administrative appeals." I asked for $200,000 for a legal defense fund that would provide legal services to farmers facing foreclosure and also allow me to bring a series of state-level cases in North Dakota and other states like the *Curry* case in Georgia as well as cases to force FmHA to comply with due process and give farmers fair hearings and force them to pay attorney's fees when farmers won those appeals.

"Legal defense for these family farmers is urgently needed if the United States wishes to avoid a massive hemorrhage in the numbers of small family farmers—the backbone of the rural economy," I wrote. "Under a very feasible scenario, the FmHA drive to 'reduce delinquencies' could have the impact of setting in motion or accelerating a chain reaction of farm foreclosures, small business bankruptcies and massive rural dislocation."

I sent it off to Chicago.

MARK COMPILED CLIPPINGS from newspapers all over the country and sent them to me and our ragtag crew of farm advocates.[7] The headlines were telegrams of distress: THE DECLINE OF THE SMALL FAMILY FARMER, MORE FARMERS FEEL THE PINCH, FARM CREDIT BLUES, ANGRY FARMERS ASSAIL FMHA LENDING PRACTICES, TIGHT CREDIT, HIGH INTEREST PINCH FARMS, FMHA STEPPING UP FORECLOSURES, AND GRAINS OF WRATH.

As the national media began to pay closer attention to what was happening in the countryside, reporters called me looking for an angle for their stories. Every call from a reporter took time away from my writing, my research, my clients, and Andrew. And, until I realized that I could call them collect and make them pay me for photocopies, reporters were also an expense.

The most irritating calls were from television news reporters who wanted me to make arrangements for them to fly in and out of North Dakota in one day to film a farm auction. In their minds, the story was already set: a crowd around an auctioneer's flatbed, the arc of the auctioneer's gavel as it fell ("Going, going, gone!"). There would be a sweeping screen shot of the red barn, the white farm-house behind a picket fence, and a close-up of tears slowly winding down the weathered face of a handsome farmer. I suspected that some also wanted to include a parting shot of a fat, pompous banker in a fur-lined coat who would smile with evil satisfaction as he climbed into a limousine and drove away.

I grew more impatient with these time-wasting calls from well-meaning reporters from big cities. At first, I'd try to explain that farm auctions occurred on the front steps of courthouses, not out on the farmstead. I also said that fore-closure sales were not common because most farmers were starved out and just quit—with great sorrow, but without the sort of drama that could be filmed by a television crew. I'd try to describe the "starve-out" process used by Farmers Home, but I learned fairly quickly that these reporters had no interest.

"Just catch the next flight to North Dakota," I started to say, "and pick up a copy of the *Green Sheet*. You'll see pages and pages of farm auctions. Goodbye."

Then one day I got a call from Richard Woodley. He said he was working on a photo essay for *Life* magazine. The magazine was iconic, but what stood out to me was Richard's open-ended approach to uncovering the toll of the farm crisis on the farmers. Rather than asking for directions to a foreclosure sale, he asked, "Would you be able to introduce me and my photographer to farmers who'll talk to us?" He promised they'd be no bother and needed only a few introduc-tions. Richard explained he'd thought of going to law school himself and had written about lawyers before. He knew I'd need to navigate the rules of ethics with regard to attorney-client privilege.

"Come on out," I said. "I'll help you."

A few weeks later, Richard, a smart and edgy New Yorker in his forties, turned up at my house with his photographer, Grey Villet, a tall, quiet man in his fifties. (Grey's particular skill was being unobtrusive. I did not find out for years there-after that he was one of the most legendary black-and-white photographers in America.) I made some introductions to farmers within a day's drive. Day after day, Richard and Grey went out and came back, sometimes briefing me on what they'd learned and other times simply hanging out or taking Andrew and me to dinner. They seemed to have an unlimited budget and unlimited time.

One afternoon, as I was preparing to leave to see a farmer facing foreclosure, they offered to drive me. Andrew and I rode in luxury in the backseat of Richard's air-conditioned rental car. I brought crayons, a coloring book, a pillow and blanket for his nap, and my fantasy briefcase, which was a real briefcase containing work that I fantasized I'd have time to work on while I was on the road. But instead of working, I played with Andrew. When he napped, so did I. We spent a long day with the farmer.

On the way home, as twilight came to the peaceful prairie landscape, I fell asleep beside Andrew. Compared to a typical drive, during which I was in almost constant fear that I would fall asleep while driving and kill myself and my passengers, it was a great day, one of the best days I'd had in months. (I learned later that this trip had cost *Life* magazine dearly, as Andrew's crayons had melted in the heat and the backseat upholstery needed to be replaced when the car was returned.)

A couple of days later, Richard dropped by.

"After going with you to the farm the other day, we think the farmers' stories would be better told if we approach it from your perspective. I called my editor to ask if we could shift to a story about the farmers' lawyer. What do you think?"

When Richard said that, I realized that my identity as a hotshot East Coast consumer protection lawyer had been eclipsed by the urgent needs of the farmers at home. I was a North Dakota lawyer in the tradition of Langer, Burdick, and Lemke. I had become the farmer's lawyer.

"Yes," I said. "But only if you do all the driving."

"No problem," Richard said. "We'll drive wherever you want to go!"

And that's how I gained companionship, free travel, many free meals, and sometimes a babysitter, courtesy of *Life* magazine, for much of the long and difficult summer ahead.

WHENEVER I HAD time, I went to the North Dakota Supreme Court law library to do research. I loved this law library, and I sometimes wondered whether Lady Justice, the beautiful Greek goddess holding a scale in one hand and a sword in the other, was peeking out from beneath her blindfold and tipping the scales to the side of the farmers. Even though I worked out of my house and was flat broke, I had access to fabulous resources, including *Newberg on Class Actions*, which covered all the arcana of Rule 23, and *Davis on Administrative Law*, which gave information on how to sue federal agencies. These texts referred me to many useful cases. More than once I pulled a volume from a shelf and the book magically opened to a case that gave me necessary insight about class actions, appeals, hearings, or due process. "Thank you, Lady Justice!" I'd whisper, in keeping with the hushed atmosphere of the library.

By studying multiple class action complaints, I learned that a key part of a class action was finding people who would serve as "class representatives." I needed to find plaintiffs whose stories would be illustrative of what was happening to all 8,400 North Dakota farmers with loans from FmHA. Don and Diane McCabe were obvious class representatives, and with them, I put together a questionnaire I could give to other farmers. There was no way I could do 8,400 individual appeals or cases, but with a class action, I could protect the family farmers in North Dakota from unfairly losing their farms to foreclosure.

I packed a stack of questionnaires in my briefcase and took off with Richard, Grey, and Andrew on our next road trip, to Richard Slabaugh's farm in Wolford, 170 miles north, near the Canadian border. I'd tried to get Richard to come down to Bismarck and save me the trip, but he said he had about fifteen farmers he wanted me to meet. "We're having a picnic," he said. Among these fifteen farmers, I thought I might find another class representative or two.

Richard and Grey had seen enough of the interstate and were delighted to take the back roads. I brought along a book first published in 1938 by the Works Progress Administration called *North Dakota: A Guide to the Northern Prairie State*.[8] It was the product of one of Harry Hopkins's Depression-era projects: to put everyone, even unemployed writers and historians, to work.

As we wound our way north on two-lane roads, I played tour guide, providing the origins of each small town's name: Medina (not named after Medina, the holy city of Islam, but rather by a homesick homesteader who missed Medina, New York); Minnewauken (an adaptation of the Dakota name Mni Wakan, which means "spirit lake"); Church's Ferry (where a guy named Church kept his ferry); Cando (delightfully named after the "can do" spirit of its homesteaders).

I relished any opportunity to show visitors that North Dakota was so much more than Sevareid's "large, rectangular blank spot in the nation's mind." The summer landscape was a vivid quilt of colors and patterns. There were fields with heavy-headed, six-foot-tall sunflowers (brought by Russian settlers and now used for oil and for snacks); there were fields of cerulean blue flax (used for oil-based paint and high-quality linen paper); there were fields of golden spring wheat used for New York City pizza and bagels, and fields of durum wheat used for pasta (townies like me had a hard time telling the different wheat fields apart). On green pastures dotted with flowers, herds of Black Angus cows or black-and-white-spotted Holsteins grazed. If you were lucky, you might see a pure white Charolais or an "Oreo" cow or bull (black with a white band around its middle, officially called a Buelingo).

The rolling hills and occasional curves gave a sense of drifting on slow ocean waves. The AM radio stations that played news and advertisements between country songs faded into silence when we weren't in range.

Any evidence of human habitation seemed superficial and transitory in this vast landscape. I found this kind of long drive through the countryside to be spiritual and meditative, but Andrew was bored and wanted to get out. "Are we there yet?" I tried to amuse him with some of the games my father had played with me, like counting red cars or tractors to make the miles go by.

"I'll pay you a nickel for every horse you see," I said. Using horses was a bargain in eastern North Dakota, where the land was so valuable as cropland that there were almost no animals, but very expensive if we crossed an Indian reservation. That day, we crossed the edge of the Devils Lake Sioux Reservation (now renamed the Spirit Lake Sioux Reservation), and Andrew made $2.00, to his vast delight.

When at last we pulled in, the Slabaugh farmstead seemed like an oasis. Surrounded by shelter belts, it also had big trees that shaded the freshly mowed lawn near the house. About fifteen people, mostly men, were peacefully standing around their pickups. A bunch of kids ran past in a game of tag, and they included Andrew right away. Mrs. Slabaugh showed us to a table with jars of lemonade and ice water, a cooler of pop, and pans of dessert bars (lemon bars, Rice Krispies bars, frosted date bars) without which no gathering of North Dakotans can occur. I made a beeline for the church-sized pot of weak coffee.

I gave a short talk to the farmers about their rights and how FmHA had violated those rights.

"You're not alone," I told them. "There was a case in Georgia that made Farmers Home follow the law and give farmers a right to apply for deferral when they fell behind and I want to file a lawsuit like that right here in North Dakota. I'd like to talk to each one of you and have you fill out this questionnaire about your story." It would take hours to meet with each of them one-on-one, but that's what I had to do.

The last farmer I met that day was Dwight Coleman.

Dwight was about my age, and he reminded me of the handsome farm boys who had driven (in their own cars or pickups!) to Mandan High School when I was sixteen. He was over six feet tall and had a huge friendly smile. He wore a brimmed cap with the Caterpillar logo.

I'd spent all day listening to farmers tell me their travails, but Dwight's was the worst story I heard. He came from a longtime farming family who had settled in the Turtle Mountains, near the Canadian border, before North Dakota was a state. The Turtle Mountains are actually hills formed by glacial deposits, but after hundreds of miles of flat prairie, they seem like mountains. As a child, he had started to farm with his father. After traveling for a while after high school, he returned home, helped out on his father's farm, and started to look for a farm of his own.

"I was doing some custom baling for people in the hills, and I stopped at this guy's farm, and we were talking. He wanted to sell his farm, so that got my interest going," Dwight said. "He told me how much he wanted for it, so I went

Dwight Coleman on one of the Turtle Mountains, photographed by Greg Booth.

to the bank. But the bank was lending money at eighteen or twenty percent. Farmers Home had this beginning farmer program with low interest, so I borrowed a hundred twenty thousand dollars for the land, borrowed another hundred thousand for cattle and machinery, and we started, we cranked her up."

The 480-acre farm needed a lot of work, and it didn't even have a house, but Dwight could see how he could succeed. The farm had some fields for farming, good pasture for the cows, and land that could be cleared of brush to become more valuable. The county supervisor agreed, and Dwight got a forty-year loan from FmHA in March 1979.

"I bought fifty heifers. I had the pasture and I fixed the fence. I bought a couple bulls, put them on pasture and bred the heifers, put up the hay, and that spring I calved all them heifers out. I saved every calf. Then it was Good Friday 1980 and in the middle of the night they were forecasting a storm, so I put all the cows and calves in the barn. About three o'clock in the morning, the barn burned down. Lost all my heifers and all my calves."

Dwight was tough, but I could see how painful it was to have to remember that night. "What happened?" I asked.

"It was a heat lamp," he said. "I had a calf with pneumonia and I had him in a little area with a heat lamp. So there we are, that's how she started, no calves, no cows, still owing fifty thousand bucks."

Dwight was able to get his operation up and running again when a neighbor, who was getting ready to retire, offered him a chance to rent land and put in wheat.

"That's how I got started back up again. In 1980, I had four hundred acres of durum, ready to combine, and we got two feet of snow. It completely ruined the crop. So I lost my cows and I lost the crop, and here's Farmers Home, 'Come on in, we got to talk to you,' and I said, 'I ain't got no money, I can't make my payments.' Well, they said, we're going to extend it, but we can't extend it very long."

In March 1981, Dwight got a harsh letter from Odell Ottmar, whom he'd never met, accusing him of "bad management" because he was behind on his payments. Ottmar's title was Chief, Reservation Programs, which was the equivalent of a district director for areas where there was an Indian reservation. Dwight had the misfortune of dealing with Ottmar because his farm was on the border of the Turtle Mountain Indian Reservation, the home of the Turtle Mountain Band of Chippewa Indians.

Ottmar told Dwight to prepare to liquidate his cattle, equipment, and land as soon as he'd harvested his 1981 crop. Farmers Home would not lend him any more money. To Ottmar, Dwight was a statistic in Shuman's delinquency reduction edict.

"I just bought that land a couple of years ago, for Christ's sake," Dwight said. "I was under the impression that this beginning farmer program was supposed to be for more than two years."

"That's right," I said. "So what did you do?"

"Last year, I had some sprouted wheat and some cattle. I had enough money to pay the interest, so that's what I did. I sent them fifty thousand dollars. That was in November. On December 10, I get a letter saying they're going to foreclose unless I pay everything I owe by Christmas Eve."

"Who signed the letter?"

"Odell Ottmar."

I was appalled.

"They said, 'Either you sell it or we sell it.' I said, 'I don't think so. I don't think that's the way it's going to be.'"

"Did they tell you that you had a right to have a hearing about the decision?" I asked.

"He told me they wouldn't stop me from having a hearing but I'd just be wasting my time. The same people on the appeals board are the ones on the foreclosure board. I said what kind of a goddamn kangaroo court is that?"

At a farm auction, Dwight heard that there was a lawyer in Bismarck defending farmers against FmHA. He decided to come meet me when he heard I'd be at the picnic.

I was impressed by Dwight. He hadn't been given a fair chance; Ottmar had decided to shut him down only eighteen months after he'd bought the farm. He had shown good faith with FmHA by making payments. I was appalled at Ottmar's demand that he pay up by Christmas Eve or lose the farm, and I imagined that when a judge heard about it, he would feel the same. The cruel deadline went against what we in North Dakota called our "blizzard ethic," which meant if you were driving down the road in winter and saw a stranded car, you stopped to help them. Did the passenger need a ride? Money for gas? Jumper cables? There were no homeless people in North Dakota. Friends or family took people in, especially around Christmas.

Sarah and Dwight on his farm, photographed by Greg Booth, 1983.

My final question to Dwight was not on the questionnaire. "Would you be a lead plaintiff in my case? Put your name on it?" I asked.

"You betcha," he said. "The war's on."

THE SUN WAS beginning to go down over the horizon as Grey pulled the car out of the Slabaughs' driveway. I sat in the front with Grey while Richard and Andrew, who'd had an uproarious day, quickly fell asleep in the back. The miles flowed by as the rental car punched a narrow beam of light down the dark two-lane highway toward Minnewauken. Only the white reflective paint on the center of the highway was visible.

Gradually, I began to notice a glow on the eastern horizon, and soon an enormous arc of reddish-yellow light appeared.

"Look," I said. "We are going to see a Harvest Moon!"

"Oh my God, it's spectacular!"

Grey and I were both quiet as the arc of light became a quarter circle hovering on the horizon, then a third of a circle, then half a circle, then three quarters, until finally a huge full moon had risen over the landscape, bathing it in bright moonlight that cast dark shadows from trees and sparkled off the sloughs.

Both the settlers and the Native Americans call this a Harvest Moon because it is so bright that harvests can be done by its light. Due to some atmospheric or meteorological fluke, a Harvest Moon appears to be much bigger than a normal full moon. This one was the largest I'd ever seen.

I heard the faint but steady beat of Native American drums, and the peculiar tones and harmonies of a Native American song. The sound was faint, but I *heard* it. The drumbeats and human voices seemed to be carried by rays of moonlight. I wasn't sure if I was having a vision or an auditory hallucination. After a moment or two, Grey very quietly said, "Sarah, do you *hear* that?"

Afraid to break the spell, I whispered, "Yes." We listened to that spirit song for miles, in the magic bubble of the rental car, enraptured by the sound of the singing and the drumming, floating down the dark highway as the moon rose higher and higher.

Suddenly the songs and drumming stopped and the spell was abruptly shattered by a hearty male voice coming from the radio: "Hel*looo* out there, all you friendly listeners! We are the Heartbeat of Mni Wakan Oyate, and you are in luck—next up, we will hear from a drum group from Tokio."[9] We were driving within the Devils Lake Sioux Reservation, home of the tribe that had once been called the Mni Wakan Oyate (People of the Spirit Lake). The station's evening programming was composed of traditional Native American music with singers and drummers.

Even if the episode was caused by technology and happenstance, Grey and I had been given a vivid reminder of the presence of the Native Americans from whom North Dakota's land mass has been taken. All of the farmers I'd met with that day, and all of the farmers I'd worked with since I'd moved back to North Dakota, were white. I knew that many Native Americans had borrowed from FmHA, and based on my experiences at the FTC investigating discrimination, and the conduct of Odell Ottmar, the "chief" of the reservations, I suspected that FmHA had treated Native American borrowers even worse than the white farmers and ranchers. That night, I resolved to find a Native American lead plaintiff.

CHAPTER 10

Here Once the Embattled Farmers Stood

While I was still waiting to hear back from the J. Roderick MacArthur Foundation, Diane McCabe had another fundraising idea. The McCabes were at the epicenter of a network of farmers who talked on the phone, shared experiences, and gave support to one another. They were regaining their sense of self-worth by lending a helping hand and sharing their knowledge of rights to appeal, rights to get records, and other available remedies. They handed out copies of the 1978 deferral law and news stories about the *Curry* case.

"Sarah, what if FFFLAP had a barn dance to raise money?" FFFLAP (pronounced "flap") was our shorthand for the Family Farm Foreclosure Legal Assistance Project. "We can have it at the Lacinas' place."

"Sure, why not!" I said.

One minute it was an idea, like a seed in rich black earth, and the next minute it was a green shoot emerging, and suddenly it seemed like there were flyers on every coffee shop bulletin board in the state. "Save Our Family Farms," the flyers said. "Come to the Country Hoe-Down August 7." There was a hand-drawn map showing how to get to the Lacinas' farm. They sent personalized invitations to state and local politicians.

Richard and Grey came along (I'd sent Andrew for a sleepover), and when we arrived at the Hoe-Down, there were farmers directing everyone where to park and collecting the $3 entry fee in a large pickle jar. Lights directed us to the brightly lit barn (actually a cleared-out machinery shed), where swirling country dancers were doing polkas and two-steps to the lively songs played by a local band from the McCabes' hometown who had renamed themselves the Farm Foreclosure Band for the occasion. Along the side of the barn were long tables (likely borrowed from schools or local churches) where Diane and other women were piling flimsy paper plates with potato salad, macaroni salad, pickles, and chips, and another table where men were slapping burgers and brats into buns. I explained to Grey and Richard that this huge spread was called "lunch" because of the time of day. Breakfast was something you ate in the early morning before the sun came up, dinner was the big meal of the day at noon, and supper was after work. "Lunch," however, was any meal served at night in conjunction with a meeting or gathering. Lunch was a cultural institution, and everyone knew their jobs.

Free beer had been promised on the flyers, so it was no surprise that there was a big crowd in front of a table where the kegs were set up. There were barrels of generic pop on ice for the kids.

Richard and Grey were stunned at the skill and stamina of all the dancers, but especially the older couples, who swiftly danced in perfect sync with their partners up and down the huge dance floor where monster tractors had recently been parked.

"You have to start young to be able to dance like that," I said, pointing to grade-school-age children dancing with their grandmas, or grandpas, as the steps and rhythms were passed from one generation to the next.

There was a pretty decent contingent of television, radio, and newspaper reporters looking for interview subjects. I saw many familiar faces, farmers I'd worked with or talked to, and they all looked so much younger that night, less tense than they seemed in my office.

The Farm Foreclosure Band put down their guitars and accordion when the time for speeches came. I spoke briefly about the case we'd file when we raised enough money, but it was the farmers' night, not mine. Don and a few others spoke about how we were going to hold FmHA accountable.

"Farmers Home is going to railroad anyone they can," Don said. "They will not go the extra mile to help the farmer. They'll walk him down a short pier—a very, very short mile, not even a block long."[1]

"That's right!" someone called back.

"We're raising twenty thousand dollars for a lawsuit and we're going to file it in just a couple weeks. They won't know what hit them."

While the crowd cheered, I stood on the side, knowing it was impossible to file the case so soon. But I didn't go up and grab the mic from Don and squash the hopes of the happy crowd. I would later come to bitterly regret my lack of courage and honesty.

State Representative Jim Brokaw (a farmer himself and the cousin of the rising TV news anchor Tom Brokaw) spoke stirringly of the farmers' cause and of his plans to secure the support of the North Dakota legislature. Tax Commissioner Kent Conrad said that the farmers were the bedrock of the state and he'd fight to protect them. Finally, U.S. Representative Byron Dorgan railed against FmHA's refusal to implement the deferral law passed by Congress and said he'd do everything he could to advocate for the farmers in Congress.

Senator Quentin Burdick couldn't make it, but Don read a telegram he had sent that day:

> I am proud that it has been the Burdick tradition to fight for the family farm. As the President of the Farmers' Holiday Association in the 1930s, my father fought against family farm foreclosures and I pledge to carry on this tradition in the 1980s.
>
> The family farm is at the heart of the American community and we will join together to nurture it back to vitality. The obstacles you face are significant but not insurmountable. Your great spirit and strength will be your most valuable assets during the struggle ahead.

When Don announced that the telegram also promised a $100 personal check from Senator Burdick, the crowd cheered and applauded. All in all, the Hoe-Down raised $1,700 and netted $270.

BACK IN MONTANA, Tom Nichols was helping farmers and ranchers navigate the maze of FmHA rules and regulations. Tom had his own copy of the Code of Federal Regulations, and he put in colored tabs so he could quickly find what he was looking for. By this time, he knew FmHA regulations better than most FmHA employees did, and he freely shared his techniques and knowledge with other farmers. What Tom had done, I realized later, was create the template for the emerging new profession of "farm credit counselor" or "farm advocate." Lou Anne Kling, a brilliant Minnesota farmer who rose to become head of FmHA's farm loan programs under the Clinton administration, was one of Tom's early long-distance pupils. Lou Anne, in turn, taught farm advocacy to hundreds of other farmers, who taught it to hundreds more. As Lou Anne won awards and accolades for her work, she often credited Tom, saying she learned how to be a farm advocate from him.[2]

Tom was trying to help a rancher named Ralph Clark, who lived in rural Garfield County, a five-thousand-square-mile area the size of Rhode Island with a single town called Jordan. "It's not the end of the world where they live, but you can see it from there," Tom said about Ralph's property.

The Clarks had started ranching in 1913 in the toughest part of Montana with the worst winters and driest summers, and they had survived for genera-tions with a mix of cattle, sheep, farming, frugality, and sheer determination. Ralph was the fourth generation of his family on the Clark place, and by 1978 he had a 960-acre farm (which was tiny in Garfield County). He'd started to borrow from FmHA in 1972, and he had generally kept up with his payments.

Then a neighbor's 7,000-acre farm came up for sale. Land values had been rising for decades, and FmHA was telling ranchers like Ralph to "get big or get out." Like many farmers and government officials and economists in 1978, Ralph believed it was a shrewd investment to buy land, even in remote Garfield County. Ralph hoped that his son Edwin, back from serving in the navy in Vietnam, would be able to farm with him. FmHA easily lent $200,000 to Ralph to make the down payment.[3]

Then everything went wrong all at once. There were natural disasters like hail, drought, and awful blizzards; prices for wheat, wool, and beef were below the cost of production, and prices for seed, fencing, fuel, and other items needed to operate an 8,000-acre ranch soared. Ralph survived by getting a couple of emergency loans in 1978 and 1979.

In August 1981, Ralph and Kay Clark had the misfortune of being debtors on at least three of the 1,094 delinquent farm loans within Montana FmHA's loan portfolio: the original Farm Ownership loan from 1972, and the 1978 and 1979 emergency loans. And, in August 1981, Charles Shuman, the national FmHA administrator, told the Montana state director that he had to reduce the number of delinquent loans in Montana by 23.8 percent, which meant that 265 delinquent loans had to be "eliminated" in order to reach the goal of no more than 834 delinquent loans.[4] The Clarks were a good target: they had multiple delinquent loans.

By January 1982, Ralph owed FmHA $825,000. FmHA sent a letter saying that he should plan to sell the farm and pay off FmHA because they weren't going to lend him any more money. Ralph agreed—in part. He hoped to sell—or "voluntarily liquidate" in FmHA-speak—the 7,000 acres, but he absolutely did not want to sell the original Clark home place. Ralph figured he could keep ranching and farming with some rental land if, on the side, he could develop a supplemental income stream by creating a guest ranch complex for hunters and fishermen from out of state, who would pay big bucks for a taste of Ralph's rugged Western lifestyle.

Ralph had confided to Tom that he also believed the home place would benefit from dinosaur tourism or actual sales of dinosaur fossils that Ralph insisted were on the property. When Tom told me about the dinosaur tourism, I found it a bit hard to believe, but it turned out to be true. Garfield County was the epicenter of paleontological research in the United States. In 1902, one of the world's first *Tyrannosaurus rex* skeletons was discovered near Jordan.

Ralph could neither read nor write.[5] (He'd "flunked out of grade school," a neighbor once said.[6]) He wasn't good at numbers either. His wife, Kay, did all the books. When he got that letter saying FmHA was done with him, he knew he needed help to develop a workable plan to submit to FmHA that would show he could sell 7,000 acres and still continue to ranch. Edwin Clark subscribed to several farm magazines, and he saw a story about Tom's work helping farmers. Tom lived 120 miles away, but in Montana, this meant you were next-door neighbors. Ralph, Edwin, and Tom soon got together to do farm plans for the revised venture. Tom crunched the numbers and they all developed a plan that they thought was feasible, shedding 7,000 acres within the next six to twelve months. Ralph and Tom went together to the FmHA office and made their pitch.

But it wasn't to be.

The county supervisor called the state office. The state director, possibly still smarting over the bad publicity after newspapers covered Tom's appeal, and his subsequent testimony to Congress about how he and Anna had been treated by FmHA, retaliated.[7] Ralph received his notice of acceleration five days later. It said Ralph had to sell *everything* within thirty days, including the home place, or FmHA would immediately foreclose. And that wasn't all. Ralph learned through the local grapevine that the county supervisor had called all of Ralph's Main Street suppliers and told them they'd better not give Ralph any more credit and hurry to collect any money Ralph owed them because Ralph was "going under." Ralph's bank account was frozen, and FmHA wanted every penny of crop insurance, wool payments, and sales of cattle or wheat.

"Ralph Clark doesn't believe in the American dream anymore," began a story in the *Billings Gazette* that ran in April 1982.[8] "If the sheriff and a posse come up here to take my property, they better be ready. It'll take the National Guard to get us off the place. We've been preparing for it, and neighbors have come to us and said that if that's the stand we have to take, they'll be with us," Ralph told the reporter.

When I read this, I thought Ralph was exaggerating, but I would later learn that he meant every word.

The Clarks had lived on very little before. When their electricity and home heating fuel supplies were cut off, the Clarks installed a woodstove and broke up an old shack for firewood. They used kerosene lamps and connected a tractor to a generator for emergency electricity. Edwin continued working as a trucker, and Ralph's daughter, who earned a small paycheck as a teacher's aide and house cleaner, also sent money.[9] The family ultimately had to go on food stamps, driving miles away to buy groceries so their neighbors would not know.

They kept grain from the market in order to feed the sheep but lacked fuel for a vehicle to get the feed to the sheep. The county committee had approved a loan for that purpose, but FmHA wouldn't release the funds. Over the winter, when the Clarks pleaded for fuel to take feed to the sheep, the county supervisor told them: "Let the goddamn sheep die."[10]

"They're making an example of him," Tom told me. "Would you come out for Ralph's state appeal hearing?"

How could I say no?

The hearing was scheduled for the Monday after the Hoe-Down, August 19, in Lewistown, Montana. I tried to change the location—Lewistown was 150 miles from Ralph's ranch, and FmHA appeal regulations said the location was supposed to be "convenient" to the appellant. The hearing officer refused to find another place, but he did agree to start the hearing at ten instead of nine.

On Saturday, Richard and Grey dropped by the house, and we planned the trip. Lewistown was 438 miles from Bismarck and just northeast of the corner where Wyoming, Idaho, and Montana meet.

"That's quite the drive," Richard said. "Same as the distance between New York City and Washington, D.C.!"

We also had two stops along the way. I had agreed to give a lecture to a gathering of folks on Sunday night at a local community hall in Fairview, and then we'd need to drive back to Ralph's place so Tom and I could prepare for the hearing and get a night's sleep.

We resolved to have an early departure on Sunday but naturally ran late. I was almost always late those days. I had to pack materials for the community meeting, notes and files and law books for the Clark hearing, and my fantasy briefcase of all the work I was behind on, including drafts of the class action complaint.

I grew anxious as we got closer to the Fairview Community Center. All I could see was miles and miles of emptiness. No signs of human habitation. In North Dakota, even if there were no houses visible, you would often see a row of giant letter T's perpendicular to a highway. This row of poles meant there was electricity going to a farmhouse at the end. It surely wasn't the case in Montana. The view was so huge and so unobstructed by trees I thought that I could see the curve of the earth.

At last, on the horizon, the outline of a plain wooden building hugging the highway appeared. *So this is the Fairview Community Center*, I marveled. *Montanans have a great sense of humor!* We pulled in to the parking lot, where there were two dusty trucks, one of which I recognized as Tom and Anna's. We went in and I met the Clarks. Ralph looked like the photo I'd seen in the *Billings Gazette*: a quintessential Western rancher complete with big hat, shiny belt buckle, white pearl-snap shirt, and scuffed cowboy boots. Edwin was much bigger, almost as big as Tom, and had a kindly face; he was dressed very plainly and frugally. Kay was gaunt and about a head taller than Ralph.

I went outside to sneak a smoke and watched headlights approach from all directions. Within a few minutes, the parking lot was full, and about forty people piled into the room, which hummed with low conversations. Everyone knew everyone, and all grabbed coffee from the big pot Tom had made.

Tom introduced me to two Montana lawyers he'd invited. I was impressed that they'd driven many miles to hear me; no North Dakota lawyers seemed interested in learning how to do what I was doing.

A little after seven, most everyone sat down on folding chairs. A few men leaned against the back wall. I launched into my talk about how to navigate the FmHA appeal process. I covered the types of issues that could be appealed, deadlines, and the right to get records in advance.

"Farmers Home told us we weren't allowed to see our records," Kay Clark called out.

"They lied to you," one of the Montana lawyers answered back.

"You have every right to see those records," I insisted. "You *need* to see your records in order to appeal." As I went on to describe the appeal process in laborious detail, I could tell I was losing my audience.

"Something has to be done to stop this, and the only ones who can do it are sitting in this room right now," the other lawyer said.[11] The room perked up.

A woman in the front row with a child by her side raised her hand. Grateful for her polite interest, I called on her.

"Can't we just shoot them?" she asked.

The room was silent as they waited for me to reply.

Was she seriously asking if it wouldn't be easier to shoot the FmHA staff than file an appeal? I waited for some sign that the woman was joking, but she just stared at me.

"No," I said. "No! We have all kinds of legal and administrative remedies we can use. We need to stay *within the system*. We have to *follow the rules* if we're going to file a lawsuit like the one in Georgia that . . ." Andrew was at my side, tugging my arm.

"Let's go!" he hissed. "It's time to go!"

I leaned down to whisper, "We will very soon." *Was he tired*, I wondered, *or was he, too, picking up on the menacing atmosphere?* One of North Dakotans' bedrock principles was faith in the government because it existed to serve the interests of the people. This was proved by the farmers of the Nonpartisan League who seized control of state and federal offices in 1917 and again in 1933. We had faith in all three branches of government. If one branch messed up, the others would correct it. I was learning that eastern Montana was vastly different from North Dakota.

Sarah speaking to the crowd at Fairview Community Center. © Grey Villet

There were no more audience questions. I exchanged cards with the other lawyers and we promised to stay in touch. Then we all went into the black night, with an incredible array of stars overhead. Ralph told Richard to follow his taillights, and Tom trailed us in case we lost Ralph. *Can't we just shoot them?* The question disturbed my thoughts. Was it hyperbole, like Ralph's statement that it would take the National Guard to get him off his place, or something more?

At last we turned off the road and bumped down a long gravel driveway that seemed to go on for miles before we pulled into the Clarks' dark farmyard. Golden lamplight flickered inside the house. Kay fed us sloppy joes she prepared on a woodstove. She seemed kind, but more worn by life on the ranch than Ralph was. Kay showed me to a bedroom down the hall, where I put Andrew to bed. Ralph escorted Tom, Richard, and Grey to a bunkhouse. Tom came right back, and he and I cleared off the dining room table. Tom laid out the papers we'd need as evidence the next day. I was grateful for his help: he made it easy for me to represent the Clarks, even though I'd just met them.

"I fully expect to lose tomorrow," I told Ralph when he came back from the bunkhouse. "But you understand that having an appeal hearing—even if we lose—is a necessary step in order to win at court later on."

"I don't know," Tom said. "We might win. They have to look at it."

I admired Tom. He was a fighter and an optimist. But I'd lost all the hearings I'd done and knew this one would be no different. Tom had more faith in me than I had in myself.

"This is part of building a bigger case, Tom."

We settled down to work, talking about the regulations we would rely on and pulling documents from the file that we would use as exhibits. I wrote down questions that I would ask. Ralph hovered around for a while but soon went off to bed.

We worked late into the night, and at some point, Richard and Grey returned to the house to quietly listen to Tom and me talk over defenses and exhibits. Grey unobtrusively took photographs. Tom and I at last quit at two thirty in the morning. I set my windup travel alarm for seven.

Sarah and Tom working at Ralph Clark's ranch house. © Grey Villet

The next morning was glorious. Pine-scented breezes wafted the sounds of nickering horses in a nearby corral. Were they greeting the sunrise? Beyond the horse corrals were the badlands, with rough broken hills and buttes in various shades of brown, yellow, green, and white, depending on the soils and the plants that managed to survive in those soils. Montana's "Big Sky" reputation was on bright blue display. A chorus of songbirds sang their hearts out from trees planted around the small white house. Tom, Richard, and Grey soon came up from the bunkhouse for coffee, eggs, and homemade venison sausage. Edwin and his wife, Janet, ambled over from their house, which was nearby. They brought a couple of friendly kids, a few years older than Andrew, who were thrilled to have another kid to play with. Janet promised me that Andrew would have a fun day, and the rest of us piled into two cars.

I rode in Tom's big truck with Ralph and Richard. The 150-mile drive seemed to pass in minutes, not hours, as Ralph went into storyteller mode. He told us tales of growing up in the Big Open: how he'd been bitten by a rattle-snake but survived; how he'd delivered mail and supplies to ranchers, on horse-back, in the Missouri Breaks of Garfield County as a child before there was rural mail delivery; how he held the world record for the most sheep sheared in one hour.[12]

Ralph had been born in 1931, but he seemed like a character in a Louis L'Amour novel set in 1882. You could tell he loved his home place and loved this part of Montana. He knew the name of every butte and "crick" for at least the first seventy-five miles of the journey, but when we approached Lewistown it was obvious he couldn't read the street signs. I chose to accept his excuse that he'd forgotten his glasses.

At the hearing, the hearing officer and the county supervisor sat so close together they seemed joined at the hip. They came together, left for lunch together, and whispered to each other as I was speaking.

For four interminable hours, Tom and I soldiered through the facts, the many laws and regulations that had been violated, and the opportunities FmHA had missed to keep the Clarks in business. Tom had brought a court reporter, and we got *Life* to foot the bill.

Despite my cautionary statements that we'd likely lose, the Clarks fully expected vindication. Ralph lived in a black-and-white world. During the hearing, I watched his expression change from confusion to rage to disappointment.

FmHA employees at Ralph Clark's hearing. © Grey Villet

"I'm mad," he blurted out at one point. So was I, but I was consoled by the fact that we had made a record for a later court hearing. I still had faith in the system. So did Tom. But Ralph, who had grown up in a county so sparsely populated that historically there had been no law enforcement apart from citizen posses (that is, vigilantes), didn't share our faith.

We lost the hearing. I wasn't surprised.

As we drove back to the ranch, Tom gestured toward the hills that bordered the narrow two-lane road. "See those hills? There are some bad people up there. If you ever hear that someone is in the Posse Comitatus, watch out. They are dangerous. Have nothing to do with them."[13]

After the hearing, I stayed in touch with Tom but lost track of Ralph. The two lawyers who had come to the Fairview Community Center meeting stepped in to work on his national appeal. As the years passed by, I sometimes wondered what had happened to Ralph Clark.

I found out in 1996, on the nightly news, when I saw aerial pictures of an isolated farmstead with two small white houses, corrals, and a few outbuildings, where a small army of armed men and a few armed women flew an American flag upside down. People wearing camouflage waved automatic rifles and vowed not to leave "Justus Township" until a constitutional government to their liking was restored. The entire farm was surrounded by a ring of a hundred armed FBI agents. It never would have occurred to me to imagine that one of the men

Kay and Ralph at their hearing. © Grey Villet

flying an upside-down flag and threatening to shoot people could be Ralph Clark, or that this "compound" filled with men in camouflage carrying automatic weapons was Ralph's idyllic little tourist/dinosaur ranch. But it was. The prediction he'd made in 1982 that he would not leave, not even if an army came after him, was coming true.

Ralph had decided to take a different route than the legal course of action I had recommended. Instead, he had followed the example of the woman who questioned me about whether it would be easier to *just shoot them* and joined the Montana Freemen.

The Montana Freemen espoused violent overthrow of the government. They threatened murder and lynching of county, state, and federal prosecutors and judges if they did not follow the Freemen's demands to recognize their "free man" status (no taxes, no driver's licenses, no obligation to follow federal or state laws). They threatened to murder law enforcement agencies that disregarded the Freemen's self-created system of courts. Some of the Freemen that Ralph associated with had violent felony convictions. They carried automatic rifles and had thousands of rounds of ammunition for the coming Armageddon. They believed the United States was a Christian republic, and Jews and Blacks were not eligible for citizenship. They claimed to have the right to print their own money and believed that federal agencies like the IRS and FmHA were part of a plot leading to a one-world government under the United Nations.

Why soft-spoken, polite, storytelling, cowboy-attired Ralph had joined up with them and started to wear camouflage was a mystery, until I learned that the Freemen had promised to get his ranch back after both the 7,000 acres and his beloved home place were sold at foreclosure sales.[14] The homestead sold for $50,000 to an out-of-state bank in 1994, and the 7,000 acres were sold to a local rancher who paid $493,000 in 1995.[15]

As eviction by a sheriff was imminent, Ralph invited the Freemen to move from their crowded headquarters in a house in the nearby town of Roundup to the Clark ranch. Some of the Freemen moved in with the Clarks (Kay and Edwin's wife, Janet, objected to no avail) while others occupied the rental cabins.

Ralph renamed the 960-acre farm Justus Township and declared independence from all county, state, and federal law. (They fancied themselves as similar to the "embattled farmers" in Emerson's poem, "Concord Hymn," about the beginning of the American Revolutionary War.) This is how matters stayed all winter, but then on March 25, the two most important leaders of the Freemen were lured out of Justus Township and arrested for multiple felonies by the FBI.

Right after the arrests, a hundred armed FBI agents in military regalia surrounded Justus Township in a massive display of force, anticipating a quick surrender by the remaining Freemen. That didn't happen. Rather, the Freemen seemed to become even more emboldened.

For eighty-one days, the world watched the standoff on TV, fearing a catastrophic end as heavily armed Freemen and heavily armed FBI agents faced each other.[16] The standoff ended on June 13, 1996, when Edwin Clark quietly took the lead in negotiating a surrender. The end of the siege was celebrated from the White House by President Clinton, in large part because there had been no ghastly deaths like those at Waco, Ruby Ridge, or Oklahoma City.

After the surrender, Ralph was booked for various crimes including participating in threats on law enforcement officials and judges who were "wanted, dead or alive." He was incarcerated for twenty months (either bail wasn't offered or he had no money for it) while awaiting trial. At the first federal trial he was tried with two Freemen leaders. They were convicted and sentenced to serious time in prison, but the jury was hung and he was acquitted. But the state continued the battle and prosecuted him for "criminal syndicalism and writing bad checks." He was found guilty for some of those charges in 1999 and received a $5,000 fine—paltry punishment after a ninety-one-day armed standoff. He moved "somewhere else" in eastern Montana, and I read that he never returned to the ranch he had fought so hard to save.[17]

"Ralph was gullible," Tom said to me years later. "He was a follower of the Freemen, not a leader. He was restless. He wanted something happening. He cut ties with me, and others that would have helped him. I couldn't go the way Ralph went. I wanted nothing to do with the Freemen."

The radicalization of Ralph Clark and the Freemen standoff did not need to happen. I still wonder how it might have turned out differently had FmHA simply given Ralph and Kay Clark a fair hearing that summer day in 1982.

CHAPTER 11

Time to Make Some Law

On August 5, I was at last sworn in to the North Dakota Bar Association. I was now a "legal" lawyer, much to my relief (and my father's). Only years later would I learn how my application had finally been processed: the clerk of court in charge of bar admissions, a friend of my father's, had paid my application fee herself.

A few days later, the phone rang.

"Is this Sarah Vogel?"

"Yes?"

"This is Lance Lindbloom. I'm the executive director of the J. Roderick MacArthur Foundation."

I gripped the receiver. If he was calling me on the phone, I thought, it had to be good news about the $200,000 grant I'd applied for.

"We're interested in your proposal," Lance said.

"You are?"

"We'd love to help but we were wondering: What would you do if you had fifteen thousand dollars?"

Only fifteen thousand dollars? I had to scale back my ambitions.

"I'd bring one class action here in North Dakota," I said. "To make Farmers Home follow the 1978 deferral law and require fair hearings." I could picture the names and faces of the men I'd be suing in court: John Block, secretary of agriculture; Charles W. Shuman, administrator of the Farmers Home Administration; Ralph Leet, state director of the North Dakota Farmers Home Administration.

"Okay!" Lance said. "I'll see what I can do."

With the prospect of funding down the road, it was time to stop fantasizing and get serious about my legal practice. I knew I was inefficient working from home.

I was in luck. The daycare at the Bismarck YMCA had an opening. The teachers were great, and the kids had access to all the facilities at the Y, including the pool. As soon as he saw the books, the toys, and the swimming pool, Andrew was eager to attend. I could pay by the week.

I signed a lease on an office in a rather run-down area of south Bismarck. The office building was on old Highway 10, squeezed between a gas station called Hawk's Pit Stop and a bar, also called Hawk's Pit Stop. My new office was in the basement and didn't have any windows. But the rent was low ($158 a month) and there was a secretarial service that I'd used before down the hall. The windowless room was starkly different from my last real office in the U.S. Treasury Building, where I'd had a huge private office with high ceilings with crown molding, big windows with a view of the interior courtyard, and a huge desk. But I was happy with my snug new office. It offered me a fresh start.

I ordered business cards and letterhead, leased a machine that "processed" my words, and bought (on time) a bunch of law books that a clever fast-talking Westlaw book salesman swore were "essential." I bought a cheap answering machine and a pricey legal billing system. All of my new purchases were on credit from downtown Bismarck businesses, who saw the last name Vogel and naively inquired no further. My girlfriend Rodine, who was a secretary for an coal lobbyist, recorded a professional-sounding message on my answering machine that said "we" would get back to the caller.

I was more efficient in the new office because I had fewer distractions, but I found that sending proper bills with my new billing system took valuable time away from my work. Within weeks, I realized that billing was futile: my clients had no money. I put the billing system in the drawer. (It was repossessed a few months later.)

In late August, Shuman sent out yet another Foreclosure Quota Memo. The House of Representatives responded with another bill that gave farmers the right to apply for deferrals. But faced with blistering opposition from

Secretary Block, who said it was equivalent to a moratorium on the collection of $20 billion, the law died on the Senate floor.

I'd started to do FmHA appeals believing that I would win if I had the facts and the law on my side. This optimism was dashed on the rocks of FmHA's obdurate refusal to back off once a decision to shut a farm down had been made.

I was cynical about any farmer's chances within the FmHA appeal system. I immersed myself in research on how to attack and improve the deeply flawed FmHA administrative hearing process. I spent hours at the Supreme Court library copying regulations, laws, and cases. I was still looking for the key that would unlock my attack against FmHA's flawed processes.

It was hard and lonely work. Andrew picked up on my mounting stress.

One day, when I picked him up at the Y, he said, "Mom, I have an idea! Why don't you get a job at daycare? You'd be good at it. Your other job is too hard!"

"I'm so sorry, honey. I just can't." As I said this, I choked up. He was right. It would be easier to be a daycare worker, and I might even net more money, and I did miss Andrew when I was away from him. But I felt that I was riding a train going a hundred miles an hour—I couldn't just jump off.

After a month at my new office, I realized I'd underestimated how expensive it could become. It wasn't just the daycare bill. My long distance phone bill was triple my rent. My name and phone number appeared in farmer newsletters throughout the country. When I worked at home, I was able to avoid long distance calls by answering the calls that came in at all hours of the day, from early in the morning (dairy farmers) to late at night (wheat farmers). When I moved to my new office, I had to return the calls that came in while I was at home or at the law library. When I got home, I had to return the calls I'd missed while I was at the office. I grew to hate the blinking answering machine light.

A typical message began with a man's quiet voice: "Hello. I guess you aren't there . . . but if you get this message, call me back at . . . I guess it's hopeless . . ." and after another long pause, I'd hear a click. There were no farm suicide hotlines back then, so returning calls like this one was my first priority. I couldn't worry about the phone bill when I heard someone in so much pain.

Magically, at my most dismal moments, the phone would ring and I'd hear Dwight Coleman's friendly voice say, "How are ya doing, Sarah!" These random calls from Dwight were enough to cheer me up for days. They reminded me why

I was fighting these battles: it was for him, it was for them, it was for all of the farmers.

I learned about the primacy of timely office rent payment the hard way. I'd prepaid September when I signed the lease in August. But on Friday, October 1, my office door wouldn't open. I went upstairs and my scowling landlord said that if he didn't have the rent check in his hand on the first of each month, he simply locked the office with a deadbolt, to which he had the only key. I could get into the office when the rent was paid.

That summer I borrowed money from Mary for food and, when I couldn't avoid it, from my father (for everything else).

A few days after I resolved the lockout, I went into the office about eight thirty in the morning, flipped on the glaring overhead fluorescent lights, and started to work. In the quiet morning, I was making good progress on a letter for the Folmers when I realized I had a question for Russel.

When I picked up the phone, there was no dial tone. My heart sank.

I walked down the hall to the secretarial service office and asked if her phone was working. It was. I called the phone company from the secretarial office and learned why my phone had been disconnected. The patient collector at the other end of the phone call said that cutoffs for nonpayment of delinquent business phones were swift compared to those of residential phones. And there was more bad news: "Your phone can't be reconnected until the last bill for $518, and the charges incurred since the beginning of the month, another $390, is paid. In cash. Have a great day!"

I walked back to my office and sank down on my desk chair, pushing the incomplete letter aside. I was in shock. Every illusion I had maintained since I left the Treasury Department about how I could succeed in this unequal battle shattered. I couldn't help Anna Mae or Russel or any of my clients without a phone. A lawyer without a phone is like a surgeon without hands. My quest to help the farmers was over.

I started to cry, for myself, for my clients, for the injustice of it all. I cried until my eyes burned from the glaring fluorescent lights. I struggled to my feet and went to the switch by the door to turn off the lights. The room was pitch black, with only a faint crack of dim light coming under the door and the blinking light of the word processor. I couldn't see my desk or my chair, so I just curled into a ball on the grimy industrial carpet like a small miserable child.

After a long while, I crawled toward the strip of light under the door, got to my feet, and went out into the hall to use the bathroom. I flinched at the bright light and was deeply embarrassed to see a man and a woman standing in the corridor. "Excuse me," I muttered, and went past them into the ladies' bathroom. I washed my red, swollen eyes with cold water and tried to pull myself together. I hoped the couple in the hallway would be gone when I came out, but they weren't.

"Are you Sarah Vogel?" the man called after me.

"Yes," I said, trying to hide my face.

"We're Richard and Marlene DeLare from near Minot. We had an appointment with you at ten. We've been in the hallway. We heard you crying and we knocked and called out to you, but maybe you didn't hear us?"

"I'm sorry," I said. "I forgot about the appointment." I quickly wiped my eyes and invited them in.

Slowly they started to tell me about their situation. In the late 1970s, they had expanded their farm with the help of a loan from Farmers Home Administration. But then they had been hit by drought, low prices for the crops, and high costs for their expenses. Things went from bad to worse and weren't helped by Richard's lack of appropriate deference to the loan officers. FmHA had accelerated the chattel loans and real estate loans, and in late June, trucks and trailers with armed federal agents had invaded their farm and taken away tractors, machinery, cattle—anything and everything that was movable.

They knew that FmHA would be back, and that the next time they'd go after the land and their home.

"It's a good farm," Marlene said.

"We'll get jobs in town. We'll do whatever it takes," Richard said. "We just can't have a foreclosure."

"I understand what has happened to you," I said. "And it was wrong what they did." I tried to choke back fresh tears. "But I'm not able to help you. I can't take a case knowing that I can't do the work. My phone was disconnected this morning."

Richard pulled out the check he'd brought with him, for $3,000, to hire me.

I shook my head. "It would be legal malpractice for me to take your money when I won't be around to do the work when FmHA sends the notice before foreclosure. I'm done. I can't do it anymore. I just can't help you. I'm sorry."

They were quiet as I wiped the tears from my face. Richard looked at Marlene, and she looked at him. Then Richard said, "We understand that you can't take this money to take our case and that you won't agree to be our lawyer. But would you accept a loan from us? We need you and I'm sure a lot of other farmers do, too. Please take this as a loan. And we'll come back later when the notice before foreclosure comes."

I sniffled as I thought about what they were saying. I had been giving hope to farmers, but now two farmers were giving hope to me. If I could get the phone reconnected, I could last until the grant from the J. Roderick MacArthur Foundation came, and then something else might turn up.

"Thank you," I said. "I'm going to write you an IOU right now. And I'll be your lawyer when you need me."

I was back in business.

ONE EVENING, I called my father and told him how frustrated I was that I couldn't find more court decisions or laws to help my clients.

"Well," he said calmly, "if you can't find a case or a law that supports the cause of your client, it doesn't mean you should quit. It simply means it's now time for you to go *make* some law."

Easy for him to say—Robert Vogel had made law on many occasions as a private attorney and North Dakota Supreme Court justice. He had stopped the inhumane practice of sending all women convicted of a crime to a distant out-of-state prison (where families could not visit and applying for parole and seeing lawyers was all but impossible), whereas men were incarcerated at the state prison in Bismarck.[1] He had stopped North Dakota's denial of educational services to students with physical and mental challenges, finding that the "right to a public school education is a right guaranteed by the North Dakota Constitution."[2] He sued the State of North Dakota to declare a law that required a copy of the "Ten Commandments of the Christian Religion" to be posted in every public school-room in the state to be an unconstitutional establishment of religion, and was hailed as a hero by the American Jewish Congress for doing so.[3] He represented numerous conscientious objectors pro bono during the Vietnam War draft.

I thought that I could be a "legal warrior" like the Nonpartisan League lawyers that I so admired. But my main strength was naïveté. I was a solo practitioner proposing a lawsuit against the U.S. government, which was represented by thousands of lawyers who fought hard and hated to lose. USDA was an ogre—big, mean, and nasty. Yet I believed I could defeat it.

I remembered the night Mary Lacina, the McCabes' neighbor, had called me because her baby was crying with an earache and there was no money for a doctor after Farmers Home seized the money in their bank account. She was in the same situation as the weeping woman I'd seen in the Bronx in 1970, sitting on a stoop with her child, her pile of belongings on the curb. Both desperate mothers had been deprived of a fair hearing.

I went to the Supreme Court law library to find the decision in *Goldberg v. Kelly*, the U.S. Supreme Court case that had protected welfare mothers from being cut off from benefits without a prior hearing and had triggered law students like me to help welfare recipients get a fair hearing. The decision was written by Justice William J. Brennan.[4]

The plaintiffs were clients of New York's Aid to Families with Dependent Children (AFDC) welfare program—mostly single mothers like me. Their payments had been cut off when social workers suspected them of welfare fraud. The state offered them the opportunity for a hearing to contest the accusation of fraud, but not until after the benefits had been lost.

I thought of the shock of families like the Folmers, the McCabes, the Nicholses, the Clarks, and so many others, when they learned their bank accounts had been emptied and their earnings had been seized by FmHA. If they wanted to appeal, the soonest they could get a hearing was weeks or months *after* the seizure of their income.

Goldberg didn't just address the timing of the hearing; it also dealt with the fairness of the hearing. Midway through the case, New York changed its policies to provide a pretermination hearing, but it still did not allow the person accused of welfare fraud the right to present evidence, to be heard orally in person or by counsel, or to cross-examine adverse witnesses.

As I read Justice Brennan's decision, I felt better and better about our chances of beating USDA. A fair hearing had to be held *before* the termination, because the recipient otherwise might lose "the very means by which to live while he waits."[5] FmHA hearings occurred *after* farmers' access to their income had been seized or frozen by FmHA. Justice Brennan said that "an impartial decision maker is essential."[6] The FmHA district directors who smugly presided over the future of small family farmers were totally biased—their bosses had made the decisions we were appealing. The parallels to *Goldberg* were obvious to me.

Goldberg provided the perfect solution, and, because it involved the Bill of Rights, I contacted the Denver regional office of the ACLU to see if they were interested in filing a case. I was vaguely hoping that because it was a constitutional issue, they would rush to my rescue and take over. I got a letter soon thereafter that said they were supportive of my theory and would be glad to consult with me going forward, but my dream that they would file the case themselves was crushed. At this point, I felt that the cost of keeping the ACLU involved was greater than the benefit, and the correspondence lapsed.

Excited as I was about using the *Goldberg* case, I worried whether the principles governing a welfare program could be applied to a multibillion-dollar business loan program. Even Dwight Coleman and the McCabes, who were very small farmers, had borrowed more than a hundred thousand dollars each from FmHA. With those loans they had purchased land, machinery, and cattle, all of which were pledged to FmHA as collateral in detailed security agreements and mortgages. Could I persuade a judge that my plaintiffs were analogous to the struggling welfare recipients living in New York City housing projects?

I remembered a United States Supreme Court case involving FmHA that my father had sent me with a memo that simply said "Thought you'd be interested." I'd read it months before and remembered that it talked about the purposes of FmHA and said something about "welfare."

Thankful that I was such a pack rat, I dug through the piles of cases and papers that were scattered in towering drifts across my desk until I found it: *United States v. Kimbell Foods, Inc.*[7] It was a unanimous decision authored by Justice Thurgood Marshall. I sat down to read it. Andrew was in bed, and I snuck a smoke in hopes of restoring my flagging energy.

The facts were simple. A Texas farmer had received a loan from FmHA and had signed a security agreement giving FmHA a lien on his equipment, including a tractor, which meant that if he failed to pay his loan, FmHA could repossess and sell the tractor and apply the proceeds from the sale of the tractor to the farmer's debt. At some point, the tractor broke down and the farmer had taken it to be repaired. The repairs cost $2,151.28. Under Texas law, the repairman was entitled to a mechanic's lien, which protected mechanics (like the tractor repairman) against customers (like this farmer) who didn't pay for their repairs.

Under the laws of every state, there are a wide variety of liens, such as seed liens (to ensure that a seed dealer is paid when a crop is sold), feed liens (to ensure that the feed dealer is paid when the cattle or horses are sold), and many others, which vary from state to state. When there's more than one lien on the same item, state laws generally set out the relative priority of the various liens. In the *Kimbell Foods* case, when the farmer filed for bankruptcy, he hadn't paid either FmHA or the tractor repairman. The repairman filed a claim for $2,151.28 and FmHA filed a claim for a much larger amount. Like a miserly Scrooge, the Department of Justice opposed paying the tractor repairman, claiming that FmHA was acting as "the sovereign" and deserved priority in all bankruptcy assets, analogous to the super-priority that the IRS had in collecting federal taxes. The trial court disagreed, saying that under Texas law, the repairman was entitled to be paid before FmHA. It seemed unbelievable to me that this was the dispute that the Department of Justice decided was worth taking all the way to the U.S. Supreme Court. But the issue of whether federal agencies like FmHA and the Small Business Administration were entitled to be paid before "Main Street" creditors was an important question of law, and the decision in the *Kimbell Foods* case would affect many billions of dollars of debt, not just the $2,151.28 owed to the tractor repairman.

In 1979, Justice Marshall flatly said "no dice" to FmHA and its claim of being "the sovereign," and as a result it was not entitled to preferential treatment vis-à-vis creditors like the tractor repairman. The Supreme Court said FmHA should be treated like any other lender—no better, no worse—under generally applicable, nondiscriminatory state laws. Under Texas law, the tractor repairman had a higher priority than FmHA did as a secured lender, so he should be paid first because he was first in line. It took nine justices of the U.S. Supreme Court, but the tractor repairman would get his $2,151.28.

What excited me about the *Kimbell Foods* decision was *why* the Supreme Court ruled as it did. Justice Marshall said that FmHA was not acting as a "sovereign" in its farm lending programs; rather, FmHA's loan programs were "a form of *social welfare legislation*, primarily designed to assist farmers and businesses that cannot obtain funds from private lenders on reasonable terms" (emphasis added).[8] As I thought back to the origins of FmHA in the depths of the Great Depression, with a mission to help struggling tenant and dispossessed farmers like the Joad family in *The Grapes of Wrath*, I was grateful for Justice Marshall's sense of history.

The *Goldberg* case was the key to get into the ogre's castle, but the *Kimbell Foods* case was the key to the treasure casket inside it. In *Goldberg*, Justice Brennan wrote,

> For qualified recipients, welfare provides the means to obtain essential food, clothing, housing and medical care . . . [Thus] termination of aid pending resolution of a controversy over eligibility may deprive an *eligible* recipient of the very means by which to live while he waits. Since he lacks independent resources, his situation becomes immediately desperate. His need to concentrate upon finding the means for daily subsistence, in turn, adversely affects his ability to seek redress from the welfare bureaucracy.[9]

And in *Kimbell Foods*, Justice Marshall said that FmHA's program was a "social welfare" program.

Why shouldn't these farmers have due process? The property that FmHA was seizing without a prior fair hearing deprived them of income that the farmers had earned from their crops or livestock. The farmers, not the federal government, had planted the crops, milked the cows, fed the calves. The money that was frozen really belonged to them; FmHA had only a security agreement covering the collateral. Seizure of their income and property was even more problematic than freezing welfare payments or trying to cheat a tractor repairman of a couple of thousand dollars.

Now I believed I could make some law.

I HAD ABOUT twenty questionnaires from farmers in North Dakota who were willing to be class representatives. I'd select farmers who best illustrated the story I wanted to tell a judge: farmers who worked hard, couldn't pay due to circumstances beyond their control, had suffered loss of their very means of survival, were entitled to apply for deferral under FmHA's own laws and regulations, and had appealed using FmHA's deeply flawed appeals system.

Gene Severens at the Center for Rural Affairs had alerted me to a case called *Hudson v. Farmers Home Administration*, filed by two Black farmers in Mississippi with small farms, on behalf of a class of similarly situated Black farmers. They alleged that FmHA was discriminating against Black small farmers by denying them access to limited resource loans, which were loans that carried a significantly lower interest rate than regular loan programs.

I had no doubt that Black farmers suffered from race discrimination. I'd seen how FmHA treated Black people in the South when I'd worked at the FTC on the Equal Credit Opportunity Act. It was clear to me that FmHA and the Department of Justice didn't want these Black farmers to have their day in court. The Department of Justice moved to dismiss the *Hudson* case because the farmers had not "exhausted their administrative remedies," and that's what the court did.

The doctrine of exhaustion of administrative remedies was developed to protect federal courts from dealing with issues that had not been thoroughly explored within administrative agencies. It was based on the idea that the federal agency should have a first "go" at fixing a problem before a federal judge was brought in. It was created by courts to reduce their caseload, but it also makes sense. Parents do the same thing when they tell two quarreling siblings to "work it out" before involving the parents.

I didn't want to repeat the lawyers' mistake in *Hudson*, in which almost two years of litigation ended in sharp criticism of the lawyers and dismissal of their clients' case.[10] The most frustrating aspect of the *Hudson* case was that the claims of race discrimination by FmHA were valid, even though it would take many years to get vindication for Black farmers in the South.[11] After reading *Hudson*, I resolved that no matter how futile it was, I would endure the FmHA appeal process so that I could someday show a court that FmHA's appeal procedures were unconstitutional. In a strange way, knowing about the *Hudson* case helped me survive the period of bitter losses that followed that summer.

CHAPTER 12

Exhaustion

By the summer of 1982, I had about twenty potential named plaintiffs, and half of them were going through appeals. I reviewed the facts and issues raised in those appeals and sorted them into three piles: strong possibilities for lead plaintiffs, maybes, and rejects. I rejected anyone who I felt could be credibly accused of dishonesty by FmHA or who had already, without excuse, missed an appeal deadline. Those folks could be part of the class, but it wasn't prudent to choose them for lead plaintiffs.

I focused on the "strong possibility" category to ensure that they illustrated fact patterns that would mesh with the two main arguments I intended to raise in the class action: failure to implement the 1978 deferral law (a copycat *Curry* case), and use of an appeal process that violated the standards of due process of law set out in the *Goldberg* case. Chief among the *Goldberg* due process issues were the use of biased hearing officers and FmHA's seizure of income and starving the farmer out before a hearing had taken place.

I gradually narrowed my list of strong possibilities down to Dwight Coleman (beginning farmer, just starting out, innocent of wrongdoing, starved out), Russel and Anna Mae Folmer (established farmers, middle-aged, falsely accused of wrongdoing by an FmHA hitman, starved out and threatened), Don and Diane McCabe (young farmers, obedient to FmHA and innocent of wrong-doing, starved out). I liked all five farmers; they were good to work with, and they'd behaved honestly with FmHA.

Now we had to exhaust administrative remedies, which meant we'd have to appeal at the state level, fight hard, and raise every conceivable argument we might want to raise later in court; once we'd lost at the state level, we would then have to raise the same arguments at the national office of FmHA and lose once more. We couldn't skip any step: in the *Hudson* case, a farmer who had lost an appeal at the state office hadn't carried it to the next level and was slammed by the Court of Appeals for having failed to *completely* exhaust his remedies. That was a fatal error that I didn't intend to make. I'd carry on with every appeal of a lead plaintiff until the bitter end.

My first adversary was Ralph Leet in the state office. Starting almost as soon as I moved back to Bismarck, Leet had been publicly bad-mouthing me, my clients, and any farmer who publicly spoke out against pressure from FmHA. Leet repeatedly denied that there was a quota, or any type of crackdown. With his sincere Norwegian face evidencing compassion and concern, he told members of the press that FmHA was only trying to help farmers become current on their loans. He claimed again and again that FmHA would stick with any farmer "who had a reasonable chance of success," implying that any farmers being shut down by FmHA were bad farmers and bad managers.[1] He seemed to dislike me intensely, and by now the disdain was mutual. I loathed Ralph Leet. I tended to take it personally when Leet told the press that "lawyers seeking clients" were in part responsible for spreading "sensationalized" accounts of FmHA.[2] My claims were sensational, but they were also true. And I didn't exactly seek the farmers as clients—they found me. Leet even dissed me in the national press, telling Richard Woodley of *Life* magazine that my work representing farmers was a "disservice" to taxpayers.[3]

Given the antipathy that Leet and others at FmHA showed to farmers who did not just "voluntarily" liquidate, I knew that the appeals would be difficult and I didn't sugarcoat it for my clients. But I also told them that every time an appeal was conducted unfairly, illegally, or harshly, our case in court would be strengthened.

I had the easiest time showing that Dwight Coleman, of all my lead plaintiffs, had exhausted his administrative remedies. After his chattel loans were declared due on Christmas Eve 1981, he went into the county office to find out whom he should contact about the "meeting" he'd been offered if he disagreed with the decision to accelerate. He did disagree. "Who do I go see?" he asked.

The county supervisor told him the meeting would be with Odell Ottmar, but any meeting with Ottmar would be a "waste of time" because it was "just a formality."

I told Dwight at the picnic up at the Slabaugh farm that he was entitled to an actual appeal, not just a "meeting" with the same guy, Ottmar, who had recommended the acceleration. FmHA had screwed up by not even following the basic appeal procedure, inadequate though it was. I drafted a letter for Dwight's signature, spelling out what had happened and asking Ralph Leet to set up a proper appeal hearing.

Had Leet responded to Dwight's letter with compassion and a sense of fairness, the case that later became known as *Coleman v. Block* might not have been filed. But that wasn't in Leet's character. Leet immediately replied to Dwight, saying he wouldn't set up an appeal because the time for an appeal had passed.

I wasn't upset by that response, because now we had two issues to raise with a court, not just one. The first violation was that FmHA didn't give Dwight a fair chance to appeal (a "meeting" isn't an appeal hearing, and he'd been misled about the process). Second, when Dwight asked Leet to correct the first violation, Leet flatly refused.

Dwight's experience would be useful in the class action, because I knew he represented many hundreds of farmers who had been similarly pressured to quit, told lies about the appeal process, and discouraged from filing or pursuing appeals. There had already been over thirty-seven hundred "voluntary" liquidations by farmers across the country during the first nine months of 1982.[4]

"WHERE WOULD YOU like to start?" the assistant district director asked. "With the delinquency or the production?"[5]

At the McCabes' July appeal hearing in a bleak conference room at the district FmHA office in Bismarck, we had to refute the accusation of "very poor" dairy production on their notice of acceleration and explain their declining net worth in order to qualify for a deferral.

"I started with fifty-two cows in 1974 and today I'm at thirty cows, with the suggestion of FmHA to cut down cows. We cut down because FmHA did not want to put up the money for feed and we didn't have room for those animals," Don said.

"Did you ask for more cows?" the hearing officer asked.

"Not at the time," Don said. "I did ask for a place to raise calves and I was denied flatly. They said it would be too high to put up a pole barn."

Diane chimed in. "We also asked to have a barn set up. We lost eight cows that winter due to the cold and their being outside. And it went on our record as poor management. We did what we were told and now it's our fault."

Dairy production had declined. Not only had their herd declined in number, but production of each cow had generally gone down too, because the cows were growing older (FmHA wouldn't authorize purchase or raising of replacement cows) and they couldn't get approval from FmHA for proper feed and nutritional supplements.

"I went into FmHA and asked for this stuff and they denied me," Don insisted.

"We really thought we owed everything to FmHA," Diane said. "What they said was law and we did not have any right to debate it in any way. That's why you don't find any problems in our record."

When the county supervisor tried to disprove Diane's depiction of complete cooperation, by pointing out that the McCabes had agreed to liquidate in 1981 but reneged on that promise, Don shot back: "This was before we knew we had any rights. We did not know at that time that we had any rights at all in this matter. What you said we figured was law. When you said to liquidate, we had to liquidate. There was nothing ever said that if we didn't agree we had the right to appeal. So I agreed because I figured you were law."

"If I have to go to an attorney to find out what my rights are from FmHA there is something wrong," Diane added.

The McCabes presented a spirited defense of their work ethic, their attempts to improve their dairy production despite extremely poor advice and little support from FmHA employees, and how hard they had worked to meet every requirement of FmHA. When Diane and Don complained that FmHA had not let their cows have sufficient feed and supplements that would have doubled milk production, I couldn't help but think of Tom and Anna Nichols and their starving hogs, let loose on a drought-stricken field in eastern Montana.

"You said good management is using what you have to get what you want. Why do they let people buy fertilizer, then?" Diane said, her voice rising. "They are feeding their ground. Why can't we feed our cattle?"

By the end of the appeal hearing, we had defended every accusation of wrongful default, proven that they were good dairy farmers (with a glowing reference from a North Dakota State University dairy expert on the high quality of their milk), and suggested a way forward (a thirty-six-month deferral and building up their herd by keeping heifer calves). Between my legal arguments and their plans for the future, I thought we'd made a very strong case that the McCabes should not be foreclosed. We walked out, exhausted but elated that we had done the best job possible.

On August 3, the McCabes received a letter, signed by the assistant district director, which said: "Based on the material in the County Office file, the hearing, and the material you have submitted, it is my opinion that there is insufficient new evidence to change the decision of FmHA." No specific reasons were given for the decision. I felt we were being hamstrung: How could we dispute reasons that were never provided to us?

I wrote a reply on behalf of the McCabes, pointing out that the agency's own appeal regulations gave him the duty of giving "*specific reasons* for the decision and the *factual basis* for the decision reached."

"I do not agree with your interpretation of our regulations," the assistant district director replied two weeks later.

I filed a formal request with Charles Shuman in the national office. In the meantime, I sought to preserve Don and Diane's factual arguments by sending a letter to the National FmHA office with legal arguments detailing how the hearing officer hadn't followed the appeal regulations. I supplemented the legal arguments with a handwritten letter from Diane. When I read that letter, it brought tears to my eyes: "We did as we were told to do, and never questioned FmHA's advice to us. We were diligent in listening to them. We have been on our farm for five years and in that time we have only left it for one day to attend my sister's wedding. We don't get vacations or even expect to, so we were diligent in being on our farm steadily."

We never did get specific reasons for the decision.

ODELL OTTMAR, THE same guy who was trying to shut down Dwight Coleman, scheduled Russel and Anna Mae Folmer's first hearing only days after we'd gotten access to the Folmers' files. We refused to attend and demanded more time to prepare. At the second hearing, the two key FmHA employees we wanted to question (and whom we'd asked Ottmar to have at the hearing) weren't there. Ottmar hadn't even asked them to attend. We walked out again.

By September 23, when we at last got our hearing, I felt hostile toward—and suspicious of—Ottmar. I brought a witness from the North Dakota Commissioner of Agriculture's Office and my own court reporter.

Ottmar listened, but it seemed he didn't understand my argument that delinquency alone wasn't a basis for a foreclosure. I handed him copies of the 1978 deferral law, the Senate resolution, and the *Curry* case, but he pushed them to the side without reading them.

"I really didn't get to hear your answer on not being delinquent. Basically our statement is that the Folmers' account does show approximately twenty thousand dollars delinquent," he said.

When I explained that the *Curry* case required USDA to follow the deferral law, Ottmar cut me off. "Ms. Vogel, if I could interject at this point, as a hearing officer I will try to stay here with the facts as to why *this* account was accelerated. We are not attorneys."

No kidding, I thought. *You are definitely not an attorney! And what's with this "we" and "our" stuff? You're supposed to be neutral and unbiased.* I began to plot how my future class action would require that every hearing officer be an attorney rather than an underling of the person who had decided to foreclose. I was tired of making futile legal arguments to bureaucrats who had been trained to follow "policy," not laws.

The Folmers' case seemed even stronger to me than the McCabes'. The Folmers' delinquency was quite small (they were only one payment behind on real estate debt), plus they had $186,000 in equity (a huge amount in 1982); their taxes weren't even due for another six months, and the idea that Jim Well, a county supervisor who had been in the county for mere days, could demand that a farmer who had been in business for decades sell his dairy herd at once or get out was crazy! Ottmar seemed bored and inattentive as I spoke, except when he became alert while seeking to fashion a way around one of my arguments.

When we finally obtained a thousand pages of their records through our FOIA request, I had the Folmers identify every action they felt was unfair. There were quite a few, but the worst was when the new guy, Well, had accused them of conversion—a felony—for selling fifty-one beef cattle that he said were secured to FmHA. This accusation against the Folmers was in a Real Estate Problem Case Report that Well sent up the chain—I wondered if anyone had ever checked to see if it was true.

It was the sale of these beef cattle that had resulted in the notice of acceleration the Folmers received, demanding they pay their loans in full or face foreclosure. But when the Folmers and I reviewed their files, we saw that when Well made the allegation of criminal conduct, FmHA didn't even have a lien on the Folmers' beef cows. The agency had a lien only on "dairy cows" and "dairy bulls."

I'd learned the Uniform Commercial Code at NYU from Professor Homer Kripke, a legendary attorney and legal scholar who had written the UCC, the law that governed secured transactions in every state (before the UCC, each state had its own commercial codes). He didn't just teach rules—he taught us *why* there were rules. One thing I remembered was that the UCC required a security agreement to "reasonably identify" collateral.[6] In North Dakota, the ubiquitous dairy cow breed was the Holstein, and there wasn't any doubt about identifying Holsteins, thanks to Salem Sue. Salem Sue is "the world's largest Holstein cow," and since 1974 she has stood on a high butte outside the town of New Salem, in Morton County, next to I-94. She is thirty-eight feet tall and fifty feet long, painted in realistic black-and-white spots with rosy pink udders under which tourists can get their photos taken.

"Well's accusation of conversion was reckless and untrue," I told Ottmar at the hearing. Any assumption that beef cattle could be covered by a security agreement that listed only dairy cattle showed appalling ignorance of the Uniform Commercial Code. I reminded Ottmar that FmHA was subject to the UCC just like any other lender, as the Supreme Court had held in the *Kimbell Foods* case. Ottmar seemed bored.

I let loose on Mr. Well, and the district director and Ralph Leet, for approving a foreclosure for the spurious reason identified in the Real Estate Problem Case Report. In the heat of the moment, I called FmHA's methods "outrageously slovenly" and said that Leet and Well had shown "willful malice" to the Folmers. Ottmar hardly reacted.

After I shoved the security agreement that said "dairy cows" under his nose and got Ottmar to agree that Herefords were not dairy cows, he finally admitted that there "might" not be conversion, but he'd need to check with an attorney. At last! I was certain that any attorney would agree with me.

As the Folmers and I walked out of the hearing, our observer from the Department of Agriculture said we'd done a superb job. But actually we'd been played for suckers.

On October 19, Ottmar sent a brief letter defending each of six reasons for the acceleration. His rationale was weak. I was most offended when he said that I, Sarah Vogel, had "mentioned but not discussed" the invalidity of the "failure to voluntarily liquidate" reason, even though the transcript of the hearing showed I had discussed this in detail. He said he hadn't had time to get an opinion from an attorney. He told us we had the right to appeal to the national office, probably assuming we'd give up.

On November 18, I sent off a twelve-page brief with voluminous attachments, giving a point-by-point rebuttal of every failure of reasoning and every factual error in Ottmar's decision. It was dense with references to sworn statements in the transcript, as well as to pertinent laws, regulations, cases, and records. And it was useless.

The national office sent a single-paragraph reply that found that the actions of the state FmHA office as to the Folmers were "proper." That was it.

In a strange way, I wasn't unhappy with the terrible way Ottmar and the national FmHA office had treated the Folmers. We had advanced one step closer to getting in front of a judge.

I SHARED MY war stories about my FmHA battles with my father and kept him updated on my progress in finding lead plaintiffs. I got sympathy and occasional laughter when I told him about the way FmHA handled hearings ("They don't follow law? They only follow policy?"). But any time I mentioned a class action, I sent my father into paroxysms of anxiety. He had done litigation for decades, had tried hundreds of cases, and he knew that class action lawsuits were one of the hardest kinds of lawsuits to bring. He feared—correctly—that I didn't fully grasp what I was up against.

One day an envelope arrived in the mail with a brochure inside for a "Special Seminar on Class Action Litigation" in Washington, D.C., sponsored by the Association of Trial Lawyers in America.

"You should register," the enclosed note from my dad said. "I'll pay."

CHAPTER 13

Competency of Counsel

The Mayflower Hotel's glorious lobby, spiffy bellmen, and luxurious furniture were a sharp contrast to my basement office, the isolated farm homes where my clients worried about their future, and the nondescript government offices where I tried to dissuade FmHA district directors from foreclosing on my clients' farms. Seeing so much wealth and luxury made me feel like a deep-sea diver coming too suddenly to the surface.

At the seminar registration desk, I received a name tag that read SARAH VOGEL, NORTH DAKOTA, and a booklet, thicker than a North Dakota phone book, that contained the materials for the seminar and biographies of the speakers. I plunked the booklet into my leather briefcase and went straight for the strong black coffee served in shiny silver urns. Most of the participants were men, sharply dressed in navy or dark gray suits, expensive ties from pricey labels, and shiny shoes. They clapped each other on the back as they regaled each other with war stories from their latest successes. The few women wore skirt suits, necklaces, and low heels. Looking at them, I felt subtly wrong: I was the J. C. Penney knockoff of the Lord & Taylor lawyers.

The first day of the seminar covered general topics like "Do You Want a Class? Factors You Should Consider" and "Management of a Large Class Action." It took me only a few hours to realize how dangerous it would have been had I filed my class action case without first attending the seminar.

I'd previously thought I could just copy the format of another case, like *Curry v. Block*. But now I was learning about the nuances of Rule 23: I'd need to show numerosity, commonality, typicality, and adequacy of representation. I felt that thousands of FmHA borrowers in North Dakota would show numerosity. The fact that all of these farmers operated under the same sets of "policies" and had the same loan documents should show commonality and typicality. But I was troubled by the phrase "adequacy of representation." This meant that the plaintiffs' lawyers had to be competent to do a class action. Even if my father joined me in filing the class action, would we be "adequate"? Neither of us had ever done a class action, and it was no secret in North Dakota that I'd never filed any case at all. Would a federal judge let two lawyers without class action experience go forward under Rule 23?

Rule 23 went on to set out the criteria for class action lawsuits seeking injunctive or declaratory relief and for monetary relief.

By noon, I realized that my class action could not seek any type of monetary damages. I already knew that it would be hard to pierce USDA's shield of sovereign immunity, a relic of the days when "the king can do no wrong," and I now learned that variation in the types of injuries suffered by my clients (loss of feed for cattle, loss of seed for planting, suffering of the family, loss of reputation) and the many ways to measure (or oppose measuring) those injuries in dollars and cents was fatal to class action status. Every lecturer who spoke about damages warned that judges wouldn't authorize a class action seeking damages if the process for calculating damages was complicated or unwieldy because of the need for mini-trials on how class members had suffered damages. To have a class action, the members had to have similar characteristics and suffer similar harm. Every farmer I'd worked with had a different set of circumstances, and I quickly abandoned the idea of trying to get monetary damages.

Instead, I'd focus on "injunctive" and "declaratory" relief. This was the type of nonmonetary remedy the farmers really needed: a court order that would tell FmHA what it could no longer do and how it had to behave going forward. This decision to abandon the dream of recovering money damages simplified the case, but there was still much for me to learn.

For the next two days, I went from session to session, furiously taking notes, as lawyers shared their hard-earned wisdom:

- KEEP ISSUES SIMPLE!
- Don't overreach
- Streamline case
- Definition of the class that isn't circular (don't use "plaintiffs *INJURED* by the defendant's dangerous product"; use "plaintiffs who *BOUGHT* defendant's product")
- Don't ask class members for money
- Named plaintiffs should come in every day so court can see them as people
- Limit number of named plaintiffs, you don't want to defend 20 depositions
- KEEP THE DEFENDANT ON THE DEFENSIVE!

At the end of day two, I flopped down on a luxurious sofa in the resplendent lobby. I'd been sitting only a few minutes when a lawyer wearing a speaker ribbon sat down on a chair next to the sofa. He couldn't have been older than thirty. He had long dark hair, a bright smile, and a friendly open face. His name tag read ALLAN KANNER, ALLAN KANNER AND ASSOCIATES, PHILADELPHIA, PA. From the biographies of speakers in the seminar notebook, I knew he was well known for using class actions in environmental litigation, and he'd won a huge settlement for people living near the Three Mile Island nuclear plant who had been exposed to radioactive gas in 1979 after a partial meltdown. But he didn't brag about his work. Instead, he opened with "I saw you are from North Dakota, and I love North Dakota!" I wasn't used to meeting people out east who had been to my state, much less who loved it.

"When were you in North Dakota?"

"I worked all through college but I took a couple weeks off one summer and drove to Glacier National Park in Montana. There was this sunset in North Dakota. It was glorious. I had to pull over. You don't see that growing up back east." I'd seen sunsets like that, and I knew exactly what he meant.

"What are you working on?"

"I'm working with farmers—"

"I *love* farmers!" Allan burst in. "My dad was a chicken farmer in South Jersey. We were an egg operation, not a meat operation. I was three and a half or four when I strangled my first rooster. They're nasty. They come after you like a dog."

I laughed. "Well, I'm here because I'm working on a class action that would stop the federal government from foreclosing on farmers. Do you know about the Farmers Home Administration?"

"Tell me," Allan said.

His eyes grew wide as I rushed to describe all the unfair hearings I'd lost and recount the stories of the farmers I'd found to be my lead plaintiffs.

"You know what they call the secretary of agriculture, John Block?" I asked.

"No, what?"

"Auction Block."

"Amazing. So, what's your angle for the case?"

"*Goldberg v. Kelly*," I told him.

Allan had learned about the case at Harvard Law School, where he'd been an assistant to Laurence Tribe, the famous constitutional law professor. He understood the connection instantly. If mothers on welfare in the Bronx got due process, why not farmers in North Dakota?

"Can I work with you on it?"

"Do you really mean that?"

"Absolutely," Allan said, with a huge grin. "I like a scrappy fight."

We rapidly exchanged cards. My entire conversation with Allan lasted less than thirty minutes, but meeting him felt like a miracle: my worries about whether we'd meet the requirements of Rule 23 on "competency of representation" were assuaged. My dad had the knowledge of trials and evidence; I knew about farmers and FmHA; Allan knew class actions.

THAT FALL, I'D identified one more farmer couple, George and June Hatfield, as prospective lead plaintiffs. They farmed near Ellendale, in the southeastern part of the state. When I first met them, I thought they were newlyweds because they were so sweet and affectionate with each other. (In fact, they had been married for decades and had grown children.) FmHA had been trying to push them off their land since 1981, but the Hatfields didn't want to sell out. To stay afloat, June worked as a bank teller and George on a county road crew.

Their loans, including a rural housing loan, had been accelerated in June. I was excited to learn they had a rural housing loan because I felt that the

Hatfields could illustrate the disparate treatment FmHA gave to rural housing borrowers (who were allowed to apply for deferrals) and farm loan borrowers (who were not). In 1978, when the AAM tractors came to Washington, D.C., Congress had modeled the farm loan deferral law on a statute that gave rural housing program borrowers the right to apply for a deferral. The two laws were almost identical, but FmHA followed one law and violated the other. The Hatfields could illustrate that disparity in court.

George and June came to my house several times, and we prepared for the hearing that had been scheduled for October 6, in Devils Lake, a city 165 miles from their farm and 180 miles from my office but convenient to the district director, who lived in Devils Lake. Just as I had done for the McCabes in July and the Folmers in September, I presented a mix of legal argument and testimony from the Hatfields that disproved the reasons they had been slated for foreclosure and explained why they should be allowed to continue farming.

The Hatfields had shared some of the mistreatment suffered by other farmers (no deferrals, unfair terms, seizure of income), but they also showed some new kinds of mistreatment. For example, FmHA ordered them to lease the farm out, and when they did, they were accused of not managing the farm. Their story was Kafkaesque.

In early November, we won—kind of. I received a letter saying the acceleration had been reversed because FmHA had not given the Hatfields a chance to apply for deferral on their rural housing loan.

It was a weird win, because the language of the law that established deferrals for rural housing borrowers and the language of the law that established deferrals for farm loans was nearly identical. We couldn't wait to point out to a judge that FmHA resisted complying with the farm loan deferral law but meekly followed the companion law for rural housing.[1] But even that victory lasted only a few weeks. Soon Ralph Leet sent out another acceleration notice on all their loans, to which he gratuitously added that the Hatfields weren't eligible for a rural housing moratorium because of their off-farm jobs. We filed another appeal.

To compensate me for my legal services, George built countertops in the unfinished kitchen of my house on the river. Every time he visited, he brought a cooler of frozen fish he'd caught, and fresh produce from June's garden.

. . .

AFTER THE CLASS action seminar, I called the Hatfields, Dwight Coleman, the Folmers, and the McCabes.

"Would you be willing to be lead plaintiffs on the class action?" I asked.

They all answered yes, without hesitation.

In his deep, rumbly voice, Russel Folmer said, "It's probably too late for me, but I'll do it if it helps someone else."

I told them I wanted the wives to be lead plaintiffs alongside their husbands. I was still carrying a grudge about the dismissive way I'd been treated by FmHA officials back at the FTC when I tried to stop FmHA from discriminating on the basis of sex and marital status. I was impatient with FmHA's assumption that the man was "the farmer" and the woman was merely the farmer's wife. They were both farmers. The women worked as hard as the men and were full partners in their farms. And, of course, every one of them would be named by FmHA as a defendant in a foreclosure suit, because FmHA demanded that the wives sign the promissory notes and mortgages.

Diane McCabe enthusiastically agreed. "Darn tootin', I'm a farmer too and have been since I was six!" she said. Anna Mae Folmer, I knew, did all the books and all the dairy work. June Hatfield worked nights and weekends on the farm and also worked full time in town.

All three women were delighted to be plaintiffs.

I told my clients that I would not bill them for my time and that we would get USDA to pay the legal fees when we won under the Equal Access to Justice Act.

Now I had lead plaintiffs, but there was much work to do before I could file. I bitterly regretted having told so many farmers that I would file "soon" or "in a couple of weeks," or that the case was "almost" ready to file.

The J. Roderick MacArthur Foundation had come through with a commitment for $15,000 for the North Dakota class action, payable to the Center for Rural Studies, the nonprofit Mark Ritchie ran, but my initial excitement was quickly crushed. I was naive and didn't anticipate all the delays as the various approvals were reached, documents signed, checks cleared, and boards of directors brought up to speed. It all took time, and my bills were pressing.

Worse, I didn't realize that the farmers who had worked on the August Hoe-Down believed that the grant would go to them. At the rally, I'd said that the

$15,000 would "support the Family Farmers Foreclosure Legal Assistance Project," but we now disagreed about what "support" meant. I thought that the grant was *my* money, to be disbursed by Mark Ritchie and the Center for Rural Studies for my expenses and legal work on the North Dakota class action, whose beneficiaries would be the farmers who belonged to the class.

But the Hoe-Down organizers thought that they, FFFLAP, should have control of the money. And Mark Ritchie, a born organizer, wanted to support the development of a farm organization as well as the lawsuit.

One afternoon, Don McCabe dropped by my basement office with a few other farmers. I recognized one, but the rest were strangers. Don introduced a farmer named Monte Haugen, who was wearing the biggest cowboy hat I'd ever seen. His attitude matched his hat. (Even in cowboy culture, it's good manners to take off one's hat indoors.) After coffee and chitchat, Monte rather abruptly said, "Okay! I'm the new president of FFFLAP, and we need to know *now* exactly *when* you'll be filing this class action."

I was surprised at his tone but calmly said, "I can't really say, because a great deal of work needs to be done before we file it. We'll have to exhaust administrative remedies by all the lead plaintiffs. And I'll need to do a lot more legal work before we file, if we want to succeed in getting class certification and a preliminary injunction." I was about to launch into the nuances of selection of defendants when Monte Big-Hat interrupted.

"Well, we went over to Mandan this morning and we talked to Joe Olson and he said he could be in court next week. So we want you to send the work you've done thus far over to Joe, and we'll be working with him from now on."

I had no respect for Joe Olson. I knew him and he could no more file a class action against FmHA than I could walk a tightwire in a circus. To dump me for Joe was sexist and insulting.

I paused to control my anger. "You do that," I said. "Go over to Joe Olson, but I will *not* give you or him one particle of the legal research I've done and I will not work *with* him, *under* him, or *for* him." My voice started to rise. "And if Joe files a complaint against FmHA next week, he will lose the case for you. But *I'm* still going forward and *you* can't tell *me* how to do a lawsuit. You aren't my client, Mr. Haugen. You can't fire me."

"But the fifteen thousand dollars is FFFLAP's money," Monte said. "We get to decide."

"Oh, no, you don't! I don't work for FFFLAP, and it sure as heck isn't your money!"

Don had never seen me mad—he looked shocked. The meeting wasn't going as Monte had told him it would go.

Monte tried another tack. "Okay, we'll work with you—but you'll get no money until after you file the case."

I scoffed at that. "What do you have to do with this lawsuit? Don is my client, but the rest of you aren't my clients. FFFLAP isn't a client. I think you need to leave now." I pointed to the door. As the five farmers trailed out, Don looked back at me with an anguished and apologetic face, mouthing *I'm sorry.*

I didn't blame Don. He was a trusting and innocent soul, and he'd been fooled by Monte's bluster.

As soon as they were safely gone, I called Mark Ritchie.

"Guess who just showed up at my office," I said. I told him about the meeting. "I'd rather quit than take direction on legal strategy from Monte Haugen or work under Joe Olson!"

"No one's going to make you work for Joe Olson," Mark said.

"I need that money, Mark. I mean I really need it. I could lose my house."

"Don't worry, Sarah. The grant will be sent to me, until I disburse the funds for the case. The money won't go to FFFLAP."

FOR THANKSGIVING, ANDREW and I drove to Grand Forks. My father again urged me to work for him, but again I found the courage (or the foolhardiness) to put him off. Among lawyers who represented people (as opposed to corporations), my father was esteemed;[2] if he had advertised that he was looking for an associate to join his practice, he would have been flooded with applicants. Yet I resisted. The thought of working for my father made me fear that we'd revert to our roles when I was a teenager (me rebellious, he dictatorial). I also thought if the class action was not ready to be filed before I moved to Grand Forks, I'd be diverted to more pressing and more remunerative work on my father's cases and my own case would languish even more.

My mother never got involved in these discussions, but it was obvious that she'd be happy if Andrew and I moved to Grand Forks. Andrew's favorite pair of jeans was raggedy and frayed. If he wore those jeans in front of my mother, there would be bags of new clothes (from pajamas to snow pants to jeans) for him when we left their house. My own clothes were well-worn because I hadn't gone shopping since I left the Treasury Department. My mother's gambit was to hand me a stack of curling white receipts and say "Share these with Mary." The fine print said they were for hundreds of dollars of store credit for clothes she'd bought and returned at Dayton's Department Store. My father paid the bills on her Dayton credit card, probably complaining about her spending, not realizing my mother had her own system of giving Mary and me presents.

At the end of 1982, a lawyer asked me to join a team of lawyers working on a class action lawsuit filed in federal court in Atlanta, Georgia called *Kjeldahl v. Block*, to force USDA to release $600 million in economic emergency loans that Congress had authorized. USDA had refused to release the funds, arguing that there was no economic emergency. The premise of the lawsuit was that USDA's decision not to release the funds was arbitrary and capricious under the Administrative Procedure Act. The lawyers envisioned massive fees—in the multimillions—if we won. I agreed to help them over Christmas vacation in Atlanta because I hoped working on this case would lift me out of debt.

My assignment was to prepare a brief to prove that there was in fact an economic emergency in agriculture. I talked to Black farmer organizations, Native American rancher associations, state and national farmers unions, economists, and academics to develop exhibits for my brief. Andrew stayed with his dad and my former in-laws while I spent weeks in Georgia on this $600 million rainbow.[3]

By this point, I was three months behind on my mortgage. Before I'd left for Atlanta, I'd put a check in the mail for $1,098.39 with a note saying "I'll forward the balance soon."

When I returned to North Dakota, a stack of mail awaited me in the mailbox at the end of the frozen driveway. The bank had returned my check to me with a letter that said if I didn't pay the full balance (over $3,000) by January 1, they would foreclose.

I had already missed the deadline. Finally I faced reality. My solo practice was a failure. I had to move. I felt too numb to cry.

It was only nine thirty. My parents would still be up. I picked up the phone.

"Dad, is the offer for me to come to work with you still open?"

"Of course it is."

"And can Andrew and I stay with you?"

"Hang on a second." I could hear a muffled conversation with my mother. "We'll set you up in the rec room downstairs."

I never told my clients about my financial problems, which seemed insignificant compared to theirs. If they knew their lawyer was in such wretched shape, they would become even more frightened and insecure. I told myself, *I might lose my home, but I still have my profession.* I had to have as much faith in myself as they had in me. Their courage to keep on fighting made me realize that I could continue to fight too.

Although we would soon lose our home, in many ways, Andrew and I were lucky. As a Christmas gift, my father forgave $10,000 of my debt to him.

PART III   # The Reaping

CHAPTER 14

Bitter Harvest

For two years, I'd resisted my father's invitations to work for him because I was afraid he'd make me work on his medical malpractice cases. I dreaded being under his thumb and fretted about losing my freedom as a sole practitioner and being told what to do. Those fears were a toxic hangover from my rebellious days as a fifteen-year-old, when I'd wanted to date an eighteen-year-old greaser with a ducktail haircut, a black leather jacket, and a hot rod without a muffler and my father had said no.

By the end of my first day working at the Robert Vogel Law Office, however, I realized that my father had no interest in having anyone as unskilled as me work on his medical malpractice cases. Medical malpractice work was high-stakes and specialized. The firm rejected nine of every ten requests for possible malpractice cases. Only my father's first hire, who had an MD as well as a law degree, and a select group of law students were allowed to work on the few cases that were accepted. The law students were bright, hardworking, and much cheaper than I was.

From day one, I was able to concentrate on my class action.

I spread three documents out on a card table. (I had arrived so suddenly, there was no time to find better furniture.) They were a forty-page complaint; a sixty-page brief that gave legal reasons for why the judge should make FmHA offer farmers deferrals when they were unable to pay due to circumstances beyond their control, and make FmHA provide fair hearings and release family living and farm operating expenses before FmHA could seek to accelerate debt or repossess or foreclose on farmers' real or personal property; and a forty-page brief in support of class action certification. These drafts were precious to me and represented a year's worth of work. They were also messy, weirdly formatted, and riddled with typing errors. I gave them to Sue, my father's lead legal secretary, to make a clean draft.

"Would tomorrow be okay?" she asked with a smile.

I was absurdly happy at the idea of not having to do my own typing.

I went to the office bookkeeper to fill out paperwork and learned that my pay would be $1,500 every other week. I learned that Andrew and I would also have health insurance—for the first time in two years.

That afternoon, a call came for me from New York City.

"Hello Sarah, this is Burt Neuborne. I'm the legal director of the national ACLU."

The National ACLU! I didn't expect to ever hear from the National ACLU. I'd been writing and calling the Denver Regional Office of the ACLU, hoping to get them to take the farmer case themselves. No dice. I'd even asked if they would be co-counsel, but the most the regional office had agreed to do was review my work and make suggestions. I'd let the correspondence lapse.

"I hear you have quite the case," Burt said. "I'd like to help!"

"Do you mean review my work on the case?"

"More than that. If you'd like me to, I would serve as co-counsel."

"You, personally, would be a co-counsel?"

"I'd be honored. You have a great case."

A huge smile broke out on my face. The ACLU had constitutional superpowers. I told Burt about the two other lawyers already on the case: my dad and the wunderkind Allan Kanner. Burt was relatively new to his role at the ACLU, and he'd promised to steer the ACLU's litigation strategy from an almost exclusive focus on First Amendment and gender equality cases to economic justice cases for people at the bottom of the economic ladder. He knew *Goldberg v. Kelly* like the back of his hand. Burt was from Brooklyn and had been educated at Harvard, but he had experience with rural issues from work he'd done for migrant laborers and for farmers and farm workers in rural Iowa who were faced with loss of their children because of poverty. When he heard about my case from the Midwestern regional affiliate I'd been corresponding with, he immediately saw that the FmHA case was made to order for the ACLU's new focus: to provide economic justice for the rural poor.

Burt agreed with me that *Goldberg v. Kelly* was the key. He saw the case's importance as the blast of a trumpet for the disadvantaged. "*Goldberg* recognized a new kind of property: the legitimate aspirations of poor people who had been led by the government to believe they had a right to certain things," Burt said. "All of a sudden, the due process clause was being transferred from being a protection of the comfortable with property to an engine that could be used on behalf of the weak." Burt also shared my anger that an agency that had been established to help the poor and the hungry had been transformed into an agency that ruthlessly hurt the weak.

After I hung up with Burt, I quickly shared the good news with my father.

"If the DOJ tries to get you on 'competency of counsel' under Rule 23, they won't stand a chance," my dad said.

NEWS THAT BOB Vogel's daughter had joined his law practice spread quickly among the gaggle of Grand Forks lawyers who met at the "roundtable" at a hotel's coffee shop for lunch each day.

Still, I was surprised when the U.S. attorney, Rodney Webb, called the office and asked for a meeting.

Ralph Leet and Shuman had been rude and dismissive to me. USDA's Office of General Counsel had been standoffish toward me, and ineffective in making FmHA employees follow the law. But when I sued in North Dakota, Rodney Webb and his assistant U.S. attorneys would have to defend FmHA in court. I was amazed that Webb wanted a meeting with me. *Maybe he wanted to settle?* If I could get the changes I wanted without suing, I'd jump at the chance. I rushed across the hall to my father's office.

"You won't believe this. Rodney Webb called. He wants to meet with me tomorrow at Bonzers. Do you want to come too?"

"Nope," my dad said. "It's your case. You handle it."

Bonzers was a popular sandwich shop that became a convivial bar after work. The owner was an avid Nonpartisan League history buff and a descendant of a manager of the State Mill and Elevator. The walls were covered with black-and-white NPL-themed posters and photographs. Right by the entrance was a large black-and-white flyer from the winter of 1932: "Grand Forks Residents! Bring winter coats, boots, hats, mittens and blankets to the train station by 4 P.M. Sunday, January 7. Train to depart Sunday night from Grand Forks to bring relief to freezing residents of western North Dakota."

I'd seen pictures of Webb in the paper, when he'd been appointed by President Reagan to be U.S. attorney for North Dakota. He was in his early forties, handsome, with thick black hair. Of course he was a Republican.

On February 3, Rodney and I sat at the counter and ordered coffee, and he wasted no time on why he had asked to meet with me.

"I hear you're planning a lawsuit."

"I am," I said.

"Why don't you tell me about it and I'll see if I can help resolve it?" I knew he'd grown up on a farm near Grafton, eighty miles north of Grand Forks, and that many of his clients in Grafton had been farmers.

I quickly told him what I was planning to do: file a class action challenging FmHA's foreclosure processes in North Dakota. He seemed to know that already, and then asked the question he had come to find out: "What do you want for relief?"

"We don't want damages," I said. "We just want Farmers Home to give notice to farmers that they have a right to apply for a deferral if they are temporarily unable to pay due to circumstances beyond their control, and we want that notice to be given before, not after, FmHA freezes access to their income or seizes money from their bank accounts. *And* we want a hearing officer to hear the farmers' appeals who wasn't involved in the decision being appealed and who doesn't work for the decision maker."

He looked at me with a little bit of surprise: "Is that all?"

"That's it in a nutshell," I said.

"That sounds reasonable."

"It *is* reasonable."

"I'll make some calls and I'll see what I can do."

"Good luck to you," I said, "but those folks at USDA are pretty dug in."

Neither of us could have known that in ten days, Rodney Webb would have a much bigger problem than my case on his hands.

. . .

I'D CAREFULLY STUDIED cases that were being rushed into court by well-meaning lawyers with desperate clients. Most of these cases were poorly prepared and had catastrophic results.

I knew the class needed to be certified before any type of relief could be given to the class. This was the harsh lesson learned by Thomas Kershaw, an eager lawyer just out of law school, as he filed several cases trying to copy the success of *Curry v. Block*. With great hoopla and publicity by the Kansas chapter of the American Agriculture Movement, Kershaw filed a lawsuit called *Matzke v. Block* in Kansas on behalf of several farmers asking for an injunction, but rather than the careful deliberative briefing Martha Miller had done in the *Curry v. Block* case, Kershaw sought a mini-trial at which he had farmers testify. His judge was sympathetic, but Kershaw made a mistake in using witnesses who were not named plaintiffs, and the judge could offer relief only to the named plaintiffs. Moreover, all but one of his lead plaintiffs were ineligible for deferral relief because they were either in bankruptcy (and therefore not facing the risk of foreclosure) or in foreclosures brought by other lenders. As a result, only one plaintiff, a woman named Janice Stoss, was protected by an injunction, and that protection was hollow, because the judge said she had to post a $5,000 bond before an injunction could be issued, in order to protect the interests of Farmers Home. A bond! If Janice Stoss was in the same boat as all the FmHA borrowers I knew, she didn't have $5,000 to put up as a bond. Requiring a bond was a poison pill.

I respected Kershaw for his eagerness to help, but I also learned from his mistakes. I'd do all my legal work well in advance of filing, and I would include a brief explaining that the judge didn't need to require a bond because FmHA already had security on all of the farmer's land, machinery, and crops.

Even lawyers who defended just one farmer at a time against a foreclosure saw their defenses go up in smoke as lawyers for USDA filed ever more sophisticated briefs. These briefs did not just argue that the deferral law was wholly discretionary with USDA ("may" meant "may"). They also argued that the farmer wasn't eligible for deferral because the farmer was not "temporarily" unable to pay, but was a bad manager—hopelessly delinquent, a lost cause, sinking like a rock with no hope of surfacing back to profitability—or a crook.

I knew the briefs I turned in would need to anticipate and fully inoculate my class members against both of these tactics. And no one before me, not even Martha Miller in the *Curry* case, had tried to attack the unconstitutional acceleration of debt, freeze of income, or unfair hearing processes being used by FmHA.

It was hard work to sue the federal government, because it could hide behind the doctrine of sovereign immunity. And even when it *was* possible to sue the federal government under one of the exceptions to the doctrine of sovereign immunity, there was a tangled maze of procedural rules and arcane requirements that a novice litigator had to navigate to avoid being tossed out of court. In contrast, the lawyers for USDA were tough litigators who were in federal court every day. They also coordinated with one another under the umbrella of the Civil Division of the Department of Justice.

When my clients expressed frustration that I wasn't filing sooner, I told them a lawsuit is like an iceberg. Only the tip of an iceberg is visible above the surface of the water, but there is a great deal under the surface. And the power of the iceberg comes from under the water, not from above it. All the preparation I was doing was making a massive iceberg below the surface that I hoped would sink the titanic response of the government.

With class members all over the state of North Dakota, I had to make a choice about which court to file in. I asked my dad for advice: Should I file at the federal court closest to us, which was the Northeast District Court across the street? Or maybe the Southeast District Court in Fargo? Both were closer than Bismarck.

My father looked at me with intense focus. "File it in the *Southwest* Judicial District in Bismarck. That's where Judge Van Sickle is chambered. He's the judge we want."

Bismarck was 280 miles away. It was hard to imagine driving so far, back and forth, to the place where I'd just lost my home. "Gee," I said. "Are you sure?"

"Don't think about the drive. The drive doesn't matter. The only place to file your case is in Bismarck."

"But what if we—"

"We don't want Judge Benson," my father said.

I finally caved and agreed. Years later, my father would say, "I didn't do much on the *Coleman* case, but the five minutes I spent persuading Sarah to file in Bismarck made the rest of the case possible."

IT WAS SUNDAY, February 13, 1983. After dinner, I was decompressing by reading one of my father's Rumpole of the Bailey books. My parents' basement rec room had bookshelves from floor to ceiling that almost, but not quite, covered the knotty pine walls. Andrew was asleep beside me in the double bed that we shared. I heard the faint sound of a phone ringing upstairs, but I ignored it.

The sound of a ringing phone no longer triggered surges of adrenaline. I hadn't gotten any middle-of-the-night calls from frightened or depressed farmers in weeks—not because their situations were any better, but because I no longer had a home phone.

Despite the appearance of an abrupt downward trajectory in my life, I was not unhappy. The basement was cozy, safe, and free, and I'd received two paychecks. Andrew had built-in babysitters (Grandpa Bob and Grandma Elsa) if I needed to work late.

"Sarah," my mother called down the stairwell. Her voice still had a Norwegian singsong from her childhood in Minnesota. "*Sarah*, there is a *man* who says he's a *reporter* on the *phone*. He *wants* to talk to *you*." I reluctantly put down the novel and went upstairs to take the call on the wall phone in the dining room. *Why would a reporter call me on a Sunday night?* I wondered.

"Hello?"

A tense, urgent man gave me his name and affiliation, then asked, "Are you the Sarah Vogel who works with farmers?"

"Yes."

"I'd like your comments on the gun battle this afternoon," he said.

"What gun battle?"

The reporter paused a few seconds, surprised that I didn't already know. "I'd like to hear what you think about the shootout late this afternoon in Medina where farmers shot and killed two U.S. marshals and wounded four other lawmen. There is a manhunt going on right now for the leader, a farmer in the Posse Comitatus by the name of Gordon Kahl."

"Why are you calling *me*?"

"Because you work with farmers—"

"Yes, I do work with farmers," I snapped. "Law-abiding farmers! We intend to use the *courts* to make USDA follow the law and the U.S. Constitution. My work will *prevent* violence, not cause it. I'm upset that you would even think about calling me about farmers using guns or shooting federal marshals. My clients and I use the *courts*! And I have nothing whatsoever to do with the Posse Comitatus!"

The reporter muttered "Sorry to bother you" and hung up.

I stood by the phone a minute or so, frozen, trying to understand how something like this could have happened. North Dakota didn't have gun battles. North Dakota was a *safe* place, and after living in Washington, D.C., and New York City, I especially appreciated that safety. Yes, many people had guns, but those guns were used for hunting pheasants, deer, and gophers. Most North Dakotans didn't even lock their houses when they left town on vacation. North Dakota farmers bragged about being first in the nation in wheat, sunflowers, honey, and flax, and its law enforcement officers bragged about being last in the nation in terms of violent crime.[1]

In the living room, my mother was reading a magazine and my father was working at his desk. Classical music played on the stereo.

"Turn on the news!" I shouted. "There was a shooting in Medina."

All three local channels were running the same story. A farmer named Gordon Kahl had been wanted for arrest by the federal government for violating the conditions of his parole after a conviction of failure to pay federal taxes. Knowing that Kahl was attending a meeting at the Medina Medical Clinic that day, the U.S. Marshals Service set up a roadblock north of Medina, a small town just north of the interstate and west of Jamestown. Kahl and his allies saw the roadblock, and instead of surrendering, they pulled over and began to fire at the marshals, using Ruger Mini-14 automatic weapons, pistols, and shotguns. The marshals fired back but they were outgunned. As the TV announcers spoke through their shock, the screen displayed a black-and-white picture of Gordon Kahl. He had a high, pale forehead, receding gray hair, a "seed cap"[2] with the brim pushed back, pale eyes, and a slight smile. It could have been a picture of an older brother of Russel Folmer, or any number of farmers in their fifties who attended county fairs and Lutheran churches across North Dakota.

The U.S. marshal, Ken Muir, and deputy U.S. marshal, Robert S. Cheshire Jr., were dead at the scene. Another deputy U.S. marshal had a brain injury, a Stutsman County deputy sheriff had lost a finger to a bullet (his trigger finger), and a Medina police officer had been wounded. My father felt sick at this news. Not only had he worked closely with the U.S. Marshals Service when he'd been the U.S. attorney, he thought that a lawyer with whom he was friends and with whom he had often worked, Robert Chesrown, was the father of the murdered Robert Cheshire Jr.

Yorie Kahl, Gordon's son, had been very badly wounded too. News anchors excitedly announced that Gordon Kahl had been briefly seen at the Medina Clinic when he dropped off Yorie. But now Kahl was missing.

"Gordon Kahl is wanted for the shooting deaths of two U.S. marshals and wounding of four other law enforcement officers. He is armed and very dangerous," the newscaster said.

We watched for hours that night, and the term "Posse Comitatus" came up many times. I'd encountered members of this racist, anti-Semitic extremist group and seen evidence of the destructive nature of their teachings a few times while working with broke farmers. The woman at the meeting in Montana who had asked "Can't we just shoot" the FmHA officials was most likely a member of the Posse Comitatus.[3] The radical man who spoke in South Dakota and disavowed the state's right to require driver's licenses was certainly a member of the Posse Comitatus.

In late 1982 and early '83, Kahl traveled the country going from one hot spot of farm suffering to another. He worked the crowd at foreclosure sales and foreclosure protests in Kansas, South Dakota, Arkansas, Texas, Tennessee, and Colorado. He told farmers that they were "victims" of a "Jewish-led, communist-supported conspiracy that had infiltrated the U.S. government, the judicial system and law enforcement and was bent on destroying the Christian Republic that had been established by the founding fathers."[4]

"We are a conquered and occupied nation," Kahl told a group of 250 farmers at a foreclosure sale in Springfield, Colorado. "Conquered and occupied by the Jews and their hundreds, maybe thousands, of front organizations doing their un-Godly work."[5]

The Posse had been chartered in 1969 in Oregon by a neo-Nazi, and once Kahl found the group, it became his passion.[6] Kahl spent the 1970s railing against the IRS and stopped paying taxes in 1973. He was sentenced to one year of prison and five years' probation and was ordered to dissociate himself from the Posse as one of the conditions of his probation.[7]

Kahl served eight months at Leavenworth, and he paid little heed to the terms of his probation once he returned to North Dakota. A lien was filed in November 1980 against his Wells County farm for nearly $35,000 (the original tax bill was only $7,074) and still Kahl refused to pay. He was ordered to appear in court to explain why he wasn't filing probation reports. His wife secretly borrowed money from her brother and paid the IRS lien. (She was also secretly saving money so she could leave Gordon.) When Kahl found out that his wife had paid the tax bill, he and his devoted son Yorie excommunicated her from Gordon's "church," the "Gospel Doctrine Church of Jesus Christ, Alter Ego of Gordon Kahl."[8]

"You usurped authority which you did not have and have attempted to negotiate and compromise by paying tithes and other blackmail payments to the tithing collectors of the Jewish-Masonic Synogogue [sic] of Satan," Yorie wrote to his mother.[9]

With the tax lien paid, the remaining issue for Kahl was a misdemeanor—failure to file probation reports. Arresting Kahl for that misdemeanor culminated in the Medina shootout.

I believed that Gordon Kahl and his fellow Posse members were engaged in massive fraud against farmers. Helping distressed farmers in early 1980s was their cover story, but what they really wanted to do was get converts to their warped belief system. I'd helped one farmer who'd been told by his Posse friends that he didn't need to respond to the foreclosure papers served by the Federal Land Bank because the debt was in Federal Reserve notes and the Federal Reserve System was a sham (an "arm of Satan"). They told my client he could pay with a "common law lien" that they could provide for a small fee and that the recorded mortgage was invalid because of a violation of the Truth in Lending Act.

I'd seen a few of these foreclosure kits. They looked "legalistic," but the words were gibberish, meaningless strings of legal phrases with occasional citations to British common law cases and irrelevant statutes. My client had been assured that these "defenses" had worked for many farmers (a blatant lie) and would save his farm too. He had faith in the people who gave him this advice.

THE FARMER'S LAWYER 179

Luckily, he turned down the worst advice that the Posse often gave: that a farmer—as a "sovereign citizen"—had the authority to issue an arrest warrant against a judge who presided over their foreclosure case.[10]

If farmers followed this stupid, dangerous, and often illegal advice, they would surely lose their farms and might even lose their freedom. And once the farmer lost their farm or their freedom, the Posse recruiter exacerbated the farmer's anger by saying that it was proof of the malignancy of the entire system and the only cure was armed revolution.

Kahl's recruitment of farmers doubled the difficulty I was facing. Not only did I have to persuade farmers that there was a way to redress their problem, but I also had to dissuade them from following the recommendations of Kahl and his ilk.

In law school, I'd been inspired by Professor Norman Dorsen, who had himself brought cases to the courts that protected the rights of the poor and powerless. As much as I deplored the conduct of the Reagan administration, I clung to the belief that the courts could be our salvation.

I believed that if farmers knew they could use federal courts, federal laws, and the U.S. Constitution to save their farms, they would not turn to the dark, apocalyptic, hate-filled message of Gordon Kahl and his allies.

In Fargo, the U.S. Attorney's Office became the epicenter of the national manhunt for Gordon Kahl, who had vanished into a dark network of Posse Comitatus members and supporters. If Webb had been trying to settle my case before I could file it, the Kahl shootout upended his best intentions. Now his office had to prepare for the biggest criminal trial North Dakota had ever seen.

CHAPTER 15

If We Eat, You Shall Eat

L ewis and Clark and their company spent the winter of 1804–5 with the Mandan tribe, and their neighbors the Hidatsa and the Arikara, on the banks of the Missouri River, forty miles north of present-day Bismarck. Upon their arrival, the Mandan greeted the explorers with gifts of corn and vegetables. Sheheke (White Coyote) famously welcomed them with the promise, "If we eat, you shall eat."[1] During the long harsh winter that followed, the expedition purchased and traded for corn, beans, squash, sunflower seed meal, and other produce for their survival.[2] In keeping with the commercial purposes of their trip, they also selected seeds to send back to President Jefferson, who planted them in his gardens at Monticello, noting their progress and their characteristics in his journals.[3]

Of the Mandan, Lewis and Clark wrote:

> These are the most friendly, well disposed Indians inhabiting the Missouri. They are brave, humane and hospitable . . . They live in forti- fied villages, hunt immediately in their neighborhood, and cultivate corn, beans, squashes and tobacco which form articles of trade . . . [4]

When they first arrived in the villages in the late fall, the expedition was too late to observe the farming practices. When they returned in mid-August 1806, they were nearing the time of harvest, the cornfields now full and beginning to ripen. Upon their departure, their Mandan hosts offered them more corn and beans "than we could take away."[5]

These agricultural tribes were able to produce a bountiful harvest in an area that gets as cold as minus 44° F in winter and 116° F in summer, with an average yearly rainfall of no more than sixteen inches.[6]

By early 1983, I was still vainly wishing a Native American farmer or rancher would call me. Who better to illustrate Native American farming and ranching than a member of one of the tribes that were known nationwide in the early 1800s as the premier agriculturalists of the Great Plains?

Since working at the FTC on the Equal Credit Opportunity Act enforcement program, I knew that FmHA discriminated against women and Black people. I assumed that FmHA also discriminated against Native Americans, and my assumption grew stronger after observing how Odell Ottmar, the so-called chief of FmHA's lending on the Indian reservations, treated Russel and Anna Mae Folmer when he served as an appeal officer. If he treated white Republican farmers like the Folmers that badly, how did he treat Native Americans?

In December, a lawyer who was a member of the Standing Rock Sioux Tribe told me he'd heard from tribal officials that FmHA's delinquency rate on the reservations had reached 85 percent. This was double North Dakota's overall delinquency rate of 42 percent.[7]

I was reluctant to solicit or advertise for a Native American farmer client for two reasons. My father was firmly against all forms of lawyer advertising. He thought it was borderline unethical; further, good lawyers didn't need to advertise. "If a lawyer doesn't get enough business through word of mouth from satisfied clients, he or she isn't much of a lawyer," he would say if he saw a lawyer's commercial on TV, or an advertisement in extra-large typeface in a phone directory. Second, for more than a year, Ralph Leet had been accusing me of being an ambulance-chasing lawyer, and I was reluctant to give Leet any credibility.

Finally it dawned on me that Native American farmers and ranchers probably weren't members of the farm organizations that carried news of my developing case, and likely didn't subscribe to the *Bismarck Tribune* or the Fargo *Forum*. They didn't go to the coffee shops where white farmers would meet to chat about the news and pause to check out the bulletin board at the door for announcements, like the Hoe-Down. (North Dakota's settlement patterns were so racially divided as to be equivalent to apartheid.)[8] I told my father about my concern that no Native American had called, and he said they were more likely to reach out for help from their tribal governments than from a white lawyer that they didn't know in Grand Forks.

Then I had an inspired idea. It was a North Dakota "gospel truth" that if one North Dakotan met a perfect stranger who was also from North Dakota, it took only a few questions to establish multiple links of commonality. I'd often experienced this phenomenon in New York or D.C. After one or two rounds of "Do-you-know," the two North Dakotans who had randomly met a thousand miles from home were no longer strangers but longtime acquaintances.

Would this strategy work at home? Maybe. There was only one way to find out: call Don and Diane McCabe and hope their phone hadn't been disconnected.

If anyone knew someone who knew someone who knew someone who was a Native American FmHA borrower in North Dakota, it would be Don or Diane. They had become mini-media stars, often contacted by press and farmers as a source of information about what was happening in the countryside.

To my relief, Don answered, and I told him who I was looking for.

"I don't know anyone, but I have an idea," Don said. "Monte Haugen might know someone. I'll call Monte and call you back."

The name Monte Haugen gave me a start. *The obnoxious guy with the big hat who'd tried to fire me?*

"Shit," I muttered.

Ten minutes later, Don called. "Monte doesn't know any, but the good news is he's going to New Town tonight for a FFFLAP meeting and he says that there are lots of Native Americans up in New Town. You should call Monte right away, before he leaves."

New Town was perfect. My ideal Native American farmer or rancher was likely to be found in New Town. Fort Berthold was the home of the Mandan, Hidatsa, and Arikara tribes, who were also known as the MHA Nation, and their tribal office was in New Town. I knew a little bit of their history[9] from growing up in an NPL family only a few miles from the Fort Berthold Reservation, and I'd studied some Indian law in law school at NYU.

As anti–Vietnam War riots were raging in the streets of Greenwich Village, I sat in the subbasement of the NYU Law School Library, with a collection of books and reference works dealing with Indian Agriculture. I was writing a paper I titled "Cooperatives and Indians,"[10] for a class called Non-Profit Organizations. I referenced the classic legal text on Indian law, Cohen's *Handbook of Federal Indian Law*, and cited sources that were sharply critical of the Bureau of Indian Affairs (BIA) and its incompetent handling of Indian property. I wrote about the abuse of children in boarding schools and the catastrophic consequences of "termination" of tribes in the 1950s. (Congress, backed by the Eisenhower administration, had tried to terminate the Mandan, Hidatsa, and Arikara Nation and the Turtle Mountain Band of Chippewa in North Dakota.) At last, at about page 30, I segued to my main topic: agricultural cooperatives. After centuries of mismanagement and outright hostility from the federal government and from white society, Native Americans could use cooperative laws and principles to develop cooperative Indian-owned and Indian-run business organizations, in keeping with their culture of sharing, generosity, community, and support for one another. I referenced examples of communal enterprises and livestock cooperatives that had been successful.

In my conclusion, I wrote: "It is important to the rest of America that Indians and their culture do survive . . . White society cannot let a century old injustice persist any longer without itself suffering a loss."

I suppressed my simmering resentment and dialed Monte's number so I could catch him before he left for the meeting in New Town. Forcing myself to be friendly, I described the person I wanted him to find.

A FEW DAYS later, I was working at my card table desk when Donna came in and said, "There is a phone call for you from a man whose last name is Crows Heart."

"Hello, this is Sarah Vogel?"

"My name is Lester Crows Heart, and I heard last night that you are looking for a Native American who is dealing with FmHA. Is that right?"

I quickly told him about the lawsuit and said that I wanted to have a Native American lead plaintiff to show a judge and the world that FmHA's conduct was affecting Native Americans as well as white farmers. "Is this something that you'd be interested in doing?"

"Yes, it is," Lester said in a firm and unequivocal voice.

I felt at that moment as though I'd found the placement of the last piece of a huge jigsaw puzzle.

Lester was the great-grandson of Paul Crow's Heart,[11] a Mandan born in 1858 who lived along the Missouri River and was the custodian of a holy shrine that was on his property. Crow's Heart had built an old-style earth lodge, and his land was a favorite place for the Mandan to gather for celebration. In 1908, Crow's Heart was photographed by Edward S. Curtis. In 1929, he was already an old man when he met Alfred Bowers, a PhD candidate in anthropology from the University of Chicago who had come to do his doctorate on the Mandan. Crow's Heart and Bowers developed a deep rapport, and they worked together

Paul Crow's Heart, Lester Crows Heart's great-
grandfather, photographed by Edward S. Curtis, 1908.

for three years, with a focus on Mandan ceremonies. Bowers's 1950 book, *Mandan Social and Ceremonial Organization*, remains the main resource on that subject. Remarkably, Crow's Heart was still alive when Bowers returned to Fort Berthold in 1947, and Bowers helped Crow's Heart complete his autobiography.[12]

I asked Lester for his own story so we could get started right away on his affidavit.

Lester and his wife, Sharon, were thirty-three years old, the youngest of the lead plaintiffs. They had three children. They had taken over Lester's father's 440-acre farm on the Fort Berthold reservation with an FmHA loan in 1977. In 1959, Lester's family had moved to a farm in the Twin Buttes area of the reservation after the rising water of Lake Sakakawea flooded the Crows Hearts' ancestral farmland along the banks of the Missouri.

"We had no bikes. We grew up on horseback," Lester told me. He and his brothers rode the fence line every day and made repairs as needed. Farming and ranching meant long hours and hard work, but it was gratifying. Even Sharon, who grew up on the outskirts of town and was more of a city girl, loved the life. She raised two buffalo from calves.

Lester had learned a lot about the economics of farming and ranching from his dad. From the very beginning of his experience with Farmers Home, Lester felt like he knew more about the business than his supervisor. "They said you have to have a budget," he told me. "We always tried to leave a cushion for the price of wheat and cattle. Like any business, you try to leave a cushion there for when things don't work out. Then they wouldn't give us the money if we didn't change it, so we had to go with what they wanted."

The Crows Hearts did what they had to do in order to get the loans necessary to build up their cattle and buy machinery. They rented and leased additional lands for a cow-calf operation. In the early 1980s, they, like so many others, were hit by the cost-price squeeze, against which Lester had tried to build a buffer in his Farm and Home plan. In January 1982, FmHA began pressuring them to "voluntarily liquidate."

By this time, Lester had negotiated leases for over 4,000 acres of grazing lands. He needed to prepay for the BIA land and the other land (owned by other members of the tribe) for the upcoming grazing season, and the payments were due in January 1982. There was ample money in the Crows Hearts' supervised bank account to pay for those leases, but when the Crows Hearts refused to quit "voluntarily," the county supervisor—without warning—accelerated the chattel debts, froze the money in their supervised bank account, and refused to countersign the rent checks. The Crows Hearts abruptly lost the leases. Now they wouldn't be able to feed their cattle. Instead of letting their cattle starve, Lester and Sharon were compelled to agree to "voluntarily" sell their cattle by May and sell the machinery by June, but they did so on the condition that FmHA would agree that some of the proceeds would go to local businesses that had been helping the Crows Hearts.

The cattle and the machinery were sold, but FmHA reneged on allowing the Main Street creditors to be paid and instead grabbed all the proceeds for itself, leaving the Crows Hearts with a ruined reputation and in debt to their local suppliers.

Lester had a trucking business on the side, and he found work hauling cattle and grain for other farmers, but FmHA seized that income, too.

I had to interrupt Lester. "Wait, I've never heard of this before," I said. No other farmer had ever told me that FmHA seized their off-farm income. Further, garnishment (the process of collecting a debt from a person's wages) was capped under federal and state at a certain percentage, and certain notices and formalities needed to be observed. (I didn't tell Lester I had recently refreshed my knowledge of North Dakota's wage garnishment laws because of my creditors' threats to garnish my own wages.) I had a low opinion of FmHA, but I doubted even FmHA would simply seize off-farm wages that weren't covered by a security agreement.

"They took everything," he said. He explained that on the Fort Berthold reservation, there were quite a few farmers and ranchers who had borrowed from FmHA during the '70s because most bankers wouldn't lend to Indians on the reservation. The county supervisors required supervised bank accounts, and they countersigned every check the farmer or rancher wrote.

"When the county supervisor saw my name on a check, he countersigned it, but instead of giving it to the guy I worked for so he could pay me, he took it all for the debt." By this point, the Crows Hearts' own supervised account had been frozen. They had no access to any of the money Lester earned. I was stunned by this perversion of the original goal of a supervised bank account. "We've lost everything but the land. Farmers Home is pressuring me to sell that, too. My dad's been a farmer and rancher all his life. So have I. We have to keep the land."

Everything Lester told me showed that he and Sharon would be great lead plaintiffs. There was one last hurdle to jump: exhaustion of administrative remedies. I asked Lester to read me the letters he'd received when his chattel loans had been accelerated. Bingo. The county supervisor had made the same mistake as Dwight's county supervisor: he'd said the Crows Hearts could "meet" with Odell Ottmar, but he'd never told them about a right to appeal.

At the same time I finalized their affidavit, I sent a letter to Ralph Leet saying that the Crows Hearts hadn't been properly informed of their right to appeal and they now wanted to appeal. Just as he'd done in Dwight Coleman's case, Leet wrote back to say it was "too late." I wasn't unhappy; now I could show that we had tried to exhaust administrative remedies.

I hoped the Crows Heart name under "lead plaintiffs" would send a message to the hundreds of farmers and ranchers at Fort Berthold, Standing Rock, Spirit Lake, and the Turtle Mountain reservations that they, too, would be protected by the *Coleman v. Block* case.

THE REAGAN ADMINISTRATION was hard on farmers, but it was even harder on Native American farmers, who were caught in a double layer of bureaucracy: the BIA (a part of the Department of the Interior) and FmHA (a part of USDA). No matter how many Native American farmers cried out for help, or how many members of Congress objected to their treatment, Reagan ignored their problems.

Ronald Reagan was lauded for his skills in negotiating complex agreements with hostile cold war adversaries, but his grasp on Native American issues was about as sophisticated as the script of a Hollywood Western.[13] Well into his second term, Reagan volunteered the following comments at a May 1988 meeting at Moscow State University:

> We have provided millions of acres of land for what are called preserva-
> tions—or reservations—I should say ... And they're [the Indians] free
> also to leave the reservations and be American citizens among the rest of
> us, and many do ... Maybe we made a mistake. Maybe we should not

have humored them in that wanting to stay in that kind of primitive lifestyle. Maybe we should have said, no, come join us; be citizens along with the rest of us.[14]

Native Americans who heard this speech were outraged. Millions of acres of reservation lands were not "provided" to the Indians by whites. Rather, the word "reservation" referred to lands that had been *reserved* by the Indians in formal treaties with the United States. Under these treaties, tribes had *given* the United States over one billion acres. And, of course, they didn't need to accept Reagan's invitation to "come be citizens." Reagan's tone-deaf statement was insulting to the original inhabitants of America and ignored the federal law that gave citizenship to all Native Americans in 1924, when the Indian Citizenship Act was passed by Congress.

In 1925, my grandfather Frank A. Vogel, who was then running for his third two-year term in the North Dakota House of Representatives,[15] was the speaker at a Memorial Day ceremony in Elbowoods, the principal town on the Fort Berthold Indian Reservation, where the tribal headquarters, rodeo grounds, hospital, high school and public and private (church) schools were located. The event was held at the Indian Scout Cemetery, which contained the graves of tribal veterans who had served as scouts for the U.S. Army against the Sioux in the Indian Wars.

There is no written record of his Memorial Day speech, but it is safe to say that he would have complimented the patriotism and bravery of all veterans and soldiers in the crowd, and then he would have launched into a request that the listeners support the Nonpartisan League platform and vote for its candidates.

My father, who was eight years old, was in the audience for this speech. It was the first political meeting he remembered attending, and he told me about it countless times while I was growing up.

"When your grandfather gave his speech, it had to be translated into three different tribal languages," he explained. "Then the responses were given, in three languages, by the elderly men representing the three tribes, and these speeches had to be translated into three languages, including English."[16]

It was a hot day, and the bench was hard. My dad twitched and squirmed in his seat during the long speeches, wishing he could leave.

"But the Indian children sat perfectly still," he said, which made him ashamed of his restlessness.

Nineteen twenty-five was a critical election year for Indians, because at last they were citizens. Despite being the original residents of the United States, they were not entitled to vote until passage of the Indian Citizenship Act in 1924.[17] Before passage of this law, Native Americans could obtain citizenship by enlisting in the military (which many did) or by agreeing to become "civilized," a status that entailed disavowing tribal membership and living on a separate piece of land called an allotment.[18]

"Allotment" was a process that began in 1887 with the Dawes Act, under which Congress established a system of dividing reservation lands into individual allotments, or small parcels, for distribution to individual tribal members. The federal government then deemed unallotted lands within a reservation as surplus or "excess" and opened up vast swaths of reservation lands to white homesteading. As James Wilson writes in *The Earth Shall Weep*, "in the first thirteen years of the Dawes Act alone, the government forced through nearly 33,000 allotments and 'released' some 28,500,000 acres of 'surplus' land."[19] One of the inducements to accept an allotment was the promise of citizenship. However, white society still sought to suppress the Native American vote. The League gave certain "civilized" Indians the right to vote in state elections in 1919, and their right to vote was upheld by the North Dakota Supreme Court in 1920.[20]

The hospitality and generosity that the Mandan, Hidatsa, and Arikara tribes had shown to Lewis and Clark was never repaid. Instead, clan and family structure, religion, way of farming, health and diet, self-reliance, wealth, commercial trade networks, governance, and population numbers suffered under the weight of white encroachment, additional waves of smallpox, loss of land, broken treaties, dishonest thieving agents, and suppression of their languages, ceremonies, and traditional ways.

But when President Franklin Delano Roosevelt was elected in November 1932, the fortunes of Indian Country and the people of the Fort Berthold Reservation began to improve. Roosevelt was appalled by the effects of the allotment era, and he put into effect recommendations of the 1928 Meriam Report, which criticized the Department of the Interior's implementation of the Dawes Act's allotment policies, the operation of boarding schools, and lack of health care.

The report said that the United States was failing at its goals of protecting Native Americans, their lands, culture, and resources.

FDR's program was called the Indian New Deal. The capstone of this new approach was the 1934 passage of FDR's Indian Reorganization Act (IRA).[21] It gave new independent powers to tribes so that tribal communities could adopt new constitutional governments, create economic corporations, and manage their own political and economic affairs.

The NPLers from North Dakota in Congress who served during all or part of the FDR years were Lynn J. Frazier, Gerald Nye, William Lemke, and Usher Burdick. The NPLers did not owe loyalty to a national party, and this made them free to act on their convictions. Langer, Burdick, and Lemke, in particular, had enormous popularity in North Dakota because of their work for broke farmers in the Great Depression, and "as a consequence they could defy both parties in the presidential campaign and spend little time mending North Dakota fences."[22] They were all intolerant of neglect of Indians.

Burdick had grown up on a Sioux reservation speaking Lakota as well as English, and he served on the Indian Affairs Committee. His biographer, Edward Blackorby, writes that "Native American leaders knew they could go to him when in need and gain his attention." Burdick wanted the BIA officials to be selected by the Indians being governed, which went too far even for FDR. In 1935, Burdick was so outraged by mismanagement of the BIA during famine conditions at Standing Rock that he sent angry telegrams to President Roosevelt, Secretary of the Interior Harold Ickes, and Commissioner of Indian Affairs John Collier. Collier soon followed up with a tour of Fort Berthold and Standing Rock.[23]

The Mandan, Hidatsa, and Arikara tribes had been so decimated by smallpox by the mid-1800s that they joined together at the Like a Fishhook Village for mutual defense from enemy tribes.[24] In the Fort Laramie Treaty of 1851, they were referred to as the Three Affiliated Tribes, and in 1934 they formally organized under that name, at the start of the Indian New Deal.

The Three Affiliated Tribes were eager to embrace their new powers under FDR's IRA and were among the first in the nation to adopt it. On June 26, 1936, the tribal council adopted a new tribal constitution under the IRA's new guidelines. One of the first projects of the council was to start a new cooperative cattle raising program funded by federal loans. The project was a huge success, and as Paul VanDevelder writes in *Coyote Warrior*, the default rate on federal loans to Indian ranchers on Fort Berthold was the lowest in the nation. By the end of the 1930s, it was common knowledge that the three tribes were weathering the '30s better than their white neighbors because of their farming skills and the excellent quality of their land. Many homesteaders from nearby towns survived the worst years of the Great Depression by finding paying work on Indian ranches and farms on the Reservation.[25]

Unfortunately, President Truman was vastly less sympathetic to Indians, and the progress promised by the Indian New Deal began to falter beginning in 1945.

After the death of FDR, federal land surveyors showed up on the Fort Berthold reservation. They didn't explain what they were doing there, perhaps because they knew how resistant tribal members would be. They were launching the first phase of a massive water development project under the Flood Control Act of 1944 that was designed to control floods and provide a panoply of other benefits to states downstream of the Missouri, while holding out the promise of irrigation to North Dakota. Colloquially, the plan was called the Pick-Sloan Plan, named after the two directors of the agencies in charge: Lewis Pick, from the Corps of Engineers, and William Sloan, from U.S. Bureau of Reclamation. The president of the National Farmers Union called the consolidation of the Pick Plan and the Sloan Plan "a shameless, loveless shotgun wedding."[26] For the Three Affiliated Tribes, the Pick-Sloan Plan meant a series of giant dams would be built and one of them, Garrison Dam, would flood the entire stretch of the Missouri River Valley where over 80 percent of their members lived.

The Three Affiliated Tribes were alarmed by the implications of the Pick-Sloan Plan. Their most precious lands and habitats could be destroyed for all time and their people might be altogether dispossessed. During the years that they fought the Pick-Sloan Plan, the MHA Nation had three key friends in Congress: Senator Bill Langer, Representative Usher Burdick, and Representative Bill Lemke. The triumvirate had worked together in the 1930s to fight foreclosures, to form the Farmers' Holiday Association, to implement the Langer foreclosure moratorium, and to craft and pass the Frazier-Lemke Farm Bankruptcy Act. A decade later, they coalesced once again on behalf of the Indians of Fort Berthold and of Standing Rock.[27]

Protesting the breaches of treaties, and the absurdly low prices that were being offered to the Indians whose land, homes, schools, and churches were being taken, they fought against Senator Arthur Watkins,[28] Republican of Utah, who wanted to terminate most Indian tribes.

President Truman was not helpful. Truman supported Native Americans' civil rights in the abstract, but he was not sympathetic to self-governance by Native Americans. Indeed, he dismantled most of the Indian New Deal programs and began the terrible programs of "relocation" (simply uprooting Native Americans from reservations and shipping them to faraway cities where they would theoretically find work) and "termination" (wholesale abrogation of treaty rights).[29] Truman did not try to stop or ameliorate the harsh effects of the Pick-Sloan Plan on the Native Americans at Fort Berthold or the other tribes impacted by the Pick-Sloan Plan.

The NPLers in Congress worked closely with Three Affiliated Tribes chairman Martin Cross,[30] who spent six years fighting the dam and the flooding of the bottomlands. At a hearing before the Senate Select Committee on Indian Affairs, on October 9, 1945, Chairman Cross explained that 220,000 acres of "the best land we have, along the river" would be flooded. Further, there were only 536 homes on the reservation, and of those, 436 were in the river valley that would be flooded. The tribal members in the river valley raised wheat, oats, corn, potatoes, and alfalfa. "We have a thriving tribal cattle cooperative," the chairman said. When asked by Senator O'Mahoney what he stood to gain from the dam, Chairman Cross replied, "We will gain nothing from this dam but our own destruction."

"I know these lands," Senator Langer said. "Everything that Mr. Cross has said is absolutely true. This dam would take by far the best land and leave the tops of the hills, which will not begin to compare with the soil in the valley."[31]

The NPLers supported a Missouri Valley Authority (which would have been similar to the Tennessee Valley Authority) as an alternative to the Pick-Sloan Plan, but that plan did not pass.

Eventually, in May 1948, a majority (625 of the 960 eligible Fort Berthold voters) agreed to accept the Corps of Engineers' lowball offer for the land (about $33 an acre for land that Chairman George Gillette, who'd replaced Martin Cross, estimated was worth over $150 an acre). They had no choice—the Corps had built the dam and the water was already rising and would flood their lands with or without an agreement.

On May 28, 1948, with flourishes of flashbulbs, there was a signing ceremony of the "taking" of MHA's lands along the Missouri River. As the secretary of the interior signed the contract to purchase the lands being flooded, Chairman Gillette put his hands over his eyes and wept. He later told the press, "As everyone knows, our treaty of 1851 and our tribal constitution are being torn to shreds by this contract. My heart is very heavy. What will become of our people?"[32]

On the floor of the house, Representative Lemke did not hold back. He said "a great crime was being committed against the Indians . . . We are again violating a treaty solemnly entered into with these tribes, a treaty in which we promised never to disturb them again. Unfortunately, the Indians have no choice. There is no honor in this settlement."[33]

Langer introduced a bill that sought $31 million in additional compensation. It was immediately shot down. Lemke fought on and managed to get the house to approve $14.6 million. Senate Republicans, led by Senator Watkins of Utah, reduced it to $4 million. After much back-and-forth, Congress agreed to a

MHA Chairman George Gillette weeping at the loss of tribal lands.

compromise package of $12.5 million. The NPLers' arm-twisting had trebled the Republicans' counteroffer, but it was a small fraction of what the Indians of Fort Berthold deserved.[34]

Lemke died in office in 1952, just two weeks after the Fort Berthold Tribal Council had sent him a resolution of thanks for his "courageous" and "valiant" work on their behalf.[35]

WHEN MY FATHER was first elected state's attorney (for some inexplicable reason, county attorneys were called state's attorneys), McLean County was still a sleepy agricultural backwater with almost no crime in the county or in Garrison, the town where we lived. But along with the population explosion when Garrison Dam construction began came crime—and the crime rate rose faster than the water. My father worked seventy-hour weeks battling prostitution, gambling, booze smuggling (McLean County was a "dry" county), and bank robbery as thousands of construction workers, grifters, and drifters moved to McLean County. I was born in 1946, so the population boom meant more playmates for me and an occasional drive out of town to watch the water slowly rise behind the dam. To the Indians living only a few miles away, it meant disaster.

I remember going for a drive in the family car, a green-and-black Hudson Hornet, and coming upon a two-lane paved road that abruptly ended at the edge of a vast body of water.

"Why does the road go into the water?" I asked my dad.

My father explained that the body of water was the consequence of the Garrison Dam. All I could see, at five or six years old, was choppy gray waves with bobbing debris. I couldn't even see the other side of the river valley. The Missouri River had become an angry lake. It was named Lake Sakakawea, after the young woman who had guided the Lewis and Clark expedition from the Mandan village to the Pacific coast and back. Sakakawea would have wept if she saw this lake.

"That's where Elbowoods used to be," my father said, pointing straight ahead. "It was a pretty little town." The original Indian Scout Cemetery, the site of the Memorial Day speeches decades before, was now underwater.

We watched this grim gray scene for a while. We tried to skip pebbles across the water but gave up—the water was too choppy. We grew bored and restless, and eventually my father climbed back into the car and silently drove us back to our little house in Garrison, where we were safe.

Of all the tragedies suffered by the peaceful and productive members of the MHA Nation at the hands of white people and the federal government, the construction of the Garrison Dam was up there with the smallpox epidemics of 1781 and 1837–38.[36] They lost population with smallpox, but they still had land. The Garrison Dam took the land. One quarter of the reservation, 155,000 acres, including 94 percent of their rich bottomlands, was lost under the waters of Lake Sakakawea. It also took their homes, their farms and ranches, their holy sites, their medicines, their history.

Ninety-five percent of the families on Fort Berthold had to move from the river bottoms, including Richard and Marie Crows Heart, Lester's parents.[37] Lester was born in Elbowoods and grew up in a log house until they were forced to relocate. "I was five years old when the water was rising," he told me. "My dad used to take us out on the lake and there would be animals stranded on little islands in the water."

Before the flood, Lester's ancestors grew everything on the fertile bottomlands. They fed their families from their gardens. Pre-dam, in 1943, the BIA published a Fort Berthold Agency Report that said that most of the people then lived on a traditional diet and few had any serious medical problems. A doctor who moved to Elbowoods in 1951 recalled that back then diabetes was unknown, kidney problems were unknown, and heart disease was very rare, as was cancer. The people of the reservation were "remarkably healthy robust people." By the time that doctor retired and moved to Bismarck, diabetes at Fort Berthold was twelve times the national average and other diseases had shot up to alarming levels.[38]

By 1982, Chairman Martin Cross's prediction of "destruction" had mostly come to pass. In *Coyote Warrior*, VanDevelder writes that "the unemployment rate at Fort Berthold had risen to 85%. Four out of five school-age children were malnourished. Infant mortality rates were quadruple the national average. Life expectancy for men had dropped below fifty years. Moreover, soaring rates of alcoholism and drug addiction among the tribe's youth had created a social climate of hopelessness."[39]

In 1980, looking back on the impact of the Pick-Sloan Plan, Vine Deloria Jr. wrote: "The Pick-Sloan Plan was, without doubt, the single most destructive act ever perpetrated on any tribe by the United States."[40]

After the flood, tribal offices, hospitals, and schools moved from Elbowoods to New Town. (It was unimaginatively named New Town by the Corps of Engineers because it was new and a town.) New Town is where Monte Haugen connected with Lester and asked him to call me.

As I finalized Lester and Sharon Crows Hearts' affidavit, I was incensed that FmHA would illegally and unconstitutionally foreclose on them. Lester's ancestors had been farming for a thousand years on lands now known as North Dakota; they had kept Lewis and Clark alive on their journey to the West; they had shared the genetic material of beans, corn, and squash that would grow in harsh northern climates; and they had been pushed off their homelands in 1954 by the Army Corps of Engineers. Langer, Lemke, and Burdick had fought for the people of the Three Affiliated Tribes against the federal government. I would too.

CHAPTER 16

Springing the Trap

I celebrated the fiftieth anniversary of Langer's Foreclosure Moratorium on Friday, March 11, 1983, in true Nonpartisan League style when at last I filed the *Coleman v. Block* lawsuit. I'd decided to list the lead plaintiffs alphabetically, and Dwight Coleman's name was first.

Like Langer's moratorium decree, the *Coleman* case sought to keep North Dakota farmers on their land. But the Coleman case differed from Langer's moratorium decree in one major way. Langer had exempted USDA and other New Deal agencies from his Moratorium Proclamation because under President Roosevelt, USDA was one of the few "good guy" lenders in the 1930s. Fifty years later, in a farm crisis that bore many similarities to the farm economic depression of the 1930s, USDA had become the worst of the "bad guy" lenders. Rexford Tugwell would have been shocked at what had happened to his programs.

The Rules of Civil Procedure that governed all federal lawsuits, and the laws that guarded historic principles of federal sovereign immunity, didn't allow me to sue USDA or the Farmers Home Administration directly. Instead, I had to sue the individuals who held official roles within the agency. The first of fourteen named defendants in the *Coleman* case was John Block, the secretary of agriculture (nicknamed "Auction Block"). The second was Charles Shuman, who had issued the infamous Foreclosure Quota Memos. The third was Ralph Leet, the smug North Dakota state director of FmHA. These three were followed by six district directors (including Odell Ottmar, the so-called chief of the counties with Indian reservations) and five county supervisors who were in charge of the counties where the lead plaintiffs lived.

Nine broke farmers against the mighty power of the federal government. A David and Goliath fight if ever there was one.

Block and all of the defendants had the benefit of free legal support from experienced litigators at the USDA Office of General Counsel, the Civil Division of the Department of Justice, and the United States Attorney's Office of North Dakota.

But my plaintiffs' weapon was the law. In order to win in time to help the eighty-four hundred farmers in the prospective class (of whom 42 percent were delinquent), I knew it was necessary to ambush Block.

I'd seen what had happened to the lawyers who had expected a normal litigation process (complaint, answer, discovery, hearing, decision). That expectation was not realistic in 1983 if you were a lawyer litigating against FmHA. When a case against FmHA was filed, the U.S. attorney in the state where the lawsuit was filed would notify the Civil Division of the Department of Justice about the lawsuit and ask for a decision on whether the U.S. Attorney's Office or the Department of Justice would handle the litigation. The Department of Justice generally let the U.S. attorney handle the day-to-day litigation, but the direction to the U.S. attorney was that the cases were to be fought tooth and nail. They had been caught flat-footed by Martha Miller in Georgia, but now the standard response was simple, and brutal: instead of filing an answer within the sixty days allowed, the Department of Justice told the U.S. attorney to file a motion to dismiss the case on or about the sixtieth day. Model briefs and affidavits were sent to the assistant U.S. attorney handling the case on which to base the response.

Somewhere around the sixtieth day, the farmer's lawyer (often a small-town solo practitioner) would get a motion to dismiss the case instead of an answer. The lawyer would need to respond within weeks to the motion and rebut the legal assertions in the government's canned brief and also the factual claims about his client in the affidavits from the State and County FmHA officials. The affidavits of the FmHA officials were invariably designed to make the plaintiff look like a crook, a deadbeat, or a lousy farmer and the FmHA officials appear tolerant, helpful, and forgiving. Too many judges had already fallen for this charade, and I didn't intend for Judge Van Sickle to be among them.

For as long as I'd been working on the complaint, I'd also been researching what I needed to get a preliminary injunction, which would provide plaintiffs with relief early on in the litigation, not at the end. (A typical federal case takes at least a year but can last for many years, and usually the sought-after relief comes only at the end of litigation.) The standards to qualify for a preliminary injunction are very difficult to meet, and I'd been working on arguments and gathering facts to show that my clients deserved help now.

In addition to my complaint and brief in support of the preliminary injunction, I had a draft brief in support of class action certification. I knew that even if I won the case for my nine lead plaintiffs, FmHA could go forward and bring collection cases against any of the other 8,391 farmer borrowers in North Dakota who were delinquent. I wanted to get relief for all 8,400 North Dakota farmers who were FmHA borrowers, so having an early class certification was critical.

Once I had all my drafts completed, I mailed fat envelopes to Burt and Allan. Despite their insanely busy schedules—Allan had many big class actions involving environmental disasters around the country, and Burt ran the ACLU's nationwide litigation program with seventy lawyers and hundreds of cases under his supervision—they both devoted many hours to the case, perfecting the draft complaint and briefs. They called me when they had questions, needed to find some obscure form or regulation, or just wanted to vent.

"How could Ottmar believe that beef cows are covered by a security agreement for dairy cows?" Burt asked. "That's outrageous!"

"They just think they can do whatever the hell they want," Allan said.

"I could understand why a loan shark would do this," Burt said. "But I can't understand why a government agency that's supposed to *help* farmers is doing this. My God, they're making it easy for us to bring this case."

Allan and Burt were brilliant legal scholars. They had fancy educations from Harvard Law and had then clerked for federal judges. They had written law review articles in prestigious journals and taught other lawyers in complex fields of law. And they needed all their education and legal skills to understand the morass of FmHA regulations and forms. It was up to us to translate it well enough so that Judge Van Sickle would understand.

. . .

ONE DAY, RICHARD and Marlene DeLare, the farmers who'd lent me $3,000 when my phone was turned off, came by. The hammer had at last fallen. They sat across from me at my card table as I read the notice before foreclosure that they'd just received.

"Is this really your desk?" Richard asked.

I laughed. "Yes, it is. And I'm happy to have it."

I had good news for the DeLares. As I'd predicted, FmHA hadn't followed the North Dakota law that gave debtors like the DeLares the right to cure the default. The DeLares' notice before foreclosure demanded full payment of the entire accelerated balance. I told them we would just sit tight, and on the sixtieth day after the complaint was served, we'd move to dismiss the case.

"Have you filed the class action yet?" Richard anxiously asked.

"I will soon," I promised. I told them the same thing I'd told other impatient farmers. "The case is like an iceberg, and I want USDA to steer straight into it."

My hope was that the Department of Justice would be overconfident. The DOJ's wins were piling up[1] while the wins by farmers were few. And even the biggest win, *Curry v. Block*, protected only Georgia farmers, and it was on appeal. The *Curry* case was the best of all the cases, but it didn't stop the starve out. No case had attacked FmHA's deeply flawed appeal process. No case had the constitutional law angle that my case had.

I wanted to surprise the Department of Justice and FmHA with the due process arguments and the challenge to the starve-out.

When the DOJ got the *Coleman* complaint, based on their experience in the other lawsuits seeking deferrals that had been filed all over the country, DOJ lawyers would naturally assume they would have sixty days to file a motion to dismiss. But that assumption would be wrong.

Right after the complaint was served, I'd call Judge Van Sickle's office to get a date and time for a hearing, hoping it would be within the sixty days. When I got my hearing date, I'd count backward to determine the last day on which I could file my motions and briefs that would provide the bare minimum number of days allowed under the Rules of Civil Procedure for the government to respond to a motion for class certification and a preliminary injunction. On the selected day, I'd hand-deliver the papers needed to get the class action certification and the preliminary injunction. (If I sent the papers by mail, USDA would get three extra days.) My plan was to spring the trap as late as possible, hopefully about twelve days before the hearing date. I felt that ten days was possibly cutting it too close.

Twelve days was still a very short period of time, and I knew the lawyers representing Farmers Home Administration would squeal that I was being unfair. But I'd show them no mercy, as they had shown no mercy to my clients.

I waited until Friday, March 11, to file the complaint, so that the first two days of FmHA's time to respond would fall on a weekend. That morning, I borrowed my mother's Oldsmobile 88 for the trip to Fargo, because it had good snow tires. Fargo had the closest deputy clerk's office.

The Oldsmobile floated along the highway like an ocean liner. The scenery was nonexistent. Between Fargo and Grand Forks is a four-lane highway with eighty miles of unrelenting boredom. The only color was the green of the ever-greens planted fifty years ago by farmers during the Depression, to prevent another Dust Bowl, with the help of USDA. I wondered how many farmers, in little wooden houses hidden from the harsh winds behind those rows of trees, were now on FmHA's list for future starve outs and foreclosure?

I parked near the federal courthouse, and walked in. To my surprise, there was a guard near the door, asking me my business. Then I remembered.

Of course, I thought, *they are worried about Gordon Kahl or other Posse members getting into the courthouse!*

When I showed the guard my bar association membership card and driver's license, he seemed satisfied that I wasn't a Posse member (the Posse didn't believe in driver's licenses). I took the elevator to the second floor. The sign above the doorway read CLERK OF U.S. COURT, and I walked into a hushed room lined with cabinets and a row of desks behind which several quiet women were seated. I laid my briefcase on the high counter and followed my script.

"I'm here to file this complaint," I said, as confidently as I could, "and I have the requisite copies and the filing fee." The check was from the Robert Vogel Law Firm account.

The woman looked at my stack of papers. "This can't be filed. It isn't in accordance with local rules."

I turned pale. "Why not?" I whispered.

"Because it isn't two-hole-punched on the top, and our rule says that it has to be two-hole-punched on the top to be filed."

"I didn't know that," I choked out.

"Yes, it is a new rule of court, as of two weeks ago." The look she gave me implied I should have known.

"I'll punch the holes right now," I volunteered. "May I borrow your punch?"

"No. I don't have one," she said and went back to her desk.

Dismayed, I walked up and down the hall, careful to avoid the U.S. Attorney's Office, and knocked on random doors until I found a friendly person at USDA's soil conservation service who could help me.

Examining my two-hole-punched paperwork a second time, the clerk said, "This seems to be in order." She gave me a receipt for the filing fee and fourteen copies of a summons: one for my file, eleven for the defendants, one for the U.S. Attorney's Office, and one for the Department of Justice. Each was embossed with the clerk of court's seal.

When I walked outside, I saw uniformed men standing outside and quite a few law enforcement vehicles. I remembered that the Medina shootout trial was going to be held in this courthouse. There were seven defendants, including Gordon Kahl's wife and son, and all of them were farmers. Several were facing trial for the murder of the two U.S. marshals. I wondered if the defendants were having a preliminary hearing in front of Judge Benson and the law enforcement presence outside was to deter supporters of Kahl and the defendants from disrupting the hearings, or worse. I was happy our case would be heard in Bismarck.

I'm sure that Rodney Webb's attention was on the Kahl case that day. In the grand scheme of things, the *Coleman* case would have seemed much less important than the trial and the ongoing hunt for Gordon Kahl, who was still a fugitive. I saw it differently. Punishment of the shootout participants was important, but I knew that Kahl used FmHA's foreclosures and harsh tactics to recruit and radicalize farmers who were bewildered and desperate. Fixing FmHA and making them implement the deferral law and give farmers a fair shot at telling their story to a neutral hearing officer would take the wind out of the Posse's sails.

By the following Tuesday, March 15, the Associated Press had discovered my case from the court filings. Their story triggered others in the Fargo *Forum* and the Minneapolis *Star Tribune*. Ralph Leet told the *Grand Forks Herald* that a similar suit in Georgia "was not favorable to most farmers," cases in Arkansas and Mississippi were "thrown out," and cases in Missouri and Kansas were not yet resolved.[2] I was relieved that Leet didn't yet understand what made the *Coleman* case unique.

The next day, I was working at my card table desk when I heard a ruckus outside my door. I peeked out and saw Richard DeLare and another big man awkwardly carrying a huge piece of furniture across the office. It was a brand-new, gleaming oak desk. The men set it outside my office door. Then, without a word, they carefully moved my card table, without disturbing the towering stacks of paper, to the far corner of my office and put the beautiful desk in its place.

"Sarah, if you are going to work for us farmers, you should work from a desk, not a card table!" Richard said. He stood, beaming, beside the desk and then handed me an envelope pulled from his pocket. Inside was a thank-you card with about ten signatures, from farmers south of Minot. Richard had gone around and collected a little bit of money from his neighbors who'd run into trouble with FmHA and then he'd used the money to buy very good quality oak boards and the necessary hardware. He'd built the desk in the shop at the farm. He pointed out the fancy trim work that he'd made out of scraps. His buddy had helped him load it into the back of Richard's pickup, drove with him to Grand Forks, and helped him muscle it up the steps to our second-floor office.

I choked up and could barely say thank you.

ON MARCH 16, I called Judge Van Sickle's secretary, Helen Monteith, to schedule a hearing. I assumed that she knew nothing about the case, but I later realized that among the staff of the federal court, gossip travels at the speed of light, and Helen probably knew within hours of my filing the case in Fargo that a big case was heading toward Judge Van Sickle's courtroom.

I spoke to her in hypothetical terms: "I'm thinking of filing two motions in the *Coleman* case and wondering when Judge Van Sickle will next have some time free for a hearing."

"I see we have one thirty on Friday, April 8. The judge will be in Grand Forks," Helen said.

This was great news. Instead of driving all the way to Bismarck, I would be able to attend the hearing in the federal courthouse across the street from our office.

"Shall I pencil it in and alert the U.S attorney's office?" Helen asked.

"Yes, please. I'll be filing the papers shortly."

The minute I was off the phone, I rushed to my calendar and counted backward from April 8. The Department of Justice was entitled to a minimum of ten days (including weekends) before a hearing on our motions. I saw that the latest day I could file the papers was March 29, so I subtracted one day for safety (or bad weather) and picked Monday, March 28, and decided to file it by hand in the afternoon. Quickly I called Burt and Allan and gave them the date of the hearing so they could book plane tickets. We knew we would likely get a response on April 6 or 7, so we'd be challenged to respond to whatever USDA filed by April 8, but the risk was worth it.

I wrote a letter to my lead plaintiffs, asking them to come to Grand Forks (and dress up) on April 8. The farmer grapevine began to hum with the news.

I was hoping that the Department of Justice in Washington wouldn't send a team of litigators to take over the case. By March 1983, there were eight cases about the deferral law that I knew of, and many more in the pipeline.[3] But I knew of no other case raising the constitutional issues regarding the starve out or issues about the unfair appeal hearings.

The *Coleman* case was assigned to Gary Annear, a longtime assistant U.S. attorney. Annear was one of Rodney Webb's best friends.[4] Years later, through a Freedom of Information Act request, I learned[5] that Webb and Annear had called and written the DOJ on March 17 to see if the Washington lawyers wanted to handle the litigation. They said we were "attempting to secure a moratorium on loan foreclosures until the Secretary of Agriculture implements a program which would allow appeals to him concerning foreclosure actions if the plaintiffs or their class action co-plaintiffs are unable to make the payments because of the economic conditions."

It is safe to say that neither Webb nor Annear had actually read the *Coleman v. Block* complaint before the call.

In the crucial days following the filing of *Coleman*, the only action taken by the Department of Justice was to gather, at Webb and Annear's request, briefs filed in various cases dealing with the deferral law. Somehow, the breadth of the *Coleman* case had managed to evade their sonar.

On Friday, March 25, I drove to Fargo to hand-deliver a stack of papers (all two-hole-punched) to Gary Annear at the U.S. Attorney's Office. These papers included a motion and brief in support of a preliminary injunction; a motion and brief in support of certification of the class; the statutory and regulatory appendix, comprising all the laws and regulations we cited in our briefs (to make it easier for the judge and his law clerk to follow our arguments); and a motion and brief to allow Burt and Allan, our out-of-state counsel, to appear. That same day, a law student who was interning for my father drove copies of the paperwork to Judge Van Sickle and the clerk of court in Bismarck.

Judge Van Sickle must have read everything over the weekend, because on Monday—without waiting to hear back from Gary—he signed an order that granted the motion to admit Allan and Burt. (Usually, judges give the opposing side the chance to respond to a motion, even if it's not controversial.)

Two days later, Annear filed his own motion asking Judge Van Sickle to change his mind and kick Burt and Allan off the case. Annear argued that so many lawyers were "unnecessary" because it was a "simple" case and my father and I were perfectly capable of handling it by ourselves. But I knew what he meant. Annear thought he could bully me, but he didn't think he could bully them. Burt and Allan took it as a compliment that their participation in this case scared the shit out of the Department of Justice.

My reply to Annear's motion gave me another opportunity to say how much our clients would benefit from the skills Allan and Burt brought to the case and to make a dig at Gary Annear, who was part of the massive Department of Justice. He had ample support, should he need it.

Judge Van Sickle issued a two-word denial to Annear's motion.

Now we waited for Annear's response to our motions and briefs. We knew he'd want the last word before the April 8 hearing.

Unbeknownst to us, Annear had called Helen asking her to postpone or reschedule the case because he needed more time to prepare. Helen brushed off his request for a delay. After all, he had said it was a simple case.

I'd noticed that requests for information on the *Coleman* case were already overwhelming my father's busy law office. The small practice just couldn't afford the time or expense to send so many courtesy copies. I called Mark and the other allies and advocates I used to meet for coffee, including Dave Ostendorf of PrairieFire Rural Action and Gene Severens of the Center for Rural Affairs, to see if they would become distribution points for the *Coleman* pleadings. They all agreed, and we set up a system whereby my office would copy any key pleadings and send one copy to each of their organizations, which would then distribute them for a small fee. Other lawyers began to do the same; soon there was brisk business in "litigation packets," and the three grass-roots organizations made valuable contacts and gained new members and visibility.

On Tuesday, April 5, three days before the hearing, Annear's response came—I was happy it came so early. I was correct in predicting that he would try to dismiss the case, but he went even further. The caption to his motion was turgid: "Defendant's Motion to Dismiss or in the alternative for Summary Judgment and Memorandum of Authorities in Opposition to Plaintiff's Motion for Designation as Class Action." A motion to dismiss meant he wanted us thrown out of court, and a motion for summary judgment in his favor meant he wanted to win the case right off the bat, without any further discovery, briefing, or trial. I got a kick out of how overconfident Annear was. The trap had worked!

One worrisome part of Annear's strategy was his request that if the judge failed to dismiss the case, then the judge should require the lead plaintiffs to put up huge amounts of money as security for any delays in FmHA's march to fore-closure and liquidation. I suppose he thought that that would be the end of the case, because the farmers couldn't afford any kind of bond—they were destitute after FmHA had already seized all of their income. However, I'd anticipated that Annear would ask for a bond, and I had a powerful brief ready to go that said no bond whatsoever should be required.

I tore through Annear's forty-eight-page brief. To my relief, I saw that we'd predicted, and inoculated ourselves against, most of his attacks. But part IV of the brief was all about why the judge should dismiss our class action, with scores of citations to cases I'd never heard of. I had no idea how to respond.

I got Allan on the phone.

"I can't make heads or tails out of Annear's class actions arguments," I said. "I need your help."

"If you can figure out a way to get me Annear's brief, I can write the response on the plane."

Time was of the essence: I felt like a doctor in an emergency room, calling for instruments. I asked Donna to rush a copy out to the airport so it could be sent to Philadelphia on the first available flight. Another copy was dispatched to Burt in New York.

It was a few minutes past noon. I wanted Judge Van Sickle to have our response by the next day, so he could read it the night before the hearing.

"Dad, you won't believe how terrible this brief is!" I blurted to my father. "Annear is saying we haven't exhausted our administrative remedies! He's relying on appeal regulations that were repealed one year ago!"

"That's great, Sarah," he said. "Now write."

For the next eighteen hours, writing is what I did, taking only a few hours off to sleep, eat, and check in on Andrew. Then I went to the airport to pick up Burt, who by this time had read Gary's brief and was as eager to destroy it as I was. Burt edited and proofread at the office while I went to pick up Allan.

Allan swooped out of the airport, his overcoat flying behind him, with a big briefcase that was so jam-packed with papers and books the top could not fully close.

"I have a draft!" he said as he leaped into my car. "I wrote it on the airplane. The seat next to me was empty so I had space to spread out my reference books." He rummaged in the briefcase and pulled out a yellow legal pad filled with handwriting. I wondered how we would ever turn this into something that could be filed by morning.

We parked and rushed upstairs to the office, where Sue was waiting to type Allan's brief. We grabbed a quick dinner while she worked, and around ten thirty, Sue gave Allan the brief to read. As he read each page, he passed it to me. I didn't see one word to change. It was a stunning brief and elegantly demolished each of Annear's arguments.

Waves of delight, gratitude, and relief passed over me as I read, and tears came to my eyes.

"Allan, it's perfect," I said.

"We can still make changes," he said.

"We aren't making any changes!"

Allan grinned.

By eleven o'clock, the brief I'd written that Burt had edited, and the one Allan had written that needed no editing, were ready for signatures. My father met us at the office to join in the fun. Sue took them to the copier, which had received quite a workout in recent days. She made three copies for Donna to deliver as soon as the courthouse opened at eight the next morning. Two copies were for Judge Van Sickle and his law clerk; the other was for Gary Annear.

On TV, lawyers spent their time in courtrooms, not at the office, working late into the night revising long briefs. The real life of a lawyer was grunge, not glamour. Still, after years of hard work, I finally would get to walk into a courtroom the next morning. And I was terrified. I didn't like my voice—it was too high, too soft. Even in ordinary conversation, people would ask me to speak up! I shivered with fear that I would sound squeaky if I had to speak in court. My memory of the law school moot court hearing, when my voice squeaked and my trembling hands made the lectern rattle, was still painful.

That night, when someone suggested we do a practice run of the argument, I wilted.

"I can't. I've never spoken in a courtroom before. I was terrible at moot court. This is such a huge case, and so many people rely on it. I'm not the right one to make the oral argument." I looked at my dad. "Dad, you've had hundreds of trials and many have been in front of Judge Van Sickle. Would you do it?"

"My main contribution to this case is telling you to file in front of Judge Van Sickle. I don't know it like you know it. You can handle it."

"Allan, will you? Please?"

"No, I agree with your dad. No one knows it like you know it."

I turned to Burt. "You know the issues in this case cold, and you participated in writing the briefs. You've been to the U.S. Supreme Court many times and have handled trials all over the country. Would you do it?"

"Why should the judge trust me? Some pointy-headed intellectual dropping down from the east? You thought up the case, Sarah. You made it happen. It's yours."

I looked at them and thought, *These are great lawyers. If they think I can handle it, I guess I can.*

I slept well that night, satisfied that we had done everything that could be done. It was the first night in weeks that I wasn't beset by waves of anxiety.

CHAPTER 17

Unity

Every café in North Dakota has a secret caramel roll recipe. The morning of the hearing, I picked up Allan and Burt at their motel and we headed downtown to a café that allegedly had the best caramel roll in Grand Forks, despite very stiff competition.

We grabbed a booth and settled in on the red plastic bench seats. Burt and Allan sat on one side; I faced them to better enjoy the show.

"You'll love these caramel rolls," I assured them.

The waitress brought us a pitcher of coffee and three large dinner plates, on which the caramel rolls were centered, fresh from the oven and steaming. This pastry bore no resemblance to the delicate croissant or pastry that Allan or Burt had imagined. Each roll was a plate-sized coil of sweetened white bread dough (made, of course, from flour from the North Dakota State Mill) drenched with sticky caramel sauce and pecans.

My co-counsel looked at their plates with awe and gamely took out their forks and knives to attack the pastries. After a few bites, Burt muttered, "Kintopnmth . . ."

"I can't understand you," I said.

With effort, Burt managed to say, "Can't . . . open . . . mouth!"

I went into gales of laughter. "That's why you have the coffee, to dissolve the caramel!"

Allan's fingers were glued together with caramel sauce.

Halfway through his caramel roll, Burt groaned, "I'll never swim again. I'll drop like a rock to the bottom of the pool!"

"Can we take a nap now?" Allan asked.

"Nope!" I said. "We've got to get ready to go to court."

"I hope the courtroom is on the first floor and I don't have to climb stairs," Burt said.

WHEN I WALKED into the courtroom that afternoon with Burt and Allan and my father, it was already half full of farmers, many of whom I recognized—Dwight, Russel and Anna Mae, Don and Diane, and George and June—and dozens more filed in behind us until the courtroom was packed. About two thirds were men (many women had full-time jobs in town that kept the families afloat).

Many of the men wore tweed woolen jackets, often with a Western cut. Not one of the men wore a suit or black dress shoes. (In the North Dakota countryside, a man wore a suit and dress shoes twice: once at his wedding and again at his funeral.) Underneath their jackets were crisply starched and ironed shirts, and some even wore bolo ties. The men's pants were tan or gray, made of the sturdy, indestructible fabrics that could resist barbed wire and long hours outside. The men with thicker hair had a distinctive indent, a hint that they usually wore a seed cap. All had squint lines on their faces from working in the hot summer sun since they were children.

The women were more dressed up than the men, some in pantsuits and others in dresses with sweaters. They'd all taken care with their hair, necklaces, earrings, and lipstick. I'd decided to wear one of my Department of the Treasury suits (which I rarely wore because they needed dry cleaning, which I could no longer afford). The skirt and jacket were dark gray, and I wore a pale turquoise blouse with a V-neck collar. A hair stylist in Grand Forks had cut my hair in a medium-length bowl cut. (I loved this haircut; it was easy to take care of.) My best jewelry was a single pearl on a thin gold chain that my sister had given me for being the maid of honor at her wedding.

The best-dressed people in the courtroom—by far—were a handsome young Native American couple with their son and two daughters. They were the only non-Germanic, non-Scandinavian people in the courtroom. He wore a Western jacket with a subtle row of beads; she had elaborate earrings and a beautiful hair ornament. The children sparkled with health and beauty and wore ranch-style clothes.

"You must be Lester and Sharon," I said.

"Follow me," I whispered to all my lead plaintiffs, and led them through the swinging gate that separated the litigants from the audience to sit on a long bench directly behind the plaintiffs' counsel table. Even the Crows Hearts' children came forward, squeezing between their parents. They represented the next generation. Burt, Allan, and my dad went down the row of plaintiffs, introducing themselves. I glanced back at the people in the courtroom. Every face seemed anxious.

About ten minutes later, Gary Annear entered. He had a lanky frame and wore a loose gray suit. His hair was pale, neither brown nor blond. He didn't come over to greet us, nor did he look at the mass of farmers seated in the courtroom. I was surprised that no one from FmHA was with him. Annear was all alone.

We faced the judge's bench at the front of the room. There was an empty jury box to our right. The judge's bench—more like a throne—was raised several feet above floor level, so the judge could easily see the entire courtroom and the audience was compelled to look up to him.

A minute or so before one thirty, Helen, the judge's helpful secretary, quietly emerged from the judge's door and sat down in the jury box.

At precisely one thirty, the deputy clerk of court came in.

"There has been a mix-up," he said. "There is no court reporter available. The judge will reschedule if you'd like, but if you are willing to go forward without a court reporter, he will go forward with today's hearing."[1]

Reschedule? I was appalled and dismayed. I glanced at my father, who subtly nodded.

I stood up. "We would like to go forward," I said.

To my relief, Annear also stood up. "The United States is willing to go forward."

The clerk then banged a gavel and said, "All rise! This court is in session, the Honorable Judge Bruce M. Van Sickle presiding."

We all stood. Judge Van Sickle had swept-back gray hair, bright blue eyes, and a stern rugged visage that spoke of many hours in the outdoors. It seemed that he had broad shoulders under his black robe. I thought he looked a lot like

Eric Sevareid, the world-famous journalist on CBS who was from North Dakota, or Charlton Heston.

"My, this is a lot of lawyers for a simple case about foreclosures," he said as soon as he sat down.

Oh, no, I thought. *Had he read our briefs?* Our case was about so much more than foreclosures.

"Ms. Vogel, I believe your side has the laboring oar. Would you proceed?"

I looked at Judge Van Sickle and took a deep breath. He was here to listen to me, and I was here to talk to him.

"Your Honor, these are my co-counsel, Robert Vogel, whom you know, Allan Kanner from Philadelphia, and Burt Neuborne from New York City. And seated behind us are the lead plaintiffs in this case, and I will ask each of them to stand up as I call their name.

"Dwight Coleman, who farms in the Turtle Mountains, near Dunseith.

"Lester and Sharon Crows Heart, who farm and ranch on Fort Berthold.

"Russel and Anna Mae Folmer, who farm in Burleigh County.

"George and June Hatfield, who farm near Ellendale.

"Don and Diane McCabe, who farm near Dickey, in LaMoure County."

The lead plaintiffs stood, frozen in an instant of time, and looked straight at the judge who held their fate in his hands, and he looked back at them. They were *people*, not simply names on a caption in the complaint or a signature on a court order.

Only later did I learn that it was unusual for a lawyer to introduce her clients to a judge. At the time, it only seemed polite and proper.

As I began to tell our story, my voice started off shaky, but I relaxed as I realized Judge Van Sickle was really listening to me, with deep and undivided attention. I wove a story that started in 1933 in the Great Depression and carried forward half a century to 1983. I told Judge Van Sickle about the laws that governed FmHA, and how FmHA would not implement the deferral law. I brought the key Supreme Court decisions into a narrative that encompassed the lives of the nine farmers who were lead plaintiffs, and the thousands of farmers in the class that they represented. I had been so immersed in this case for so long, the arguments flowed like a river. (Part of me seemed to be watching from the sidelines, surprised that I was so articulate.) I felt the support of the farmers in the courtroom and the solid phalanx of brilliant co-counsel seated beside me. Sometimes I turned to look back, drawing the court's attention to the row of my lead plaintiffs, as I described a particular violation of constitutional or statutory law that had happened to one or more of them.

"The lead plaintiffs and the eighty-four hundred farmers that are in the class are hardworking people entitled to equal protection and due process of law, but FmHA has flouted the deferral law and denied these farmers inalienable rights guaranteed by the Constitution," I said as I wrapped up. "That is why we are in this courtroom today. That is why we are asking this court to certify the class under Rule 23. That is why we are asking this court to issue a preliminary injunction. Thank you, Your Honor." I sat down.

Judge Van Sickle said, "Mr. Annear, you may proceed."

Annear began on a querulous note.

"I don't even know why we are in court. These farmers are hopelessly delinquent, in over their heads, and bad managers. The United States should not be a defendant. We should be the plaintiff. I propose that this case be dismissed, and then FmHA will bring two cases for foreclosure that would be test cases. One foreclosure would be in the west, before you, and one foreclosure would be in the east, before Judge Benson."

I was incensed by Gary's opening argument. It was patronizing and just plain stupid. It was like a five-year-old going to a friend's birthday party and declaring, "This shouldn't be your birthday; it should be *my* birthday and you must give me your presents now."

The remainder of Annear's arguments were more rational. He made the same arguments that USDA had made in *Curry* and other cases. He said FmHA's loans were business loans, and the farmers were delinquent, entitling FmHA to foreclose and collect as it saw fit. He emphasized that a number of courts had found that giving or not giving a deferral was purely discretionary with the secretary of agriculture, and it was perfectly legal for the secretary to decide not to implement 7 USC 1981a. His final suggestion was that Judge Van Sickle just park this case to the side, wait for the government's appeal of a Missouri case similar to the *Curry* case but only on behalf of one farmer, *Allison v. Block*, to the Eighth Circuit, and let the decision in that case govern this one.

"Ms. Vogel, have you any comments in rebuttal?"

I rose and said, "Of course, we disagree with Mr. Annear's proposals. We are in court now, and we believe this case is ripe for a decision on the class certification motion and on the preliminary injunction. Under no circumstances will we dismiss this case, nor would we think of proceeding with Mr. Annear's 'test case' scenario. We also disagree with waiting for the Eighth Circuit to rule on the *Allison* case. It could take a year or more to get a decision, and it would be useless to wait. The *Allison* case only deals with interpretation of 7 USC 1981a, the deferral law. It doesn't deal with the other big issues in *this* case: the biased hearing process and the *unconstitutional* way FmHA starves farmers out before they can even apply for a deferral."

I felt myself getting worked up over Annear's arrogance.

"Further," I added, "if the Supreme Court of the United States says that the mothers in the *Goldberg v. Kelly* case deserve due process of law before they lose welfare benefits that are the very means of their survival, then the farmers of North Dakota deserve due process of law before FmHA deprives them of the very means of their survival, especially because the income at issue is income that the farmers have earned from their own labor! And if the Supreme Court of the United States in the *Kimbell Foods* case says that FmHA loans are a 'social welfare' program, they are—even if Mr. Annear claims that FmHA loans are just ordinary business loans. These decisions of the U.S. Supreme Court *compel* this court to require that FmHA compassionately and fairly administer these FmHA loans in order to help family farmers in distress due to no fault of their own. The court should quickly certify the class and issue a preliminary injunction applicable to all eighty-four hundred farmers." I sat back down.

Judge Van Sickle did not ask me or Gary any further questions. He looked out over the courtroom, sweeping his eyes from Gary sitting alone, to me, my father, Burt and Allan, the lead plaintiffs—and then he paused as he looked at the rows of farmers who were looking at him with hope in their eyes. "Thank you all very much," he said. "I anticipate that you will have my decision in about two weeks."

The deputy clerk banged the gavel again and cried out, "All rise! This hearing is now concluded!"

We all stood up as Judge Van Sickle walked out, his black robe swirling behind him. The minute the door shut, the room hummed with muted conversations.

"Good job!" Burt whispered. Allan and my father echoed him. I stuffed the papers back into my briefcase, realizing I had not glanced at them once. I turned and looked back at the lead plaintiffs; they looked happy and relieved.

"I think the judge understood what you said," Dwight said quietly.

"I think so too," I whispered back.

As we walked outside, other farmers stepped forward to congratulate me on a job well done. The tension that had been so visible on their faces before the hearing seemed to be gone, but I didn't have time to chat. I evaded two reporters who were trying to corner me and hurried back to the office to fill my briefcase with paperwork in case I found time to work on the plane. Allan, Burt, and I had a plane to catch to Des Moines for a big national gathering of farmers and farm advocates.

It was called the Emergency National Meeting of the Farm Crisis and had been organized by Mark Ritchie. There were farmers there from all over the Midwest, as well as California, and even a contingent from the Canadian Farmers Survival Association. We met farmer after farmer who had all heard about our case in North Dakota. Many of them asked the same question: Could we file a lawsuit in their state, too?

THE TRUE EXTENT of FmHA delinquencies was not yet known, not even to me. For more than a year, Block and his underlings had been fighting congressional proposals for a national moratorium. They claimed that USDA was compassionate, the farm economy was solid, all "deserving" farmers were being helped, and delinquencies were confined to a small subset of farmers.[2] In reality, the rate of delinquencies was getting worse. By March 31, 1983 (three months after most payments should have been made), the delinquency rates on FmHA loans had skyrocketed. In powerful, fertile, productive California, the delinquency rate was 52 percent. In Arizona, 64 percent. In Texas, 60 percent. Florida and Georgia were at an astonishing 66 percent. North Dakota—with "only" a 42 percent delinquency rate—was in the middle of the pack.[3] Other lenders' delinquencies were rising too, and land values were beginning to dip.[4]

And then another bomb dropped. Someone on one of the congressional committees noticed an addendum to the 1983 budget from David Stockman's office. Despite the frequent protestations that FmHA was trying to help farmers and wasn't interested in foreclosures, the addendum said that the Office of Management and Budget was planning to intensify its crackdown on debtors and speed up collections of overdue debt by using ninety-four United States

Attorney's Offices. Their goal was to reduce FmHA delinquencies by seventy thousand.[5]

In early April, around the time of the preliminary injunction hearing, the national office of the Farmers Home Administration told its local offices to develop emergency plans "to protect the offices, employees and files in case hostile farmers should storm the offices."

"I think this is why Gary Annear was all alone on Friday," my dad said when I got back from Iowa, passing me a clipping from the *Jamestown Sun*. "Farmers Home is scared of their own clients."

The headline read ARE FARMERS FIGHTING MAD? FMHA PLANS FOR THE WORST. Ralph Leet said that he now required each county office to develop an emergency plan complete with directions to call law enforcement "if irate farmer borrowers disrupt the office's normal workings or take over the office." Even though he admitted that such action had never before been necessary in his twenty-six years at FmHA, Leet said the emergency plan was a good idea "because confrontations have always been a possibility since FmHA is a lending agency of last resort for farmers in financial straits."

I was also worried about organizations like the Posse Comitatus, but I was convinced that the way to defeat the Posse's recruitment strategy was for the federal government to follow fair procedures. The farmers gathered in Des Moines had declared "We believe firmly in nonviolence." Could FmHA not distinguish honest farmers' legitimate complaints from the warped beliefs of Gordon Kahl and his ilk? My clients and I were using the constitution and the laws and the judicial branch to obtain justice, but apparently Ralph Leet was afraid even to enter a courtroom where farmers would be present. *What a pity*, I thought. *He might have learned something if he had come.*

I showed my dad the clipping about Stockman's plan to more deeply involve United States attorneys in collections of FmHA loans.

"That is a tremendous number of farmers to push out of business," he said. "When I was United States attorney, I was there for six years and I had only three foreclosures and they weren't due to nonpayment."

He pulled out a calculator and divided 70,000 FmHA farmers by forty-eight states (Hawaii and Alaska didn't have FmHA offices then). If every state had the same number of delinquencies, that would be 1,458 farms per state on the auction block by November.

"It's looking more and more like the thirties," my dad said. "Those were tough times. There were farmers marching in the streets and the Farmers' Holiday Association was stopping sheriff's sales. That's when Governor Langer issued his foreclosure moratorium. One thing they learned back then was that the more land that goes on the market, the more land values drop, and then more loans are in trouble, and the cycle can get bad, very bad, very quickly. Your grandfather, when he ran the Bank of North Dakota, did everything he could to avoid foreclosures. That was the NPL way."

I nodded.

"You know, Dad, Ralph Leet should be grateful to me."

"Grateful? Why?"

"For putting Farmers Home back on the right track, the way it was designed to work back in the thirties. Back then, Farmers Home didn't need barricades. They were the farmers' savior."

We looked at each other and cracked up at the absurdity of Leet ever being grateful to *me*. His plans for barricading offices and calling sheriffs wouldn't keep his people safe. Trusting the farmers and treating farmers compassionately would keep his people safe.

I put a big star on my calendar for exactly two weeks from Friday's hearing date, April 22, and wrote DECISION DUE FROM JUDGE VAN SICKLE.

CHAPTER 18

The Dead Chicken Argument

As FmHA farmers began to sell all or parts of their farms, land values began to dip, which caused the huge network of Federal Land Banks and Production Credit Associations to get nervous and ratchet up pressure to collect on their borrowers. They too began to sell, and farmland values dropped even lower. Further, with low prices, high interest, and concerns over land values, many lenders refused to lend to long-standing customers to help them put their crops into the ground in the spring of 1983. The trends looked ominous.

I was frustrated by Ralph Leet's mantra that only inefficient farmers were being weeded out. As the eminent lawyer and economist Dr. Neil Harl wrote in his 1990 book, *The Farm Debt Crisis of the 1980s*, if a farm was in financial difficulty, it typically wasn't due to inefficiency. The farmers being pushed out were among the *most* efficient. Instead, the main predictor was age: "young farmers . . . had purchased land and other assets during the boom time of the 1970s and had large payment obligations to meet."[1] Put very simply, younger farmers had more debt. Of all farmers in the United States under thirty-five years old, 44.9 percent had debt to asset ratios over 40 percent; of farmers sixty-five or older, only 3.5 percent had debt to asset ratios over 40 percent. Harl wrote, "Those who had the lack of foresight or good sense to be born late enough so they started farming after about 1970 were disproportionately impacted by the phenomenon [of the farm debt crisis]."[2]

Family farms were often multigenerational. Farms were the original "home-based businesses," and most farmers wanted to help their children farm, some-times with tragic consequences. In the late 1970s and early 1980s, expanding a family farm to provide opportunity for a son or daughter to join as partners in the parents' operation, or offering a parent's guarantee to a lender to get a loan to start a child's own operation, could lead to the loss of not only the child's farm but also the parents' farm.[3]

In Grand Forks, I learned about a young go-getter who decided to raise chickens and provide fresh eggs to regional buyers. His father, an established farmer, guaranteed the loan for buildings for the chicken farm, start-up expenses, packing equipment, and trucks. But the burden of debt grew too big to bear. Two years later, I sat at the back of a starkly modern Lutheran church at the young farmer's funeral. He had committed suicide, naively believing that life insurance would pay the chicken farm debt so his father wouldn't have to pay the guaranteed loan by mortgaging his own farm. His grieving parents greeted people as they arrived, hiding their unspeakable pain under the shell of Norwegian stoicism. From then on, I begged every young farmer I met never to ask for—or accept—a loan guarantee from their parents. I told older farmers, "Love your children, but don't ever guarantee or cosign their debts."

Farm debt was ballooning. Between 1971 and 1976, the total outstanding farm debt in the United States grew from $54 billion to $91 billion. By 1984, that figure had more than doubled to $215 billion.[4]

Farm income couldn't keep up. Farm debt was 334 percent of net farm income in 1975 and skyrocketed to 795 percent of net farm income in 1981.[5] By 1983, it had risen to 1,350 percent of net farm income.[6]

When land values began to decline, at the same time the Reagan administra-tion was trying to wring inflation out of the economy, lenders withdrew, too nervous to continue to invest. The drop was cataclysmic and cut enormous amounts of equity from farm balance sheets. In Iowa, farm values peaked at $2,147 per acre in 1981 and fell to $1,054 in 1985. The value of agricultural land nationwide fell by more than $300 billion.[7]

As news spread about my case, distraught farmers from all over the nation called and wrote. Letters addressed simply to "Sarah Vogel, North Dakota" reached me by postal service. The network of advocacy groups had grown stronger, and now I could send farmers to other sources of help. By early 1983, the Center for Rural Affairs had published a *Farmers Guide to FmHA* with detailed information on how to file appeals. PrairieFire Rural Action was developing a cadre of trained farmer advocates in Iowa. In Minnesota, two fiery Norwegian women farmers—Lou Anne Kling and Anne Kanten—put the principles of the Farmers' Holiday movement to work and led farm protests, plowed up fields in a graphic demonstration showing how worthless the crop was in the market, and trained farm advocates. Mark Ritchie kept on sending out *Ammo*, which provided updates on developments all over the country.

I hadn't forgotten about the MacArthur Foundation grant that Mark was funneling through his nonprofit, the Center for Rural Studies, but it was hard to keep good records of my time when every day it seemed there was a new fire to put out, and the need for the grant money had become less urgent once I was on salary at my dad's firm. Finally, in May, I pulled together a detailed bill for Mark of all the hours I'd spent on the *Coleman* case so far. When Mark sent me a check, I turned it over to my dad to cover all the expenses my case had been racking up: the long distance phone charges, the photocopies, Allan's flight to North Dakota (Burt's travel was covered by the ACLU).

While I worked long hours, Andrew spent his days with my mother (often shopping in department stores, where Andrew often scored new clothes, toys, or books) or playing with friends across the street. He was now four and a half and seemed a little bored with his peaceful life ("Mom, let's go *do* something!"), so I found a Montessori preschool ten minutes from home. After rustling up extra money from his father, I enrolled Andrew, and he loved it from the first day.

I reconnected with a few friends from college and joined a small Friday night book club. It was a treat to read *Beowulf* and Shakespeare instead of the Code of Federal Regulations. While we sipped cheap wine and ate cheese and crackers, our kids played in the next room.

At my parents' house, the television was always tuned to public TV. In the evenings, I'd read one of the thousands of books that lined the walls of the basement rec room. I discovered that my mother was a secret feminist (I'd had no idea) when I found her copy of Betty Friedan's *The Feminine Mystique*, in which she'd underlined lines such as "The feminine mystique has succeeded in burying millions of American women alive."

With grit and determination, my mother had managed to leave her small town for the big city of Minneapolis to get a college education, and then she married my father. She worked as a secretary while he finished his law degree, but she never finished college, and she never again held a paying job once he started as a lawyer. In that era, if she'd worked, it would have stained his reputation ("He can't support his family"). My father's career had benefited from her sacrifice. The few months I spent in the basement showed me the advantages that men like my father had by having women like my mother at home while they pursued their careers without worrying about housework, meals, or childcare.

I realized that my own idyll of not worrying about housework, meals, or childcare courtesy of my mother could not, and should not, last. I was almost thirty-seven. Pleasant as it was to live in my parents' home, it was also humiliating and infantilizing. The last time I'd lived with them was during high school. I'd gotten married when I was nineteen. I was used to being on my own, difficult as it might be. I needed to find a home in Grand Forks for myself and Andrew.

On May 3, my thirty-seventh birthday, I awoke hoping that Judge Van Sickle's decision would be my gift. It was well past the two weeks he'd promised at the preliminary injunction hearing. At the close of the day, as I had a birthday party with Andrew and my parents, I thought about everything that had changed since my thirty-fourth birthday. Then, I'd had a lovely two-story colonial town home and a nice car. I'd had a high salary and low debts. I represented the secretary of the Treasury. Now I was camping out in my parents' basement and deeply in debt; my clients were insolvent, and I had a charity job (for which I was very grateful) courtesy of my father. What would happen to me and Andrew if Judge Van Sickle did not rule in our favor?

On May 5, the call finally came. I was sitting at the desk Richard DeLare had built for me. Back then, clerks of court had the humane practice of calling lawyers to tell them about a judge's decision as soon as a decision was signed but before it was filed or became accessible to the public or the press. This gave the lawyers a brief heads-up so they could alert their clients of a win or a loss before it became public.

"This is Vivian, the chief deputy clerk of court. Judge Van Sickle just signed a preliminary injunction in your favor today. Would you like me to read the order to you?"

As I listened to Vivian read slowly, so I could take notes, my relief was so great, I felt my spirit leave my body. Judge Van Sickle had denied FmHA's motion to dismiss and its motion for summary judgment. He'd certified the class as all North Dakota farmers who had farm loans from FmHA or were eligible for them in the future. He had enjoined FmHA from proceeding with any foreclosures, accelerations, or refusals to release income that had been planned for family living and farm operating expenses unless FmHA first told farmers about the deferral and gave them personal notice of the right to apply for deferral. He said hearing officers had to give the specific reasons for their decisions and the hearing officer could not have been involved in the initial decision. There would be no bond.

But I hadn't heard any mention of administrative law judges. "Vivian, would you reread the part about hearing officers?"

"Sure. Defendants shall give at least thirty days' notice . . . that informs the borrower of the official before whom the borrower may request a hearing. The official designated shall not have been actively involved in the initial decision of termination."

My spirits fell a bit. Without fair hearing officers, the other rights granted by the preliminary judgment would be on shaky ground. But I shook off that concern for the moment. I'd won half a loaf at least. District directors could no longer be hearing officers on accelerations of chattel loans within their own district on decisions that they had already approved. And apart from the problem of having district directors who worked for Leet as hearing officers on real estate foreclosures, everything in the order was perfect!

"Judge Van Sickle has set up a status conference on May 23 in Bismarck to discuss how he'd handle wrapping up the case. Will plaintiffs' counsel attend at ten A.M.?" Vivian asked.

"Yes, we will," I said. "Thank you!"

I leaped to my feet to cross the hall to tell my father and then raced back to my desk to start calling the lead plaintiffs and Burt and Allan. I reached all of them by the end of the afternoon. June Hatfield was at her bank job and said, "Thanks to you and thanks to God!"

I couldn't disagree—it did seem that God was on our side; after all, the Bible was full of verses supporting farmers, but I wasn't aware of any that supported foreclosures. June said she would find George, who was graveling a road somewhere, and share the news. Anna Mae went to the pasture where Russel was working to tell him. Dwight had no phone but I told his mother. Sharon Crows Heart said Lester was out but she'd tell him. She said it was a relief that she didn't need to live in fear of a federal agent knocking on their door to deliver foreclosure papers.

When Dwight called, he whooped with enthusiasm. "We won! Damn right, they deserved to lose!"

In every conversation, I had to temper my enthusiasm. It was a preliminary injunction, not a final permanent injunction. But it gave me hope.

There was a pink message slip buried under the clutter of papers on my desk from a woman whose son was a farmer.

Robert and Sarah Vogel in their downtown law office   Photograph: Vivian Kellowod

The law's a family affair for Grand Forks' Vogels

Sarah and Robert Vogel in his office.

He'd been pressured by FmHA to schedule an auction sale for all his equipment, and the auction was set for May 6. She asked me to urgently call her back about my case, because if the lawsuit was successful, maybe her son could cancel the sale.

"Hi, this is Sarah Vogel. We talked yesterday, and I have good news . . ."

"I'll call my son right now," she said, choking up. "He'll be so happy. He wants to keep farming."

The Robert Vogel Law Office was usually quiet and peaceful, but not on May 5, after the phone call from Vivian. Reporters from TV and radio stations and newspapers lined up in the reception area, and the stack of pink phone messages grew higher. I was interviewed by an Associated Press reporter who then told me that Gary Annear and Rodney Webb weren't available for comment, and Ralph Leet refused to talk.

During all this, Sue, my father's main legal secretary, burst into my office to tell me John Block, the secretary of agriculture, was on the line. He wanted to talk to me.

Holy buckets!

I swiftly got off the call I was on and, suppressing my excitement, said, "Hello, Secretary Block, this is Sarah Vogel."

I was met with a tiny pause and a muffled chuckle. Then a delightful happy voice with a Southern accent said, "Actually, this isn't old Auction Block. This is Dale Reesman, from Boonville, Missouri; I'm the lawyer in the *Allison v. Block* case, and I just lied to your secretary so I could jump to the head of the line." Dale went into gales of laughter at the absurdity of the idea of John Block's calling me, and I collapsed in laughter too.

We swiftly shared compliments (me praising the *Allison* decision that said that FmHA had to implement the deferral law and tell farmers about their right to apply for a deferral, he praising the *Coleman* case). Like all North Dakotans, I believed I had no accent myself, but I certainly noticed his. His first name took two syllables: "*Day*-ull." Missouri was pronounced "Miz-*ur*-ah."

"You know, they're appealing *Allison* to the Eighth Circuit," Dale told me.

"Uffda!" I said.[8] That raised the stakes. If *Allison* was upheld by the Eighth Circuit, that meant Judge Van Sickle would have to rule in our favor, but if Dale lost at the Eighth Circuit, we would lose, too.

It was obvious. My co-counsel and I needed to do everything possible to help Dale. By the end of the call, we were pals, and I said I'd call Burt to see if he would write an amicus brief on behalf of the Coleman plaintiffs to alert the Eighth Circuit Court of Appeals that a case involving the same legal issues about deferral and other constitutional issues was pending in North Dakota.

That night, the ten o'clock news had stories about the *Coleman* decision, but the big story was that federal officials feared Gordon Kahl would resurface on May 9, when his wife, Joan, his son Yorie, and four followers went on trial for murder and other felonies. His wife was later acquitted by the jury. The federal courthouse in Fargo had imposed ultra-high security to protect against violent assault by Kahl or other members of the Posse. As I sat in my parents' living room watching the news, I hoped that farmers would connect the dots between the Kahl shootout and the *Coleman* case and see that farmers could still look to the system for help.

"I hope the DOJ sees that fighting us is only going to provide fuel for the Posse philosophy," I told my dad during a commercial. Like me, Gordon Kahl preached that the farmers had done no wrong; they were the victims.[9] But his solutions were vile: they would not save farms, and they'd put farmers in danger of prison or worse.

My hope that Block, Shuman, Leet, and other FmHA officials would see the light and stop fighting the simple, practical relief we'd obtained in the preliminary injunction lasted only a few days.

By Monday, May 9, there were many signs that the federal government was not going to comply with the order. As farmers went to county offices, they were told, "We don't know anything about that order." Even the county supervisor in Don and Diane McCabe's county, who was a named defendant, said that he couldn't release money without permission from Ralph Leet.

The most disturbing story I heard was that a Native American couple from the Fort Berthold Reservation had gone to Leet's office on May 9, along with their legal aid lawyer and a copy of the *Coleman* decision, to ask for urgent release of funds from cattle sales for purchase of seed and fuel so that they could plant feed crops before it was too late to plant. Leet flatly said he hadn't received advice from his attorney and would not authorize any releases until he heard back. Their lawyer demanded a hearing on that refusal, but Leet said that the only way her clients could get a hearing was for Leet to send an acceleration notice first. When the lawyer again objected, Leet threatened to send her clients' names to the U.S. Attorney's Office for felony conversion.

On Tuesday, I called Annear. He "wasn't available."

The next day, I wrote a letter warning him that "as a matter of professional courtesy," I would ask Judge Van Sickle for assistance to make him promptly implement the order. I was happy to have sent that letter, especially once I read that Annear had complained in the Fargo *Forum* about Judge Van Sickle's order and said it would be "several weeks" while FmHA readjusted to the order.[10] This meant the starve outs were still going on. Nothing had changed.

I furiously filed a motion to hold the defendants in contempt and asked Judge Van Sickle to consider this motion at the status conference on Monday, May 23.

EARLY ON THE morning of the status conference, I went to the clerk's office to deliver a brief with more arguments about the need for administrative law judges (in lieu of district directors) on FmHA appeals.[11] In the sub-basement of the UND law library, I had uncovered a treasure trove of regulations and administrative law judge decisions that arose out of USDA's meat inspection program.

I wrote pages of gruesome information on the "rights" that USDA gave to spoiled and rotting meat. I found that a condemned poultry carcass enjoyed greater due process rights than a FmHA borrower. I thought my "dead chicken argument" would surely win Judge Van Sickle to my side.

At the preliminary injunction hearing, Annear had been alone and we'd had a courtroom full of supporters. Now, in Judge Van Sickle's office on May 23, Annear had brought five FmHA employees to back him up. They sat stiffly on one side of a long conference table and did not answer my father's or my greeting as we came in and sat down on the opposite side. My father cast a twinkling glance at me, somehow conveying that, from his perspective of over forty years of litigation, their rude behavior was a good sign for us.

After a few minutes, Judge Van Sickle swept in. He opened with a bang, saying that he wanted to wrap up our case quickly so that USDA could appeal it. This meant that he was wedded to his preliminary injunction decision, and I hoped that meant he would make it permanent.

But then he threw icy water on my request for administrative law judges, saying it would result in "hamstringing" the administrator.[12]

I tried to keep a poker face and clung to the hope that Judge Van Sickle would change his mind after he read my dead chicken argument.

"Does either side feel that they need more than a hundred twenty days in order to close all trial preparation?" the judge asked.

I looked at my father.

"A hundred twenty is about right," he said.

Judge Van Sickle looked at Annear. "Are you ready to live under the existing temporary restraining order for a hundred twenty days?"

"Well, I guess," Annear waffled. "That's of course one of the reasons I thought we were having this meeting. We are prepared to show the court the type of action that we contemplate taking during this period of time in implementation of the court order."

My spider senses tingled when Gary said *We are prepared to show the court.* What was he going to show the court? How was he going to follow the order? I'd received nothing on FmHA's plans for implementation—despite my motion to hold FmHA in contempt. Before I could ask for more, the judge had moved to a new topic: setting a strict 120-day limit to gather all the evidence. To do all the discovery in this case within 120 days was quite fast, but my father answered, "The plaintiffs will have no problem with that requirement."

Annear hemmed and hawed but eventually said yes. Then Judge Van Sickle looked at me directly and said, "I intend to make this meaningful, and I'll make an order that amended pleadings must be served within ten days from today."

"That's fine," I said. I'd worked hard on the documents I'd already filed and I thought they were perfect. No amendments would be needed.

Annear said he wanted to file briefs that would challenge every legal conclusion in the preliminary injunction, including whether there should be a class action.

"Now," Judge Van Sickle said, "is there any reason why this type of information cannot be furnished on affidavit? The only reason I suggest furnishing them on affidavit is if you have to prepare the affidavit, the presentation will be orderly and I won't have to take up court time. I can keep moving the other cases along and then sit down and read this. What is your feeling? Do you feel that it is a matter that should be handled in a manner of a hearing?"

"I think affidavits and depositions and motions for admission and interrogatories should do it. I don't see any need for a live trial," I said.

"How do you feel?" Judge Van Sickle asked Annear.

"At this stage I would say that it could be handled that way, yes," Annear said.

The deputy clerk of court wrote: "Counsel agree that fact material may be presented by affidavit. Court will set hearing on motion for permanent injunction for Tuesday, September 20, 1983."

I tried to steer the discussion back to FmHA's noncompliance and my request for sanctions. I asked Judge Van Sickle to instruct Annear to send corrective notices to FmHA offices, so as to comply with the order.

Judge Van Sickle agreed and, gesturing to the deputy clerk making notes, said, "Defendant must recommend a notice program to the plaintiffs within ten days." *That's better than nothing*, I thought, but I was irked that FmHA was stretching compliance out to an unreasonable length.

Then, to my surprise, Annear volunteered that he already had a notice program ready to go. He handed a slim document, perhaps five or six pages, to Judge Van Sickle.

"Do you perhaps have a copy for the plaintiffs, Mr. Annear?" I asked. He handed it to me with a smirk. The first thing we noticed was that it was dated May 19, the day after I'd served the motion to hold USDA in contempt. As my father and I pored over the document, we were stunned. It was defiant of the order; it was defiance of the court order!

To our delight, Judge Van Sickle studied the document and then began to cross-examine Gary. His critique was polite but ruthless.

"You are enjoined from terminating the living and operating allowance previously determined until the victim of your decision has been given thirty days' notice of a right to a hearing to contest the termination," he said to Annear.

Victim! I marveled at his word choice. My father and I looked at each other, trying to hide our glee.

Judge Van Sickle read a long paragraph from FmHA's May 19 memo and summarized it: "What you are saying is 'Okay. We've decided that you're out, Buster.'" Annear sputtered with indignation, but the message had been delivered.

I harbored hope that Judge Van Sickle would channel his unhappiness with the May 19 memo with a contempt order, but he said that "only under extreme circumstances would I be willing to use any contempt procedure."

He spelled out exactly how he wanted me and Annear to work together to come up with a mutually acceptable notice and compliance procedure for implementation of the preliminary injunction. Annear and I loathed each other, but we gritted our teeth and agreed.

THAT SPRING, I started looking around Grand Forks for an affordable rental home, and I found a tiny house off an alley near downtown. It was a converted garage but I thought it was fine. It was all Andrew and I needed, and the rent was low. There was moss on the roof and roses climbed up the kitchen window wall. I signed a lease for one year, starting June 1. Most of our belongings were still back in Bismarck, and I rented a one-way U-Haul. I didn't want to remind Andrew of how much he'd loved going to the sandbars with me at the river house, so I left him with my mother.

On Memorial Day, I walked through my beloved river house one last time. I stood on the deck facing the sparkling river and whispering cottonwood trees and shed tears for all my lost dreams. But eventually, resolutely, I straightened up, climbed into the U-Haul, and drove away, lighting a cigarette before I'd hit the interstate.

On the drive back to Grand Forks, I decided to press forward on the administrative law judge issue. I'd been stunned when Leet wrote to all his minions that he intended to reaccelerate every loan that had been deaccelerated by the order. This was one more reason why district directors could not be impartial.

On Tuesday, I called Helen to get a date for a hearing on two issues: whether Judge Van Sickle would modify the preliminary injunction to require administrative law judges, and whether he would issue a new order to fix the incorrect information that Leet had sent to FmHA county office employees. Helen said Judge Van Sickle's calendar was jammed; he was taking cases from Judge Benson while Benson focused on the Kahl trial. But she was friendly and said she'd try to find a time.

When she called back, she told me that Judge Van Sickle could fit us in on June 8 or June 10. I told her either date worked for me. But Annear said he was busy both days. When Helen said the hearing would be on the tenth, and suggested that if he couldn't make it, he could send another lawyer from the U.S. Attorney's Office, he blew up. He sent an angry brief in which he humble-bragged about how busy he was on other important cases, complained of Helen's late notice, excoriated my "unnecessary" briefs, and accused me of simply trying to generate higher attorney's fees. *Did Gary Annear simply dislike women?* I wondered. Criticizing me was one thing; criticizing the judge's longtime secretary was a really dumb move.

Annear sent another assistant U.S. attorney to the hearing in his place. The entire status conference lasted only twenty minutes. Judge Van Sickle said that he found my criticism of Leet's deeply flawed "implementation" of the preliminary injunction to be "valid." But to my intense disappointment, instead of accepting my plain-English revised notice, he looked sternly at me and said that I would have to work with Annear to reach a notice agreeable to both of us. My heart sank.

As he stood up to leave, Judge Van Sickle told the assistant U.S. attorney to give me a copy of the May 24 notice. I was bewildered—I had not heard of any May 24 notice. Leet and Annear had taken one message from the May 23 status conference: neither was in any danger of a contempt citation. They felt free to disregard the order.

I thought the second notice was no better than the first notice, which had triggered my request for a contempt motion. Both reaffirmed Leet's expectation that all farmers with loans that had been accelerated would be reaccelerated. It seemed FmHA had no intention of following the preliminary injunction order in good faith; without the hammer of a contempt charge, they'd do the very minimum and dare me to stop them.

As my father and I drove back to Grand Forks, I fumed. It was so obvious to me that USDA was in contempt. *Why didn't the judge see it the same way?*

While my father and I drove five hundred miles round trip for a twenty-minute hearing, Annear was at last writing a reply to my motion to require administrative law judges and to make USDA meaningfully implement deferrals.

It arrived a few days later. As soon as I had the opportunity to read his brief, my mood improved, and pretty soon I was laughing. His brief was terrible. The punctuation was bizarre; sentences were long, rambling, and confusing; paragraphs went on for multiple pages. He hadn't even proofread it. I was grimly amused at his accusation that my legal arguments on due process were "frivilious." Remarkably, the entire brief contained not one citation to a court case. Much of it was written in jargon-ridden FmHA-speak that even I could barely understand.

Before closing, Annear again slammed the lead plaintiffs ("The reason that they failed is mainly because of the management problem"), but he failed to attach any affidavits to support that accusation, even though Judge Van Sickle had already said that FmHA would need to rebut plaintiffs' affidavits with sworn affidavits of its own.

This badly written and poorly reasoned brief was like a tonic for my mood. I did not think Judge Van Sickle would find it persuasive.

I WAS CONFIDENT in the North Dakota preliminary injunction, but I was growing increasingly distressed about the fate of similarly situated farmers across the country.

Roger Allison Jr., the son of the plaintiff in Dale Reesman's *Allison v. Block* case in Missouri, had been elected chair of the farm credit committee of the

North American Farmers Alliance (NAFA), an organization that had been formed at the national gathering in Des Moines. He called to say his committee had met and authorized him to call to ask me to file a national class. I avoided giving him an answer. I was frightened by the responsibility of a national class, but at the same time I felt that if I turned my back on them, it was the same as driving by a person stranded by the side of the road in a blizzard.

I was waiting to see if anyone else would bring a national class—or if lawyers in other states would bring cases like the *Coleman* case, with its unique due process argument. There were now dozens of cases involving the deferral law. But only one case was similar to the *Coleman* case. That case was *Gamradt v. Block*, filed by Minnesota Legal Services on behalf of a class of Minnesota farmers who had borrowed from FmHA. The lead attorney on the case was Jim Massey, and it was closely based on the pleadings in *Coleman v. Block*, which I'd sent to Jim after Mark Ritchie introduced us.

Then, one night in the middle of June, I was woken by the shrill of the telephone. I stumbled over to the phone, still half asleep. I heard a man's voice with a thick Southern accent. He sounded desperate but proud. "I'm from Mississippi and I'm losing my farm to FmHA and so many other farmers down here are losing their farms too. We've heard about what you're doing in North Dakota. Can you help us too? Please? We can make it if we could get some extra time. Please." The pain in his voice doubled me over. I could hear thousands of farmers' voices in his. It overwhelmed me.

"Could you please call me tomorrow?" I asked. "At the office?"

There was a pause.

"I don't know if I can make it that long," he said.

And for the first time I said, "Maybe. I'll try."

I told Allan and Burt about the calls, and they endorsed the idea of a national class. Allan pointed out that there had never been a national class action filed out of North Dakota (North Dakota was the second-smallest state in terms of population after Wyoming), but he saw no reason why that would be a barrier.

Even my father—who had a lot to lose since I hadn't earned a penny since I'd been at his firm—looked at me soberly, and said, "If you want to make it into a national class action, I'm okay."

Dale Reesman agreed to co-counsel with us on the national case, and he said he'd find the proper national class representatives.

Everyone seemed to want me to convert *Coleman* to a national class action, with one exception: Jim Massey. Jim was adamant that it would be better to proceed with a series of state class actions, as he was doing in Minnesota, and develop the law carefully, and slowly.

We would meet that objection by defining our case as a national class covering all states except those where state class actions had been approved or where requests for class action status were pending. This way, Jim's *Gamradt* case would not be affected.

A deeper concern was that at the May 23 status conference, Judge Van Sickle had given us a ten-day deadline to amend the pleadings, and that deadline had long passed.

In early July, I received a copy of FmHA's quarterly report on its Farm Program loans.[13] The cover of this report had a drawing of a happy rural scene, complete with a movie-star-handsome husband in work clothes and boots, and a beautiful young woman—presumably the farmer's wife—wearing go-to-church clothes. I knew that the status of real-life borrowers would not match this cheerful illustration. As I and a handful of other underfunded lawyers were working to stop farm foreclosures, thousands of FmHA officials and their attorneys at the Department of Justice were working too. And they were having greater success than we were. From October 1982 to June 1983, FmHA reported:

- 3,172 chattel liquidations were approved
- 2,931 bankruptcy petitions were pending
- 1,095 borrowers discontinued farming due to bankruptcy
- 2,801 acceleration letters had been sent to farm borrowers
- 1,737 foreclosure cases were pending
- 971 foreclosures were completed
- 2,223 "sales other than foreclosures" were completed
- 1,172 voluntary conveyances were registered
- 454 transfers and assumptions have been finalized.

I felt sick as I totaled it up: as many as 16,500 farm families were on Auction Block's chopping block. And there was still one quarter to go in the fiscal year in order to reach Stockman's goal of a seventy thousand reduction in delinquencies. Only a miracle, or a national class action, would stop them.

I thought about the farmer who had called me from Mississippi. His voice did speak for thousands of other farmers. Suddenly my indecision and reluctance disappeared. I had no choice. I had to do the class action, or thousands upon thousands of additional farmers would be lost.

I would file a motion to make the *Coleman* case a national class action, and if Judge Van Sickle rejected the amended complaint because of the ten-day deadline, so be it. He might be angry at me, but I wouldn't go to jail. I wouldn't be fired. And if Judge Van Sickle wouldn't allow us to do it, our team would find another judge in another state.

My first call was to Dale, accepting his offer to join as co-counsel. He said he would find new lead plaintiffs to represent the national class. Then I called Allan and Burt. It was time to put the pedal to the metal, as the hot-rodders used to say in high school.

CHAPTER 19

The Front Steps of the Courthouse

Russel Folmer rarely called me. He was a patient sort. But just after the Fourth of July, he rang.

"Sarah, I was just served papers by the sheriff." His voice broke. "The Bank of North Dakota is going to sell our farm on August 4. And there is a notice of the sale of our farm in the *Bismarck Tribune*." Russel paused for a moment, and then angrily said, "This is all FmHA's fault. The Bank of North Dakota has the first mortgage. Our cattle sales were more than adequate to pay the bank, but that damn Leet refused to pay the bank from the cattle check. What should we do?" His voice was trembling, and I thought he was probably crying.

I suddenly realized why Annear had been so quiet all summer. He had argued that all of the lead plaintiffs were such bad farmers that it was inevitable that their farms would be lost. Annear intended to prove that point by having the Folmers, our most respectable lead plaintiffs, lose their farm.

It was a vicious tactic. The Bank of North Dakota was the same bank that my grandfather had run, and it had helped many farmers survive the 1930s. Because of the trust that the legislature had in the Bank of North Dakota, it was the only lender in the state that could foreclose by simply advertising the property for a sheriff's sale. The Folmers could only stop the sale by filing their own lawsuit against the Bank of North Dakota.

"Russel, I know you're upset, but I'm sure we can beat it back," I said. "I discovered a law passed in 1933 by the Nonpartisan League called the Confiscatory

Price Law. It says that when the prices you receive are below the cost of producing that farm product, North Dakota judges don't have to approve a request from a creditor to foreclose on a farmer. Instead, the judge can stop the foreclosure until farm prices are no longer confiscatory. We just need to sue the Bank of North Dakota. Is that okay by you?"

"You bet it is," Russel roared so loudly that I had to move the receiver away from my ear.

ON THE AFTERNOON of August 3, Russel, Anna Mae, and I climbed the front steps of the Burleigh County Courthouse. I was dressed in my best lawyer uniform (suit jacket, skirt, peach-colored blouse with a floppy bow at the neckline). Our mission was to stop the foreclosure sale that was set to occur on those same steps the following morning.

The courthouse had been built in the art deco style in 1931. In the entry was a mural of the French fur trader and explorer Pierre La Vérendrye paying a visit to the Mandan tribe in the winter of 1738. Leaving the sweltering heat of an August day, we found it restorative to look at the winter scene, with smoke rising peacefully from the mounded earth lodge homes as La Vérendrye and the Mandan greeted each other. The painting corrected the myth that Lewis and Clark had "discovered" the Mandan in 1803. In fact, the Mandan were traders with coast-to-coast networks long before the arrival of Lewis and Clark.

We walked up wide marble steps to the second-floor courtroom to which we'd been assigned. The Folmers followed me through the swinging gates and we all sat down at the table on the right side. A few minutes later, a man from the attorney general's office came in and shook our hands. He didn't seem hostile, nor did he radiate the disdain that I'd felt from Gary Annear.

At two thirty P.M. sharp, a clerk walked in.

"All rise!"

We all stood for a hawk-faced man in black robes coming in fast through the side door. He held a clutch of papers that had to be my legal brief and the three supporting affidavits. One was from Russel and Anna Mae about their farming operation and the low prices they received for their milk, their crops, and their cattle. Another was from a North Dakota State University economist who presented data on the "parity ratio," which measured the "disparity" between what farmers paid for the costs of production and what they received; he said that the parity ratio in 1983 was the lowest since the Great Depression. The third affidavit was from Larry Remele, a historian who worked for the North Dakota Historical Society and the nation's top expert on the history of the Nonpartisan League. Larry's affidavit (which he did for free) eloquently told the story of the dramatic 1933 legislative session when the confiscatory price law had been adopted.

"Proceed," the judge said.

"Your Honor," I began confidently, "we are asking you to stop the foreclosure sale of the Folmers' farm tomorrow because prices of the farm products grown by my clients, the Folmers, who are sitting beside me, are confiscatory. The legislature in 1933 said that when prices are confiscatory, or under the cost of production, it is the public policy of the state that the courts of this state can find a foreclosure to be unconscionable. This means that the Folmers can use the 'confiscatory price' law as a defense. And if a person who is facing a foreclosure by advertisement has a defense, this court *must* halt the foreclosure by advertisement, and the Bank of North Dakota *must* sue the Folmers in a regular foreclosure action where they can file and answer and defend themselves. As I state in my brief—"[1]

"Ms. Vogel, but why do you believe this so called 'confiscatory price' law is still in effect?"

Mystified, I said, "Because it is printed in the North Dakota Century Code."

"But doesn't Section 28-29-04 say that '*until* the price of farm products produced in this state shall rise to a point to equal at least the cost of production.' *Until*. I'm sure you are aware that the Great Depression ended in the 1940s."

"Yes, of course, but as shown by our economist's affidavit, farm prices are again below the cost of production and this means—"

"But doesn't section five say that 'Whenever any foreclosure proceeding is pending in any *court* . . .' and isn't the Folmers' farm being sold under the foreclosure by advertisement method? No court is involved in a foreclosure by advertisement. Isn't that right?"

"Your Honor, yes, the Folmers do face foreclosure by advertisement, but the law says that we can stop a foreclosure by advertisement by presenting a *defense*, and the confiscatory price defense is a *defense*."

"But this is a foreclosure of real estate, and real estate is not a 'farm product' like wheat or corn. Isn't that right?"

"Yes, but the law says that—"

Suddenly—without even hearing from the lawyer for the Bank of North Dakota—the judge banged his gavel and barked, "Motion denied. Case dismissed."

The clerk swiftly said, "All rise."

I was outraged. The judge had treated us as though we were one of the "pro se" litigants who were clogging court dockets with bizarre legal theories from "foreclosure kits" sold by fraudsters and members of the Posse Comitatus. I remained seated in my chair and glared at the judge as he swirled out of the courtroom. I hoped he saw that I hadn't risen for him, but he didn't even look back. Less than ten minutes had passed.

Russel and Anna Mae sat frozen beside me. I crammed my papers back into my briefcase. The lawyer for the bank seemed surprised. He hadn't said a word.

I raced down the staircase, Russel and Anna Mae struggling to keep up with me. I wanted to be outside before I started to cry, but I was sobbing by the time I reached the ground floor. When the Folmers caught up with me, I was incoherent, unable to catch my breath. Russel looked around and saw a fluorescent sign flashing MAIN STREET BAR only a block away. He grabbed my briefcase and led us into the dark, cool interior. It was empty except for two sad hunched men at the bar. I followed Russel to a booth.

"Don't cry, Sarah. You did your best. We'll be okay," he said.

Through a throat so tight I could barely speak, I said, "That judge is wrong! He is wrong!"

Russel had brought three beers to the booth, and I drank mine fast. I lit one cigarette, then another. Gradually my breathing returned to normal. The Folmers kept comforting me. "There, there, Sarah, it will be okay," Anna Mae insisted. Soon the three of us realized the absurdity of the situation. They were the ones whose farm would be sold the next day. And they were consoling me!

I told them that despite the sale, they'd still have a one-year grace period to live on their farm. This period was called the redemption period because at any time during that year they could "redeem" their title by paying the Bank of North Dakota the amount paid at the August 4 foreclosure sale plus interest at the "legal rate." The year of grace was due to the wisdom of the Nonpartisan League, and it would not expire until August 1984.

"Plus, we are going to file a notice of appeal," I said. I took a blank piece of paper from my briefcase and printed "Folmer v. State" and the case number at the top. I added a caption: "Notice of Appeal of Denial of Injunction." I wrote, "Russel and Anna Mae Folmer hereby appeal the court's refusal to enjoin the foreclosure by advertisement scheduled for August 4, 1983. Sarah Vogel, Attorney, for the appellants." If this wasn't the proper format, I was confident the clerk would tell me what I had done wrong (just as the federal court clerk had told me about the two-hole punch) and I'd just redo it until I got it right.

We walked back to the courthouse and went to the clerk of court's office. I put my handwritten document on the counter and paid the filing fee. The clerk looked over my notice of appeal, stamped it August 3, 1983, and kindly made a copy for me.

The next day, the Folmers' farm was sold on the front steps of the Burleigh County Courthouse. The only bidder was the Bank of North Dakota, and it bid the exact amount of its debt. I never asked Russel and Anna Mae whether they were on the lawn of the courthouse when the sheriff held the sale, but I hoped they were not. I hoped they still had faith in me and in the legal system.

IN JULY, I had two grueling days of depositions in Room 460 of the United States Courthouse in Bismarck, where I questioned Ralph Leet, five district directors, and several other farmer program officials under oath. One afternoon, I was walking toward the women's room when I heard someone from behind me urgently calling "Ms. Vogel, Ms. Vogel!"

A fresh-faced young man was walking toward me at a fast clip. When he caught up with me, he said, "I'm Lynn Boughey, Judge Van Sickle's new law clerk."[2] He looked up and down the long hallway, as if to ensure he wouldn't be overheard. Then he whispered, "This is a somewhat unusual situation, and I'd appreciate it if you never told anyone about this conversation, but Judge Van Sickle told me to tell you that you don't need to write any more long briefs."

I thought about this advice as I drove home from the Folmers' hearing. Judge Van Sickle didn't yet know that the stakes were much higher than North Dakota. This case wasn't just going to be about eighty-four hundred North Dakota farmers—if we could amend the class definition, it would cover about a quarter of a million farmers nationwide. By this point in the case, I felt I was being dragged along by forces beyond my control. To leave the case would have been like jumping out of a car speeding down a highway. All I could do was hang on. And

I didn't want to deprive Judge Van Sickle of all the new information and evidence I'd gained from the depositions. As soon as I could put all this new material in front of Judge Van Sickle, I was sure he would be as appalled as I was. I still harbored hope that he would require FmHA to replace the incompetent, biased district directors with competent, legally trained neutral hearing officers.

A few days later, Andrew and I were at the Grand Forks city swimming pool. I sat at a table with an umbrella, my briefcase open beside me, as Andrew splashed in the shallow end. Every few minutes, I glanced up to make sure he was okay. But I lost track of time, and when I looked again, he wasn't among the little kids in the shallow end. I frantically scanned the kiddie pool area. Then I noticed a small blond boy standing at the edge of the deep end, looking at the water, ready to jump in. Fear flooded my body. Would I or the daydreaming teen lifeguard on the other side of the pool be able to reach him in time?

As soon I started toward Andrew, his small figure stepped back from the edge and came running toward me.

"Mom, I went to the deep end and I looked in! But I decided it was too deep for me."

I hugged him and told him how smart he was to make that decision all on his own. He hadn't learned prudence from me. Being with Andrew was my rare escape from the unbelievable pressures of the case.

As the summer progressed, I gathered information on other agencies' use of administrative law judges and drafted a brief on the requirements laid out by the United States Supreme Court for administrative hearings in the 1976 case *Mathews v. Eldridge*. But I couldn't complete it until I got the deposition transcripts back from the court reporter. Even though we were paying double the standard rate for a quick turnaround (Burt had volunteered to pay the costs of the depositions, which was many thousands of dollars), the depositions didn't arrive until the end of August. The hearing was scheduled for September 20.

I sank into despair when I looked at the stack of depositions, containing more than four hundred pages of testimony, and the boxes of documents I'd received from Annear, which contained thousands of pages of unorganized reports and records.

How would I keep all this straight in my head? My eye fell on the tattered hardback copy of the Code of Federal Regulations that I'd first used with Tom

Nichols, and at every FmHA hearing since. My copy of the CFR was color-coded with plastic paper clips.

Since coming to Grand Forks, I'd been on a shopping "diet." If I never went into a store, I reasoned that I wouldn't be tempted to buy anything. But now it was time to break that rule, and I went on a run to K-Mart with Andrew to buy office supplies for me and a luxury for him: a fresh box of Crayola crayons. He was thrilled—his old crayons were worn to nubbins. While Andrew played school with two girls from the neighborhood, I put boxes of colored paper clips on a TV tray in front of me and began reading the depositions for evidence to insert into the brief.

I decided to use a blue paper clip to mark issues related to a failure to implement the deferral law; a green paper clip whenever Leet or one of the others admitted that there had been droughts or that prices were at historic lows; an orange paper clip for testimony that showed the hearing process was unfair and biased. A yellow paper clip would represent seizure of a farmer's income before there was a due process hearing; red would be for admissions of FmHA's "from-the-top" hierarchical structure that meant subordinates of a state director couldn't be neutral hearing officers; purple was for failure to comply with the preliminary injunction order; and white was for everything else.

Back at the office, the brief on the administrative hearing officer issue swelled to over a hundred pages with every assertion meticulously referenced to a deposition with the page and line numbers. The final brief in support of a permanent injunction was only about fifty pages. My father read both and gave me some advice: "Sounds like you are on the right track . . . but I think both briefs are a little on the long side." He had a point.

I called Burt and Allan and told them I didn't see any need for them to come to Bismarck on September 20. I'd have all the briefs filed by then and didn't think the hearing was worth the time and expense. They agreed. I anticipated the only excitement at the hearing would be Annear's screams of outrage when I gave him a copy of the motion to turn the case into a national class action on the morning of the twentieth.

I wrote a short letter to the lead plaintiffs saying they could come to the September 20 hearing if they wanted to, but I thought it would be only an hour or two long, and I'd understand if they didn't want to spend gas money.

On Friday, September 16, I mailed my magnum opus, the document that I believed would change Judge Van Sickle's mind on the need for administrative law judges, captioned "Brief in Support of Disqualifying District Directors and the State Director of FmHA from Ruling on Foreclosure Appeals." I'd cut it down to sixty-one pages.

On Monday afternoon, I was ready. I had a suitcase in my mother's car and I'd told Mary I'd be at her house in Mandan by nine o'clock. My mother had already collected Andrew from Montessori. A big brief bag (borrowed from my father) contained the pleadings in the case, the Code of Federal Regulations, and a few key cases: *Goldberg v. Kelly*, *Mathews v. Eldridge*, *Kimbell Foods*, and *Curry v. Block*.

In my briefcase, I had a legal atom bomb: multiple copies of a motion to change the case into a national class action and a national class complaint. The complaint was virtually the same as the one I'd filed in March, but now the class was defined as "all farmers with farm loans from Farmers Home Administration," and there were eight new lead plaintiffs located by Dale Reesman.[3]

I saved room in my briefcase for five copies of the final document, the Plaintiffs' Brief in Support of Permanent Injunctive Relief. It was based on the words of the defendants during the depositions and FmHA internal documents. I'd changed a few words in the brief and fixed some awkward punctuation that afternoon, but it was as perfect as I could make it. Donna was making copies, some for me to take to Bismarck, three to mail to Dale, Burt, and Allan and several more to be mailed to the nonprofits to be used in "litigation packets." I heard the hum of the copier cease as Donna left it to answer the phone.

"Sarah, Lynn Boughey is on line one."

Shit, I thought. *I bet he's calling to complain that I haven't turned in the final brief on the permanent injunction.*

"Hi Lynn, I bet you're calling because you're wondering where my brief is. I'll hand-deliver it to you tomorrow morning."

"That's not why I'm calling," he said. "I wanted to find out which witnesses you were bringing to the trial tomorrow."

Witnesses to the trial tomorrow?

BY FIVE FORTY-FIVE, I was on the road in my mother's huge Oldsmobile. At the same time, Dwight Coleman was heading south from up near the Canadian border, in a rickety old junker that could go no faster than sixty miles an hour, wearing his work boots and jeans, with a clean shirt in the backseat. The Folmers and the Hatfields said they'd meet me at the federal courthouse at nine the next morning. The Crows Hearts and the McCabes wouldn't be able to make it.

As I drove, I pondered Allan's advice: "Call the defendants as your opening witnesses." I had the color-coded depositions with me. I knew what to ask them, and I knew how they'd answer. I also knew what questions to ask Dwight, the Folmers, and the Hatfields: I'd simply follow the arc of their affidavits and rely on their honesty for the rest.

Dwight arrived at my sister's before I did. She welcomed him even though I'd forgotten to tell her that Dwight (who I knew couldn't afford a hotel) would be another guest. We had bologna sandwiches for dinner, and glasses of milk. I'd asked my father for advice on preparing my clients for testifying the next day, and I practiced first on Dwight.

"I've never been in a courtroom before," Dwight said.

"That's all right."

"I've never testified about anything."

"All you have to do is tell the truth," I said. "Answer the question they ask you if you know the answer but don't try to guess if you don't know the answer."

"Okay," Dwight said.

"After you answer the question, *stop*. Don't volunteer more information!"

"Don't give them any extra words, huh?"

"Right! And try not to argue. Try not to get mad."

"You bet."

"How do you feel?"

"Like a chicken about to get his neck wrung," Dwight said, grinning.

We both laughed. Dwight's good mood lifted mine.

The next morning, I ran through the same instructions for testifying with the Folmers and the Hatfields. Everyone was cheerful and optimistic: I realized that they viewed Judge Van Sickle as an ally. I told them about decorum: they were to be quiet and respectful and try not to show reactions, even if Annear was a jerk. I led them to the left side of the courtroom and they sat down behind me. (I realized later that I'd made a real rookie mistake in sitting on the wrong side of the courtroom. The tables weren't labeled, but traditionally the one next to the jury was for the plaintiff.) I had the entire counsel table to myself, so I spread out all the depositions and briefs. I put the preliminary injunction order in the center for symbolic strength. On a fresh yellow legal pad, I wrote an outline for an opening statement: (1) deferral; (2) fair hearing.

Magically, adrenaline overcame my desire for a cigarette.

Annear entered with an overstuffed briefcase, followed by about ten FmHA employees. I recognized some of them from their depositions. He noisily unpacked a mess of papers.

I am better organized than he is, I realized.

Helen Monteith and Lynn Boughey quietly entered from a side door and sat in the jury box. I cast a grateful glance toward Lynn, who kept his poker face.

At ten ten, the deputy clerk came in and called out, "All rise, the Honorable Bruce M. Van Sickle is presiding!" The court reporter (who had also recorded the depositions) came in and set up his machine. The deputy clerk and the court reporter looked alike—I realized they were brothers, both with the last name Emineth.

Judge Van Sickle began by saying that the trial would involve the "root merits" of the case, not the contempt motions, and also that it would not involve the "motion to amend the complaint to extend the scope of the class to all debtors within the jurisdiction of the federal courts."

That's a funny way to describe the national class, I thought, not realizing that Judge Van Sickle was already wrestling with the implications of encroaching on the jurisdictions of other district court judges throughout the country.

"Since the laboring oar is with the plaintiffs, would the plaintiffs proceed?"

My first trial had begun.

I walked to the podium with my two most recent briefs. "During the course of this trial we will seek to establish two main principles," I said quietly. The first was that farmers had a legal right to apply for a deferral, and that right was not being provided by FmHA. The second was that under principles set out by the United States Supreme Court, farmers had a right to a package of rights that could be summarized as a "fair trial and fair tribunal" and that those rights were being disregarded by FmHA.

I walked back to my chair and Annear approached the bench to make his opening statement.

Annear started with the same "mountain out of a molehill" argument that had failed to persuade Judge Van Sickle at the preliminary injunction. He complained that the court and the plaintiffs hadn't accepted his offer to dismiss the *Coleman* case so that FmHA could bring two foreclosure cases against two guinea pig farmers, one in the east before Judge Benson and one in the west before Judge Van Sickle.

I was stunned. He'd had months to develop a substantive response to the arguments I'd made at the preliminary injunction hearing. And here he was still telling me how I should run my case! How ridiculous to suggest that after I'd won round one, I should just fold up my tent and creep out of the courtroom, so he could win round two. No way was that going to happen! I stared daggers at the back of his gray suit jacket. But as he kept speaking, in a loud combative voice, with obvious irritation directed toward Judge Van Sickle for not having dismissed the case outright, my mood improved. I wasn't a trial lawyer, but I had enough common sense not to attack a judge to his face—in his own courtroom!

Annear eventually moved to the merits, repeating the argument made in March that there were only a handful of foreclosure cases, while there were 8,400 farmer borrowers. He claimed that this proved there was no need for an injunction. He asserted that FmHA employees were magnanimous and offered an "informal-type" deferral. He complained that the preliminary injunction was overbroad, and covered people who were so well off that they should graduate from FmHA or that people that needed to be foreclosed on due to divorce (*Huh?* I thought marital status was a prohibited consideration under the ECOA) or other factors.

"So, all in all, the proof by the United States or by the individual defendants in this particular case, we feel, will be that they have done the job that Congress set out and they have done it adequately," Annear concluded.

"Miss Vogel," the judge asked, "will you please proceed with your evidence?"

Game on!

I walked back to the podium and said, "Plaintiffs call Ralph Leet as their first witness."

CHAPTER 20

Nothing but the Truth

R alph Leet was not happy that I called him as my first witness. He whispered to Annear, and Annear whispered back. Finally, Leet rose to his feet and went to the witness chair, where the deputy clerk of court swore him in: "Do you agree to tell the truth, the whole truth, and nothing but the truth?"

"I do," said Leet.

I intended to ask Leet questions about the FmHA appeal process and to have his own words show Judge Van Sickle how grotesquely unfair the FmHA appeal process was for farmers who were struggling to retain their farms against false accusations by incompetent FmHA employees. Even with all the material I had, I knew it wouldn't be easy. Leet was self-righteous and defensive. He also despised me and had told Richard Woodley, the *Life magazine* reporter, I was wasting taxpayers' money by delaying "the inevitable demise" of poorly managed farms.[1]

It was very difficult to win an FmHA appeal. Farmers had the "burden of proof." This meant they had to show that FmHA was wrong in accelerating the farmers' loans and deciding to foreclose. FmHA's statements in the notice of acceleration—such as accusations of conversion, bad management, or failure to cooperate—were deemed to be true and the farmer had to prove that each of those accusations was wrong. To do that, the borrower often needed FmHA witnesses and documents, but the appeal regulations gave farmers no power to make the necessary FmHA-employed witnesses come to the hearing, and often farmers could not get copies of important documents necessary to make their case from FmHA. The cards were dealt by a crooked dealer, and the farmers got only bad cards.

"Are you aware of the fact that the burden of proof is on the borrower to prove that the decision being appealed is wrong?" I asked Leet.

"No," he replied. "I don't think that's true."[2]

I felt like a predator who caught scent of its prey. I'd been through so many hearings that I knew the appeal regulations by heart; Leet obviously did not know them. In fact, he had never once attended those hearings. At his deposition in July, he'd told me that early in his career he'd attended one hearing, but as state director, he'd attended "none."

"Are you aware of the fact that 7 CFR 1900.57(a) states that the appellant will bear the burden of proving the original decision erroneous?"

"No."

"Could I show you a copy of the regulation?" I asked as I handed it to Leet.

"Is that the FmHA regulation?"

I glanced at Judge Van Sickle to see if he noticed that Leet couldn't even recognize an FmHA regulation. He was looking on with interest.

"Yes, it is," I said.

"Okay," Leet said, weakly.

"Could you read the first sentence of 1900.57(a)?"

"Okay, 'The hearing will be—'"

"Excuse me," Annear said. "I'm going to object to this question. If she wants to have [the regulation] marked properly and have an instrument introduced according to the Rules of Evidence, then I'd have no objection; but just to read from something that we don't know what it is and isn't of record, I would object to it."

Surely it wasn't proper for Annear to object to having an FmHA employee read one of its own agency regulations? I panicked: my whole case depended on arguments about law and regulations. I had no idea how to introduce the regulation into evidence. I hadn't needed to know the Rules of Evidence since law school.

Judge Van Sickle saved me. "Well, of course the regulations—the Court can take judicial notice[3] of them . . . I overrule. Would you please go ahead."

Now Leet had to read the regulation. "The hearing will be an informal proceeding at which the appellant will bear the burden of providing the initial decision erroneous," he read quickly.

"Excuse me, Mr. Leet. Is that '*proving* the initial decision erroneous'?"

"Yes."

Leet's inquisition went on for two hours, as I asked questions starting with "Isn't it true that . . ." followed by description of an abusive practice by FmHA. Leet had started his testimony in a foul mood and became more and more defensive and argumentative, which was fine by me. Sometimes he changed his story from what he'd said at his deposition. I had every page color-coded and could quickly find what he'd said then and make him read the answers he had given previously. It gave me a chance to show he was not a truthful witness.

The first time he lied, I picked up the deposition transcript and was walking toward Leet when I noticed the court reporter urgently shaking his head and rolling his eyes in the direction of the deputy clerk, who was curling his left index finger in a *come here* gesture. In his right hand, he was waving a sticker marked "Plaintiffs' Exhibit 1."

Obediently, I walked over, and tentatively asked, "Could I mark this Exhibit one?"

With his eyes cast downward on a blank sheet marked "Exhibit List," the clerk whispered, "Show it to Annear, say what it is, and come back to me."

I walked over to Annear and held the deposition transcript in front of him and said, "July 18, 1983, Deposition of Ralph Leet." Annear said nothing, so I walked back to the deputy clerk, who promptly put the Plaintiffs' Exhibit 1 sticker on the cover of the transcript. There was no objection from Annear. Apparently, I'd done it right! This was the first of many times that the court-room staff took mercy on me and guided me around the courtroom with smiles, frowns, glances, and gestures—none of which were recorded in the final transcript, but I will never forget the brothers Emineth, who were fond of my father and decided to teach me the ropes that day in the courtroom.

One point I wanted to make during Leet's testimony was that farmers had a property interest, protected by the due process clause in the Fifth Amendment to the U.S. Constitution, in the amounts of money that were listed in the Farm and Home Plan for family living and farm operating expenses. I needed to show that receipt of family living and farm operating expenses was a "property right" deserving of protection by the Constitution, not a "mere expectation."

"Do you view the Farm and Home Plan as a contract?" I asked.

"I view it as a very strong agreement between our borrowers and the government," Leet replied. "Whether it's a legal contract, I don't know."

I asked whether he recalled, during his deposition, saying, "A Farm and Home Plan is really the contract between Farmers Home and the borrower."

"Mm-hmm," Leet acknowledged.

I made him read out loud the various times on July 18 that he had said that Farm and Home Plans were contracts, on which both the farmer and FmHA could rely. These statements by Leet firmed up the property right that could not be taken from the farmer without a fair hearing.

Leet seemed to be under the impression that if FmHA won all—or almost all—of its appeal hearings, that meant everything was fine. He bragged that FmHA won over 90 percent of its appeals. He likely wasn't aware of the briefs I had submitted to Judge Van Sickle that compared FmHA appeal statistics to the Social Security Administration and Veterans Administration appeals. The latter agencies used administrative hearing officers who were independent and neutral and the agencies lost about 50 percent of the time. I hoped that Judge Van Sickle would see that the high success rate enjoyed by FmHA was in fact proof that the process was unfair.

After I thought I'd asked enough questions to establish the flaws in the appeal process, I asked, "Is it true that on January first, 1983, that operating loans of Farmers Home were fifty-eight percent delinquent?"

"They're forty-two percent delinquent now."

"Is it true that the farm-ownership loans were thirty-eight percent delinquent?"

"That is correct."

"And emergency loans fifty-six percent?"

"Correct."

"And economic emergency loans sixty-one percent?"

"Yes."

"Have those delinquency rates risen since 1978?"

"Yes."

"Are they the highest that you have ever known?"

"Yes."

"Is it not true that farmers are in an economic squeeze?"

"Yes."

"Do you recall the plaintiffs requesting that you produce all documents pertaining to the implementation of 7 U.S. Code 1981a?"

"Yes."

"Do you recall admitting that the only document that referred to 7 U.S. Code 1981a was the statute itself?"

I waited for his answer. By admitting that no regulation or document referred to 7 USC 1981a, it would be tantamount to admitting that FmHA had never implemented the law.

"No; I think we proceeded with the procedure—our reamortization procedure, and produced that for you."

Leet had obviously been coached. One of the recent gambits of the national office in defending FmHA's failure to defer debts was to equate deferral with reamortization (in which overdue interest was rolled into principal and a new loan made with a much higher interest rate).

I made Leet admit that reamortization increased farmers' interest payments; for farmers who had received loans in the 1970s, their interest expense could double. He resisted giving forthright answers, but overall his testimony demonstrated that reamortization and deferral were not the same.

After grilling Leet, I was satisfied I had shown through his testimony that FmHA had not implemented the deferral law, and that FmHA routinely denied farmers due process of law by freezing the income of the farmers months in advance of a deeply flawed hearing run by biased hearing officers.

Now it was Annear's turn. He didn't use the podium, as I had done. Instead he strode up to the witness chair, where Leet beamed at him like a teenaged girl in love. Annear paced back and forth, shooting well-researched questions to Leet, and Leet shot back well-rehearsed answers. It was like a scene in a television courtroom drama.

"What were your instructions from the national office concerning reamortization as far as farm programs are concerned and operating loans?" Annear asked.

"We should reamortize or consolidate or defer when that action will be to the benefit of both the borrower and the government; and this is one reason why we left so many accounts delinquent. We carried them delinquent; we had in fact a moratorium already."

"You're talking about an unofficial moratorium. What are we talking about as far as period of time is concerned for some of these borrowers?"

"Well, some borrowers are delinquent for five or six, seven years, and we'll continue with them if they have a reasonable chance for success. That's the key."

"Pardon?"

"That's the key. If our borrower has a reasonable chance of success, delinquency is not a factor for action on our part," Leet said.

If our borrower has a reasonable chance of success. Where were these two lovebirds going with their choreographed "unofficial moratorium" argument? Plain and simple: they planned a character assassination of my lead plaintiffs.

As Leet and Annear tossed well-rehearsed questions and answers back and forth, Annear's storyline of the case emerged. According to the defense, FmHA was not a "social welfare" program but rather a commercial-style lender that, due to the compassion of its loan officers, always stuck with honest hardworking farmers even if they were five or six years delinquent. Further, FmHA employees sent delinquent farmers helpful letters and met in person with those farmers to give them advice on how to improve their management skills and profitability. FmHA gave that advice long before an acceleration notice was sent.

Leet proclaimed that delinquency was "not a factor for action on our part" as long as the farmer had a reasonable chance for success. Only a tiny handful of bad managers, who didn't deserve to keep farming, did not qualify for this "unofficial moratorium."

Annear coaxed Leet to give examples for why FmHA might stop working with a particular farmer despite the "unofficial moratorium."

"Well, like say we have a mortgage on some crops or on livestock, and they sell it at a livestock ring or at the elevator and they put it in their name only and use the funds or put it in their children's names, or put it in their wife's name, and then use the funds as they so desire, therefore defeating the effects of our lien."

It wasn't hard to interpret this. Leet was saying farmers like my clients were probably crooks.

Annear asked for more examples of why an account might be accelerated.

"Leasing a farm without permission, keeping the money thereby," Leet rattled off. "Failure to cooperate to any degree with the farm plan or cooperate to any degree with FmHA clientele; extremely unwise management decisions consistently that happen over a period of time and we cannot correct by our supervisory guidance; refusal to accept advice."

"Excuse me, Mr. Annear," Judge Van Sickle interrupted. "When the decision is made to accelerate, the Farmers Home Administration must proceed with the acceleration; it can't withdraw from the decision, is that true?"

"No, sir," Leet said. "That's not true."

"All right. How and when do you withdraw?"

Leet said if a borrower corrected the problem on his account, Leet could personally withdraw the acceleration.

"Are you the only officer who can?" the judge asked.

"Yes, sir," Leet replied.

Annear continued: "There was a reference in [the preliminary injunction order] to a social welfare program. Has there been any determination made by FmHA as to whether or not this is a welfare or a social-welfare-type program?"

"I've never known that to be, never thought it to be, and never heard it to be," Leet replied.

I was stunned at Annear's gall. Did Annear think that Judge Van Sickle had invented the "social welfare" concept in his preliminary injunction order? Did Annear—an assistant U.S. attorney—think a judge could disregard the United States Supreme Court's unanimous ruling in *United States v. Kimbell Foods* that explicitly found that FmHA was a social welfare program?

"What type of people or borrowers do you receive out of the flow from the farming industry?" Annear asked.

"We receive many, many good people who are beginning farmers, who have low-equity situations; we receive people who have had adverse situations that need refinance; we receive the people who other creditors will not make a loan to and therefore have a higher risk involved. That doesn't mean they're not good people."

I glared at Leet. *Good people, my eye!* My clients were good people too! He was acting like God Almighty, deciding who to let into heaven and who to keep out. I was furious at his sanctimonious satisfaction with the arbitrary and cruel FmHA process of selecting the "bad people."

"And what have been your instructions concerning these farm programs and going along with the farmers during this period of time?"

"Our instructions from the national office and the instructions from our state office is we're going to continue with all farm borrowers that have a reasonable chance for success, delinquent or not. That has consistently been the policy of my administration; it's been the policy in Farmers Home in as many years as I can remember. You collect according to ability to pay."

What a bunch of bullshit, I thought. Leet's testimony was completely at odds with what I knew about Charles Shuman's delinquency reduction memos.

I jumped up for redirect.

"Is it not true that the notice of acceleration specifically says to the borrower that even if the borrower cures the default that that will have no impact on FmHA's decision to foreclose?"

"I don't recall that terminology," Leet said.

"Mr. Leet, you do sign these letters, don't you?"

"Oh, yes, sure."

"And you're not familiar with that paragraph?"

I made him read the paragraph from the Folmers' real estate acceleration that said, "If you submit to the United States any payment insufficient to pay the entire indebtedness which has already been accelerated or insufficient to comply with any arrangements agreed to between FmHA and yourself, such payments will not cancel the effect of this notice."

As Leet left the witness stand, he looked at me with contempt and loathing. I didn't give a damn. I turned to look back at my five clients for the first time that morning and their tense gazes met mine. I turned away quickly. I didn't need a reminder of the extraordinarily high stakes that they were facing. I knew they were rooting for me, even if it seemed I didn't know much about how to do a trial. I'd introduced one exhibit and questioned one witness, and I already felt worn out.

During the lunch break, I reviewed the Hatfields' and the McCabes' affidavits and appeal files before I examined my next witness, Harold Aasmundstad, their district director in southeastern North Dakota. I now could anticipate that Annear's plan was to use Aasmundstad's testimony to drag my clients through the mud.

I had the courtroom to myself, except for one quiet security guy in the corner. I assumed he was not watching me, but rather keeping watch *for* me, in case a Gordon Kahl supporter showed up. Kahl had died in a fiery shootout in Arkansas on June 3, after killing another law enforcement officer.

When the Hatfields came back from lunch, I warned them I would call them to the stand after Aasmundstad was done testifying. They were ready.

At one thirty-three P.M., the clerk called "All rise!" Aasmundstad took his place on the witness chair, and I stepped back behind the lectern.

"Mr. Aasmundstad, is it not true that prior to the preliminary injunction it was the practice within your district not to release any funds for family living or farm operating expenses to the farmer once an acceleration had been approved?"

"Yes, ma'am."

"Is it not true that the income was cut off to the farmer before the farmer had an opportunity to have a hearing?"

"Yes."

"You have an agricultural economics degree; is that not correct?"

"Yes."

"You have no legal training."

"No, I haven't," Aasmundstad said.

Aasmundstad's testimony showed he believed he was part of a smoothly functioning system. If one of them accelerated a chattel loan, a fellow district director serving as a hearing officer would be the hearing officer for him, and he would reciprocate on their accelerations. He socialized with Leet, other district directors, and county supervisors. Before and after a hearing, he felt free to call county supervisors with questions about the borrower, and he felt no need to advise the farmer or the farmer's lawyer of those calls. (Any administrative law judge who did the same would be violating ethical rules about ex parte contacts.) I hoped these admissions would make Judge Van Sickle realize the deep unfairness of the FmHA appeals system even when the hearing officer appeared to be a pretty good fellow.

I moved on to how he handled appeals of real estate acceleration notices that had been signed by his boss, Ralph Leet. A theme of my briefs was that hearing officers who worked for Leet, and whose job evaluations were done by Leet could *never* be neutral. When Aasmundstad said he got advice on how to rule in the hearings he conducted from the head of the farmer loan programs section,

LeRoy Nayes, I asked, "Are you aware that Mr. Nayes works for Mr. Leet?" I thought it an innocuous question, but I'd pushed one of Annear's buttons.

"I don't believe the record indicates that," Annear said, jumping up to object. "I think the record indicates that Mr. Nayes was an employee of the government of the United States."

I froze, and then to my relief Judge Van Sickle stepped in to give me an on-the-spot lesson on how to rephrase my question.

Judge Van Sickle leaned over his bench to look down at Aasmundstad. "It is correct, isn't it, you're an employee of the United States?"

Aasmundstad answered, "Yes."

"Your supervisor is Ralph Leet; is that right?"

"Yes, sir."

"Please go ahead," the judge said to me.

After a few more questions, I passed the ball to Annear.

Annear led Aasmundstad through a series of background questions designed to show his experience (he'd been with FmHA for thirty-one years) and data showing FmHA's general benevolence to farmers. Annear questioned Aasmundstad on the purpose of the Farm and Home Plan, and I was delighted to hear Aasmundstad call it an "agreement, informal contract, on how the operation is going to be carried out."

"In other words, is it in the form of a budget?" Annear asked.

What? I thought. I should have objected, because that is not at all what Aasmundstad said during direct examination or at his deposition, but I was too slow. Before I could even rise to object, Aasmundstad said, "Yes, it is."

They went through a long give-and-take about how hard FmHA employees worked to resolve farmers' problems. Annear smoothly transitioned to questions about *Mr.* McCabe and *Mr.* Hatfield. I stiffened with anger. Diane McCabe and June Hatfield were farmers too; their names were on the promissory notes. I'd had enough of the agency's sexism.

"How long has FmHA been dealing with Mr. Hatfield?" Annear asked.

I jumped to my feet.

"Your Honor, could I interject a moment? It's Mr. *and Mrs.* Hatfield. They're both borrowers."

Annear cast a withering look at me, but thereafter he began to use "they," "them," and "the Hatfields" and "the McCabes."

I flashed a glance back at Anna Mae and June, and they nodded with approval. Their posture said, *Damn straight! We're farmers too!* Three of our four female lead plaintiffs were full-time farmers and one (June) farmed nights and weekends and worked off-farm on weekdays to pay farm bills.

"And what is the status of *Mr. and Mrs. Hatfield* at this time, then, as far as farming operations are concerned?" Annear asked Aasmundstad. "In other words, are they farming or are they not?"

"I understand they are not," Aasmundstad answered.

I struggled to keep a poker face. *The Hatfields were still farming!* Aasmundstad's assumption that they weren't farming was a perfect illustration of FmHA's practice of using gossip, unfounded assumptions, and outright lies to deprive hardworking farmers of their homes, farms, and dreams. I couldn't wait to cross-examine him.

"And was their account ever accelerated by FmHA?"

"Yes, sir."

"When would that have been?"

"There was an acceleration January 18, 1983."

Annear had Aasmundstad read aloud the reasons for the Hatfields' and the McCabes' loan accelerations. I did not object at all. I wanted all this in the record. Annear wrapped up by emphasizing the low milk production of the McCabes, implying that they were lazy, incompetent farmers.

"I have no further questions," Annear said.

"I have some questions," Judge Van Sickle interjected, before I could cross-examine. I sank back in my chair and watched Judge Van Sickle cross-examine Aasmundstad on behalf of the absent McCabes with a skill I only aspired to have. First, he showed that delinquency was not the reason for the acceleration of the McCabes.

"So while that [delinquency] was a factor of concern, that was probably not what triggered your decision at this time; is that right?"

"Yes, sir; that's right," Aasmundstad answered.

"All right. Another reason you gave was failure to pay taxes . . . was that a triggering factor or was that also something that . . . didn't trigger the decision?"

"I would say that it did not trigger the decision, sir."

"Now I read this, 'failure to liquidate voluntarily when requested,' that as you recited it sounds as though, 'Well, if you won't cooperate with me, I'll nail you';

but I interpret that rather to be that 'given we are denied that option, we must use the mandatory procedure to protect our equity'; is that how you reason?"

I squirmed in frustration on my hard chair. *Why was Judge Van Sickle giving FmHA a break?* "Failure to liquidate voluntarily" wasn't a verbal shorthand for a different rationale. FmHA employees meant it literally. I'd learned that FmHA had fostered a culture within which its employees had an exaggerated view of their own wisdom. When farmers who had the temerity to believe they knew best how to manage their own farms rejected their advice, FmHA staff often retaliated. "Failure to cooperate," "failure to follow advice," and "failure to liquidate voluntarily" were often used by sanctimonious FmHA employees to "nail" farmers who thought for themselves. I felt Judge Van Sickle was cutting Aasmundstad and his co-defendants undeserved slack.

"Yes, sir."

Aasmundstad's only rationale left standing was the drop of dairy income. I wished Don and Diane were there to talk about how FmHA wouldn't release income from the dairy assignment to buy feed or supplements. I remembered Diane's protest at the appeal hearing the summer before: *Farmers get to feed their soil. Why won't you release money so we can feed our cows?* In fact, the reason Don and Diane weren't at the trial was that they were desperately haying ditches to provide feed for the cows for the coming winter.

"Don't you feel as you review the record of McCabe that in your Farm and Home plans where you accepted or agreed to a program which would require a production in the neighborhood of eight or nine thousand pounds of milk per cow per year . . . don't you think you were assisting him to get into trouble?" the judge asked.

In other words, Judge Van Sickle was asking whether FmHA was *also* a bad manager, if its accusations against the McCabes were true.

"I hope not, sir," Aasmundstad said.

Finally, Judge Van Sickle asked Aasmundstad about the Farm and Home Plan.

"What type of factor or what type of incident would cause you to accelerate before the annual plan has had a chance to run its course?"

"The one I could think of immediately, sir, would be a grain or livestock conversion."

"Anything else? Any other typical problem?"

"Well, if they just left the farm, just dropped everything, which very seldom happens, but it has."

Judge Van Sickle homed in on this answer. Earlier, Aasmundstad had said that the Hatfields had quit farming.

"Do you have a policy against continuing—and I look now to the discussion of the Hatfield case—do you have a policy that if you engage in a loan program with someone who is a farmer and that farmer retires or leaves the operation, you feel it is advisable to pull the money in and put it back out on an operating farm? Is that one of your policies?"

"Yes, sir; because the objectives for the loan will never be reached."

"I see. The primary objective of preserving the farm operation by a family."

"Yes, sir."

Now Judge Van Sickle looked at me.

"I would like to call George Hatfield to the stand, please," I said.

George confidently came forward. His brown hair was neatly combed, and it had the type of ridge that showed he usually wore a cap. His neck was reddened by the sun. His hands—huge and gnarly—demonstrated he'd worked hard as a farmer and in all weather. His eyes crinkled with a smile as he was sworn in. He was very happy to be on the witness stand.

"Mr. Hatfield, are you a plaintiff in this case?"

"Yes, I am."

"Are you a Farmers Home borrower?"

"Yes, I am."

"Are you a former farmer?" I asked.

"A former farmer?"

"Yes."

"I'm a former farmer and a present farmer," George answered.

"You presently are farming?"

"Yes."

I turned around to give Annear an evil smile.

"How many acres does your farm have?"

"Eight hundred acres."

"How many acres did you plant this year?"

"Approximately seven hundred seventy acres."

"What crops did you plant?"

"Wheat, barley, and corn."

"And you're living on the farm?"

"That's correct."

"And working on the farm."

"That's correct."

Even Judge Van Sickle was suppressing a smile.

"Do you have any explanation for Mr. Aasmundstad's belief that you aren't farming any longer?" I asked.

"Well, we did rent it out last year."

"Why did you rent it out last year?"

"Well, we were told that that would be probably be best."

"Who told you that?"

"The county director."

Like every other farmer in the state, the Hatfields had suffered from drought, low prices, and high costs. In addition, they'd been mistreated by FmHA with respect to their dairy herd and the milk assignment. George explained that he'd been told by FmHA that he had no options other than to sell out. He was never offered a deferral of payments. At FmHA's request, he sold most of his good machinery (at low prices) and tried to sell the land, but there were no bids, so he and his wife decided to go back to farming with a loan from the local bank. I asked George if he also had a job.

"Yes. I'm the Dickey County highway superintendent." I knew Judge Van Sickle would understand the significance of that job. Dickey County was a farm and ranch county, and George was the person that the county commissioners relied on to keep the roads in good shape so farmers could get their crops and cattle to market. George was the person who made sure the roads were plowed in the winter so children could get to school, workers to work, and sick people to hospitals. Having this job meant George was among the most reliable and respected people in Dickey County. And Judge Van Sickle would also know that a substantial loan from the local bank—even after FmHA dumped them— meant the Hatfields had good character and good reputations in their own community, among the people who knew them best.

I asked George about how their delinquencies started. First, they had decided to buy cows rather than rent them. The local bank had advanced the money to purchase the cows, on an oral promise by FmHA that it would reimburse the bank. Then FmHA reneged on that promise.

Further, FmHA had a dairy assignment of 70 percent of the Hatfields' dairy income (even though Farmers Home hadn't lent them the money to buy the cows in the first place) and wouldn't release any income from the cows, not even enough to pay the bank's interest. For two years, George and June begged FmHA to release the dairy assignment so they could pay the bank, but FmHA ignored their requests. At last, they sold the cows—at a loss—in order to pay the bank, but it wasn't enough. They still owed $20,000, and June was making a monthly payment to the bank from her paycheck. It was the same bank she now worked at, and FmHA's conduct had even jeopardized her job.

"Did Farmers Home later accuse you of being a bad manager because you sold off your dairy herd?" I asked.

"That's correct," George said.

I asked George if he had ever had a hearing on an acceleration. Yes, he had. And he had won the hearing. Why? Because FmHA had failed to tell the Hatfields about their right to apply for a deferral on their rural housing loan. What happened next? They applied for the deferral on that loan but were denied because of their off-farm jobs.

I asked George to read from his own hearing transcript, about the reasons (such as drought) that he was asking for a deferral on the farm loans.

"I'm going to object to this unless the transcript is marked and offered in evidence," Annear said.

I was walking toward the clerk to have the transcript marked when I was stopped in my tracks by Judge Van Sickle.

"I have a problem," he said. "It seems to me that what that gentleman said about the drought is hearsay. Could we go on to something else?"

I had no idea how to respond to the assertion that the drought was "hearsay," so I responded by doubling down and offering another example of "hearsay," by saying, "Well, even the county supervisor said that there had been a very severe drought."

Now the judge and I were in a debate.

"What is your point? That despite the fact of the drought, he made the decision?"

"Despite this, they accelerated the loans and they did not allow the Hatfields the opportunity to apply for deferral because of the drought."

Judge Van Sickle now realized that I didn't know how to dig myself out of a hearsay objection. I only dimly remembered from law school that the "hearsay rule" (a rule that kept statements that were other than first-person statements from being considered as evidence) had many exceptions. I couldn't remember either the rule or the exceptions. I could sense Annear enjoying my confusion and humiliation.

After what seemed like an eternity, as I stood frozen, Judge Van Sickle decided that he wanted to know what George's answer would be, and to do that he needed to help me. He proceeded as though he were a law school professor giving a demonstration.

"Were you present when whatever was said was said?" the judge asked George.

"Yeah. This is the transcript from our hearing."

"All right then. What you can do is *refresh your recollection* from the transcript and tell us what was said."

Then Judge Van Sickle looked meaningfully at me, and I took my cue.

"Mr. Hatfield, would you look at this transcript and *refresh your recollection* about what the county supervisor had said about why your farm hadn't sold?"

"Sam said there weren't even any bargain hunters buying at this time," George replied. "The way he put it, 'The people who have money aren't spending, and the ones that don't have money can't spend.'"

"And to *refresh your recollection*, did you during that hearing ask specifically for a deferral under 1981a?" I asked.

"Yes, we did."

"No further questions."

Now Annear stood up to cross-examine George. He started with how much money the Hatfields owed FmHA (quite properly, George gave only estimates) and how much he and June made at their jobs. When he asked about farm income, George explained how the years of drought, heat, and grasshoppers had reduced their expected income. When Annear aggressively demanded that George tell the court how much they owed on their chattel debt to FmHA, George patiently told him that it had been paid in full in 1981. It seemed to be news to Annear that the Hatfields owed FmHA money only on a farm ownership loan and rural housing. I smiled at Annear's lack of preparation and how badly his "ambush" was going. The more aggressive Annear got, the more reliable, honest, and hardworking George seemed. Finally Annear quit.

"You are excused, Mr. Hatfield," said Judge Van Sickle.

Now I called June.

June briskly rose from her seat, and the couple smiled at each other as they passed. She was brown-haired and petite, neatly dressed in a pantsuit with earrings and heels. I knew the Hatfields had woken up at about three that morning to get to Bismarck in time, but she looked fresh and alert.

I asked about her job at the First National Bank of Ellendale. She brightly answered that she had been a teller, but now she was an assistant cashier and the manager of Student Loans and Installment Loans. I hoped Judge Van Sickle would see what I saw: June was trusted, reliable, and highly regarded in a town where everybody knew everybody else. She was trusted with the bank's own money. She certainly didn't look like a "bad manager."

June had started at the bank in 1975 or 1976, because there was not enough money from the farm for medical insurance, which they needed because they had an asthmatic daughter. Very precisely, she said she made $1,000 a month and $353 went to pay the bank for the deficit on the loan for the dairy cattle, after FmHA had reneged on its promise to issue a loan that would pay off the bank loan. I clumsily tried to get June to tell the court that the bank president had contemporaneous written records of this promise, but Annear objected ("hearsay") and the objection was upheld. Still, the message had been delivered to Judge Van Sickle that the bank and the Hatfields had been grievously misled by FmHA.

"How much family living expenses has Farmers Home released to you in, say, the last four years?" I asked.

"They released one thousand dollars to us, in three years."

"Do you believe your job is in jeopardy right now?"

"Yes, very much so."

"Because of this cattle loan?"

"Yes. In fact, I know it was classified by bank examiners."

"I have no further questions," I said.

Annear walked toward June for cross-examination, scowling, intending to intimidate her. *Good luck*, I thought. I didn't think Annear had a chance in hell.

"Mrs. Hatfield, with regards to the visitation by FmHA, I believe that you'd be working during the day so *you* wouldn't know whether FmHA was coming out to visit *your husband* or not."

"That is not correct," June said. "I read the letter too and I would take time off. In fact, many of the visits were made while I was at home."

Annear pivoted to his argument that the Hatfields' farm had never made any money. June reminded him that before they sold the cows, "you were taking seventy percent of our milk check, which gave you between forty and fifty thousand dollars from that alone a year."

Annear changed the subject again, asking the amount of the initial loan to buy the dairy cattle. June said it was $77,000.

"And it was paid off, all but the twenty thousand dollars?" Annear asked.

"That is correct."

"Do you know why it [the sale] didn't pay it all off?"

"Yes, I do." I was proud of June for following my instructions. *Answer only the question that you are asked. Don't volunteer.*

"Why was that?" This was a rookie mistake: Annear asked an open-ended question to which he didn't know the answer and June took the bit and ran.

"Because cattle prices dropped terrifically," June said. "We paid between thirteen seventy-five and fourteen hundred dollars for each cow that we purchased. When we went to sell them, the market was down and you were lucky to get a thousand."

"Doesn't dairy livestock bring a premium price compared to slaughter cattle?"

"It depends on whether you have buyers there to buy them."

It was now my turn for redirect. I asked June where the income from the cows went before they were sold. She answered that 70 percent went to FmHA and they had to buy feed and pay all their living expenses out of the remainder.

"Have you ever asked Farmers Home to release some of that income to the bank so that you could keep the cows?"

"Yes, we did. Many times."

"What happened?"

"They declined. They wouldn't."

"Did you ever try to reach Mr. Leet and explain your situation and request relief from him?"

"Yes, my husband called him many times and no answer. The phone would ring and ring and ring and there wasn't an answer."

"Have you ever met with Mr. Leet?"

"Yes, we did."

"Did Mr. Leet offer any relief to you?"

"We met with Mr. Leet in Fargo in [U.S. senator] Mark Andrews's office and no, he didn't. He said there wouldn't be any more operating money for us. We wanted to explain our situation and we still feel that we can come out of this, and he says, 'What do you want to keep that farm for anyway?' Quote, unquote."

When she'd finished her testimony, June calmly walked back to her seat beside George and they clasped hands. Her major accomplishment had been shattering Leet's claim that FmHA did everything possible to help farmers succeed.

"Miss Vogel, is this a convenient place to break?" the judge asked.

"It certainly is."

"At this time we'll stand in recess until nine o'clock tomorrow morning." We all stood. It was four thirty and I felt as though I had been flattened by a bus. Every joint in my body hurt. Dwight grabbed all my briefcases and we crowded into the elevator. When we got out, there was a television crew in the lobby, which I ignored. I was too exhausted to talk to the press. June asked Anna Mae to walk in front of her and whispered, "If the bank knows I was here at this trial, I'll be fired."

Dwight drove us back to my sister's while I slumped down with my eyes closed, wondering how real trial lawyers like my father, or Burt, or Allan could do this day after day, and sometimes week after week. I obviously wasn't that type of lawyer. I was a desk lawyer, a paper lawyer, an office lawyer. I'd barely survived one day of a trial with a compassionate judge who was sympathetic to my clients. If there had been a jury present . . . or if I'd had Judge Benson . . . no . . . I didn't even want to imagine how much worse it could have been.

"MR. BINEGAR, IF A farmer came to you at an appeal hearing and said, 'Yes, I am delinquent, but I am unable to pay due to circumstances beyond my control,' would the acceleration of that loan be an error by Farmers Home?" My first witness the next morning was Glen Binegar, the district director for Burleigh County, where the Folmers farmed.

"I don't believe that the mere fact that it's delinquent would be a reason to foreclose in most cases."

"If a loan is accelerated, may the farmer still be considered for deferral relief?" I asked.

"Under most circumstances, I think they would not."

"You know of no reason you would—"

"Consider deferral," Binegar said.

"Are you familiar with 7 U.S. Code 1981a?" I asked.

He was not.

"If somebody says to you '7 USC' something or other, what does that mean to you?" I asked.

"It doesn't mean much to me."

"If somebody said '7 CFR' something or other, what would that mean to you?"

"Nothing."

I asked if anyone in the state FmHA office had legal training, and Binegar said he wasn't aware of anyone who did.

"If a legal question arose during a hearing, what would you do?"

"I would contact the State Office and they would probably get an answer from the United States attorney or the general counsel."

"But you don't know for sure."

"It would depend on the case, I'm sure."

"It would depend upon their perception of whether there was or was not a legal issue?"

"It could."

"But you're not sure."

"No, I'm not."[4]

"So you're basically familiar with FmHA procedures, is that correct?"

"I'm somewhat familiar with them, yes. I don't know them word for word—they are on file in our office and if we need to look it up, we can do so."

"You are aware, are you not, that when you're serving as hearing officer, you are supposed to be making decisions in light of applicable statutes and regulations?"

"Yes, I am."

I hoped that Judge Van Sickle would see the danger of having district directors who were ignorant of the law serve as hearing officers. "I have no further questions."

Annear rose to his feet and asked Binegar which of the lead plaintiffs resided in his district.

"Mr. and Mrs. Russel Folmer," Binegar answered.

"And have you brought the county file on Mr. and Mrs. Folmer?"

"Yes, I have."

I didn't object. I knew the Folmers' files backward and forward. This would be war, but unlike Annear, I knew the battlefield. Annear asked Binegar to recite the stated reasons for the June 30, 1982, acceleration of the Folmers' real estate debt.

"Is there an indication as to whether or not there was any livestock or cattle that were mortgaged to FmHA that had been sold without your agency's consent?" Annear asked.

"There are several indications in the file," Binegar answered, sounding well rehearsed. "There's a letter from a farmer program specialist to the county supervisor at Bismarck. It said, 'the file has been reviewed in regard to conversion of 51 head of livestock without proper release.'"

This false accusation had been thoroughly addressed during their appeal. It was total crap, but now, in open court, the Folmers were again accused of a crime for which they could be sent to a federal penitentiary for years.

Annear, satisfied that he'd delivered a fatal blow to the Folmers' credibility, rolled on with questions designed to show the Folmers were bad farmers, had low dairy production, and were delinquent on their taxes and loans. Binegar was cagey when asked about the value of their property compared to the value of the debt (the Folmers still had substantial equity in their farm), and said that "FmHA was *approaching* a deficient position with taxes and interest accruing."

"Is there any way that Mr. and Mrs. Folmer can survive this family-farm operation as they have it now?" Annear asked.

"The county supervisor and the county committee and myself and the hearing officer do not believe so."

Satisfied with his assault on the Folmers, who sat behind me trying very hard not to look humiliated, Annear said, "I have no further questions."

I began to stand up when Judge Van Sickle said, "I have some questions."

Immediately, the judge homed in on the dual role of district directors in accelerating debts and then serving as an appeal officer on the debts that were accelerated. After Binegar laid out the process, Judge Van Sickle paraphrased it.

"All right, so the county supervisor comes to you, who are the district director, and he says, 'This is a bad loan . . . I think we've got to accelerate it,' and you and he decide to accelerate. Now then the debtor says, 'Wait a minute. That's not what I think is a correct answer. I want to appeal.' Who does he appeal to?"

Binegar was boxed in. "That would be to me," he said.

"How do you tell him?"

"This instrument [the notice of acceleration] is sent to him and he has the opportunity for a hearing and if he would like to have it, he notifies us."

"But at this level, you don't say to him, 'You have a right to a hearing,' or anything like that. You don't invite him to come in or advise him that you will listen if he does come in anyway; is that correct?" Judge Van Sickle asked.

Binegar dodged the question by saying that the farmer had a right to meet with the county committee. I knew that a meeting with the county committee—which was only an advisory committee—wouldn't alter a decision made by FmHA staff. I also knew that Dwight Coleman and the Crows Hearts had only been offered a "meeting" with the county supervisor and then denied an appeal when they asked for one. Nope. FmHA wasn't eager to let farmers have real hearings.

"How does he know these things?" the judge pressed. "Does he get it in the literature which you send to him when he took out the loan? Does somebody walk up to him and say, 'I'm going to accelerate. If you want to complain about it, go in and see the supervisor.' How does he *know* he can talk to the county committee? How does he *know* he can come back and talk to you?"

"Well, I would think that most of it would be in conversations with the county office."

"So it's just sort of passed by word of mouth? How does that real estate debtor know about his appeal procedures? Do you tell him in any way?"

"He receives a certified letter," Binegar said, referring again to the acceleration notice.

Judge Van Sickle turned to the Folmers' file and the reasons for their loan acceleration. "I think that actually what you were doing was trying to say in a nice way that he converted the cattle and that you weren't going to continue a loan to a person that converted cattle. And then that failure to liquidate voluntarily, that's another kind of canned reason, the way I see, because if you've got to liquidate them and he won't liquidate voluntarily then you've got to liquidate him—to protect your security. Is that just about what it adds up to?"

"No," Binegar answered. "I would say that his debt structure was such that it didn't appear that he could make it."

He assumed this statement would pass muster with Judge Van Sickle. It didn't. Instead, Judge Van Sickle asked a series of basic questions about the Folmers' debts and farming operation, which Binegar struggled to answer.

Finally, he confessed, "I'm not entirely familiar with the file because I just got it yesterday."

"Well, thank you very much," the judge said, signaling that Binegar was all mine.

I started with a series of rapid-fire questions about his claim that the Folmers hadn't paid real estate taxes. Wasn't it true under FmHA's own regulations it was Binegar's duty to ensure the taxes were paid before FmHA took a penny from a payment by the Folmers to pay a debt to FmHA? He didn't seem aware of that requirement, so I had him read the section of the Code of Federal Regulations on tax servicing, which explicitly said that payment of taxes was a higher priority than payment to FmHA.[5] I asked him to admit that FmHA had received vastly more money from the Folmers through cash payments and through the dairy assignment than was needed to pay the taxes *before* the Folmers' loans were accelerated. Binegar helplessly shuffled through the file, until Judge Van Sickle declared a short recess for Binegar to "familiarize himself with the file."

When we reconvened, Binegar had found an "extra payment" on the chattels on June 22, 1982 of $18,878.68. I asked him whether this amount was more than the taxes due.

"Yes."

I looked up to be sure Judge Van Sickle "got it": the only remaining reason for what happened to the Folmers was the accusation of conversion.

"So, the real reason for accelerating Folmers was they had sold fifty-one head of cattle, without an accounting—that they had converted fifty-one head of cattle, is it not?" I asked.

"I thought that had been answered when I read the portion of the letter from Bernie Kyllo on May fourth," Binegar snapped. *Good!* That was the answer I wanted.

"Now, you keep a record, don't you, called dispositions of chattel security, and in the final column of that form you have a place for the county supervisor's initials where he can either approve it or disapprove it, is that correct?"

"Yes."

"And what is the number of that form?"

"462-1, Farmers Home Administration form," Binegar answered obediently.

"Would you please remove that document from the Folmers' file? I would like to introduce it into evidence." I was proud of how *I would like to introduce it into evidence* just rolled off my tongue. As much as I disliked him, at least I'd learned a little bit from watching and copying the format of some of Annear's questions.

Binegar seemed shocked at the very idea.

"I'm sure the clerk will make a duplicate copy," I added.

Judge Van Sickle stepped in. "Is there any objection if counsel for the plaintiff make a copy of that instrument and then it is received as a copy? Any objection for the defense?"

Annear choked out, "The government has no objection." I noted that Annear was beginning to become irritated at Judge Van Sickle's involvement.

"Exhibit Five is received."

Now I ran with it. Annear should have known what was coming, but he hadn't bothered to depose the Folmers that summer or prepare Binegar. He hadn't troubled himself to read the legal arguments I'd made during the Folmers' appeal to the national office. I felt that the exhibits and arguments from that appeal were certain to convince Judge Van Sickle that there had been no conversion. A summary of the Folmers' defense against conversion was in their affidavit that was filed with the court at the end of March. It said:

> In 1982, a new County Supervisor, James Well, was transferred to our county. He accused us, *falsely*, of converting 51 head of cattle that he said were secured to FmHA. For example, he said we had sold calves on April 8, 1981 and April 29, 1981 in violation of a security agreement.

However, we didn't even have a security agreement with FmHA until May 7, 1981. He also accused us of converting beef cattle on July 1, 1981, October 28, 1981 and January 27, 1981, even though the May 7, 1981 security agreement covered only our *dairy* cattle, while our beef cattle were secured solely to the Bank of Steele. While we did sell two day old dairy cows on July 25, 1981, the previous county supervisor explicitly authorized sales of day-old calves.[6]

I knew that Judge Van Sickle would see very quickly that the Folmers hadn't converted anything. It was obvious: all someone needed to do was compare the dates of the sales to the dates of the chattel security agreements. At the FmHA hearing in September, I had made those same arguments to Odell Ottmar who was serving as the "judge," but none of my legal arguments made a whit of difference to him.[7]

However, I now had Judge Van Sickle listening to those arguments.[8] Unlike Binegar and Ottmar, he knew that the Uniform Commercial Code was the law adopted by North Dakota and forty-eight other states (the outlier in 1982 was Louisiana, which still followed the Napoleonic Code). With regard to secured transactions involving cattle, grain, and livestock, FmHA did not enjoy a special status as the "sovereign"—thanks to the *U.S. v. Kimbell Foods* decision by the U.S. Supreme Court.

I unleashed a torrent of confrontational leading questions at Binegar.

After making him recite the dates and numbers sold at the "unauthorized sale" on April 8, 1981, and asking him to note the May 7, 1981, date of the first security agreement, I asked, "You did say earlier under Mr. Annear's examination that the Folmers were accused of converting fifty-one head of cattle; is that correct?"

"Yes. I read from the letter."

"Do you now believe that this was inaccurate, to say that it was fifty-one head of cattle, because these sales occurred *prior to the time* that Farmers Home had a security agreement?"

"That could very well be."

I wasn't happy with that answer.

"Could you make a mistake?" I asked.

"Did I make a mistake?"

"Did Mr. Kyllo make a mistake?" Bernie Kyllo was an administrator in the state office who'd signed off on the chattel debt acceleration.

"There's a possibility that he did from the information that was furnished to him; yes."

"Then Mr. Well must have made a mistake?"

"That could be."

"Mr. Well is your subordinate; is that not correct?"

"Yes; he was a new county supervisor at that time."

"He hadn't been there very long when he discovered that the Folmers had converted fifty-one head of cattle; is that not correct?"

"That he felt that they had, yes."

"And Mr. Kyllo confirmed that, I take it."

"In effect, yes."

"But they were both wrong with respect to the sales that occurred prior to the time that Farmers Home had a security agreement."

"I believe that is correct, yes."

I looked at Judge Van Sickle. His jaw was set and his gaze was fixed on Binegar. He realized what I was saying.

Now I moved on to the sales after the May 7, 1981, security agreement but before the May 30, 1982, security agreement.

I made Binegar read a list of cattle owned by the Folmers: "71 cows, Holstein, black and white; one bull, Holstein black and white, two-years," followed by 55 other "mixed" cows, aged one to eight years old, 63 short yearlings, "mixed," and 22 "mixed color" calves as well as one brown Tarentaise bull. I'd been taught by the Folmers that the description of "mixed" and "mixed color" cows and calves meant that they were beef cattle of no particular breed.

"Does that description indicate to you that the Folmers had two kinds of cattle: beef cattle and dairy cattle?"

"Yes, it does."

I forced Binegar to admit that a sale of twenty-four steers on July 1, 1981, and more on July 25, 1981, were sales of beef cattle over which FmHA had no claim because the May 1981 security agreement listed only dairy cattle as collateral. A local bank had a security agreement on the Folmers' beef cattle. I glanced up to see that Judge Van Sickle knew exactly what this admission meant. Another one of FmHA's accusations of conversion—the sale of beef cattle—was false.

I showed the May 14, 1982, acceleration of the chattel loan, signed by Jim Well, to Binegar and asked if it told the Folmers that they could have an appeal.

"I don't see the word 'appeal' exactly. I see, 'You have an opportunity to have a meeting before this foreclosure takes place.'"

"You are familiar with your appeal procedure 1900-b, are you not? You do conduct hearings under that regulation?"

"Yes, I do."

"Then you must be aware of Exhibit B4 to that procedure?" I facetiously asked. Exhibit B4 was a form letter that explicitly gave farmers the right to a "hearing."

Showing a spark of gumption, Binegar said, "I might if I had a copy of it here."

I immediately gave him a copy of the form letter that the Folmers should have received but never did. They should have been told of their right to a *hearing* when their chattel loans had been accelerated. But it was soon clear that it didn't matter to Binegar whether the Folmers were offered a "meeting" or a "hearing"—it was all the same to him. I looked at Judge Van Sickle to make sure he had noticed this blasé reaction.

I spent all my remaining anger on my final question to Glen Binegar.

"And item six on that real estate acceleration, it says, 'failure to liquidate voluntarily,' is that not correct?" I never lost the shocked feeling I'd had when I first read "failure to liquidate voluntarily" as reason for an acceleration. We lived in the United States—these farmers weren't prisoners in a Siberian gulag run by sadistic guards. FmHA had no right to make such demands!

"That is correct."

"No further questions."

Farmers needed fair, well-trained, neutral hearing officers. Glen Binegar was Exhibit A on why administrative law judges were needed.

I questioned two more district directors that afternoon. Both gave testimony that provided even more proof that the hearing process for farmers was unfair and exploitive, and by now Judge Van Sickle knew that FmHA did not allow farmers to apply for a deferral based upon 7 USC 1981a. Annear's cross-examinations weakly reiterated the claim that FmHA was a beneficent lender and only "crooks" and "bad managers" had problems.

I had saved Odell Ottmar, whom I believed was the worst of the FmHA district directors, for last.

"Would you please state your name for the record?"

"Odell Ottmar." He was about forty, white, plain, and smug; he may have looked like any other district director, but I thought he was the most heartless.

"And you are a district director of Farmers Home?"

"I'm the *chief* of Reservation Programs of Farmers Home," Ottmar replied. I had expected he would correct me.

"Pardon me," Judge Van Sickle interjected. "What are you? The district supervisor? What is your position?"

"My position is actually *chief* of the reservation programs, Your Honor."

I suppressed a grin as Judge Van Sickle asked follow-up questions on Ottmar's duties, which were identical to the duties of all the other district directors, and then concluded: "So you would be the same as a district director."

"That's basically correct."

I resumed my questions, establishing that delinquencies in Ottmar's districts were as high as they'd ever been—and higher yet among the Indian population. Ottmar had recommended accelerations and liquidations on loans within his district and had served as hearing officer on real estate accelerations outside his district.

"You have no legal training," I said.

"That's correct."

"You have no knowledge of statutory interpretation."

"I have not."

"Have you ever encountered a legal question at a hearing?"

"Yes, I have."

"Whose hearing was that?"

"Mr. and Mrs. Russel Folmer."

"With respect to Mr. and Mrs. Folmer, what was the nature of the legal issue that arose?"

"If I remember correctly, the question that arose as to whether the beef cattle that were listed in the security agreements actually were Farmers Home Administration security or not."

"Did you agree at the time that that was a legal question which was beyond your capability of answering?"

"Yes."

"Did you promise the Folmers that you would request a legal opinion on that issue?"

"I did."

"You did not receive a legal opinion on that issue, however, did you?"

"I received it orally."

Orally? I was stunned. In his deposition, he'd told me under oath that he hadn't sent any documents for review and had only talked to an attorney, who told him the question was too complex to answer over the phone. Damn! I didn't expect much of Ottmar, but now he was committing perjury in front of a federal judge.

"You didn't so state at your deposition though, did you?"

"I don't have it with me," Ottmar said.

"Just a moment, please." I walked back to my table, picked up his deposition transcript, and stalked back to the podium. I had the page marked with a colored paperclip.

"I would like you to read page fourteen," I said.

Ottmar read aloud his own words from the July deposition at which he said he *hadn't* sent documents to USDA's Denver Office of General Counsel and he'd been told it was too complex a question to answer over the phone. The last question I'd posed during his deposition was: "So did you make your rulings without the answer from your lawyers?"

"Yes, I did," Ottmar had answered then.

Judge Van Sickle had the look of a Marine captain ready to send someone to the brig.

Annear attempted to repair Ottmar's credibility on cross-examination, by asking how many years Ottmar had worked at FmHA, the positions he'd held, the number of borrowers within his Reservation Program district.

Annear's final question was an attempt to rehabilitate Ottmar. "*Now*, as I understand it, right *now* you recall securing advice from the Office of General Counsel before making a decision on the Folmer case. Is that your testimony *now*?"

"That's right," Ottmar said.

I was disgusted by the two of them.

"Now, Mr. Ottmar, I believe under your supervision there are two plaintiffs that are involved in this action personally. Is that correct?"

"That's correct."

"And who would they be?"

"It would be Dwight Coleman and Mr. and Mrs. Lester Crows Heart."

"With regard to the Dwight Coleman case, do you have the file with you? And also the Crows Hearts'?"

"Yes, I do," Ottmar replied with a smirk.

Annear and Ottmar went through a long recitation of Dwight's loans, starting in 1978, with dollars lent, terms, and interest rates. I noticed no mention of the payments Dwight had made. Ottmar expounded at length on a letter he'd sent in March 1981 about Dwight's various "failures" of "good management." He moved on to the December 9 acceleration of Dwight's chattel loans, emphasizing each of the reasons for the acceleration.

After Ottmar summarized the total owed by Dwight (about $380,000) and Ottmar's view of the value of his assets (about $250,000), Annear asked:

"Has Mr. Coleman asked for a hearing?"

"Negative."

I didn't look back at Dwight; I hoped he would see this as I did, as an opportunity to expose Odell Ottmar.

Annear, feeling confident, now turned Ottmar's attention to the Crows Hearts with a series of questions and answers designed to show that the Crows Hearts were terrible farmers and ranchers, had committed conversion, had "voluntarily" sold their cattle but had breached commitments to sell their other personal property, thus "forcing" FmHA to repossess and sell their machinery and equipment. Ottmar concluded with numbers: after the Crows Hearts had been stripped of everything, they still owed FmHA $273,000 with remaining assets of about $50,000 in land.

Lester was not a quitter. His ancestors had been farming along the Missouri River for thousands of years. Despite the ferocious onslaught coordinated by Ottmar, culminating in U.S. marshals seizing every speck of the personal property they used to farm, plus Lester's off-farm wages, without a judgment or a garnishment order, the Crows Hearts were still there, and Lester wasn't giving up his scrap of land.

"Any redirect?" the judge asked me.

You betcha, I thought.

"Mr. Ottmar, on both of those chattel acceleration notices directed to Mr. Coleman and the Crows Hearts, to whom were they directed to go with their appeal?"

"I believe to me." I let that sink in: Ottmar had fully exposed his disdain for Dwight and the Crows Hearts during Annear's questioning.

"But you had already recommended that these actions [the acceleration of their loans] take place; is that not correct?"

"That's correct."

I moved on to Dwight. I asked Ottmar to open his file and provide the precise amounts Dwight had paid in 1981. Reluctantly, Ottmar admitted that Dwight paid $10,830 on November 12, $8,270 on November 24, $19,168.25 on December 1, and $9,889.67 on December 8, 1981. I figured that Judge Van Sickle would realize this was not a guy who was trying to get around paying his bills.

"And his chattel loans were accelerated December 9, 1981?"

"December 24."

"They said, 'pay it all on Christmas Eve,' hmm?" I asked.

"That's what it said. That's true."

The court reporter's fingers froze over his keyboard. Judge Van Sickle looked down at Ottmar in shock. North Dakota was an overwhelmingly Christian state and almost everybody went to either a Lutheran or Catholic church. *Christmas Eve!*

"I have no further questions."

I hoped I would never have to see Ottmar's face again.

It was now time to go on offense. I felt I had built the basic outlines of the case by the testimony of the FmHA district directors. Now I could fill in the human angles—the effect that the illegal and unconstitutional practices used by FmHA had on real live suffering, struggling people who had stepped up bravely to be lead plaintiffs on behalf of thousands of other farmers.

"MR. FOLMER, COULD YOU please state your name for the record?"

"I'm Russel Folmer. My mailing address is Wing, North Dakota."

"How long have you been farming on your land?"

"On my land since 1949."

"Could you please describe some of your civic responsibilities?" I asked.

"Well, at the present time I'm chairman of the township board, chairman of the Burleigh County School Reorganization Board; I've been a school board member for about twenty-four years. I've been district chairman of District 31 Republicans for six years; I was extension chairman for Lions International covering the western third of the state for two years, and I guess that's about all I can remember. Oh, I was also a candidate for agriculture commissioner in 1980. I mustn't forget that."

"Mr. Folmer, did you at one point borrow from FmHA and then pay them off in full?"

"Yes, on two occasions that I can recall."

I asked about weather conditions in Burleigh County from 1978 on, and Russel recited a list that reminded me of Job's troubles in the Old Testament: successive years of droughts, grasshopper plagues, early freezes that killed every growing plant, and in 1980–81 the harshest winter he could remember. Only other North Dakotans could truly understand what "six weeks of twenty-plus degrees below zero" meant! Everyone in the courtroom seemed to shiver, remembering that winter. Living in D.C. at the time, I'd only heard about it.

The series of weather catastrophes had impacted their ability to feed their cows and their dairy production. Russel said that they hadn't been able to grow feed themselves due to drought in 1980 and there was a statewide shortage of feed. "We couldn't get quality feed that dairy cows really need. We had to buy hay that was two years old."

I walked Russel through his arrangements, set up during George Weber's time as county supervisor, under which the Bank of Steele handled the beef cattle and FmHA had a lien only on the dairy cattle. Russel explained that FmHA had a 40 percent milk assignment, which was generally sufficient to handle the Folmers' annual payments to FmHA. Mr. Weber had explicitly given his okay on the sale of day-old dairy calves, and so Russel sold his unnecessary bull calves in the spring. He'd been doing that for years, and it was a common practice.

Then in March 1982, James Well, the new county supervisor, showed up.

Russel said he was called to a meeting with Glen Binegar and James Well, who told him there were problems with his site inventory (where FmHA officials came to check on the collateral). Russel disagreed. Everything was there;

nothing was amiss. A short while later he got a "thirty-day" letter. I asked him to identify that document. It was the notice of chattel acceleration. We introduced it as an exhibit.

"Was there talk during this [thirty-day] period by Farmers Home that they had accused you of conversion and that conversion was a felony?" I asked.

"Oh, yes, there was talk of that. I wasn't too impressed by it because I had enough security on hand," Russel said proudly. "I could have sold out and paid them off with no effort whatsoever."

"But thirty days after you received the notice of acceleration of your chattel debt, you did sell your entire dairy herd, did you not?"

"Yes. We sold the majority of our dairy herd on June fourteenth."

"And the notice of acceleration on your chattel debt was May fourteenth."

"Mm-hmm." Russel seemed choked up.

I proceeded gently. "And did you understand that if you did sell the dairy herd as FmHA requested, that you would be able to hang on to your real estate?"

"Well, I was given that impression by Mr. Well. He sat in my living room and had coffee with me and told me that the FmHA was not going to accelerate the real estate loan." Russel took several deep breaths to compose himself, then continued, looking down and shaking his head in disbelief.

"The papers had already been made out and signed before he came out." He was referring to the real estate acceleration. "We got it in the next mail. After he got back to the office, he obviously mailed it."

I needed Judge Van Sickle to understand that FmHA's playbook for getting farmers to "voluntarily liquidate" was to first take away the farmer's means of earning a living by forcing a sale of livestock and machinery, and then—after the farmer was stripped of earning potential—to force a sale of the land.

I continued by asking Russel about the reasons given for the acceleration, starting with Leet's accusation that Russel had operated the farm in an "unhusbandlike" manner. In farm country, this was a serious insult. To be "husbandlike" meant that a farmer was good to his animals, planted and harvested on time, maintained his machinery, didn't spread weeds, and was a good neighbor.

"I'll tell you," Russel said, "I moved there in the fall of 1951 and there was one building on the place and we put about . . ." He stopped to clear his throat. "Could I have a drink of water, please?" I realized he was fighting back tears. "I've got diabetes and I have to drink constantly."

Judge Van Sickle poured a glass of water from his own pitcher and passed it to Russel. The courtroom was quiet. I felt very sorry for Russel. He hadn't broken down when the judge ruled against us on the Bank of North Dakota foreclosure sale, and even though he knew his farm would be sold the next day, he'd somehow found the strength to comfort *me* as I cried in the booth of the Main Street Bar. It was clear to me that the stress and worry (our appeal of the Bank of North Dakota's foreclosure sale to the North Dakota Supreme Court hadn't yet been decided) were mounting.

"We put about three hundred fifty thousand dollars of improvements on that farm, and compared to our neighbors who have been there forty years longer, I would say that it looks pretty good," Russel continued, his voice growing stronger.

I handed him a copy of the aerial photograph that he'd shown me when I'd visited his farm. "Is this a fair and accurate representation of your farm in 1979?"

"Yes." It showed the shelter belts surrounding barns, outbuildings, and a couple of houses with a tidy driveway and parking lot.

"Do you have an exhibit number?" Judge Van Sickle nudged me to correctly introduce it.

"This is marked as Plaintiff's Exhibit Number Twelve," I said.

Utterly exhausted by now, I clumsily ran Russel through the appeal of the acceleration of the real estate in order to get the key appeal documents introduced into evidence. It didn't go well. When I tried to introduce my brief to the national office in the Folmers' national appeal, Annear objected because it was "self-serving." The judge sustained Annear's objection, saying "the internal procedural papers have no value." I moved on to my next planned exhibit as soon as Judge Van Sickle hinted that the ruling on the national appeal "may be a different matter."

"I offer Exhibit Fifteen," I said.

"Now is that the ruling?"

"Yes, it is."

I asked Russel to identify it. Instead, he read it: "We have completed a review of the county case files, the hearing transcript, and all other pertinent information relative to the decision to accelerate the Folmers' loan accounts. Based on our review, we find this decision to be proper; therefore, we must continue with the acceleration of the loan accounts."

Annear objected. "I guess I don't understand the materiality of it, Your Honor."

"Overruled," Judge Van Sickle snapped. He seemed not to believe what Russel had just read. He reached toward Russel and gestured that Russel should hand the letter to him.

"Did the United States Department of Agriculture, anyone in the Office of the Administrator, send you anything in the form of a decision other than this letter?"

"That was all," I blurted, before Russel could answer.

"But don't you have anything else from the people in Washington?" Judge Van Sickle was angry—it was an unusual display of emotion from him.

"No," I said. "That's all."

"That's the only communication you have had from the Farmers Home Administration in Washington relative to your attempted appeal to Washington after the Ottmar decision," the judge repeated.

"That's the only thing."

"The only thing your client has." The judge looked at Russel.

Russel nodded.

"Yes," I said.

When it was Annear's turn for redirect, he changed the topic. "Mr. Folmer, during this period of time, did you have occasion to go to Hawaii?" he asked.

"No. I've been to Hawaii, but it's been several years."

"When?"

"It's been at least four years ago, I would say."

"During this period of time when you had loans from FmHA?"

"No," Russel said. "I didn't have a chattel loan at the time. I had a real estate loan."

In North Dakota, only wealthy people went to Hawaii. Other questions about a new pickup truck and a fancy irrigation system followed, as Annear attempted to show that the Folmers lived high on the hog. Russel did his best to be accurate and honest, but he didn't remember dates or numbers, and he grew confused under Annear's relentless questioning. It got even messier when Russel tried to explain that three of his children also had some cattle on his farm. Annear eagerly followed this trail, as if trying to catch Russel in a lie about which cows belonged to whom. I was shocked. The Folmers' farm was a "family farm," and farm kids were encouraged to start with calves that they'd show at county fairs and breed so that in a few years the kids would have a small herd that might pay for their college tuition or be used as a down payment on their own farm. I began to realize that Annear knew that Russel was our most credible plaintiff, and Russel's credibility needed to be destroyed in order for FmHA to win any kind of public relations battle.

Annear spewed out more questions: he wanted to know precise acres, land values, crops in storage, and other data that Russel helplessly said he'd need to see his records to answer. Annear implied that it was lack of candor, not lack of records, that was Russel's problem. To my chagrin, Russel volunteered to bring the records. I had coached my plaintiffs never to volunteer anything.

"When?" Annear asked.

"Tomorrow," Russel promised.

It was time to adjourn for the day. I felt I'd done better on the second day than on the first, but I felt guilty about Annear's mistreatment of Russel. If I had more trial experience, I could have protected him better.

Dwight and I headed to the Big Boy drive-in for pizza burgers flying style, French fries with gravy, and cinnamon Cokes. As soon as we got to Mary's, I called Andrew and told him I missed him and that I'd be home tomorrow.

That night, my dad walked in the door with a huge smile on his face. After his trial had ended in Fargo that afternoon, he'd hitched a ride with his opposing counsel. I was grateful he had come for the moral support. When my father had come with me to hearings or status conferences, he'd made subtle gestures that provided quiet guidance, as when he wordlessly communicated that I should go forward on the preliminary injunction hearing even though there was no court reporter, or when he silently signaled that I should let Annear keep talking because all he was doing was irritating Judge Van Sickle. I thought he might be able to pass notes to me or even elbow me and whisper "Foundation" or "Hearsay" so that I'd make proper objections. By the end of the second day, I could see that Annear was stretching the bounds of proper questioning, but I didn't know how to stop him. And, most selfishly, I was happy that my father, not I, would be driving us back to Grand Forks tomorrow. I wanted to get home to Andrew and not die in a crash caused by falling asleep at the wheel.

· · ·

AT PRECISELY NINE the next morning, Judge Van Sickle gaveled the court into session and said, "Miss Vogel?"

"Mr. Folmer is parking the car," I said. "He should be here any moment. I have several documents I could introduce."

I started with an FmHA report on national accelerations, foreclosures, subordinations, and other data. Annear had no objection. I moved on with a cost-benefit analysis of FmHA's appeal system that had been done by a private contractor in the Carter administration. It concluded that a system of neutral administrative law judges (ALJs) would be more fair, and would cost only slightly more than using FmHA's current system. Unfortunately, the Carter administration had decided against ALJs in order to save money. The findings of this report were a core part of my argument in favor of ALJs in the brief I'd turned in.

"We are not familiar with that and we would object to that as no foundation," Annear said.

I froze.

"How did you get this report?" Judge Van Sickle asked. "Was this something that was produced by Farmers Home in your discovery process?"

"No." I'd found it on my own and proudly explained the sleuthing I'd done to find it. I'd first seen reference to the report in a Carter-era *Federal Register* notice about FmHA appeals, and then I'd contacted the contractor Systems Science, Inc., and asked for a copy. My plan was to get it into evidence as a government record; I'd gotten the idea because the Folmers' final national decision had been admitted as a government record, and just that morning, by looking at one of my father's books, I'd found a rule of evidence allowing government reports to be evidence.

"I believe it's admissible under Rule 803, subsection 8, as a record, report statement, or data compilation in any form of public offices or agencies setting forth in civil actions—"

"Of course, Systems Science, Incorporated, is not a public officer or agency," the judge gently corrected.

"But it was used by Farmers Home."

"I'm sorry. I'll need a little more. I find that I must sustain the objection."

I glanced at my father, hoping for sympathy, but he looked unhappy. The rules of evidence were like a second language to him, developed over decades of practice and hundreds of trials. I immediately switched into defensive teenager mode and thought, *Not my fault. If I'd had more than a half hour's notice that there was going to be a trial, I might have been better prepared.* There were probably other ways to get that study into evidence, but I didn't know the rules.

Russel Folmer arrived, looking pale and stressed. I should have asked for a short recess to talk to him, but I was too inexperienced, and I felt pressure to meet Judge Van Sickle's expressed wish that we wrap up the trial by noon.

"Are we ready to go?" Judge Van Sickle asked. It was Annear's turn for cross-examination.

It started badly: Russel didn't wait for a question from Annear, but instead said that overnight, he had done a new livestock inventory by hand and wanted to correct any errors "so I'll not be falsely accused of conversion again." Russel meant the best, but his new list was like throwing raw meat into a pool of piranhas. Annear had a field day examining Russel about his cattle, his son's cattle, and his daughter's cattle, implying throughout that Russel had been converting cattle for decades (even though most of the time Russel hadn't even been borrowing from FmHA). Once in a while I looked over at my father's face. He didn't like to see a witness browbeaten, and his posture and stern visage showed me he wouldn't have allowed it for a client of his. As the lawyer for Russel, I should have been leaping to my feet, breaking up Annear's rhythm, and making Annear back off on his most aggressive questions. But I didn't know how to make those objections, and my father didn't know enough about the facts to step in either.

One small note of humanity came out when Annear, trying to imply that Russel was playing a shell game with his kids' cows, asked him an open-ended question:

"How do you tell your own cows from your daughter's?" Annear asked.

"Well, it's just like looking at your kids; they all look different."

Anna Mae leaned over my shoulder to whisper to me that I should ask Russel about when they had taken the Hawaii vacation. I followed that advice when it was my turn for redirect.

"Mr. Annear asked you yesterday about a vacation that you took. How many years had it been since you had taken a vacation?"

"Well, after we got home last night, my wife and I were discussing that very thing and she happened to remember that she was forty-five years of age at that time. Well, that would make it eight years ago, and that was the first vacation we had ever taken."

"And how long had you been married?"

"About thirty years, at that time."

Russel and Anna Mae had taken but one vacation in over thirty years of marriage. It was obvious he was devoted to his farm, his children, his crops, his cattle, his church, his community. He'd come to that farm as a teenager; he was the opposite of an unhusbandlike farmer.

I called Anna Mae as a witness and asked her to describe the psychological effects of the actions taken by Farmers Home. As always, she looked impeccably put together, with dark shiny hair framing her exquisitely beautiful face.

"Could you describe in your own words what life has been like since Farmers Home started certain actions against you?"

"Well, at our age, which I think was a factor in this case, it's been horrendous. As soon as we found out about this, both my husband and I did very little sleeping at night. In fact, when I did fall asleep all I did was have nightmares about the FmHA and that's all I dreamt about for months, but now I've gotten a little more calloused to the fact and I've kind of gone with the tide, but it has totally wrecked our lives."

Annear prudently had no questions. I think Anna Mae was disappointed, as she very much wanted to give him a piece of her mind.

My final witness was Dwight Coleman.

Dwight confidently walked to the witness stand and sat down, gazing over the courtroom. Despite more than two days in the stuffy courtroom, he still seemed to carry fresh cool air from the hills with him. Where he farmed, near the Canadian border, the air had a scent of pine, herbs, grasses and sunshine. It was delicious.

"Could you describe the kind of land and the kind of farming you do?" I asked.

"It's mostly pasture—cow pasture and wheat farming. It's hilly—lots of valleys and sloughs."

"Did you grow up in that area?"

"Yes, I've been there all my life."

"And your family?"

"Yes."

"For about how long?"

"Well, I'm thirty-seven years old and I've been there all my life."

"I meant your family," I said.

"They've been there all their life, too."

I wanted Dwight to tell Judge Van Sickle that the Coleman family had come to that region before North Dakota had become a state, but Dwight was following my precise instructions to answer each question without volunteering more information.

Dwight received his first operating loan from FmHA in 1978, for land he was renting, and he paid it off in full. He then began looking for a farm of his own to buy, and in 1979 he received a second loan from FmHA to buy some good land he'd found. He'd hope to build a house and buildings for machine storage on that land, but FmHA had said no.

What happened then? I asked.

"In 1979 we had a drought." Hardly anything grew.

"Did FmHA offer you a deferral?" I asked.

"No."

"What happened in 1980?"

"We had a good crop in 1980 but we never got to combine it. September came along and we got fifteen inches of snow on it."

"And how were cattle prices in 1980?"

"Not good."

He'd bought ninety-one heifers, but the market for pasture cattle dropped, so he decided to breed the heifers and keep them over the winter—he had been able to gather quite a bit of hay. He planned to sell calves in the spring of 1981 and thereby recoup the money he'd spent for the heifers and make a profit.

"Were you able to make the December 31, 1980, payment?"

"No, I wasn't. They said they'd give me one more year to get my act together. If progress wasn't made in 1981, they were going to foreclose."

I asked Dwight if he remembered Ottmar sending him a "servicing letter" about having machinery scattered around and being a bad manager for having a poor calf crop.

Dwight turned to address Judge Van Sickle with his answer. "Well, I farmed several different areas of the Turtle Mountains, anywheres from one to four miles from one piece of land to the other, and since I wasn't living on the place, I couldn't leave my machinery at the farmstead—there was no farmstead—so I had to leave it with people that were staying on their farms throughout my farming area."

Instead of selling ninety-one heifers at a loss, he kept them over the winter and bred all of them in the fall. Before spring calving, he'd traded thirty of his worst heifers for forty good cows.

"Did it work out well?"

"It worked out fine."

"Did you make payments to Farmers Home in 1981?"

"Right around fifty thousand dollars," Dwight answered.

"And you made your last payment around December eighth?"

"I think so."

"What happened on December ninth?" I asked.

"I got a letter of acceleration. I had fifteen days to come up with two twenty-five or two hundred thirty thousand dollars for the chattel acceleration."

"And what did that letter tell you you could do?"

"I could have a meeting at the county supervisor's office within fifteen days."

"Did you go in and talk to Mr. Schaefer?"

"Yes, within the fifteen days I went to the office to see what it was all about. They said if you wanted to you could meet with the district director and have a hearing—he said it would be just a waste of time because a hearing is just a formality. He said to go home and get ready to be sold out."

"What happened after that, then?"

"I waited until spring to see what they were going to do and I went to Nolan Anderson's auction sale. He's a young kid that was getting sold out by FmHA, and at that auction sale I found out that a person could hire a lawyer and the hearing is *not* just a formality. It's more than just a formality. I had decided to sell out before that day; I had the auctioneers and the clerk. I had it ready to go, but when I got back from that auction sale, I decided I was going to cancel that."

"Did you try to do anything further with FmHA after that point?"

"Yes. I wrote a letter to Mr. Leet requesting a hearing after I found out it was more than a formality. He said that the case has been closed and sent to general counsel for foreclosure action."

"Have you ever been given the opportunity for a hearing?"

"No."

"How often has your county supervisor come out to your farm?" I asked.

"He's never come."

"Did he send assistants?"

"If you could call them that. One of them didn't even know the difference between a cow and a bull."

"No further questions," I said, smiling as I remembered the story that I'd heard Dwight tell at the Slabaughs' farm. His county supervisor sent an underling to count the cattle in the fall. Dwight sent a crowd of farmers into hysterics when he told them what happened next: *So he's counting the cows and he's looking at my huge Charolais bull and he says, "Gee, that's an awful big cow." Really? I mean you're out here, you're telling me what you're going to do for me, counting my cows, and you don't know the difference? That just burned my ass.*

Now Annear had a chance to cross-examine.

"Mr. Coleman, I take it that Mr. Schaefer knows the difference between a cow and a bull, does he?"

"Yeah," Dwight answered. "But not his assistant."

Annear moved on, trying to make Dwight into a villain and a bad farmer.

"With regards to the snow in September, when did that occur?"

"I think that was about the fifteenth of September."

"Isn't that kind of late for combining?"

"No, not in the Turtle Mountains. The Turtle Mountains is always the last part of the state to be combined."

Now Annear focused on Dwight's debt. It was clear that Dwight was underwater: he owed more than his land and cattle and machinery were worth. If he sold out, he'd still be in the hole. Dwight readily admitted this.

"I was just a beginning farmer. I started with nothing, and it takes time to get things going."

"You have a net worth of a hundred thousand?"

"A net worth?"

"Yes," Annear said.

"Oh, no. I think my net worth is nil," Dwight said.

Annear, satisfied, said, "I have nothing further."

I began to rise from my seat, but then I saw Judge Van Sickle lean over and begin his own line of questioning.

"What goes through my mind is aren't you actually ahead to chuck it and start over again? I mean you'll never get out from under the load, will you?"

"Well, actually, there's things going on now that we probably have a chance to get started." Dwight's optimism had kept me afloat for many months and now he was sharing it with Judge Van Sickle, who was looking down at Dwight with compassion and understanding. Judge Van Sickle had grown up on a farm in the 1930s. Possibly he saw a younger version of himself in Dwight. Based on his own life experiences, possibly he believed that if a young man like Dwight was in a hole, why heck, he'd find a way to get himself out.

"In effect you're saying to me that it's cheaper to work your way out of this debt than it is to chuck it and start over again."

"Oh, definitely! I've got things just starting to roll now instead of having to start all over again. I've got my cattle herd and I've started a new business. I'm in partnership with another guy and we started a landfill business in the Turtle Mountains and it's just getting off the ground now."

"And you want the profits you're going to make from that to go to pay for the farm loss?"

Dwight nodded.

"You'd rather sink it in there than enjoy it yourself."

"I'd like to keep my property at all costs," Dwight said.

"Ms. Vogel, does plaintiff rest now?"

"Yes, we rest."

I turned to look at my father, who managed a small smile for me.

Annear now called his only witness: LeRoy Nayes, former head of farmer programs in North Dakota. He had retired one month before the trial, but he'd been with FmHA for a quarter century. He was smart and articulate and was there to shore up the government's case. He said all the right things, about how FmHA was there to help farmers—but Dwight's testimony still reverberated in the room. To my surprise, Annear had Nayes introduce the two delinquency reduction memos, the infamous Foreclosure Quota Memos. I didn't object to either one.

But then I detected something amiss. Annear was having Nayes talk about a report I'd never heard of that had very low loan acceleration and foreclosure numbers.

"Your Honor, I object. I haven't seen the document that he's testifying about."

Judge Van Sickle snapped a quick "Sustained" but changed his mind when Annear said, "I was laying a foundation." The exhibit was marked "Exhibit 31."

Annear and Nayes continued to volley numbers of accelerations and foreclosures back and forth. These numbers were far lower than what I knew to be the case, and I realized that this exhibit was being offered by Annear to support his "mountain out of a molehill" theme.

I couldn't take it anymore and stood up again to object.

"What is your objection, Ms. Vogel?"

"It's not true!"

The courtroom was completely silent. I glanced at my father, who had his head down on the table and appeared to be writhing in pain. I had the sinking feeling that he wished he had never come to the trial.

I figured out that I had made a mistake with my "It's not true" objection.

"It doesn't match other official reports that they have previously submitted," I clarified.

Judge Van Sickle asked to see Exhibit 31 himself, and asked Annear, "Is this some kind of an official publication or is it a summary?"

"This is a summary by support personnel down at FmHA on figures that they had on file concerning real estate foreclosures in the state office."

Judge Van Sickle appeared to ponder this and then announced, "This is an exhibit under Rule 1006." *What in the world is Rule 1006?* I wondered.

"I'm going to require some more foundation," the judge added. "Unless this witness knows that these figures are accurate or somebody knows they're accurate, why, the plaintiff is entitled to have some basis for testing the source of this information. At this time I sustain the objection as to Exhibit Thirty-One."

Hurrah! Having Judge Van Sickle on the bench was like having Santa Claus as my uncle. He'd saved the day. Annear and Nayes's cooked-up report didn't make it into evidence.

The rest of Annear's questions to Nayes were innocuous and aimed at showing that the lawsuit caused bad morale at FmHA. *What about the damn morale of the farmers you are running off the land?* I fumed. At last Annear ended.

Now I was able to ask Nayes questions of my own, and I focused on issues having to do with the deeply flawed appeal process. Nayes was repeatedly boxed into corners and eventually had to admit that the hearing officer on a chattel acceleration was in all cases deeply involved with the decision to accelerate. Nayes verified that Ralph Leet was the decision maker on acceleration of real estate loans. I asked Nayes why, if Leet was the decision maker, Leet never came to appeal hearings? Nayes said the county supervisor represents Leet at the hearing as a decision maker. It was clear that LeRoy Nayes was a total company man—even in retirement. He'd never admit that FmHA did anything wrong.

At last I said, "I have nothing further," and Annear said the same.

"All right," Judge Van Sickle said. "With that, court will stand adjourned."

The court reporter added the precise time that the trial was concluded. It was eleven forty-six A.M., September 22, 1982.

No members of the press awaited us on the ground floor, and Russel, Anna Mae, Dwight, and my father and I said our farewells in the lobby. The Folmers returned to their farm in Wing, Dwight headed back north in his run-down car, and my father and I piled the briefcases in the backseat of my mother's huge Delta 88 Oldsmobile.

Fifteen minutes after we'd left Bismarck, he began his law lecture. My father had been in agony all morning as he'd watched me fumble about introducing evidence and asking questions in the wrong format. The first thing I learned was that Rule 1006 allowed use of a summary or chart to prove the content of voluminous writings that cannot be conveniently examined in court. There are some restrictions: the proponent must make the originals available for examination to the other party, and the summaries must be neutral, accurate, and straightforward. Rule 1006 was not a backdoor vehicle for the introduction of evidence that would be otherwise inadmissible, and he thought Judge Van Sickle had used it properly that morning.

My father then moved on to how to get documents admitted into evidence, how to prevent the other side from admitting their documents, how to question adverse witnesses, how to protect your clients from unfair questions from the other side, and, most of all, how not to shame your own father in front of a federal judge. The scant three hours he'd suffered through that morning as he'd watched me flail about gave him more than enough material for a three-hour lecture. It was a lecture that most lawyers in North Dakota would have paid big bucks to attend.

I listened politely, but the blizzard of excellent advice on how to be a trial lawyer was irrelevant to me. I'd already decided that I would *never ever* again handle a trial. This was my first trial, and I intended it to be my last.

CHAPTER 21

Wouldn't Bill Langer Be Proud

A week after the trial, when I went to pick up Andrew at his Montessori school, the head teacher had a complaint about Andrew. *Oh, no*, I thought. *I can't handle any more problems.*

"I'm worried about the influence Andrew has on the other children," she said.

"Oh?"

"He has too much imagination. He believes he has magical powers, and he's telling the other children they have magical powers too."

I looked over at Andrew, happy, smiling, adorable, and confident. *Good for you, kid!* I thought.

On the drive home, Andrew shared the news that he had started a new club he called the Bullies. That did concern me.

"Why are you calling yourselves 'bullies'? What kind of club is it?" I asked.

"It's just me and my friends from across the street, Mom. We want to be the Bulls, but we're little. So we're Bullies."

I took a rare weekend off: no work, no office, no paper, no phone calls. We did whatever Andrew wanted to do. *Let's go to the park! Let's play with the Bullies! Let's go to the Dairy Queen! Let's order pizza for dinner! Read this book (and this book and this book) to me!* By the time I went back to work on Monday,

I felt refreshed, rejuvenated, and empowered: I was now an honorary member of the Bullies.

Helen Monteith, friendly as ever, called on Wednesday.

"Are you available on October seventeenth for a hearing on the motion to amend the complaint to become a national class?"

"Yes!"

This was terrific news. If Judge Van Sickle intended to toss the national complaint, why would he bother having a hearing? I immediately called Burt, Allan, and Dale. This time they had enough notice to join me in person at the hearing. But first we needed to hustle to get the briefs written and filed. Burt and Allan were available to consult, but the writing fell to me. Our legal work on the national class action had to be impeccable. The stakes were enormously high. I needed Andrew's magical powers.

Late in the evening on October 5, I mailed a fat express mail envelope with five documents that would, I hoped, change the North Dakota class into a national class. I knew Annear would explode.

On October 12, Annear asked Judge Van Sickle to disallow the national class action complaint because I'd narrowly missed the deadline to file the accompanying brief with the motion. I was shocked that Annear would be so persnickety. The sanction he sought didn't match the gravity of my violation.

We celebrated Andrew's fifth birthday at Grandma and Grandpa's house with balloons and a living room full of Bullies drinking lemonade. But the next day I had to leave once more, to go to St. Paul to hear USDA's appeal of the *Allison v. Block* case.

I waited until we'd parked at the Montessori school before telling Andrew that Grandma Elsa would be picking him up after school. His face fell.

"I'm sorry," I said. I hugged him goodbye and watched him walk into school with his little shoulders slumped in the black and red Bulls T-shirt he'd gotten for his birthday. Tears stung my eyes.

In St. Paul, I met up with Burt (who had written the amicus brief), Jim Massey, and our hero, Dale Reesman. Because Missouri, Minnesota, and North Dakota were all within the same region (the Eighth Circuit), the ruling that came down in the *Allison* case on the deferral law would be decisive. If Dale won *Allison*, we would all win.

Late in the afternoon, we did a mock argument for Dale, impersonating judges who would pepper him with questions. Then we traded roles and helped Burt practice the oral argument he would make on behalf of the *Coleman* class.

That evening, we met with a slew of rowdy and enthusiastic Minnesota farm advocates led by Lou Anne Kling. Lou Anne was a little older than I, and she had learned how to be a farm advocate from Tom Nichols; now she was teaching others how to be farm advocates too. She was like a virus spreading across the countryside: every farmer she helped she turned into a farm advocate, who helped other farmers, and they helped more farmers. Soon, Don and Diane McCabe would come to Minnesota for one of Lou Anne's training sessions, and then they too would become "viruses" in North Dakota, carrying their color-coded Codes of Federal Regulations and accompanying farmers to meetings and hearings.

The hushed courtroom of the Eighth Circuit was awe-inspiring. Even its ceiling was paneled in carved glowing walnut. Judge Van Sickle's courtroom was plain in comparison. The three judges asked searching questions of Dale and Burt, and of the attorney for USDA. Dale and Burt were eloquent and persuasive. The assistant U.S. attorney from Missouri was awkward and stumbled in his answers. We walked out on a cloud of optimism.

On the five-hour drive home to Grand Forks, I felt exhausted. To stay awake, I smoked—a habit Andrew hated. Even though I never smoked in front of him, he was no fool. I resolved that as soon as I got back home, I'd quit. I knew I'd have Friday night and Saturday before I'd have to tell him that I was leaving again Sunday morning for our hearing in Bismarck. I waited until the last possible minute to tell Andrew on Sunday.

"No, Mom! I want you to stay with me!" Tears came to his eyes, and to mine too.

"I'm sorry, kiddo. I have to leave."

I met Allan, Burt, and Dale at the Bismarck airport on Sunday evening and they all wanted to go to a restaurant where they could have a drink.

"Sorry," I said, "but North Dakota still has blue laws. There's no liquor for sale on Sundays, not even in restaurants."

"Are you serious?" Allan asked.

"But I have another idea! I'll take you out into the country!" They were dubious but went along. We left Mandan on Old Ten going west and I pulled over at the top of a butte. The air was scented with sage and there were millions of stars in the blue-black sky. All around us, there was silence.

"The sky is one of the reasons why farmers and ranchers don't want to lose their land," I said.

A few miles later, I pulled off the interstate at the exit marked CENTER, where there was a brightly lit truck stop.

"You will love this," I promised. The café—in the exact center of nowhere—was about two-thirds full of truckers, going from coast to coast. We sat down at an empty booth.

"Look," I said, pointing at a pay phone at the end of the table. The pay phones were for the convenience of cross-country truckers, but cross-country lawyers could take advantage of them too. We gathered up some coins and Burt called his wife to report he was calling from a table at a North Dakota diner in the center of nowhere. He vowed that as soon as he returned, he'd encourage Manhattan lunchrooms to get pay phones too.

After sadly cruising up and down deserted Main Street back in Bismarck (they still couldn't believe that an entire state could go dry, without at least one bar cheating), I took them to the Fleck House, a one-story concrete block motel near the courthouse. I went off to my sister Mary's house—only belatedly realizing that I could have stopped by Mary's and asked her for a bottle of wine for my thirsty passengers.

At eight the next morning I parked at the Fleck House and knocked on Burt's door.

"Look at this," he said, beckoning me in. Over the bed, and on every wall, hung framed pictures of Jesus and cross-stitched samplers of psalms. Apparently, the Fleck family were serious Catholics who didn't expect to encounter East Coast Jewish lawyers. Allan's room was the same. Even Dale, a good Methodist, agreed the décor was over the top.

At breakfast, I was edgy. My skin felt prickly and my mind was skittering in circles. My nicotine craving was being set off by nervous energy and the sugar from the caramel roll (I'd eaten my share as well as Burt's and Allan's shares).

By ten thirty, we were seated in the courtroom. The gavel was pounded and we all rose for Judge Van Sickle.

"Ms. Vogel, you may proceed. Do you want to use the podium?"

I wasn't thinking straight and did not get the hint that he would prefer it if I used the podium, as my voice didn't carry well. Instead, I declined. It felt more comfortable with Dale, Allan, and Burt right next to me.

First, I had to get Dale admitted to practice in the United States District Court of North Dakota. I listed Dale's qualifications, adding that he had been counsel for a number of cases involving similar issues from Missouri. Politely, Judge Van Sickle asked Annear if he had any objections, and Annear did not disappoint.

"We objected to out-of-state counsel before, and we would again voice an objection. No doubt he is well qualified, but we again feel that it's unnecessary to add additional members to this staff, or *this army*, whatever the case may be."

I glanced at my "army," who seemed delighted at the appellation.

Judge Van Sickle brushed off this objection ("Assistance of counsel is always desirable") and admitted Dale. "By the way, Mr. Reesman," the judge asked, "do you not have one of those cases on appeal before the Eighth Circuit right now?"

"Yes, sir." Dale stood to answer. "It was argued last Friday in St. Paul."

Judge Van Sickle asked whether this covered the deferral law.

"Yes, sir. It, in fact, was a pure 1981a issue, the only issue involved."

Dale sat down, and I continued, reminding Judge Van Sickle that the defendants had introduced a map of the United States showing delinquencies in every state, and many states had higher rates of delinquency than North Dakota's 42 percent. The government's own data proved the "profound need" for national relief. I went on to say that the legal issues raised in the North Dakota case were "precisely" the same nationwide. Jittery from sugar and lack of nicotine, I jumped around in my presentation: I mentioned Supreme Court cases authorizing national class actions when national regulations were involved, and interspersed criticism of USDA for defending its foreclosure practices in case after case, even after federal judges had ruled against USDA.

"Undertaking this as a national class was something the lawyers all, you know, struggled and wrestled with," I admitted. "We were really hoping that after the *Coleman* case, after the *Matzke* case and the other cases throughout the country, the government would change its practices and would make it unnecessary to bring a national class action, but as the summer progressed, the phone calls came in from all over the country to me and to the other lawyers here. It was very clear that the national class was the best mechanism and the most efficient mechanism to address the law violations that we raised in the *Coleman* case."

My stream-of-conscious statement had been from the heart, and, over-whelmed, I sat back down, hoping my team could take over.

"If these gentlemen have anything to say in support of the argument that this should be an expanded class action, I would like to hear it," Judge Van Sickle hinted.

"If it please the court, I would speak from whence I come, Your Honor, from the state of Missouri, particularly with regard to what I see as a need," Dale said. He spoke in the measured drawl of a Southern gentleman. "In Missouri, we do not have a class action pending. So far as I know, the primary reason for that is nobody has come up with the money to fund such a thing. I have had a number of individual clients and none were able to afford any more than to take care of themselves."

Dale went on to say that he had won four deferral cases but still had ten cases pending, and that FmHA continued to fight against farmers "tooth and toenail." He spoke of the impact these tactics had on his clients, especially because Missouri used a power of sale foreclosure process. Some farmers were facing liquidations by other lenders because FmHA had seized all the income from the farm.

Dale's presentation was calm, logical, and utterly convincing. He bowed courteously and sat down.

Burt then reiterated Dale's point about how hard it was to wage battle against Farmers Home. "If you're wealthy enough to afford a lawyer to go in and stop FmHA, then as to that particular farmer, his constitutional rights are protected. But as to those farmers who either don't know their rights or are too poor to hire a lawyer to enforce those rights, nothing seems to change.

"None of us wanted to do a national class," Burt continued, looking at the somber row of lawyers seated beside him. "Sarah Vogel has carried an enormous burden here in North Dakota and was justifiably concerned about being respon-sible for a national class action. *I* was concerned about the expenditure of resources that the enforcement of such a national class action would entail."

Burt said we were all cognizant of the responsibilities that would be trig-gered by a national class, and then he dropped his bombshell: "I have been authorized by the ACLU's board of directors to represent to the court that the resources that would be necessary to implement a national class action will be made available on a voluntary basis, on an unpaid basis, by the American Civil Liberties Union. We have affiliates in forty-eight states, approximately a thousand active volunteer attorneys, who I will urge strongly to make their services available to farmers who need it in order to enforce any such decree, as well as the seventy full-time lawyers of the organization, to the extent that is necessary, who will make themselves available as well. Once the national class is certified and appropriate orders were entered, my experience with the government is that this government obeys the law and that once such a clarification were to be forthcoming, I would expect it to be implemented without the need for acrimonious enforcement procedures. But if such enforcement proceedings are necessary, the resources are there to bring them. Thank you."

Ha, I thought, *we do have an army of lawyers! So there, Gary Annear!*

Now Judge Van Sickle turned to the U.S. attorney's table, where Annear and another attorney sat. The new lawyer stood up and said, "I am Norman Anderson, assistant United States attorney here in Bismarck. We oppose certification of the national class at this late date."

Anderson waved a copy of the June 1983 ACLU newsletter, *Civil Liberties* magazine. I recognized it because Dwight and his cows were on the front page. Anderson used an interview Burt and I had given in the newsletter about the *Coleman* case as evidence that I'd been thinking in late May of amending the lawsuit but didn't file the paperwork until September.

"Case law establishes that if a party who wishes to file an amended complaint fails to act in a timely manner, they have the burden of proving that their reason for delay was due to *oversight, inadvertence, or excusable neglect*. The plaintiffs haven't even *attempted* to make that showing," Anderson said. "The time for discovery has ended and the evidentiary hearing for the permanent injunction has been held and is past." He concluded with an argument that I expected: on May 23, Judge Van Sickle had said that any amendments had to be filed within ten days. I'd long since blown by that deadline.

"Ms. Vogel, do you have anything in rebuttal?"

I had an extreme urge to ask for a recess so I could run out of the courtroom and light up a cigarette. I struggled to string my thoughts together.

"I think that there should be a distinction drawn between new theories of law and the need for new evidence and the need for expanded relief," I rambled incoherently. "I believe, at the trial, the bulk of the atmospheric evidence . . . if we ignore that and focus on what required the violations of which the plaintiffs were complaining, we'll find that they were the national regulations. Ralph Leet testified again and again, 'I had no choice but to do it that way. The national regulations told me I had to do it that way.' I believe that every argument we made was based on the results of the requirements of the national regulations, so if new evidence is required, I would think it would be very minimal."

I was humiliated; my brain wasn't sending timely signals to my mouth.

"What you are saying is that you can present these issues as a matter of law?" Judge Van Sickle helpfully suggested.

"Yes. They talk about the need for discovery," I said. "I don't see where the need for discovery would arise. The government has all the facts on this. They know what the regulations are. They published them. There are thousands and thousands of unrepresented farmers who simply can't survive through the starve-out period, who are losing their farms, and those quiet people who never get to court are the ones that we are the most concerned about."

Not to be outdone, Annear got in the last word.

"I have been associated with the U.S. Attorney's Office for twenty-some years, and of all the government agencies and all the government employees, at Farmers Home they are the most conscientious and most dedicated of all. They have one concern, and that is the success of the family farmer."

Judge Van Sickle adjourned the court and promised to make his decision as soon as he could.

For lunch, we found a restaurant that served liquor and had a cigarette machine in the entry. I lit up and resolved not to quit smoking again until the *Coleman* case was done.

ON OCTOBER 19, JIM Massey called with bad news on the Minnesota case. Even though he'd modeled the complaint and much of the briefing on the *Coleman* case, his judge had "cut the baby in half." Farmers had a right to apply for a deferral, but they were not entitled to releases of family living or farm operating expenses. In other words, Minnesota farmers could still be starved out and deprived of all income needed to survive months before there would be a hearing on a deferral. Jim said he wanted to ask the judge on his case for permission to bring his Minnesota class into the *Coleman* case, if *Coleman* was certified as a national class.

"Is that okay? Would you support adding the Minnesota class to Coleman?"

I didn't remind Jim that he had vehemently argued against turning the *Coleman* case into a national class action.

"Of course," I said.

I didn't expect an apology from Jim, and I didn't get one.

A week later, Donna appeared at my office door and said Vivian from the Clerk of Court's Office was on line 1. "She wants to talk to you. Says it's urgent."

I grabbed a pen and a yellow legal pad. When I answered, Vivian's voice was clipped and businesslike; I felt that was a bad sign.

"I'm ready," I told her.

"I'll start on page five, with the order that the plaintiffs' motion to amend the complaint is granted and that this case is designated as a national class action. The class is certified as: 'All persons who have obtained a farmer program loan from the Farmers Home Administration . . .'"

I felt as if I was on a roller coaster that had crested to the top of a steep climb, right before it rushed down the drop. I'd hoped for this news, but I also dreaded the descent. The case was about to barrel ahead with new force and momentum.

"Thank you! Would you read it again?"

Vivian laughed and obliged. She highlighted the key dates and deadlines I needed to know. All discovery had to be wrapped up by the end of the year and there would be a trial for the national class in January. It was daunting news—but good news. I zipped across the hall and told my startled father: "Judge Van Sickle approved the national class!" Then I called Dale.

"Please tell Mr. Reesman that John Block is calling and he's *very mad*," I told his secretary.

"Yee-haw!" Dale hollered when I told him the good news. He said he'd call our national lead plaintiffs right away.

I called PrairieFire Rural Action and the Center for Rural Affairs and asked them to spread the word to their networks. By the time those calls were over, calls began to flood in from national newspapers, magazines, and news services. I took care to call Jim Corcoran at the Fargo *Forum*; his anxiety over the rise of the Posse Comitatus would be assuaged if he knew that farmers would be getting due process of law from USDA. If FmHA followed the laws and the

Constitution, the Posse would lose a key recruitment method. Jim shouted, "Good job!"

I was on the phone for five solid hours, interrupted only by TV and radio interviews.

By the time I picked up Andrew, he was waiting near the door with a tired teacher. I usually did my best to leave work by five, but too often Andrew was the last kid to be picked up by the six o'clock deadline.

"Mommy won!" I told him. "Let's go out for pizza!"

When I finally got a physical copy of the decision, I saw that Dale's and Burt's persuasive arguments at the hearing, when I was too nicotine-deprived to think straight, had influenced Judge Van Sickle's decision to support the national class. The order said, "The plaintiffs have repeatedly asserted, and the defense has not denied, that the Department of Agriculture's policy is to accept a trial court's order as to the plaintiffs in that particular case, and to continue to apply its own interpretation of the law in all areas where it has not been specifically challenged. This policy, while perhaps proper as a tactical decision, invites numerous lawsuits, all of which must be funded by persons who are suffering financial hardship."

On October 29, 1983, an Associated Press story reported that "Sarah Vogel said this is going to stop the Farmers Home Administration from commencing foreclosures. They have . . . 17,037 farmers who were sent to the Office of General Counsel to start foreclosure as of June 30." (This was in addition to the 16,500 farmers who had already been forced out of business or had loans accelerated prior to being sent to the Office of General Counsel and the United States Attorney's Offices.)[1]

There was jubilation all over the nation, felt most intensely in small-town coffee shops, as the network of farmers and farm advocates shared the news. The grapevine worked faster than the AP! Messages of congratulations flooded in. It had been so long since farmers had heard good news. People felt hope again.

Then I got a call from Ward Sinclair, a reporter at the *Washington Post* who had been closely following the rural crisis for months. In D.C., he was in the belly of the beast—the epicenter of formation of agricultural policy.

"Sarah, are you aware that USDA is saying that Judge Van Sickle's injunction order only covers the North Dakota class?"

"What!" I gasped. "That's impossible."

As Ward understood it, USDA was taking the position that the judge might have changed the class definition, but his preliminary injunction order still covered only North Dakota. *Those bastards*, I thought.

"Well, they're wrong," I said. "USDA was preliminarily enjoined from taking certain actions on the class of North Dakota farmers. It is now preliminarily enjoined from taking the same actions on the national class of farmers."

"Well, they seem to disagree with you. I just got off the phone with the Office of General Counsel in Washington and they told me that there is a national class, but the restraining order that is in effect in North Dakota does not apply to the rest of the nation. And the clerk of court in Bismarck just told me that Judge Van Sickle wouldn't provide interpretations of the order. She said, 'If it is unclear, it is up to the lawyers to come before the court.'"[2]

The bad news flashed across the country with the speed of light, and for two weeks, I writhed in a weird mix of agony, anger, guilt, and confusion. The newspapers were the slingshots for ferocious threats from me ("We will see Secretary Block in court for contempt")[3] and even more ferocious threats from Burt ("If I find FmHA officials are in violation of that order I'm going to move that they are in contempt and insist that they be jailed").[4] I felt sick when I saw a *Bismarck Tribune* headline that said NO MORATORIUM SEEN ON LOANS. Similar headlines ran in papers all over the country.

I asked my mother to watch Andrew while I stayed out all night at the UND law library, dining on candy bars and pop, reading hundreds of pages of legal analysis by lawyers, judges, and law professors on injunctions. I then wrote a letter to the general counsel of USDA and said that FmHA offices nationwide were covered by the injunction. I reminded the general counsel that John Block and Charles Shuman were defendants bound by and subject to the injunction and we didn't need any more defendants. Block and Shuman's lawyers had fought certification of a national class and they'd lost. For Block and Shuman to now argue that they weren't subject to the injunction was frivolous and contemptuous. I warned that his clients Block and Shuman needed to correct their error or face future sanctions. I salted the letter with quotations and citations. It was a powerful letter and I was proud of it. I sent copies to Judge Van Sickle and to Annear.

I grimly wished that I could be a fly on the wall when the lawyers in the Office of General Counsel read my words. I hoped they realized that we were serious about sanctions and that the ACLU had litigators ready to pick up the fight.

Meanwhile, I was supposed to be working on discovery. Allan had recommended scheduling depositions of higher-ups in Washington, D.C., starting with Block and Shuman. "They'll hate being deposed!" he said, laughing, which of course was an incentive for us. We'd also bring in our own witnesses who would testify about the foreclosures, starve outs, and unfair hearings.

My father came into my office while I was working and handed me a sheet of paper. "You must read this," he said.

Now what have I done? I thought.

It was a letter to my parents, dated November 4, from Agnes Geelan, a well-known NPL old-timer.[5]

> Dear friends,
>
> You must be very proud of the excellent and successful way Sarah is handling the FmHA case. Wouldn't Bill Langer be proud to know that the grand-daughter of his most trusted advisor and friend is carrying on his fight for people? My admiration for Sarah and my best wishes for you.
>
> Sincerely,
> Agnes Geelan

I looked up at my father and noticed that he had taken his glasses off and was rubbing his eyes. He turned around and left without saying another word. But I knew he was very proud of me. *I was carrying on Bill Langer's fight for the people. I was carrying on Frank Vogel's fight for the people.*

My pride was erased the next afternoon with a one-minute call: "This is the assistant cashier of the Dakota State Bank. I am calling you to tell you that a notice of levy was received on your checking account with us. Your balance of twelve hundred twenty-six dollars and eighty-four cents has been debited and we have issued a cashier's check for that amount to the creditor."

William "Wild Bill" Langer, undated.

"Could I talk to you about it in person?" I whispered.

I told Donna I had to run an errand and rushed out of the office. The bank was one block away. As I hurried, I realized that if the bank's cashier had not called me, I would never have known that my account was empty, and all the small checks I had sent out to repay my many debts would have bounced, in the same way my farm clients' checks had bounced after FmHA seized their supervised bank accounts.

When I saw the notice of levy, my eyes widened in shock: it was for $3,350.95. Even after the $1,226.84 that had been seized, I still owed $2,124.11! It had been issued by a Grand Forks lawyer, based on a Virginia default judgment for unpaid condo fees, plus additional interest and costs. I'd made a few payments on the overdue condo fees, but I'd assumed they were nullified by the foreclosure and sale of the condo itself. Besides, that debt felt far less immediate than all the North Dakota bills that kept the lights on and a roof over my head.

When I got outside, I lit a cigarette and gathered my courage. If the levy wasn't lifted, my salary (which the office sent directly to the bank) would be seized and I'd have not a penny of income until the middle of December. I had no savings. And now my checking account was empty too.

I went directly to the office of the lawyer listed on the levy, a block away. The man had white hair and bushy eyebrows above sharp intelligent eyes. I thought he must be at least eighty years old, which meant he'd made it through the 1930s. Maybe he'd have compassion. I asked him if he would lift the levy if I agreed to make payments to him of $100 a month until it was paid. He countered me at $150, and we agreed on $125.

I'm sure he wondered why I didn't do what all the other deadbeats did— close the bank account and cash future payroll checks at random banks or check cashing services, or just file a Chapter 7 bankruptcy. But changing banks would lead to a citywide hunt for hidden assets that would destroy my reputation as a lawyer, and maybe my father's as well. Even though I was a perfect candidate, I ruled out bankruptcy. A Vogel would never file bankruptcy. Somehow I would repay all my debts. Eventually.

On November 14, Vivian called with good news. The May 5 preliminary injunction that covered the North Dakota class now definitively covered the national class too.

Judge Van Sickle was tactful, but he let his disdain for USDA's tactics show by adding a new paragraph—aimed squarely at Block and Shuman—to the original injunction:

> IT IS FURTHER ORDERED that defendants John R. Block and Charles W. Shuman are required to give notice upon their agents, subordinates and employees who are charged with implementing FmHA loans, of the contents of this order.

CHAPTER 22

Discovery

When my father and I showed up at the status conference on November 21, Gary Annear had another lawyer with him. The dark-haired man was wearing the kind of well-cut navy-blue suit, crisp white shirt, and shiny black shoes I'd seen on the best-dressed lawyers, from the most prestigious firms, at the class action seminar I'd attended in D.C.

Aha! I thought. *The frigging Department of Justice has arrived.*

Annear set a pile of papers in front of his fancy colleague and they both stared straight ahead. The awkwardness was too much for my father.

"Hello," he said, extending a hand. "I'm Bob Vogel."

"I am Sarah Vogel."

We were met with an angry glare. "And I'm Arthur Goldberg!" he announced. We were startled. The "real" Arthur Goldberg was a famous labor lawyer appointed by President Kennedy to the Supreme Court. He'd resigned to become President Johnson's ambassador to the United Nations. Justice Goldberg was an icon to liberal lawyers like us. But this imposter Arthur Goldberg wasn't a liberal, that was for sure, and he certainly wasn't interested in having a collegial relationship with us. Gary Annear managed to grump out "Good morning." The conversation was over. My dad and I went back to our seats, sharing a glance that meant *That was sure weird.*

When Judge Van Sickle came out, he did not seem to be in a good mood either. After calling the hearing to order, Judge Van Sickle asked Goldberg to introduce himself. Arrogantly, Goldberg announced that he was now lead counsel for the federal government in *Coleman v. Block*. The judge did not welcome him to North Dakota, as he had Burt, Allan, and Dale, but proceeded to rattle off a series of upcoming deadlines, without asking either party if they were workable.

By December 8, each side had to submit an outline of every argument made during the litigation thus far. A week later, each could respond to the other's outline. By December 22, all briefs on the merits had to be filed. Responses could be filed by December 31. All discovery had to be completed by the end of December. My heart sank: if briefs were due by December 22, discovery (the process of getting the other side to answer your questions and produce documents) would need to be completed before December 22. I groaned at this schedule: to finish by December 31 was impossibly tight and included three major holidays—Thanksgiving, Christmas, and New Year's.

As I was trying to wrap my head around the deadlines, Judge Van Sickle surprised us all. He said he'd instructed Cletus Schmidt, the clerk of court of the District of North Dakota, to write to his counterparts throughout the country to inform them of the injunction. There were more than eighteen hundred foreclosure actions pending against individual farmers in United States District Courts, with thousands more about to be filed by U.S. attorneys. The clerk working for Judge Van Sickle notified those courts that they could send those cases to North Dakota if they so chose.

I almost leaped to my feet and cheered!

I marveled at how deft this maneuver was on the part of Judge Van Sickle. Judge Van Sickle knew that the clerks of court were the key. Across the country, clerks were struggling to schedule criminal and civil trials with overworked federal judges. Judge Van Sickle knew that clerks of court with full dockets would *welcome* any good excuse to bounce a bunch of foreclosures over to Judge Van Sickle. Those clerks would swiftly inform their judges of the chance to nicely prune the docket, and the judges would sign orders to make that happen.[1] It was a slick offensive maneuver of a combat officer to outflank an enemy force. I'd never heard of a court's doing anything like that—before or since—and neither had my father.

Then the judge asked whether Annear and I would get together to resolve discovery issues. It wasn't really a question.

Annear and I both stood up.

"Yes, Your Honor," I said.

"Yes, Your Honor," Annear agreed.

Judge Van Sickle declared the status conference concluded with a bang of the gavel. My father and Goldberg, his face reddening, stood up too. Goldberg had flown in all the way from Washington, D.C., and all he had done was introduce himself. He walked out without a word, leaving Annear to pick up the papers on their table like a servant.

Goldberg reminded me of the arrogant Department of Justice lawyers I'd worked with when I was head of the Equal Credit Opportunity Act enforcement program at the Federal Trade Commission. Now I saw that the DOJ lawyers from Washington also treated the U.S. Attorney's Office in "flyover country" like pond scum.

ANNEAR WAS ALWAYS "too busy" to come to our office in Grand Forks, so I drove to Fargo for our discovery meeting. I knew it would be a wasted trip: Annear wasn't the type to cooperate, and Goldberg wouldn't have allowed it anyway.

I told Gary I'd identified the USDA witnesses I wanted to depose: Shuman and one other official in Washington and another official in St. Louis, where the finance office was. I said I would take two to three hours maximum each, and I could do them at any time during a two-week period in December. This flexibility in scheduling gave Annear and Goldberg no chance to credibly claim that these witnesses were "unavailable." Annear fussed, but agreed to pass the request along to Goldberg.

Back in Grand Forks, I focused on gathering more evidence through requests for documents and requests for admission. As hard as I tried to concentrate, my workdays were interrupted by a host of calls that were urgent ("a farmer is calling with a sick child"), important ("the *New York Times* is on line one") or necessary ("Burt is back in his office and he can talk to you now"). The calls wouldn't quit. I'd look at the clock at the end of the day and think, *I got nothing done today.* But brick by brick, I was building an edifice.

My social life was limited to lunchtime. Lawyers and businessmen had been meeting at a male-only "round table" at the back of a local café for decades. I had integrated the table soon after I arrived in Grand Forks. Why? Because they'd tried to keep me out!

Every day at noon, I got forty-five minutes of teasing, jokes, and repartee, and then it was back to work. I taught the guys the FmHA cheer I'd learned from a farmer: "Shout it out with feeling! Liq-ui-date! Ac-cel-er-ate! Fore-close! Ter-mi-nate!"[2]

The only time I could do any concentrated legal work was late at night.

I found teenaged babysitters who lived near my little rental house who could watch Andrew until nine o'clock, but that's when I'd just be hitting my stride. And I dreaded hearing him say, "I don't want a babysitter! I want to be with you!"

We began to eat a simple dinner at home, pack some snacks and drinks, and then head back to the office together. Andrew was content to play with his crayons, his writings, and the books he had memorized. When I got him a pile of "new" used books, he made up his own stories to go with the pictures. While Andrew played, I worked.

I was designing a very simple trap. By forcing Goldberg and Annear to make Shuman admit or deny statements about how FmHA operated nationwide, I could prove that the laws, regulations, policies, and practices that governed FmHA offices in North Dakota also governed every other FmHA office throughout the country. I wrote eighty-six separate requests for admission, and each one said: "Plaintiffs request that Defendant Charles W. Shuman admit or deny that [statement of fact] is true." For example, Request for Admission 43 was "Admit or deny that only a State Director or an Acting State Director may accelerate a loan secured by real estate . . ."

Underneath my desk, I put a couch cushion and some blankets so when Andrew grew sleepy, he could curl up there until I finally quit at one or two in the morning. I'd carry him out to the car fireman-style. He'd sleep through the ride home and then we'd both curl up in the double bed in the tiny bedroom until morning.

Working late at the office had another advantage besides silent productivity: warmth. I was finding it impossible to heat the little garage house. It had no insulation. The wind whistled through the upstairs walls, so I abandoned the upstairs as uninhabitable. We were almost always cold, even though our November heating bill exceeded the $230 monthly rent. I lamented not getting an apartment with utilities included: the house wasn't such a bargain after all.

On Christmas Eve afternoon, Andrew and I drove around looking at Christmas lights (it got dark by five o'clock) and then went to my parents' house.

My brother Bobby was there, and we called the other siblings (Mary in Mandan, Frank at Harvard getting his doctorate in Arabic studies). My mother had decorated her houseplants and a potted orange tree in a sunny corner of the dining room with twinkly white lights. Presents were piled beneath the tree branches. The dining room table was dressed up with a vivid Norwegian tablecloth and napkins and red Norwegian wooden candlesticks. There was mulled wine for the grown-ups, warm cider for Andrew.

The phone rang with a call from my mother's older brother, Cal, in Minnesota. My mother's Mork siblings almost never called or visited. Their rare communications were by round-robin letters. One sibling would write a letter to another, who would add news of his or her family and send both letters to another, who would forward again until all six were in the loop, and after the letters had circulated to all the siblings (which might take a year), a new round-robin would start. My mother held the receiver out so we could all hear.

"Elsa, this is Cal. I just read a front page story about farm foreclosures and it says that there is a Sarah Vogel from Grand Forks who is fighting farm foreclosures? Is that Sally?"

"Yes!" my mother proudly answered.

"I'm glad. Okay now. Merry Christmas."

"Okay, Cal, Merry Christmas."

Decades later, a cousin sent me a letter with some Mork family history my mother had never shared. I knew my Mork grandparents, Edvard and Evelyn, were immigrants from Norway. I knew they met and married in Minnesota. I did not know that Edvard and Evelyn were farmers in Minnesota who lost their farm in the 1920s. The couple and their seven young children moved to town, where Edvard became a carpenter and handyman. Then more tragedy struck. Evelyn died soon thereafter and some of the children had to "board out." My mother was sent to stay with one of her aunts in St. Cloud for about two years. I knew my mother had "visited" her aunt after her mother had died, but she never spoke of her mother, her aunt, being very poor, or of the farm. Apparently, losing the farm was a shameful Mork family secret. I didn't learn of the lost family farm until after my mother died (at age ninety-seven). I remembered my mother's quiet remark in the abandoned sod house: "These houses were hard to clean."

When it was time to open presents, Andrew got toys (no guns), clothes, and books. I got a check for $3,000. (Equitable as always, my parents gave Frank and Mary the same; Bobby was on a disability program so he got "extras" on a daily basis.)

When we got home that night, I parked by the front door, leaving the car running to keep Andrew warm while I opened the door. It was a bitter cold night and my breath went up in clouds of steam, almost obscuring my vision. But through the fog, I saw water seeping out from under the doorsill. It sparkled darkly against the white snow as it turned to ice. I slowly stepped forward, pulled the door open, and flipped on the light switch (a truly stupid move, as I was standing in water, but I realized my error too late to withdraw my hand). My pupils hurt as the ceiling fluorescent light stuttered to full brightness and I stared into the kitchen at the water shooting out from under the kitchen sink. The pipe had burst, and the kitchen floor was covered with several inches of water, flowing down the sloping floor to the door I'd just entered. At the edges it was turning to ice. The counters were covered with droppings from the mice that had escaped from the frozen water that filled their regular living spaces under the counters. I realized that the mice had sought cover when they heard me come in. I backed out, switching off the light, and climbed into the car. I covered my face with my mittens to muffle my crying.

But it was too cold to stay in the car, even with a heater going full blast. I drove down the brightly decorated streets back to my parents' house.

"Is that you, Sarah?" my mother whispered, as she heard me come in.

My father was awake, too. They were happy to see us out of the "shack." In the morning, I told Andrew we had to move back to Grandma and Grandpa's, which was fine by him.

USDA HADN'T SENT me any discovery requests. They hadn't asked to depose any of my original North Dakota plaintiffs or any of the new lead plaintiffs Dale had found. USDA had agreed that the written evidence could be used in lieu of depositions, so it wouldn't be necessary to depose Shuman and the other two officials. Thankfully, I didn't have to spend days traveling to D.C. and St. Louis. The January 9 trial date was less than two weeks away.

On December 27, I found out what Arthur Goldberg had been up to when I received a FedEx envelope containing two documents. The first asked for a postponement of the January 9 trial. The second was captioned "Defendants'

Supplemental Memorandum in Opposition to Plaintiffs' Request for Permanent Injunctive Relief and in Support of Defendants' Motion for Summary Judgment."

As I skimmed the supplemental memorandum, I was dismayed at its high quality. It was much better written—and better researched—than anything written by Annear. It cited cases and made arguments about the constitutional issues that Annear had never raised.

By that afternoon, I was on an emergency conference call with Burt, Allan, and Dale. We agreed we wouldn't back off on the January 9 hearing; our clients couldn't afford any more delays. We were ready for a trial. Our witnesses from around the country were lined up and were arriving the weekend of January 7–8. All we needed now was a reply brief—an unbelievably powerful reply brief.

Dale volunteered for the legal arguments having to do with the deferral law. Burt would gather some ACLU attorneys and they would dive into the constitutional issues. Allan would prepare a summation of the national class issues. I had to gather evidence from the trial testimony, the admissions, the depositions, and boxes of evidence to buttress my co-counsel's legal arguments.

The day after our planning call, Dale called me back.

"Well, I've finished my 1981a argument on deferrals! And it's brilliant."

"How'd you do that? You've only had a day. I've barely started."

"*Well*," Dale drawled slowly for effect, "I just got a call from the clerk of the Eighth Circuit."

I held my breath.

"A three-judge panel unanimously affirmed *Allison*! My assignment is done!"

"Dale, you are my hero!"

"Aw shucks, it was nothing, but thank you anyway, ma'am."

The news about *Allison v. Block* spread like wildfire. Judge Van Sickle had to follow the Eighth Circuit's ruling on the deferral law in *Allison*. If the *Coleman* case did nothing else, it would give farmers in forty-six states the right to apply for a deferral.

Later that day, I got a call from Annear. I was distrustful but tried to be polite. He didn't beat around the bush or engage in useless pleasantries. Instead, he bluntly asked, "What do you think about doing a stipulation saying that FmHA in North Dakota is typical of FmHA nationally?"

My mind began to whirl with speculation. Was this proposal because they were confident of winning based on Goldberg's very strong brief, or was it because we had them on the run? Had they arrived at the sensible realization that FmHA loans were in fact uniformly run nationwide, or did Goldberg just not want to come to North Dakota in January, when the weather was truly awful? Was it because they weren't prepared for the trial?

I took a deep breath, and said, "Send me something in writing and we'll look at it."

By New Year's Eve, we had worked out language that my co-counsel and I agreed to on behalf of the farmers:

> It is hereby stipulated between the parties that both parties agree that the Court's final judgment on all claims in this action may be based on the evidentiary record made before the Honorable Bruce M. Van Sickle on September 20, 21, and 22, 1983, and all other pleadings, affidavits, admissions and depositions which have been submitted herein to the extent deemed necessary by the court.
>
> After filing the Defendant's Response to Plaintiffs' Request for Admissions, it is further stipulated that the evidentiary record shall be closed.
>
> It is further stipulated, subject to Court approval, that the hearing on January 9, 1984, shall be limited to oral argument on the law and on evidence already in the record and that no witnesses shall be called by either party.

My very first trial—for which I'd had less than twenty-four hours' notice—was now going to be "the evidentiary record" for the more than 240,000 farmers in the class. There would be no trial for the national class—only one last oral argument in front of Judge Van Sickle on January 9.

I wasn't a gambler, but I felt like a character in an old *Gunsmoke* episode, facing Goldberg across a poker table. I was the honest, hardworking cowhand who'd bet the ranch. Goldberg was a card shark from the east. I thought my cards were good; so did Goldberg. Soon we would see who had the stronger hand.

CHAPTER 23

The Biblical Injunction

T he small crowd of farmers who'd come for the hearing were shedding their heavy jackets, earflapped hats, and gloves in the back of the courtroom, whispering among themselves and sharing news. The Folmers, the Hatfields, the McCabes, and Dwight Coleman were all there. This time, I didn't feel so alone. I had Allan, Dale, and our newest co-counsel, Jim Massey, with me. There were several reporters with notebooks. Even the security people seemed relaxed: it was obvious that this was no Posse crowd.

Gary Annear and Arthur Goldberg sat alone on the defendants' side. It was like a country wedding where the bride comes from a huge Catholic family and the groom is an orphan.

We all stood when Judge Van Sickle entered. He also looked relaxed, likely because he didn't have to conduct a multiday trial.

Our team had divided the argument, and Dale went first, to say that the Eighth Circuit had correctly interpreted the deferral law and it was a good thing that USDA's five-year delay in implementing this law had at last ended. Allan spoke without notes about how the farmers in the class were a perfect fit for the rules governing class actions, and he answered several questions from Judge Van Sickle with ease. I wrapped up by summarizing the constitutional principles that supported the preliminary injunction's guarantees of a fair hearing before farmers could be deprived of essential family living and farm operating expenses.

I asked, again, that Judge Van Sickle issue a final permanent injunction that would require neutral administrative law judges as hearing officers.

Goldberg took the opposite side of all these arguments, but it seemed he was saving his true thunder for an appeal. Annear sat silent—it seemed that his relationship with Goldberg had become even more fraught.

The hearing was over in less than two hours. I gathered up my papers with a light heart and told the lead plaintiffs, "Meet us at the East 40 Restaurant for lunch!"

Everyone followed me back to the Fleck House parking lot. The icy cold was brutal. I jumped into my car; Jim jumped into his. My passengers shivered as the car croaked back to life. We arrived at the restaurant well before noon and had a large room to ourselves. We rearranged tables so the lawyers and the clients could all sit together. That's when I realized we were missing someone.

"Didn't you bring Dale?" I asked Jim.

"I thought he was riding with you," Jim said.

I grabbed my coat and keys and flew out the door. Ten minutes later, I found Dale standing in the motel parking lot in his thin city shoes and lightweight black overcoat, his gloved hands shoved into his armpits. He was wearing the stocking cap he had borrowed from me pulled so low it almost covered his eyes.

"I'm so sorry! I thought you'd gone with Jim," I said as I jumped out to grab his suitcase and briefcase. Dale stiffly climbed into the passenger seat. His eyelashes and eyebrows were dusted with frost. As he defrosted in the car, Dale shivered out his first words: "I thought you'd never come!" Dale explained that he'd gone to his room to grab his suitcase and he saw the cars pulling away when he left his room. He'd locked the door to his room behind him and the motel office was locked, too.

Dale was met with cheers at the East 40. He ordered a hot toddy, and like a master storyteller (I'm sure he charmed every jury he encountered), he began his tale of how "the Dakota Witch" (his new nickname for me) had abandoned him, an innocent Southerner, to almost certain death. Northern hospitality, indeed!

The North Dakota farmers tried to one-up him by telling him stories about worse winters: winters when the cows froze to death on their feet, winters when the blizzards were so bad that farmers needed guide ropes to walk between house and barn, winters when their houses were covered by drifts of snow, winters when it stayed twenty below for weeks at a time.

"Pshaw!" Russel Folmer said. "This is *good* weather, Dale!"

Over the years, Dale's story of the twenty minutes he spent in a North Dakota parking lot grew ever more colorful. "Dale, tell us the story about how you survived after Sarah abandoned you in a blizzard!" Dale was always happy to oblige.

IN EARLY JANUARY, Charles Shuman had issued a new directive called "Pretermination Notice for Farmer Program Borrowers." It seemed strangely secretive—neither Annear nor Goldberg had mentioned it at the hearing. Maybe they didn't know about it. Even with my network, it took me weeks to get a copy.

The first few pages instructed FmHA employees to follow Judge Van Sickle's preliminary injunction order: no repossession of livestock, no loan accelerations, no seizing income that should be released for family living expenses.[1] Shuman gave his employees a template letter to send to tens of thousands of farmers whose loans had been accelerated, to offer them relief "as a result of pending litigation." I had hoped for a notice exactly like this one, but as I read it closely, I realized that this letter was only the first of many. The relief being offered was only "for the present." Additional form letters followed, and none of them were written in plain English. They were written in the jargon of FmHA-speak. Even I had a hard time understanding them. I asked an English professor to analyze one of them and she determined it was written in language more difficult to understand than the *Harvard Law Review*. I feared that farmers who didn't have guidance on how to properly fill out the forms wouldn't be able to properly apply for deferrals and other relief.

It was time to amend the FmHA chant: *"Liq-ui-date! Ac-cel-er-ate! Fore-close! Ob-fus-cate!"*

I didn't just dislike the content of the notice—I objected to the word "pretermination" in the title. It wasn't a letter to encourage farmers to come in and visit about how they could work out of their current difficulties. I believed it was a notice *preceding* termination, which meant that termination remained Shuman's end goal.

I submitted a brief to Judge Van Sickle about the pretermination notice, but he brushed it aside to be dealt with after his decision.

By mid-February, I was still waiting for that decision. The farm crisis was turning into one of the hot political issues of the 1984 election. The harsh effects of David Stockman's policies spread from FmHA to the Federal Land Banks, and even to the better-off farmers who did business with banks. Congressman Dorgan had created a farm crisis task force, and on February 17, I flew to Washington to brief members of Congress and their staff on the *Coleman* case.

I took a cab straight from the airport to one of the House office buildings and spent the afternoon in a room packed with members of Congress and their staff convened by Congressman Dorgan. I shared numbers, statistics, strategies, and a dire prediction: the *Coleman* case might buy farmers time, but Congress would have to develop better prices and bring interest rates down. Even though tens of thousands of farmers were now protected by the injunction, they couldn't last much longer unless the economy improved.

Before I left I made another request: "If Judge Van Sickle doesn't require administrative law judges for FmHA hearings, you have to fix the law. The hearings are the farmers' last chance, and they deserve fair and impartial hearing officers."

Later that afternoon, I wearily pulled my suitcase to Senator Quentin Burdick's office, where my friend Sara Garland worked. Our plan was to go to dinner to catch up on our lives and our kids; I'd stay the night at her house on Capitol Hill and leave for the airport at five the next morning.

"Something's up," Sara told me as soon as I got there. "Your office has been getting press calls. Your dad called me a little bit ago and said that the word is that Judge Van Sickle is going to come out with a decision soon. I'm waiting for the Bismarck office to call me back."

I sat in Sara's small cubicle and worried.

The phone rang. Sara picked up and put it on the speaker.

"You won't believe it," her Bismarck staffer reported. "A bunch of reporters with TV cameras are hanging out in the hallway outside the judge's office. NBC News is here; they flew in on their own jet. Helen just came out and said the decision will be ready soon."

I started pacing the office. After working on the case for years in North Dakota, I was now a thousand miles away from my office, only a half mile from the USDA headquarters of Auction Block and Shuman.

The phone rang again. It was five o'clock in Bismarck and the scout wanted to know if he could go home.

"Not yet," Sara said. "I checked with the senator and he said it's absolutely essential that he be notified as soon as the decision comes out."

When she hung up, I raised my eyebrows.

Sara smiled and said, "The senator is at home. We don't need to call him. I know this is exactly what he'd want me to say. He defended farmers in the 1930s; his dad ran the Farmers' Holiday Association; he supports you and your case. Don't worry."

I remembered what Senator Burdick had said in his telegram, when he sent $100 to the fundraising Hoe-Down the McCabes had organized: *The obstacles you face are significant but not insurmountable. Your great spirit and strength will be your most valuable assets during the struggle ahead.*

Hours passed. In lieu of dinner, Sara and I raided the office fridge and visited the candy machine and juice dispenser. We talked nonstop. We'd been friends since we were thirteen, almost shared a first name, and had been born two days apart. We'd gone to the same college and had both left home for the East Coast. Our professional lives had run on separate tracks but toward the same destination—a better society for all. At my darkest times during my separation from James, I'd taken Andrew to her house to get a break and support. While we waited for the call from Bismarck, we shared the intimate details of our lives that we shared with no one else.

At eight the scout called Sara again. "Still nothing. May I go home now?"

"The senator is sorry you have to stay so late, but it is *essential* that he have a copy of the decision tonight. As soon as it comes, get a copy and fax it to me here and I'll get it to the senator."

I looked at her, bewildered. "What is fax?"

Sarah explained it was a new technology ("facsimile") that could transfer documents over a telephone line. I thought that sounded like science fiction. I couldn't wait to tell Andrew. It was like *Star Wars*, a document flying through space.

Time slowed to a crawl. I looked at the clock but it seemed to have stopped moving. Sara and I stared at the phone, willing it to ring.

Finally it did.

"Yes?" Sara answered. "Uh-huh, okay . . . send it by fax."

I could hardly breathe as I followed her to a room filled with copy machines, paper, and a whirring machine that was already pushing a long curling scroll of paper out of its maw.

I dropped to the floor, even though I was wearing my best suit, and lay under the machine on my back, reading the pages as they emerged from the miraculous fax machine. I shivered as I lay on the concrete floor, but it wasn't due to the cold; my shivers were due to unbearable tension. So much was at stake.

Of the roughly 240,000 farmers in the national class, FmHA had reported that 77,111 farmers were delinquent, and almost 14,000 of those delinquent farmers had received the so-called "servicing" letters that led to freezes of income, starve outs, and demands that the farmer "voluntarily" quit.[2] Moreover, 1,800 cases were still pending in courts across the country.[3] And this data was six months old. I knew—everybody knew—that the next statistical report by FmHA would be worse unless something was done.

The fax was spitting out pages faster than I could read them. I flashed on a sentence that crushed one of my hopes: the judge didn't think Farmers Home needed neutral hearing officers from outside the agency. I had hoped outside hearing officers would bring law and order back to FmHA. My eyes flooded with bitter tears. *All that work for naught.*

"What's wrong?" Sara asked.

"I lost the administrative judge issue," I said.

I forced myself to continue reading.

"Oh my God, Sara," I said.

"What now?"

"I think we actually won," I said. I had won a final permanent injunction for the national class of 240,000 FmHA borrowers.[4]

Judge Van Sickle opened his decision with the big picture: FmHA existed because "a strong and stable farm economy is vital to the welfare of the nation." I'd grown up with this mantra. He said FmHA had been set up "to help farm families retain their land despite droughts and depression" and now was a "far-flung undertaking by the United States government to bolster the credit position of practically all farm operations, farm related businesses, and rural towns and communities."[5]

Judge Van Sickle went on to say that under current leadership (he meant Reagan, Stockman, Block, and Shuman), FmHA's guiding principles had been abandoned in a zealous mission to reduce delinquencies. I thought about the way the Resettlement Administration had worked in the 1930s to improve the lives of tenant farmers by helping them buy their own land and get modern conveniences like electricity. I remembered Ralph Clark's dining room, where Tom Nichols and I developed arguments to fight his foreclosure by oil lamp light because the electricity had been cut off. I remembered Tom's anguish about his starving hogs. I remembered Diane McCabe asking, "Why do they let people buy fertilizer to feed the ground and we can't feed our cows?"

Even though the decision was written in formal legal language, Judge Van Sickle's compassion for farmers shone through. My father had been right when he told me I needed to file the *Coleman* case before Judge Van Sickle.

At the heart of Judge Van Sickle's decision was a biblical injunction: *The laborer is worthy of his hire.* It said,

> The "hire" of the farm operator is basically the crop he raises, whether it be a crop of produce for commerce (wool), produce for animal use (hay), or produce for human use (vegetables or fruit). Various examples in the law, such as wage protection in garnishment statutes, wage claims priorities in bankruptcy proceedings, specific exemptions of growing crops from process ... and specific restraints as to crop production liens ... all reflect a concern for the person without whose labor the production would not occur ... [6]

I remembered that the Saint Paul version of this biblical injunction[7] was carved in stone on the face of the United States Department of Agriculture building in D.C.: THE HUSBANDMAN THAT LABORETH MUST BE FIRST PARTAKER OF THE FRUITS. It was fitting that Judge Van Sickle brought USDA back to its original mission.

And it was fitting that Judge Van Sickle used the Folmers to demonstrate how FmHA had violated the biblical injunction. Russel had been accused of "unhusbandlike" farming practices, and Judge Van Sickle used the Folmers' security agreement to explain the harsh consequences of an acceleration: "The debtor ... now receives nothing towards support of his family from his effort

[yet] must care for the animals and the crops on the place, let them starve or waste, or 'voluntarily' sell out."[8]

The Folmers and all of the other families deserved to be able to provide for their own sustenance and to care for their animals before an agency of the federal government could deprive them of the very means of their existence. And they deserved due process of law, as enshrined in the Fifth Amendment of the United States Constitution.

The biblical injunction would no longer just be carved in the stone façade of USDA's building and the due process clause would no longer be just on paper; they would be implemented in people's lives.

But the judge and I disagreed on who was to blame for the conditions that led me to file the lawsuit. Judge Van Sickle held the national FmHA office accountable, not the state or county bureaucrats I'd done battle with for two years. In fact, he wrote sympathetically, "These state employees have had the unenviable task of balancing the FmHA's function as a form of social welfare with the realities of operating a loan program. Their task has not been made any easier by confusing legislative enactments and a plethora of complicated and interconnected regulations."

I wasn't that charitable; I had seen too much gratuitous cruelty from county, district, and state FmHA officials. The Crows Hearts and their neighbors often faced racist conduct at their local county office. FmHA employees often behaved worse than private lenders. The local bankers didn't rub salt into the wound by accusing the borrower of bad management, "unhusbandlike" farming practices, or dishonesty. They didn't demand slavish behavior ("You must sell out") or use "failure to voluntarily liquidate" as a reason for foreclosure.

The government wanted permission to proceed straight to acceleration, seizure of income, and foreclosure—bypassing any rights to appeal—whenever FmHA came up with one of several plausible rationales. But the judge ruled that an accusation of conversion (as in the case of the Folmers) or abandonment (as illustrated by the Hatfields' being accused of having quit farming) would not justify the loss of any farmer's right to appeal, nor would an FmHA borrower lose their rights to appeal if another lender commenced foreclosure, because Judge Van Sickle realized such a foreclosure could be created by FmHA's refusal to release income to pay that lender, as had happened to the Folmers and the Bank of North Dakota.[9]

I remembered telling my clients, "Someday a judge will hear about this." As I turned the pages of the decision, I saw that Judge Van Sickle had listened to the lead plaintiffs' stories, and now he was giving hundreds of thousands of farmers protection from similar mistreatment.

He devoted only two short but powerful sentences to reject FmHA's argument that it did not have to provide notice to the farmers of their right to apply for a deferral: "The ruling in *Allison* is controlling law in this case. Therefore, the Court rejects the government's arguments that 1981a is permissive and that the FmHA existing deferral regulations are adequate."[10] It had been more than five years since President Carter had signed the deferral law, saying that it would "prevent foreclosures." Now, at last, it would be in effect nationwide.

Judge Van Sickle emphasized that a decision to foreclose by FmHA was not based upon delinquency, but rather on "highly subjective" decisions of the FmHA employees and therefore the farmers deserved due process of law and the right to present their own case at a hearing before a neutral hearing officer.[11]

Despite how unskilled I was as a trial lawyer, I had convinced Judge Van Sickle that due process (a notice, a neutral hearing officer, a fair process) was necessary. Fifty-five lawsuits had been filed against FmHA by January 1, 1984,[12] and only two challenged the starve out and the hearing process: *Coleman* in North Dakota and *Gamradt* in Minnesota. *Gamradt* had flopped. *Coleman* wasn't perfect (I still wanted administrative law judges) but it protected a quarter million or so farmers from violation of their rights to proper notice and a fair hearing.

Good job, Sally Vogel, I said to myself. I imagined the old NPLers would have been proud of me.

The decision included three pages of directions to FmHA going forward. The starve out would be a thing of the past. I thought of the DeLares, who had federal agents descend on their farm to seize their cattle and machinery. I thought of the Nicholses, whose innocent attempt to have the state office require that their county supervisor treat them fairly resulted in vicious retaliation and seizure of all their income. I thought of all the times I'd gone to FmHA hearings where the result was predetermined and the hearing officer had already approved the action we were appealing or his boss was the decision maker. "That's a kangaroo court," Dwight had said.

The magic words of the order left no wiggle room for the lower-level officers of FmHA: it applied to "defendants, their agents, subordinates and employees."

Before any liquidation, foreclosure, freeze of income, or similar action could be taken, FmHA had to provide at least thirty days' written notice of its intentions to the farmer. This notice had to tell the farmer that she or he had a right to a hearing and also had to give the reasons for the proposed liquidation or termination.

FmHA had to tell the farmer who the hearing officer would be, and, crucially, "the hearing officer *shall not have been actively involved in the initial decision* of liquidation or termination" (emphasis added). I didn't get neutral hearing officers from outside the agency, but in one short sentence, Judge Van Sickle had upended the process FmHA used to shut down farmers. Now, there would be—at a minimum—a fresh set of eyes on the conduct of the district directors.

Judge Van Sickle required that the hearing officer had to give the decision "in writing, giving his reasons therefore, which decision shall be furnished to the borrower." I remembered Judge Van Sickle holding the national office's one-paragraph rejection letter and asking Russel Folmer, "Is this all you received? This is it?" That wouldn't happen again.

The order did not just affect what FmHA officials did. It also reached the vast network of U.S. attorneys in courthouses throughout the United States, who would have to file motions to dismiss thousands of pending foreclosure cases. Annear and his counterparts in other states would have to dismiss the foreclosure cases against the DeLares and nearly two thousand other farmers who were already in court. Many more farmers' files were stacked up in regional offices of USDA's Office of General Counsel being prepared for foreclosure cases; they would have to be returned to the state and county offices. The burden wouldn't be on broke farmers to reverse their accelerations or fight their way out of court. They would be set free, as a bird is set free when the door to the cage is opened. And FmHA would have to start over—from scratch—with notice, opportunity for a hearing, and so on.

Judge Van Sickle was clearly aware of FmHA's evasion of his earlier orders, and so he reiterated that "defendants John R. Block and Charles W. Shuman shall give notice to their agents, subordinates and employees who are charged with implementing FmHA loans, of the contents of this order."

BACK HOME AT my parents' house the next day, I dropped my briefcase on the floor as Andrew came running to greet me. I spun him around in a huge hug, and then I gave my father a copy of the decision.

"We've gone and made some law," I said.

On Monday, I sat at the desk that Richard DeLare had built and wrote a letter to the lead plaintiffs. It said:

> We won!
>
> To those of you who put their lives and reputations on the line to become named plaintiffs, I want to express our sincere thanks. Some of you told me early on, "I don't know if this will help me or not, but I will be happy if others can't be treated like this in the future." Others said, "I just don't want to go down quietly." As it has turned out, we have helped *thousands* of others. The final order affects about 240,000 farmers, of which 52% were delinquent on January 1, 1983.

A reporter from the *Grand Forks Herald* interviewed me soon after the decision came out.

"I got most of what I wanted," I told her. "I wanted a *lot*."

I still do.

PART IV

The Saved Seed

CHAPTER 24

There Is One Bright Spot
Where the People Rule

On January 1, 1989, I looked out a sixth-floor window of the North Dakota State Capitol in Bismarck. As the sun cast weak shadows from the bare tree branches on the capitol grounds below me, I looked out at the frozen horizon. My new office was even bigger than the office I'd had at the Treasury Department, and the view was far better. From the huge windows, I could see most of Bismarck, parts of Mandan, and the escarpment on the far side of the Missouri River that marks the beginning of the vast Missouri Slope that stretches west to the Badlands where Teddy Roosevelt once ranched.

In November 1988, I had been elected the North Dakota agriculture commissioner, and I now held one of most powerful positions in North Dakota government, with thirty-five full-time and many part-time and temporary employees working for me.

After the election, I'd called my friend Norma in New York City to brag a little about my achievement. I was the first woman elected to this office in the history of the United States.

"Hey, Norma, I was just elected ag commissioner of North Dakota!"

"Gee, that's great! Congratulations! Are you the first woman to be egg commissioner? Do chickens have a commissioner too, or just eggs?"

In North Dakota, at least, I was now a "somebody," but one thing hadn't changed—I was still fighting to save broke farmers.

It was a Sunday and the office was quiet. I half wished Andrew was with me, but he was ten years old now, and very skeptical of my invitations to come with me to the office, to a meeting, or on a "trip." Instead, he was with his uncle, watching football, while I organized my new office. I had carts of boxes to unpack from my previous office on the first floor, where I had been a North Dakota assistant attorney general. Dozens of cardboard supermarket boxes that had previously held green beans and apples were crammed with files and bore legends like THE CRAZIES, COLEMAN, and 87 AG CREDIT ACT in bold black marker. Those files held documents going back a decade.

From the time I'd tried to help Chuck Perry get his farm records, the farm economy continued to fail. By New Year's Day 1989, it wasn't just FmHA borrowers who were suffering. It was virtually all farmers, except those farmers (usually in their sixties) with no debt who could survive long periods of selling their farm products at a loss. USDA officials kept up their mantra that times were good and getting better, but absolutely no one believed them. The agriculture economy was in free fall. By 1986, the impact extended beyond the sectors of the economy that depended on farmers (seed, feed, fertilizer). It was also beginning to drag down pension funds and insurance companies that had invested in bonds secured by farm loans. Farmers' contributions to the national economy weren't appreciated until their troubles affected Wall Street.

Ironically, agriculture economists were very late in acknowledging the crisis.[1] They looked backward at abstract data like trends in farmland values or the value of lenders' portfolios but didn't consider the condition of the people on the farms. Lawyers, politicians, musicians (Willie Nelson), actresses (Jessica Lange), and tiny groups of young activists (Mark Ritchie, Danny Levitas, Dave Ostendorf) knew how bad it was years before the economists began to churn out tables with lines that sank into the red zone that at last "proved" that hundreds of thousands of farmers were going down.

Many powerful Republican officeholders had joined farm advocates in putting pressure on President Reagan to do "something" for farmers.[2] In the fall of 1984 (right before the midterm elections), Block announced a new Debt Adjustment Program, but Stockman thwarted its potential success when he "vetoed" any interest write-downs. Only principal could be reduced.[3]

Testifying before the Senate Budget Committee on February 7, 1985, Stockman said, "For the life of me, I can't figure out why the taxpayers of this country have the responsibility to refinance the bad debts willingly incurred by consenting adults who went out and bought farmland when the price was going up because they could get rich, or who went and bought machinery and production assets because they made a business judgment that they could make some money."[4]

Dr. Neil Harl later wrote, "Every tragedy needs a villain; Stockman qualifies easily for that role in the farm debt crisis of the 1980s."[5]

As I gazed out the window of my new office, I was grateful that most of the leaders in both the state and the nation now recognized that the farm economy was in dire shape.

My predecessor as agriculture commissioner, Kent Jones, a Republican, had founded a farm advocate program in 1984 and invited me to be one of the trainers of the first group of advocates. My topic was how to do FmHA appeals, while Lou Anne Kling from Minnesota taught them how to do farm plans and how to effectively mediate and resolve disputes. The advocates now worked for me. Between November and January 1, the Agriculture Department had hired and trained more than eighty new farm advocates[6] (now called mediators and farm credit counselors). We were expecting thousands of seriously delinquent FmHA borrowers to ask for help. The *Coleman* injunctions had been a thumb in the dike until Congress passed the 1987 Agricultural Credit Act and FmHA wrote the regulations implementing that act. But now, the new regulations were in place, and in days, a tsunami of cases would emerge from FmHA offices. The farm advocates were the human shields that would save as many farmers from foreclosure as possible.

I suspected that some of them were already working, even on a holiday. I walked down the hall, in the direction of the fresh coffee I smelled. There was Roger Johnson, my choice to head the Farm Mediation Program; his family had been NPLers too. His administrative assistant was Jet Collins, a miraculously cheerful and hardworking person.

"Howdy!" they both said with huge smiles.

I didn't expect much chitchat; they had hardly taken a day off since the election.

I filled my cup with hot coffee. "If you can take a break, come visit me," I said. "I'm unpacking."

John Baer cartoon, January 6, 1919.

"You bet, boss lady," Jet said.

Back in my office, I took the certificate of my election, embossed with the Great Seal of North Dakota, out of its envelope and put it into the frame. Hanging the certificate on the wall made the office my own.

Next I hung a poster with an NPL cartoon by John Baer, the political cartoonist A. C. Townley had hired for the *Nonpartisan League Leader*. It showed a picture of Lady Liberty, a beautiful young woman wearing a loose Greek tunic, standing behind a dejected Uncle Sam seated at a desk. Lady Liberty's right arm is raised and her hand points to a map of the United States. Her index finger touches the state of North Dakota, which is bordered by rays of light as though the state were a sun. Her other hand compassionately rests on the slumped shoulder of Uncle Sam, who is pondering papers on his desk labeled "Other States."

"Don't become discouraged," the caption next to Lady Liberty says. "There is one bright spot where the people rule and we have real democracy in America—your day is coming!"

After we won the *Coleman* case, I'd sent copies of this poster to Burt, Allan, and Dale to thank them for helping the farmers of the United States. The poster wasn't their only reward; they'd also been paid attorneys' fees through the Equal Access to Justice Act. I'd been paid too. And it was a miracle.

Ever since EAJA had become law in 1980, a battle had been raging between the Department of Justice and attorneys like me in private practice. EAJA was modeled after civil rights laws, and if a plaintiff in a civil rights lawsuit against a state won any significant issue or was a catalyst for positive change, the state *had* to pay the plaintiff's attorney's fees. Many people believed that EAJA would be interpreted in the same way, based on its language and legislative history. But the Department of Justice argued that payment of attorney's fees by parties who won cases against the federal government should be reviewed under a more rigorous standard; EAJA payments should be granted only if the party won *and* the government's position was "unreasonable."

Too many judges were agreeing with the highly polished arguments of the Department of Justice that its defenses were "reasonable." I knew Goldberg and Annear would argue that their resistance to the legal arguments I'd made was reasonable. After all, no one had ever filed a case like *Coleman* before; it was a case of "first impression." I feared EAJA was a chimera; it held out the hope of payment, but courts rarely made federal agencies pay attorneys fees under EAJA.

Then, on January 9, 1984, one week before Judge Van Sickle issued the final permanent injunction in our case, the Eighth Circuit came out with a wonderful decision in an EAJA fee award. The case was called *Premachandra v. Mitts*. Two of the three judges applied the same liberal standard that the courts had been using in civil rights litigation; one judge dissented and said no fees should be awarded if the government's position was reasonable, even if it had lost the case.

I rejoiced. Because this was a decision from the Eighth Circuit, Judge Van Sickle would be required to follow it, just as he had to follow the *Allison* case. I relied heavily on the *Premachandra* decision when I turned in our fee application in February.

Collectively, my co-counsel and I asked for a total EAJA award of $186,386, and over $20,000 in costs. Plus, because of our great results, we asked for an enhancement of 25 percent for the time of every lawyer except me; I—not so modestly—asked for an increase of 50 percent.

Predictably, Goldberg and Annear went nuts.

They filed a long, detailed brief nitpicking almost every minute for which we wanted to be paid. I'd expected that, but what I didn't expect was that the Department of Justice would be successful at getting all the judges of the Eighth Circuit to agree to review the *Premachandra* decision to see if it had been correctly decided (this process is called an en banc review). Goldberg and Annear put in a motion for Judge Van Sickle to hold our fee petition in abeyance until the en banc review was completed. An en banc review could take at least six months, so I begged Judge Van Sickle not to hold up the fee petition. Why wait up to a year to decide, I argued, when the en banc decision might be the same as the panel decision and Annear and Goldberg would appeal the fee decision no matter what?

In June, Judge Van Sickle issued a decision in which he relied on *Premachandra*. He awarded $179,382, including $101,837 for me and $4,680 for my dad.[7] We high-fived on the win, but there was no doubt in our minds that Goldberg and Annear would appeal within the sixty-day window they were allotted, especially because *Premachandra* was still being reconsidered.

August 14 was the sixtieth day from Judge Van Sickle's fee decision, and I hadn't heard a thing from Annear or Goldberg. "Should I call the clerk's office to find out what's up?" I asked my dad.

My father straightened up as though he'd had an electric shock. "Absolutely not," he said. "If you call the clerk, the word will get to the U.S. attorney. Don't call until tomorrow."

The next day, I did call the clerk's office, and the same day, Annear (probably alerted by the clerk's office) filed a notice of appeal, together with a motion for extension of time.

They were one day late.

"Dad, I think God is on our side in this case," I said. "There's no other explanation."

As Judge Van Sickle pointed out when he denied Annear's motion, an appeal deadline is a firm deadline, and the only way it can be extended is by "excusable neglect"; neither Annear nor Goldberg showed excusable neglect. The reason Goldberg gave for missing the deadline was that he had gone on vacation and assumed someone else would take care of it. Annear's defense was that Goldberg had told him the Department of Justice was now in charge.

On January 14, 1985, the Eighth Circuit, by a 7 to 2 majority, vacated the original *Premachandra* decision on which Judge Van Sickle had relied and instead came out with a tough standard; fees under EAJA would not be awarded if the government's defense of its action was "reasonable."[8] The unimaginable excuse of Arthur Goldberg had saved us from almost certain reversal of all or a big part of Judge Van Sickle's fee award.

When a $101,837 check from the federal treasury finally arrived at the Robert Vogel Law Office, my father sent it to me with a note, "Please endorse and return to firm." I'd been on salary at the firm for almost all the hours I'd listed in my fee application. The money wasn't mine; it belonged to the Robert Vogel Law Office.

And I was fine with that. If not for my father, I would never have been able to do the *Coleman* case. He'd lent me money when I was developing the theories of the case in Bismarck; he'd sent me to the class action seminar; he'd given me the credibility of his name on the pleadings; he'd paid overtime to secretaries who worked until midnight typing my long briefs on impossibly short deadlines.

And this support wasn't just because I was his daughter. It was because this case was a legacy of the Nonpartisan League philosophy that he'd been taught by his father and that he'd passed down to me. I thought it was possible to get a moratorium on farm foreclosures because my father's hero, Governor William

Langer, had done it by decree. My father helped me win a similar result by an injunction. Robert Vogel was the real hero of the *Coleman v. Block* case.

I took another searching look at the NPL poster. Lady Liberty's index finger was pointing at the exact spot in North Dakota where I now stood: Bismarck, the state capital, the "one bright spot where the people rule." It was the people who had put me in the office of agriculture commissioner, and it was my NPL inheritance that had brought me here.

When the Department of Justice missed the appeal deadline on fees, I had then attributed it to an act of God. But now I realized it wasn't God at all. It was the NPL's Lady Liberty, and she had picked Arthur Goldberg as her agent.

The Department of Justice filed an appeal of the *Coleman* decision to the Eighth Circuit, but on the day their brief was due, they threw in the towel. I'll never know the reason, but 1984 was an election year, and I suspect that Reagan wanted the farmer vote and many Republican farm state candidates for Congress were pressuring him to "let up."

After the DOJ dropped their appeal, I accepted a job offer from the North Dakota attorney general to be an assistant attorney general to work full time on farm crisis issues.

Three of the boxes from my time as assistant AG were labeled THE CRAZIES. I opened each one and glanced at the captions on the file folders: UNLICENSED PRACTICE OF LAW, THREATS AGAINST JUDGES, LOONY DEFENSES. I'd spent a lot of time trying to suppress extremist right-wing organizations and individuals that pitched solutions to farmers in crisis.

After the Medina shootout trial, the name Posse Comitatus disappeared, but the group's philosophies resurfaced in other organizations. I did battle with all of them.

They often preyed on farmers by preparing legal papers (for a fee) or selling "foreclosure kits." Using these papers virtually guaranteed the farmer would lose his farm. They also created the risk that the farmer might lose his freedom, because the language in those papers caused judges to feel threatened, and threats against judges were illegal. I fought against these wacky theories by giving speeches, writing letters to the editor, and doing public service announcements.

The most success I had in deterring sales of bogus legal remedies was by referring one particularly blatant offender, Charles Niska, to the Morton County state's attorney for practicing law without a license. (The law gives everyone the right to represent himself or herself "pro se," but only licensed lawyers can represent another person.) Niska was charged with four counts of Class A misdemeanor unlicensed practice of law after he prepared four faux legal documents for an overly trusting farmer who believed his false claims of legitimacy. One of those documents was a direct threat against a local judge. A search of Niska's home uncovered an office full of virulent anti-Semitic propaganda.

At his trial, Niska predictably acted as his own lawyer, and I was the main witness against him. His first question for me was: *What do you think of the papers that are the basis of the charges against me?* This open-ended question was a gift that allowed me to deliver a half-hour lecture to the jury on how dangerous those papers were to the farmer because they included threats against judicial officers, and how ineffective his defenses were in actually helping that farmer/victim. It took the jury less than fifteen minutes to come back with a unanimous guilty verdict. Niska was sentenced to prison, which had a deterrent effect on the sale of foreclosure kits.

Another right-wing radical with more violent tendencies was Larry Humphreys, the wealthy, sharp-suited operator of a white power survivalist camp in Oklahoma. He openly advocated use of guns and violence to "protect" farmers from foreclosures. He'd been given significant credibility on a multicity Midwestern tour because he was accompanied by Tommy Kersey, a former national president of the American Agriculture Movement, who had led the 1979 tractorcade. When Humphreys scheduled a meeting in Jamestown, I decided to attend.

The Humphreys meeting had been heavily advertised and was held in an old hotel ballroom. I walked in and saw a large crowd of North Dakota farmers seated on folding chairs as though they were at a normal farm organization meeting. A dissonant note was the presence of several heavily muscled men wearing camouflage leaning against the side and back walls of the meeting room. Humphreys was introduced by Kersey and began to speak about his program to "help" farmers. I stood up to interrupt him at almost every statement.

"That's not correct!" "That's wrong!" "That tactic won't work here in North Dakota!"

At first Humphreys ignored me, but then he started to shout, "Sit down!" "Shut up!" "This is *my meeting*!"

I kept standing with my arm up as a signal to the audience that he was incorrect. He screamed at me to put down my hand. Two German-Russian farmers sitting in front of me turned around and one of them said with a warm smile, "Don't cha worry, Sarah. We'll protect cha." I whispered "Thank you" and remained standing. Suddenly, Humphreys jumped off the low riser and ran down the middle aisle toward me. His eyes were on me and I could see the spittle around his mouth. Time seemed to stop.

Tommy Kersey rushed after Humphreys, grabbed him from behind, and wrestled him out the side door like he was a balky hog. I was irked that Kersey had given Humphreys credibility on his Midwestern tour, but I was also grateful for the rescue. In the chaos, the meeting broke up. I was suddenly aware of what I had done. I'd taunted a neo-Nazi who advocated armed violence and won the showdown. In retrospect, it had been rash, but the result was very satisfying.

I saved all my THE CRAZIES files for Roger and Jet. The first place these toxic characters would be discovered would be out in the countryside, where the farm advocates were working.

The next box was labeled CONFISCATORY PRICE DEFENSE. I had taken Russel and Anna Mae Folmer's case against the Bank of North Dakota all the way to the North Dakota Supreme Court, and it was a beautiful moment when I called to tell them that the chief justice had authored a unanimous decision in their favor and ordered the Bank of North Dakota to give their farm back.[9] *Folmer v. State* stood for the principle that North Dakota courts had "special equitable powers to protect debtors when the price of agricultural products are below the cost of their production or when the debtor would lose his equity in a home to foreclosure or execution [and that courts may] stay foreclosure proceedings on public policy grounds."[10] *Folmer* had brought the NPL's confiscatory price laws back to life after fifty years of dormancy.

WHEN I TOOK the job as assistant attorney general, I asked Jim Massey from Minnesota to step in as lead counsel in *Coleman v. Block*. At the time, we both assumed the case was over. The injunction was final. But we had underestimated the enemy.

Although USDA dropped its appeal, FmHA came out with regulations designed to override every protection Judge Van Sickle had incorporated into the *Coleman* final permanent injunction. FmHA fought us "tooth and toenail," as Dale would say.

Jim Massey and other co-counsel filed an amended complaint in 1986 raising fourteen new causes of action. This became known as *Coleman II*. *Coleman I* was a case in which we asked the court to *enforce* the Constitution, law, and regulations. *Coleman II* was built upon the success of *Coleman I*, and it aimed at *preventing* FmHA from undercutting the constitutional rights provided by *Coleman I*.

Coleman II was litigated ferociously in front of Judge Van Sickle from 1986 until 1989 with dramatic twists and turns. I followed the litigation closely not only because I'd been the original lead counsel, but also because I now represented the State of North Dakota as a "friend of the court" on the side of the farmers along with other states.[11]

As the *Coleman II* litigation raged on in the judicial branch, the legislative branch of the federal government stepped in. The entire farm economy was in a free fall under President Reagan. Delinquency could no longer be described as a problem that a few "bad managers" at FmHA were having; it was bigger than that and everyone knew it. The opening paragraph of a report by the Brookings Institution in 1986[12] said that from 1980 to 1984, the average real value of U.S. farmland dropped by 29 percent, and in some states by 40 percent; the massive government-sponsored Cooperative Farm Credit System (FCS) faced an imminent threat of insolvency; total outstanding farm loans likely to default were between $80 billion and $100 billion.

But I was sick of reading statistics by economists who had been so slow to recognize the crisis and who obviously cared more about lenders' and investors' balance sheets than they cared about living, breathing, suffering farmers.

What ultimately turned public opinion toward the side of the farmers was not any statistical report. It was a Hollywood movie. *Country* was released on September 28, 1984, and it dramatized the struggles of farm families against the juggernaut of Charles Shuman's delinquency reduction goals.

Jessica Lange, who was also a co-producer, conceived the idea for the movie when she saw a photograph of a farm couple at an FmHA auction of their farm. "There was something about the expression on their faces . . . that triggered the idea for a movie on the economic plight of the American farmer."[13] She wanted to make a contemporary *Grapes of Wrath*—and she did.

Jessica's sister Jane was my college roommate, and when Jessica heard about my case, we talked by phone. I mailed her my clients' affidavits. In Iowa, she connected with Dave Ostendorf and Danny Levitas, who became her local guides to real Iowa farm families who were in the same situation as my clients in North Dakota. She used mostly local Iowa farmers as actors. Sam Shepard, her real-life partner, costarred.

Jessica and Sam played Jewell and Gil Ivy, farmers facing acceleration, foreclosure, and stress. Their neighbor commits suicide. They face unsympathetic FmHA officials who tell the farmers they have "no choice" but to collect the debt or repossess the cattle. In my mind, the *Coleman* case and the movie *Country* were inextricably connected.

The lives of the characters and the lives of the real farmers overlapped in real time. In the fall of 1983, when I filed the papers for the national class action and for a national permanent injunction, it would have raised the hopes of the fictional characters in the movie and the real-life farmers who were extras in the movie and lived in the area of Iowa where the movie was shot.

The final scene in *Country* is a chattering teletype machine printing these words:

February 16, 1984. A federal judge in North Dakota ordered the U.S. government to stop all FmHA farm foreclosures until the farmers of this country receive their rights of due process under the law.

As hundreds of thousands of people watched *Country* in movie theaters and saw Jessica nominated for a Best Actress Oscar, the nation's sympathy for farmers grew.

It continued building when Willie Nelson, John Mellencamp, and Neil Young organized the first Farm Aid concert in Champaign, Illinois, on September 22, 1985. In addition to the organizers, Bob Dylan, Billy Joel, B. B. King, and many other musicians performed for a crowd of eighty thousand. An astonishing $9 million was raised and rapidly and efficiently distributed. Farm Aid money from other concerts in 1986 (Texas) and 1987 (Nebraska) followed and was also distributed to farmers and farm groups and to support advocacy for farmers.

One of the ways Farm Aid helped was to pay for the expenses of broke farmers to come and testify before congressional committees. Hearing from the actual farmers—not slick lobbyists and heartless economists—played a critical role in persuading Congress to adopt laws supporting farmers.

Farm Aid money was also a lifesaver for tiny grassroots organizations. An early Farm Aid grant helped Jim Massey start a nonprofit law firm called the Farmers' Legal Action Group, Inc. (FLAG) in Minnesota. Another grant supported Roger Allison Jr.'s work with Missouri farmers.

Even after we'd won the final permanent injunction, Reagan was still denying the existence of a farm crisis. He dismissively wrote in his diary on February 28, 1985 that "only 10.4 percent of the 2.2 mil. Farmers are involved in the financial and farm crunch" and "the farm [economy] is 90 percent sound with the crisis all bunched up in one area." Reagan blamed Democrats who were "demagoguing all over the place, smelling an issue for 1986."

From the outside, the Reagan administration and Republican leadership looked unified and unrepentant of their treatment of farmers. But inside there were vicious drag-down fights. Midwestern Republican governors were being pressured by farmers and farm organizations to urge Reagan to back off.

One of those governors was Republican Terry Branstad in Iowa, who visited Reagan several times to talk about the "farm problem." In October 1985, he told Reagan there had been three farmer suicides in Iowa. Reagan shrugged it off: "I feel as bad as he does but what can we do? We are spending more on the farmers plight than any admin. in history."[14] Branstad was next mentioned when George Bush came back from Iowa where he had attended a fundraiser for Governor Branstad. Reagan confided to his diary that Branstad "has been kicking my head in" and that Senator Grassley (also a Republican) "has really mobilized the farmers against me."

"I have compassion for them," Reagan wrote, "but there is a limit to what we can do to help them in this situation & we're doing all we can."[15]

The president watched *Country* at Camp David, noting in his diary that it was "a blatant propaganda message against our Agri. programs."[16]

In response to farm crisis data brought to Washington by politicians, economists, farm leaders, and lenders, the Reagan administration's response was a "drumbeat of ridicule," writes Neil Harl.[17] Harl saw firsthand how USDA had been taken over by David Stockman at a meeting in the White House in January 1985. In attendance from Iowa were Harl, Governor Branstad, and the head of the Iowa Bankers Association. Secretary Block and his undersecretary Frank Naylor were there too. But it was clear that David Stockman was in charge.

When it was Harl's turn to speak, he said that 30 percent of all farmers were facing "severe financial and economic turbulence."

"Just let them fail," Stockman snapped in reply. "We'd have a blow off. Lose a few thousand farmers, even a few hundred bankers. But then we wouldn't need to spend $18 billion a year on farm programs, right?"[18]

Stockman resigned from the Office of Management and Budget on August 1, 1985. During his term, the deficit had ballooned from $907 billion in Carter's last year to $1.8 trillion. And the farm economy was a wreck. Stockman's "Grand Doctrine" turned out to be a grand disaster.

In 1985, a farm bill designed to help farmers was vetoed by Reagan. In 1986, an election year, Reagan briefly implemented a new program, which basically gave everyone who had received a loan from FmHA in prior years another loan. It didn't stop the slide of the farm economy, but it did help many Republican members of Congress avoid being thrown out of office.

By 1987, many farm state members of Congress were incensed at the conduct of FmHA, Block, and his successor as secretary of agriculture, Richard Lyng. They saw an opportunity to make lasting change in late July 1987 when the massive Farm Credit System came to Congress begging for a bailout. The coalition of attorneys general, along with the Farmers' Legal Action Group, and a host of farm organizations from every corner of the country realized that this was an opportunity to make farmer protections a precondition of the bailout. Our mantra was "no bailout without help for the farmers."

When I sat down at my new desk to reflect on the dramatic twists and turns the *Coleman I* and *II* litigation had taken over the past few years, it seemed that victory was finally obtained with passage of the Agricultural Credit Act of 1987. Congress put the key provisions of the *Coleman I* decisions—due process, notice, fair hearings, and release of income—into permanent law along with scores of other protections and safeguards.

This time it seemed impossible for FmHA to evade the law. Having witnessed how FmHA tried to evade its obligations under previous laws such as 7 USC 1981a (the deferral law), Congress tightened the language governing FmHA so thoroughly and so exhaustively that FmHA officials were fenced in like cattle. There was only one way to get out, and it was the way that Congress said FmHA had to go. Congress even made a law saying that FmHA had to submit its regulations to Congress for approval. At last, FmHA would have to live up to the motto carved in stone on its headquarters: THE HUSBANDMAN THAT LABORETH MUST BE FIRST PARTAKER OF THE FRUITS.

Title VI of the Agricultural Credit Act dealt with the Farmers Home Administration, and I was proud when I saw that Congress called these new reforms the "Coleman reforms." The law had provisions on release of income for family living and farm operating expenses, precise instructions on how administrative appeals had to be conducted, and exact directions on how notice to farmers was to be provided. The law also gave farmers a yearlong de facto moratorium by prohibiting further foreclosures until regulations that implemented the Coleman reforms were in place and farmers had been given direct personal notice of all the rights that were provided by the new law.

As to those farmers who had already lost their land, Congress also set out procedures for FmHA to follow to sell off its massive portfolio of "inventory farms" to family farmers, and to provide the buyers with financing to do so. The first priority was given to the previous owner to repurchase the land he or she had lost. All the people forced to "voluntarily" convey their land to FmHA now had a way they could recover the land. Native Americans were given special rights: if the original tribal member didn't recover the previously owned property within a reservation, the tribe could acquire it. One of the most significant pieces of the law gave farmers the option of having debt written down (a mini Chapter 12 bankruptcy) to reflect the lower land values due to land devaluation. It was modeled on laws from the 1930s.   .

After the bill passed the House and Senate, President Reagan signed the Agricultural Credit Act of 1987 into law on January 6, 1988. Petty and vindictive to the end, he asked Congress to repeal the parts of the law that protected FmHA borrowers. He said Congress should "take its responsibility for the deficit seriously and to work with us to amend or remove" the provisions that provided "additional forbearance to producers who have been substantially delinquent" on FmHA loans.[19]

As agriculture commissioner, I was going to benefit from the ACA too. Recognizing the complexity of the restructuring process, Congress said it would finance state agriculture mediation programs (up to $500,000 per state) for the first time, as a cost share, and compelled FmHA and the Farm Credit System lenders to participate in good faith in mediations and negotiations. I thought it was wonderful that the new farm credit advocates in my office were paid through a grant from FmHA.

Congress had brought FmHA back to its Resettlement Administration origins and purposes. The new goal was to keep farmers on the land, not to push them off the land.

Roger popped his head into my office to see how unpacking was going. I gestured at a pile of boxes I hadn't even opened yet.

"If you need a break, check this out," he said.

He handed me a folded sheet and I spread it out on my desk. It was a game board, made to look like Monopoly, to help farmers and farm advocates navigate FmHA debt restructuring options.

"This is brilliant!" I said.

Instead of "Go to Jail," this game board said "Go to Cash Flow Land to prepare for your mediation meeting," or "You win your appeal, go to Lease."[20]

"We've ordered three thousand copies," Roger said. "FmHA will be going after twenty-six hundred farms that have been held up by the Coleman orders, but there may be more than that."

After Roger left, I sat at my new desk and thought of all the farmers I hadn't been able to help. I remembered the farmers who had slipped through the cracks because I could not respond to every tactic being used by FmHA to force them out. I felt guilt over the farmers who had missed deadlines or failed to apply for remedies because the pretermination notices they'd received were written in gibberish. I tried once to stop the use of those pretermination notices, but when I failed, I gave up. I should have kept fighting. When I'd gone to see the movie *Country*, I couldn't help but weep through the entire movie. Had I filed the national class sooner, or been a stronger advocate, the farm families represented by the Ivy family would not have faced the threat of foreclosure or the danger of suicide.

The ACA was giving many farmers I'd failed a second chance. It was giving me a second chance too. The Coleman reforms in the appeals process would protect farmers' rights to a fair hearing. I was in a position to help the survivors of this cataclysm recover their land, their home, their future, and their hope.

EPILOGUE: STRENGTH FROM THE SOIL

December 2020

By the end of the month, I'll have been able to haul thirty boxes filled with legal research, farmers' budgets, correspondence, yellowed news clippings, and assorted paper detritus back to the North Dakota State Historical Society Archives, where they will be shelved with about sixty other boxes within Collection #10721, also known as the Sarah Vogel Collection.

During the years that I worked on *Coleman v. Block*, I had no time to reflect. I only had time to react as I struggled to save my clients. I knew I should have been keeping a diary—even then I realized I was engaged in a historically significant legal battle—but that was impossible. Instead of a diary, I kept every scrap of paper that crossed my desk or was given to me in a farm kitchen or a courthouse hallway. I kept farm budgets and plans for the 1982 growing season, bills (mostly mine, mostly overdue), phone messages, drafts of long legal briefs, copies of federal and state decisions, legislative history, letters, news clippings, notices of foreclosure (some of which were mine), answers to complaints, and worried letters from my father.

As the years passed, these mounds of paper were tossed into cardboard boxes that I retrieved from the alleys behind grocery stores. These boxes moved with Andrew and me from house to house, office to office, town to town. Eventually they migrated to the attic of my house in Bismarck, until one day a historian came by and said I had a massive firetrap. He told me I should call an archivist at the North Dakota Heritage Center, who would be delighted to take them. There were about seventy boxes in that first haul. When I learned that other files related to the *Coleman* case were in storage with another legal group in Minnesota and might be destroyed for nonpayment of storage fees, I paid the fees and brought another twenty or so boxes back to North Dakota. I asked the federal court for access to its stored files, and we discovered that they were in a warehouse down south and would have been destroyed in six months.

At the Archives, Collection #10721 started with 48 feet of shelving. I used to wish that a scholar of Midwestern farm history would someday realize that there was valuable information—maybe even a book—hidden within all those boxes. My clients' suffering, courage, and endurance reminded me of the plain, stoic, ordinary farmers and workers who had survived similarly difficult economic times in John Steinbeck's *The Grapes of Wrath*, Upton Sinclair's *The Jungle*, and Ole Edvart Rølvaag's *Giants in the Earth*. I waited for someone else to write the story of the *Coleman v. Block* case, but no historian stepped forward.

After almost three decades, I realized I was the only one who could write this story. I went over to the Archives and began the Herculean task of organizing the documents with labels and dates. When Covid-19 struck North Dakota, I brought the boxes that dealt with the *Coleman* case back to my house. This time they migrated to my basement, not to the attic.

Among these papers was an article written by Judge Van Sickle for the summer 1999 edition of the American Bar Association's prestigious magazine, *Litigation*.[1]

Judge Van Sickle was scrupulously ethical. He would never have invited me to lunch when the case was active, but by 1999, long after he'd gone into senior status and long after the case was closed, having lunch together wasn't an ethical concern for either of us. I joined him at the Elks Club dining room one sunny summer day. He told me he had been asked to write an article about the *Coleman* case and asked if I would write a short postscript about what had happened to the North Dakota Nine.

"The North Dakota Nine? Who are they?" I asked.

Judge Van Sickle's blue eyes twinkled as he explained. "During the trial, I began to call your lead plaintiffs the North Dakota Nine because I thought that in their own way they were as radical as the defendants who protested the Vietnam War in the Chicago Seven trial in Chicago, who created such a ruckus in front of Judge Julius Hoffman." I got the joke, and from that point forward, I also called them the North Dakota Nine. They didn't dress as outrageously as the Chicago Seven, and they wouldn't have dreamed of disturbing the decorum of Judge Van Sickle's courtroom, but their courageous support of the Bill of Rights was equal to that of the Chicago Seven.

When I pulled the article from a box, more than twenty years after I'd last read it, I noticed Judge Van Sickle's use of the word "whiffletree" after he had summarized a long series of orders against USDA. He wrote, "Finally—at least for a while—the whiffletree was straight across the wagon tongue."[2]

"Whiffletree" isn't a word in any law dictionary. But, in a regular dictionary, I learned that a whiffletree is a crossbar attached to a harness. The whiffletree was located between the horses and the plow for the purpose of equalizing the disparate forces of two unequally matched horses pulling the plow.

The whiffletree provided an elegant analogy to describe justice in a case about farmers. After all, this case involved farmers who plowed, planted, and knew how important a balanced effort was to a good harvest. Judge Van Sickle gave a story that illustrated this at the very beginning of his article:

> As the oldest son at home in the midst of the drought and depression that was 1934, I tried to farm a quarter of a section [160 acres] of land with one team as my power source. Queen was a strong, reliable mare. She did what I needed her to do when I needed her to do it. Prince was a lazy, rawboned gelding. No matter how hard I drove him, I could never get Prince to keep that whiffletree at right angles to the wagon tongue and do his share of the work.

He explained that during the litigation of the *Coleman* case, he viewed the local FmHA employees as being like Queen, but he viewed the national USDA officials who triggered the lawsuit as being like Prince.

In the bitter years that I worked with the farmers who were suffering under the harsh and adversarial policies of the Reagan administration, I was so caught up in my day-to-day struggles that I did not realize I was living within an inflection point in history, similar to the inflection point in the 1930s.

The "whiffletree" of federal farm policy had been askew in the 1930s when the teenaged Bruce Van Sickle tried to farm with horsepower. President Franklin Delano Roosevelt straightened out the whiffletree of federal farm policy with a suite of New Deal programs to raise the income of farmers to an equivalence

Abandoned farm machinery in Dust Bowl North Dakota.

("parity") with townspeople, stop foreclosures, and set up new loan programs for farmers. And those New Deal programs (and returning rains) worked—family farmers again began to thrive. Serious economic problems within farm country again surfaced in the late 1970s, but when President Ronald Reagan was elected, he didn't straighten the whiffletree out: he made the imbalance worse. With David Stockman as his budget ax man and John Block as secretary of agriculture, decisions were made in Washington, D.C., that had catastrophic impacts in the countryside.

During the 1980s, I was often demoralized and uncertain. Especially at the beginning of my work on the case, I had little support and not much reinforcement. But I could look back to the 1930s and find inspiration and courage in the oral and written record of the Nonpartisan League. I knew the leaders of the League had faced challenges even worse than what I was facing, and they didn't quit. They persisted. The League's motto was "We'll Stick. We'll Win." The League mascot was a goat, "because a goat is an animal that works with its head when attacked." The lawyers for the League were smart; they did careful research; they proposed thoughtful solutions based on facts and law. Above all, they sought justice for the common people.

Today's whiffletree of agriculture policy is pulling too far toward the side of industrial-scale and corporate farm agriculture and too much in favor of massive seed, feed, and chemical agribusinesses. Further, the reins to the plow are being held by politicians who are okay with a crooked whiffletree because of the donations they get from those who benefit from it. As the Nonpartisan League farmers understood almost a century ago, the financial incentives of corporations providing "inputs" (patented seeds, fertilizers, pesticides, insecticides, credit, and so on) do not necessarily align with farmers' well-being.

However, we can straighten the whiffletree by looking to the past—for example, the profound public policy shifts that occurred under Franklin Delano Roosevelt and the initiatives of the Nonpartisan League in North Dakota such as the anti-corporate farming law. The shift to bigger and bigger farms and "corporatized" farming is *not* inevitable. Solutions, already researched, vetted, and implemented in the field are available.

FDR once said, "A nation that destroys its soil destroys itself." It is possible to overcome the devastating economic and soil health consequences caused by too much dependence on fossil fuels and agrochemicals. Innovative farmers using regenerative and conservation farming practices (such as minimal soil disturbance, integration of cover crops, and diverse crop rotations) have demonstrated that, by focusing on soil health, they can restore life and fertility to their land, and profitability to their farms, with techniques that blend traditional knowledge with modern science. Examples of farmers who practice this type of agriculture can be found in the inspiring book *Growing a Revolution: Bringing Our Soil Back to Life* by David Montgomery.[3]

Organizations like Farm Aid, Farmers' Legal Action Group, National Farmers Union, the members of the National Sustainable Agriculture Coalition, and the Institute for Agriculture and Trade Policy have been working on solutions and have ready-made public policy solutions waiting for acceptance and implementation. Organizations that specifically support minority and women farmers include the Federation of Southern Cooperatives, the Women, Food and Agriculture Network, the Intertribal Agriculture Council, and the National Latino Farmers and Ranchers Trade Association. Go to their websites, join their organizations, subscribe to their mailing lists, and donate what you can. You can find local organizations by checking with Farm Aid's database of 750 farmer support organizations. Every one of these small nonprofits and coalitions would welcome your support.

In the United States today, we can look to three farmer-philosophers, Wendell Berry, Wes Jackson, and Fred Kirschenmann, as our guides in this difficult work. Kirschenmann is a North Dakota farmer and longtime mentor of mine and his passion is the survival of the middle-sized family farmers. In his 2020 book, *Perilous Bounty*, the journalist Tom Philpott says:

> Although the farmers market model can work for farms small enough to sell all or most of their produce directly to consumers, it makes only limited economic sense for diversified midsize family farms. As a group of agriculture scholars, led by Fred Kirschenmann, wrote in a seminal paper titled "Why Worry About Agriculture in the Middle?," midsize farms get squeezed in this arrangement. They are "too small to compete in highly consolidated commodity markets, and too large . . . to sell in direct markets." National distributors stocking huge grocery chains have the leverage to push down prices paid to farmers, and they can put midsize farmers in a particular region into competition with massive California or foreign operations.
>
> And yet, Kirschenmann shows, it's precisely those midsize farms that have the scale to grow local and regional food chains to a point where they supply a large part of the American diet. For the past several decades, midsize farms have operated under severe pressure; they close at a rate of more than 10 percent every five years. Meanwhile, the number of large and mega-farms—the kind that dominate in the Corn Belt and California's main valleys—grow steadily. *Finding economic models that allow midsize producers to thrive is crucial to the needed transformation of our food system.*[4]

The North Dakota Nine had small to middle-sized farms. In the 1980s, their lives were very difficult. In today's economy, they wouldn't have a prayer. But farmers like them are exactly the kind of farmers we need today: farmers who will love their land, grow crops as well as communities, plant trees, care for their animals, and leave the earth better than when they found it. In the big picture, farmers like them can help solve global warming, revitalize the countryside, and provide abundant, healthy food—but they need a balanced whiffletree to do that.

We can save farmers, protect the environment, solve the hunger crisis, and rebuild rural and urban economies from the ground up after the ravages of the Covid-19 pandemic—if we act soon.

I hope this book will sow seeds for a future agriculture system that is based on human needs and human values. The people who can grow that system are on farms in the countryside right now, and they have city counterparts who are pioneering new methods of urban agriculture. They need our support. They are America's family farmers.

POSTSCRIPT

THE FARMERS

Dwight Coleman freed himself from FmHA's bad management advice and paid off FmHA's real estate loan with a loan from the Rural Rehabilitation Association (a legacy of the Resettlement Administration). He paid off his FmHA operating loans with financing from his local bank and the sale of most of his cattle herd and kept farming. In 2007, he sold his farm to two Wisconsin hunters who loved his land: the beautiful wooded hills, wetlands, and meadows that Dwight's cattle had loved to graze. He paid all his debts, bought a condo in Nevada, where he lives with his longtime girlfriend, and is now a snowbird: he lives and works in North Dakota in the spring, summer, and fall and goes south during the winter. When in North Dakota, he operates huge construction equipment and spends weekends helping his sister farm "back in the hills." In recent years, he learned that his ancestors were farming on the East Coast since colonial times.

. . .

Lester Crows Heart still has his land on the Fort Berthold Reservation. He farmed and ranched until 2000 and also worked at the coal gasification plant in Beulah for fifteen years. In 2000, he began a new job as the director of the Three Affiliated Tribes' water department, where he led the installation of a reservation-wide rural water system. He tried to retire but was pulled back to full-time work for the tribe as the head of maintenance for the tribal headquarters district. One of his proudest achievements is being an original founder of MHA Nation Tribal College, Nueta Hidatsa Sahnish College, located in New Town. It offers four-year degrees, with programs and courses in agriculture, food sovereignty, holistic gardening, traditional foods, seed keeping, equine studies, and other legacies of the MHA Nation. Sharon passed away in 2017. Lester and Sharon have five children and many grandchildren.

. . .

Russel Folmer passed away in 1994 at age sixty-nine. His family was so proud of what he did to stand up for other farmers in the *Coleman* case that his role as a lead plaintiff was included in his obituary. The North Dakota Supreme Court decision in *Folmer v. State* protected many farmers during the 1980s by encouraging lenders to come to the table to work out solutions that kept farmers on the land. The *Coleman* case affected only FmHA borrowers, but *Folmer v. State* helped all North Dakota farmers who faced summary judgment motions. It meant that lenders were incentivized to sit down and talk to farmers about ways to restructure debts and avoid foreclosures. The precedent that the Folmers set was used many times in the ensuing years to make lenders realize that they couldn't just grab farms away from farmers without the intervention and review of a judge.

. . .

Anna Mae Folmer, remarkably, still lives in the same house that Andrew and I visited back in 1982. She turned ninety-one in February 2021. After Russel's death, she farmed on her own for two years before she reconnected with the man who would become her second husband at a Wing High School reunion. She was forced to sell some of the land to reduce her debt, but she still has the homeplace, some acres, and a few cattle. I recently asked her how she had managed to farm during all those years of hardship: "I loved animals. I loved farming." Anna Mae now has six grandchildren and four great-grandchildren. She remembers the trial vividly and is still upset that she was unable to give Gary Annear a piece of her mind because he was too cowardly to question her.

One of Anna Mae's daughters-in-law decided to go to law school after seeing the mistreatment of Russel and Anna Mae by FmHA. She is now the general counsel of the North Dakota Tax Department.

. . .

George Hatfield kept working on the road crew, and June kept working at the bank, and they kept farming for many years. They paid off Farmers Home in the late 1980s. Ten years later, when they decided to retire, they sold all of their farm except for the home quarter at a good price and used some of the surplus to buy an RV. When I had the opportunity to catch up with them, they told me they loved their semivagabond life, popping in and out of North Dakota during the glorious spring, summer, and early fall months and finding long-term camping spots in warm climates while North Dakotans suffered in the deep freeze of winter. George was bereft when June passed in 2010 (they were second-grade sweethearts). He stopped RV traveling and instead devoted his time to hunting, fishing, riding his motorcycle, and achieving a lifelong dream to get an airplane and a pilot's license. George died at almost eighty years of age in October 2017. He and June had three children, six grandchildren, and eleven great-grandchildren. The couple are buried side by side in Ellendale, North Dakota.

. . .

Don and Diane McCabe had the most difficulty after the Coleman case. In 1985, USDA decided to make an example of the McCabes, who were then nationally known farm advocates who spoke out for the rights of farmers. Farmers Home refused to allow them any income whatsoever from their farm after the injunction. The McCabes endured that treatment, but when an old bull was about to die, they sold him for $300 and used $200 for taxes and $100 for groceries. This was the crime for which they were prosecuted by the Department of Justice. I helped them find good criminal lawyers, and Diane's father lent them money to pay their legal fees. The trial was held in August for three days in front of Judge Paul Benson, who issued orders that prevented Don's lawyers from showing that the use of the money from the sale of the bull was in full accordance with Judge Van Sickle's order and FmHA rules. I was a character witness for Don, but I was forbidden by Judge Benson even to bring up the *Coleman* case. Even though Don couldn't mount a defense, the trial resulted in a hung jury. Don didn't want to risk another trial, especially if Diane would get dragged in. He pleaded guilty to a misdemeanor and was on probation for one year. They stayed on their farm for another ten years. During those years, Diane came across a displaced homemakers program, which paid for tuition, books, gas money, and a stipend, and she became the first person in her family to finish college. While she was in school, Don commuted to a farm machinery repair job in Jamestown. They moved to Fargo, where both found work: Diane became a deputy clerk of court and taught school, which she still does part time today. Don has retired and suffers from long-term effects of cold weather and crouching to milk cows by hand. They are tremendously proud of their role as lead plaintiffs. They watched the movie *Country* and said to each other as the excerpt from the *Coleman* injunction rolled across the screen at the end of the movie, "We did that. That was us."

. . .

Tom Nichols is still on his farm in Montana, having beaten back FmHA and other lenders over the years. Anna passed away in 2012.

. . .

Chuck Perry disappeared for a long time. His 2019 obituary said that for the twenty-five years prior to his death he had been an organic gardener near Walhalla, North Dakota.

THE PLAINTIFFS' LAWYERS

My father, Robert Vogel, was the unsung hero of the *Coleman v. Block* case and a role model. He stopped actively practicing law in 1997 to write a book, *Unequal Contest: Bill Langer and His Political Enemies*, about the conspiracy trials of his father and Governor Langer during the early 1930s when they were falsely accused by the United States attorney of defrauding the federal government of $179.50 by engaging in twenty-seven overt acts to support the conspiracy. (Yes, that really happened.) When he died in January 2005, we had to have two funerals: one in the afternoon for the lawyers and judges and politicians who came from all over the state, and another in the evening for friends and family.

. . .

Burt Neuborne is a longtime professor of constitutional law at New York University School of Law and also serves as a visiting professor at the University of California, Berkeley, School of Law. He and Professor Norman Dorsen (who taught me constitutional law at NYU) co-founded the Brennan Center for Justice at NYU. Over the years, Burt has litigated hundreds of important constitutional cases in state and federal courts, including many at the United States

Supreme Court. He has written four books and more than twenty law review articles and even had a brief stint as an actor (he played Jerry Falwell's lawyer in the movie *The People v. Larry Flynt*). He still has his NPL Lady Liberty poster on his office wall at NYU.

. . .

Allan Kanner has a litigation firm in the French Quarter of New Orleans, where he focuses on environmental law and complex class actions. He is routinely listed as among the 500 best lawyers in the United States. He also writes prolifically and lectures about class actions and environmental law. I once had a difficult case involving defective sunflower seeds costing a hundred farmers many millions of dollars. When I brought Allan in as co-counsel, as soon as his name appeared, the defendant who had been fighting me as though it was World War III meekly settled. Allan also has his Lady Liberty poster, which survived Hurricane Katrina.

. . .

Dale Reesman continued to practice law in his two-person law office in Boonville, Missouri. He was one of the first board members of the Farmers' Legal Action Group and served on its board of directors up to his death in 2011. Dale achieved remarkable success for a small-town lawyer: in 1986, he received the American Bar Association's most prestigious award, the Pro Bono Publico Award, given to only a few lawyers every year in recognition of their love of justice and willingness to fight for the downtrodden. He passed away in 2011, at the age of eighty.

THE JUDGE

Judge Van Sickle went into senior status in 1985, but he continued to serve as presiding judge on the second phase of the *Coleman v. Block* litigation through the end of 1988. As significant as the *Coleman* decisions were, his most important case may have been the *ARC v. State of North Dakota* case. In this lawsuit, which was filed in 1980 and lasted until 1996, Judge Van Sickle required North Dakota to release people with mental and physical disabilities from harsh conditions within state institutions and to provide proper care, housing, and educational services to them. Judge Van Sickle passed away in 2007, after a difficult illness. By then, he had a towering reputation within North Dakota legal circles and even had a federal courthouse named after him. When I attended his funeral, I learned from the pastor's sermon that Judge Van Sickle's professional life was a manifestation of his very private religious faith and his belief that justice on Earth was possible.

ACKNOWLEDGMENTS

More than a decade ago, I began to dream about writing this book. Now it is done. These are some of the people who helped me get to this point.

I owe so much to the farmers who shared their lives, hopes, dreams, and futures with a novice lawyer who didn't know the meaning of "heifer," "gilt," or "combine," or the significance of myriad strings of initials, until they educated me. I learned that farmers are born teachers and love to talk about their passion and share their knowledge.

I am grateful to the archivists who treated my messy stacks of paper as though they were relics of Hemingway or Rølvaag, not the detritus of a disorganized wannabe writer. Jerry Newborg, Ann Jenks, Shane Molander, Jim Davis, Sarah Walker, Emily Kubischta, Daniel Sauerwein, and others were unfailingly kind and polite as I requested particular documents or boxes of documents (especially during the Covid-19 pandemic).

They also made their huge conference room available to me and Amanda (Mandy) Kubik for months on end as we put the files in chronological order. Mandy Kubik saved the day for me. She spent months at the archives, steadily and competently organizing thousands of files so I could begin to write this book. Mandy was a godsend: Thank you!

I found that writing a book while I was practicing law more than full time didn't work out at all. Annie Kirschenmann and her executive coaching service helped me move out of law and into writing by thinking about "mission, vision, planning, and core values" and having fun and laughing along the way.

I'd been vain about what a good legal writer I was (or thought I was), but I had a hard time not writing for an audience consisting of a panel of appellate judges. I signed up for several remote classes at the Loft in Minneapolis. One of the classes I took in 2018 was called "Writing in the Margins: Developing a Sustainable Writing Habit" (I called it the class on "how not to procrastinate"), and in the last session the teacher mentioned Leigh Stein, a writing coach on the

East Coast. I immediately sent her a long, sad, urgent, hopeful message begging for help.

One of the best things that happened to me in the ten years I spent developing this book was meeting Leigh Stein. She guided me through the intricacies of writing, editing, and publishing *The Farmer's Lawyer*. Without her, this book would not have ever come to be. Leigh also introduced me to Andrea Guevara, marketing magician and website designer, making the launch of this book a success. Thank you, Leigh!

I am grateful to Jessica Lange for creating, and starring in, the movie *Country*, which so accurately depicts what happened to my clients, and I am grateful to John Hanson for the movie *Northern Lights*, which shows the drama of the early NPL movement.

My friend and mentor, the philosopher/farmer Fred Kirschenmann, educated me on sustainable agriculture, and his writings and our conversations have given me hope for the future of family farm agriculture.

Alan Guebert, Jerry Hagstrom, and Mikkel Pates, my friends, mentors, and esteemed agricultural journalists, have for decades been my guides to understanding the complexity of national agriculture developments.

Thank you to all the journalists who fought the false narratives of the Reagan administration in the '80s.

Dwight Coleman, Don and Diane McCabe, Tom Nichols, Lester Crows Heart, Anna Mae Folmer, and Lynn Boughey all took time to speak with me about their recollections; their insights and memories helped to paint a more vibrant picture of the events described in the book.

Many people took the time to read this book and give me thoughtful and constructive comments: Jayanti Tamm, Rudra Tamm, Frank Vogel, Annie Kirschenmann, Fred Kirschenmann, Marilyn Stuckey; my wonderful friends known as the BadAss Grandmas (Dr. Ellen Chaffee, Dina Butcher, and Kathy Tweeten); my friends from high school through today, Sara Garland and Rodine Durgin; the director of Humanities North Dakota, Brenna Gerhardt; and the *Coleman* co-counsel, Allan Kanner and Burt Neuborne. Thank you all!

Gary Cunningham and Betsy Hodges: Thank you for listening to me and telling me to "go for it" that day we had the three-hour lunch in Kīlauea!

Willie Nelson, Carolyn Mugar, Glenda Yoder, and the Farm Aid family: Your vision doesn't just illuminate a way forward for family farmers all over the United States, you also illuminate the way forward for farmer's lawyers like me.

Jim Massey, Lynn Hayes, and Randi Roth worked for years on *Coleman II* and did exemplary work educating farmers. The lawyers at FLAG continue this important work. The organizers are my heroes: Mark Ritchie, Danny Levitas, Dave Ostendorf, Denise O'Brien, and so many others. Since the mid-80s, Janie Hipp has been my guide to the intricacies of agriculture law and Indian law. Our ache of missing Lou Anne Kling, Anne Kanten, Dale Reesman, Dixon Terry, and so many other valiant farm advocates and lawyers won't diminish . . . ever.

Roger Johnson, Jet Collins, Jeff Weispfenning: Yup, them were the days—twenty-four-hour days! Thank you! You guys were my teachers and I appreciate all your hard work and dedication to the farmers and the people of North Dakota.

I'm grateful to Loren and Jennifer Morlock for introducing me to bicycling (a great way to decompress after frustrating hours at the desk) and to Lance Larson for keeping my bikes tuned and running; to Kathi Aspaas, who is the best swim coach ever; and to the teachers at Proximal50 fitness and the instructors at exercise and yoga studios in Hanalei and Bismarck. One of these decades, I'll be good at what I attempt to do; after all, the book project will no longer be a valid excuse.

Sarah Murphy—the Marie Kondo of Bismarck, North Dakota—came in like a prairie gale and helped me create lovely spaces to write. When the pandemic is over, she'll need to make a return trip. Becky Charvat and Debby . . . can't tell you how much I miss you!

Mackenzie Brady Watson at Stuart Krichevsky Literary Agency: I am grateful for your guidance and your support. You and Aemilia Phillips have done more than simply sell the book: You've made it better.

Thank you to Anton Mueller, Morgan Jones, Patti Ratchford, Barbara Darko, Emily DeHuff, Megha Jain, Krister Swartz, Marie Coolman, Nicole Jarvis, Ellis Levine, and the team at Bloomsbury for bringing my story to a larger audience. Anton's understanding of the causes of the Great Depression, knowledge of modern far-right extremism, and love of family farm agriculture were instrumental in the creation of this book. You have turned *The Farmer's Lawyer* from an idea I carried with me for decades into a published book, and I can't thank you enough.

My son, Andrew, is a wonderful son, a loving husband, and a SuperDad to his children—his family has brought me so much joy. I'm so proud of you. I love you all!

And as for Rudra Tamm, I won't embarrass you except by saying, I thank you.

IMAGE CREDITS

NOTES

PREFACE

1. Roberto A. Ferdman, "The Decline of the Small American Family Farm in One Chart," *Washington Post*, September 16, 2014.

2. U.S. Department of Agriculture, "2017 Census of Agriculture Data Now Available," April 11, 2019, https://www.usda.gov/media/press-releases/2019/04/11/2017-census-agriculture-data-now-available.

CHAPTER 1: THE PLATFORM

1. U.S. Census Bureau, "QuickFacts: North Dakota," https://www.census.gov/quickfacts/ND.

2. Eric Sevareid, *Not So Wild a Dream* (Columbia: University of Missouri Press, 1995), 2.

3. 1950 Census of Population, https://www.census.gov/library/publications/1951/dec/pc-12.html.

4. Bruce Nelson, *Land of the Dacotahs* (Lincoln: University of Nebraska Press, 1971), 309.

5. Robert Loren Morlan, *Political Prairie Fire: The Nonpartisan League, 1915–1922* (St. Paul: Minnesota Historical Society Press, 1985), 7–16.

6. Ibid., 16–17.

7. Michael J. Lansing, *Insurgent Democracy: The Nonpartisan League in North American Politics* (Chicago: University of Chicago Press, 2015), 1.

8. Morlan, *Political Prairie Fire*, 17–18.

9. George McGovern, ed., *Agricultural Thought in the Twentieth Century* (Indianapolis: Bobbs-Merrill, 1967), 81.

10. Baer is also credited with coining the term "New Deal" in a 1931 cartoon that shows Hiram Rube facing off against Big Biz, Crooked Politician, Congress, and Speculator at a high-stakes gambling table in a room labeled "The U.S.A."

11. Readers interested in learning more about the NPL may wish to watch Prairie Public's three-part series *The Rise and Fall of the Nonpartisan League*, available on YouTube. John Hanson and Rob Nilsson's award-winning 1978 movie *Northern Lights* is from the perspective of a farmer who is an early NPL organizer. For further reading, check out Robert L. Morlan's *Political Prairie Fire: The Nonpartisan League 1915–1922* (St. Paul: Minnesota Historical Society Press, 1985); Michael J. Lansing's *Insurgent Democracy: The Nonpartisan League in North American Politics* (Chicago: University of Chicago Press, 2015); Robert Vogel's *Unequal Contest: Bill Langer and His Political Enemies* (Mandan, ND: Crain Grosinger, 2004); and Bruce Nelson's lyrical *Land of the Dacotahs* (Lincoln: University of Nebraska Press, 1971). Biographies have been written about Usher Burdick, Quentin Burdick, William Lemke, and William Langer (an excellent biography of Langer is Agnes Geelan's *The Dakota Maverick* [Fargo, ND: Kay's Printing Company, 1975]). Numerous scholarly articles about the League have appeared in the *North Dakota Quarterly* and other publications of the North Dakota Historical Society. A particularly fascinating history of the NPL's empowerment of women farmers is Karen Starr's "Fighting for a Future: Farm Women of the Nonpartisan League," *Minnesota History*, Summer 1983, 255–66.

Two books have been published about the Bank of North Dakota (the only state-owned bank in the United States): Rozanne Enerson Junker's *The Bank of North Dakota: An Experiment in State Ownership* (McKinleyville, CA: Fithian Press, 1989) and Mike Jacobs's *The Bank of North Dakota: From Surviving to Thriving—the First 100 Years*, published in December 2018 by the Dakota Institute Press (Bismarck) for the centennial of the creation of the bank by the NPL in 1919.

12. Lorena A. Hickok, *One Third of a Nation: Lorena Hickok Reports on the Great Depression*, ed. Richard Lowitt and Maurine Beasley (Urbana: University of Illinois Press, 2000), 11.

13. Nelson, *Land of the Dacotahs*, 299.

14. Elwyn Robinson, *The History of North Dakota* (Lincoln: University of Nebraska Press, 1966; reprinted 2009), 424–25.

15. Nelson, *Land of the Dacotahs*, 301.

16. University of North Dakota, Bureau of Business and Economic Research, Statistical Abstract of North Dakota 238 (2nd ed., 1983).

17. See Sarah M. Vogel, "The Law of Hard Times: Debtor and Farmer Relief Actions of the 1933 North Dakota Legislative Session," *North Dakota Law Review* 60 (1984), 491–92.

18. Harry Hopkins, the head of the Federal Emergency Relief Administration (FERA), sent the journalist Lorena Hickok across the country to talk to teachers, workers, farmers, and the unemployed during 1933 and 1934 and report back what she found. Hickok's heart-wrenching stories of North Dakota farmers during this time may be found in Hickok, *One Third of a Nation*.

19. North Dakota Session Laws, 1933, 494–95.

20. Ibid.

21. Ibid., at §2. The anti-corporate farming law has always faced stiff opposition from corporations, and legal challenges continue to pop up from time to time. See *Asbury Hospital v. Cass County*, 326 U.S. 207 (1945) and *N. Dakota Farm Bureau, Inc. v. Stenehjem*, 333 F. Supp. 3d 900 (D. N.D. 2018). The law has been amended over the years, most notably in 1981 to allow family farmers to incorporate as "family farm corporations." However, the basic prohibition against corporations farming or owning farmland in North Dakota remains. There are now eight other states—South Dakota, Oklahoma, Iowa, Minnesota, Wisconsin, Nebraska, Missouri, and Kansas—that have some variant of an anti-corporate farming law. These laws have uniformly been upheld as constitutional, with the exception of when they discriminate against out-of-state owners.

22. Address by William Langer, incoming governor, before the North Dakota legislature (January 5, 1933), reprinted in 1933 ND House Journal 56.

23. Robinson, *History of North Dakota*, 405.

24. Vogel, "Law of Hard Times," 493n23.

25. Edward Converse Blackorby, *Prairie Populist: The Life and Times of Usher L. Burdick* (Bismarck: State Historical Society of North Dakota and North Dakota Institute for Regional Studies, 2001), 179.

26. Ibid., 185.

27. Ibid., 184.

28. This executive order was issued in March 1933. It is reprinted in Vogel, "Law of Hard Times," 509–10.

29. Walter C. Anhalt and Glenn H. Smith, "He Saved the Farm? Governor Langer and the Mortgage Moratoria," *North Dakota Quarterly* (Autumn 1976).

30. Robinson, *History of North Dakota*, 405.

31. The Farm Relief Bill was part of the massive Agriculture Adjustment Act, 48 Stat. 31.

CHAPTER 2: THE FIRST FARMER

1. See, generally, Michael Johnston Grant, *Down and Out on the Family Farm: Rural Rehabilitation in the Great Plains, 1929–1945* (Lincoln: University of Nebraska Press, 2002).

2. The Resettlement Administration lasted from 1935 to 1937, followed by the Farm Security Administration (1937–1946) and the Farmers Home Administration. The acronym "FmHA" was used from 1946 until 1994, when USDA reorganized under President Clinton. In 1994, the farm lending programs begun under FDR were folded into a Consolidated Farm Service Agency, which is generally called the Farm Service Agency or FSA.

3. Sidney Baldwin, *Poverty and Politics: The Rise and Decline of the Farm Security Administration* (Chapel Hill: University of North Carolina Press, 1968), 93.

4. Ibid., 90–91.

5. Ibid., 93.

6. Ibid., 103.

7. Ibid., 102.

8. Rexford Tugwell, "Resettlement to End Human Erosion," in *Agricultural Thought of the Twentieth Century*, ed. George McGovern (Indianapolis: Bobbs-Merrill, 1967), 208–16.

9. Ibid., 213–14.

10. Baldwin, *Poverty and Politics*, ix.

11. Ibid., 93.

12. Amity Shlaes, *The Forgotten Man: A New History of the Great Depression* (New York: HarperCollins, 2009), 256–57.

13. SERA was the acronym for the State Emergency Relief Administration in every state; each SERA received federal funds from FERA.

14. Milton Meltzer, *Dorothea Lange: A Photographer's Life* (New York: Farrar, Straus & Giroux, 1978), 92–100.

15. Ibid., 100.

16. Ibid., 101.

17. John Steinbeck, *The Grapes of Wrath* (New York: Penguin Classics, 2006), 307.

18. Baldwin, *Poverty and Politics*, 166.

19. Ibid., 29.

20. Today, USDA farm loan regulations require an individual borrower be the operator of "not larger than a family farm and the owner of the farm after the loan has closed." See, e.g., 7 CFR §762.120(j)(1). If the applicant is an "entity," there are elaborate requirements to impose linkage of individuals to that entity. See, e.g., 7 CFR §762(j)(2). USDA also requires that that "entity" be "authorized to be an operator of the farm in the state or states in which the farm is located," which is a reference to the anti-corporate farming laws that still exist in North Dakota and some other states (see note 21 to chapter 1 above). 7 CFR § 762(j)(2)(i).

21. Baldwin, *Poverty and Politics*, 250.

22. Ibid., 249.

23. Ibid., 252–53.

24. Jon Meacham and Tim McGraw, *Songs of America: Patriotism, Protest, and the Music that Made a Nation* (New York: Random House, 2019), 126.

25. Edward Steichen, ed., *The Bitter Years, 1935–1941: Rural America as Seen by the Photographers of the Farm Security Administration* (New York: Museum of Modern Art, distributed by Doubleday, 1962), iii.

26. The position had been created by an executive order of Jimmy Carter that set up a Presidential Consumer Affairs Council. Every member of his cabinet had to create a new position of Consumer Affairs Advisor. Executive Order 12160 of September 26, 1979.

27. Roberta Walburn, "Brash N.D. Farmer Battles Bureaucracy," *Minneapolis Tribune*, August 2, 1981.

28. Even today, many farmers remember the days of parity as good ones. And even though parity is no longer the governing principle of farm bills, Congress still

requires USDA to calculate and publish parity for many crops using the original formula based on 1910–1919 values and also under an amended version
with a rolling base of the prior ten years. See 7 CFR Part 5 (7 CFR
§§5.1–5.6).

29. Prior to 1948, parity was measured by comparison to the base years of 1909 to
1914. Source: U.S. Department of Agriculture, Economic Research Service,
Bulletin #485, "History of Agricultural Price-Support and Adjustment
Programs, 1933–84," 3. Hereinafter ERS 1933–84 Report.

30. *Perry v. Block*, 694 F. 2d 121 (1982), the appellate decision, is the most enduring
legacy of Chuck Perry's battles with USDA. It has been cited as authority in more
than 680 cases involving how to measure federal agencies' compliance with the
FOIA.

31. Al Gustin, *Farm Byline: Reflections on North Dakota Agriculture, 1974–2013*
(Bismarck: Smoky Water Press, 2013), 11.

32. Clifton B. Lattrell, "The Russian Wheat Deal—Hindsight v. Foresight," Federal
Reserve Bank of St. Louis, October 1973, 3.

33. Scot A. Stradley, *The Broken Circle: An Economic History of North Dakota*
(Grand Forks: Bureau of Business and Economic Research, University of North
Dakota, 1993), 183.

34. Seth King, "Farm Income in 1978 Put at 2d-Highest," *New York Times*, January 25,
1979.

35. Jerome E. Johnson, "North Dakota Farmland Values and Rentals," *Farm Research*
42, no. 1 (Jul/Aug 1986), 26, https://library.ndsu.edu/ir/bitstream/handle
/10365/5917/farm_42_01_06.pdf.

36. May Peters, Suchada Langley, and Paul Westcott, "Agricultural Commodity
Price Spikes in the 1970s and 1990s: Valuable Lessons for Today," United States
Department of Agriculture, Economic Research Service, https://www.ers.usda
.gov/amber-waves/2009/march/agricultural-commodity-price-spikes-in-the
-1970s-and-1990s-valuable-lessons-for-today/.

37. Frazier's bill would have created a federal agency to buy 90 percent of the nation's
wheat, corn, and cotton. It died a quick death in the Senate committee. USDA,
ERS, Ag. Info. Bull. 485, History of Agricultural Price-Support and Adjustment
Programs 1933–84, 2 ("ERS—1933–84 Report").

38. The CCC was created by Executive Order 6340 on October 17, 1933 (ERS 1933–84 Report, 6). The CCC has become a mainstay of many subsequent farm programs, and it was the source of President Trump's multibillion-dollar payments to farmers hurt by the tariff wars with China in 2018, 2019, and 2020.

39. ERS Report 1933–84, 10.

40. A good description of the corporate campaign to end the parity programs can be found in Mark Ritchie, "The Loss of Our Family Farms: Inevitable Results or Conscious Policies?" (published by League of Rural Voters in March 1979), https://www.iatp.org/documents/loss-our-family-farms-inevitable-results-or -conscious-policies.

41. USDA Census of Agriculture Historical Archive, *1969 Census of Agriculture*, chapter 2, "Farms: Number, Use of Land, Size of Farm," http://lib-usda-05.server farm.cornell.edu/usda/agcensusimages/1969/02/02/1969-02-02.pdf.

42. William P. Browne and John Dinse, "The Emergence of the American Agriculture Movement, 1977–1979," *Great Plains Quarterly* (Fall 1985), 225.

43. Ibid., 227.

44. Ibid.

45. Jo Freeman, "Farmers Occupy the Mall—Winter 1979," jofreeman.com/photos /Farmers79/Farmers.html.

46. Daniel Roth, "The Ray Kroc of Pigsties," *Forbes*, October 13, 1997.

47. A transcript of this October 1979 episode of *60 Minutes* is included in the congressional transcript (see footnote 48 below).

48. *Farmers Home Administration Loan Programs: Hearing Before a Subcommittee of the Committee of Appropriations*, U.S. Senate, 96th Cong., 1st Sess. (1979).

49. Roberto A. Ferdman, "The Decline of the Small American Family Farm in One Chart," *Washington Post*, September 16, 2014.

50. Tom Philpott, *Perilous Bounty: The Looming Collapse of American Farming and How We Can Prevent It* (New York: Bloomsbury, 2020), 178–79.

CHAPTER 3: COTTONWOOD HAVEN

1. U.S. v. Perry, 706 F. 2d 278 (8th Cir., 1983), at 279.

2. See S. Rep. No. 96-253, 96th Cong., 1st Sess. (1979).

3. "Overview: Farmers Home Administration 1979," USDA, available on Google Books, 2–4. Hereinafter "1979 Overview."

4. Ibid., 6–9.

5. Ibid., 3.

6. "A Brief History of Farmers Home Administration," reprint from the collection of the University of Michigan Library, published 1979, revised March 1984, digitized by University of Michigan Library, available at lib.umich.edu, 10. Hereinafter "Brief History of FmHA."

7. "1979 Overview," 5.

8. Ibid., 3.

9. Ibid., 4.

10. Letter from Senator Melcher of Montana to one of Tom's lawyers in 1981: "Art Lund [the state FmHA director] has told my office that should the present county supervisor choose to be transferred, there is no other employee of the Farmers Home Administration in Montana who would agree to serve at Wolf Point."

CHAPTER 4: CUT, SLASH, CHOP

1. David Stockman, *The Triumph of Politics: Why the Reagan Revolution Failed* (New York: Harper & Row, 1986), 1.

2. Ibid., 2.

3. Ibid.

4. Ibid.

5. Ibid., 74.

6. Ibid., 53.

7. Kimberly Amadeo, "US Budget Deficit by Year Compared to GDP, Debt Increase, and Events," *The Balance*, updated October 08, 2020, https://www .thebalance.com/us-deficit-by-year-3306306.

8. Stockman, *Triumph of Politics*, 11.

9. Ibid.

10. Ibid., 153.

11. Ibid., 53–54.

12. Unemployment rates hovered between 7 percent and 8 percent from the summer of 1980 to the fall of 1981. By December 1982, it had reached 10.8 percent. Richard C. Auxier, "Reagan's Recession," Pew Research Center, December 14, 2010.

13. Stockman, *Triumph of Politics*, 54.

14. Sidney Blumenthal, "David Stockman: The President's Cutting Edge," *New York Times*, March 15, 1981.

15. Stockman, *Triumph of Politics*, 32.

16. Ibid.

17. Meg McSherry Breslin, "Charles B. Shuman, 92, Advocate for Farmers," *Chicago Tribune*, October 27, 1999.

18. *Time*, September 5, 1965.

19. "Brief History of FmHA," 31.

20. Ibid.

21. Mont. Code Ann. Section 45-8-211: "A person commits the offense of cruelty to animals if without justification the person knowingly or negligently subjects an animal to mistreatment or neglect by:... failing to provide an animal in the person's custody with... food and water of sufficient quantity and quality to sustain the animal's normal health."

22. "U.S. Increasing Pressure to Collect on Delinquent Farm Loans," *Washington Post*, February 4, 1982, A5.

23. Don Kendall, "Farm foreclosures expected to rise," *St. Cloud Times*, November 21, 1981.

24. Ward Sinclair, "FmHA staff pressured to collect loans," *Clarion Ledger*, February 6, 1982.

25. 97th Cong., 1st Sess., S. Res. 257, December 11, 1981, Cong. Rec. Senate at pages 30853–55.

26. Randy Bradbury, "New FmHA Head Set for Challenge: FmHA Head Cites Goals," *Bismarck Tribune*, April 27, 1981, 1–2.

27. Ibid.

CHAPTER 5: THE STARVE OUT

1. Gregory Jaynes, "U.S. Farmers Said to Face Worst Year Since 1930's," *New York Times*, March 28, 1982, nytimes.com/1982/03/28/us/us-farmers-said-to-face-worst-year-since-1930-s.html.

2. Neil Harl, *The Farm Debt Crisis of the 1980s* (Iowa City: Iowa State University Press, 1990), 28, Table 2.1, "Total Farm Debt Outstanding, Jan. 1, 1950–1987."

CHAPTER 6: A LITTLE BIT OF NOTHING

1. National Farmers Union newsletter, April 30, 1982, page 4. On file with author.

2. "Farm, Ranch Bankruptcies Rising in Tri-state Region," *Bismarck Tribune*, May 3, 1982.

3. Don Kendall, "Value of U.S. Farmland Declines," *Bismarck Tribune*, May 13, 1982.

4. "Value of Nation's Farms Down; First Drop Since 1954," *Des Moines Register*, January 14, 1983.

5. Rob Swenson, "Farmers Told Not to Give In to Government Agencies," *Sioux Empire*, April 27, 1982.

CHAPTER 7: THE ORGANIZERS

1. Chapter 156 of the 1933 Session Laws of North Dakota. It is still law. See N.D.C.C. Section 32-19-20, *Notice Before Foreclosure,* and N.D.C.C. Section 32-19-21, *Content of Notice*: "The notice of foreclosure shall contain . . . (3) The amount due to bring the installments of principal and interest current as of a date specified . . . (4) A statement that if the amount due is not paid within thirty days from the mailing or service of the notice, proceedings will be commenced to foreclose the mortgage."

2. Tom O'Connell and Steve Trimble, Twentieth Century Radicalism in Minnesota Oral History Project: Interview with Clarence Sharp, February 24, 1977, http://collections.mnhs.org/cms/display.php?irn=10444484.

3. See William C. Pratt, "Using History to Make History? Progressive Farm Organizing During the Farm Revolt of the 1980s," *Annals of Iowa* 55 (Winter 1996),

doi.org/10.17077/0003-4827.9988, for a detailed overview of the organizations and key people that were involved in this movement. Pratt believes this coalition might have been the "the last significant progressive rural insurgency in American history."

4. Stuart Taylor Jr., "Legal Aid for the Poor: Reagan's Longest Brawl," *New York Times*, June 8, 1984.

5. Vincent Coppola, *The Sicilian Judge: Anthony Alaimo, an American Hero* (Macon, GA: Mercer University Press, 2008), 114–15.

6. *Williams v. Butz*, No. 176-153 (S.D. Ga. Oct. 7, 1977). The law in question was 42 USC Sec. 1475.

7. Curry v. Block, 541 F. Supp. 506, at 510–11 (S.D. Ga. 1982).

8. Coppola, *Sicilian Judge*, 13–18.

9. *Curry*, 515–16, quoting *Paelo v. Farmers Home Administration*, 361 F. Supp. 1320 (D. D.C. 1973).

10. *Moskiewicz v. Block*, September 7, 1982; *U.S. v. Hamrick*, November 15, 1982; *Rowell v. Secretary of Agriculture*, December 6, 1982; *Neighbors v. Block*, December 15, 1982.

CHAPTER 8: PROBLEM CASE

1. Adapted from Sid Behrman, *The Lawyer Joke Book* (New York: Barnes and Noble Books, 1991).

2. The term "pin money" came over from England, where it meant money given to married women by their husbands to run the household, including buying pins for sewing purposes. But in rural North Dakota, the women weren't *given* pin money; they *earned* it. Ironically, these farm women thought the origin of the expression was that female farmers safety-pinned their hard-earned $1, $5, and $10 bills inside their bodices as they left town for home.

CHAPTER 9: THE FARMER'S LAWYER

1. *Depression in Rural America*, National Farmers Union (May 1982). The report states that copies of the transcripts and materials from the nine hearings are housed at the Western Historical Collections at the University of Colorado, Boulder.

2. *Depression in Rural America*, 29–33, appendix I, "Assessment—Financial Conditions of Farm Borrowers, American Bankers Association, March 1982."

3. *Depression in Rural America*, 5.

4. Dale Lyon, Kansas, quoted in *Depression in Rural America*, 5.

5. "A Message to the American People from America's Family Farmers," special order of business of the 80th annual National Farmers Union convention, three unnumbered pages prior to page 1.

6. The J. Roderick MacArthur Foundation was started in 1978 to support civil rights. J. Roderick was the son of the MacArthurs who founded the massive John D. and Catherine T. MacArthur Foundation famous for the "genius" grants.

7. Within a year, the stacks of clippings had become a bound publication that Mark captioned "AMMO: Information and Analysis to Defend Our Farm Communities." Starting in early 1983, AMMO came every other month or so, with hundreds of scrupulously organized pages on farm crisis news, action strategies to stop foreclosures, economics, history, legal rights, organizing assistance, legislative updates, and educational materials, with a $20 annual subscription or $40 for express delivery.

8. *The WPA Guide to 1930s North Dakota* (Federal Writers Project, 1938; reprinted with new introduction, Bismarck: State Historical Society of North Dakota, 1990).

9. Mni Waken Oyate means "People of the Spirit Lake." Tokio, North Dakota, is a town on the Spirit Lake Reservation. Some say it was named by a railroad official based on the Dakota phrase *to ko*, or "center of the region"; others say it was named after Tokyo, Japan.

CHAPTER 10: HERE ONCE THE EMBATTLED FARMERS STOOD

1. Skip Seiser, "Farmers' Group Fighting FmHA," on file with author.

2. Lou Anne was interviewed in 1990 for the book *Breaking Hard Ground: Stories of the Minnesota Farm Advocates* by Dianna Hunter (Duluth, MN: Holy Cow! Press, 1990). Lou Anne is quoted as saying, "I didn't know much about FmHA because Wayne [Lou Anne's husband] and I aren't FmHA borrowers, but I heard

there was a guy in Montana, named Tom Nichols, who had filed a lawsuit against FmHA. I called Tom Nichols, and he told me where to get information. I sent for the Code of Federal Regulations that governs FmHA. They were absolutely Greek to me! But I just kept reading and reading, and every time I was in an FmHA office, I asked a lot of questions." Hunter, *Breaking Hard Ground*, 51.

3. Steven E. Shay, *"Here Once the Embattled Farmers Stood": The Rise and Fall of the Montana Freemen*, PhD diss., copyright 2008 Steven E. Shay, Washington State University Department of History. The quotation "get big or get out" is at page 49.

4. AN 580 Memo.

5. Lorna Thackeray, "Foreclosure Fight Turns Dream into Nightmare," *Billings Gazette*, April 25, 1982.

6. James Brooke, "Freeman Depended on Subsidies," *New York Times*, April 30, 1996.

7. Thackeray, "Foreclosure Fight."

8. Ibid.

9. Shay, *"Here Once the Embattled Farmers Stood,"* 55.

10. Shay, page 57, quoting "Brief in Support of Supplemental Motions to Dismiss," page 20. This brief would have been filed in the criminal case accusing him of conversion, filed in 1984 which the federal judge dismissed because FmHA accused him of conversion when it didn't have a lien on the wool or the crop. See also "Bitter Harvest," ABC, 20/20, March 24, 1983, #311, pp. 11–12 of transcript published by Journal Graphics (interview of Ralph Clark by Geraldo Rivera).

11. Shay, *"Here Once the Embattled Farmers Stood,"* 60.

12. Ibid., 54.

13. Years later, I learned that the woman at the Fairview Community Center "came out" in 1993 as a Freemen supporter and a member of the Posse Comitatus. Shay, *"Here Once the Embattled Farmers Stood,"* 173.

14. See Shay, pages 44–243, for a thorough discussion of the Clarks' farm history and encounters with the federal government. Nicholas Munion, the local prosecutor who stood up against the Freemen, is covered in *Profiles in Courage for Our Time*, ed. Caroline Kennedy (New York: Hyperion Books, 2002).

15. Brooke, "Freeman Depended on Subsidies."

16. A fascinating insider account of the Freemen occupation of the Clark ranch and the 81-day standoff was written by an undercover FBI agent and published in 1998. Dale and Connie Jakes with Clint Richmond, *False Prophets: The Firsthand Account of a Husband-Wife Team Working for the FBI and Living in Deepest Cover with the Montana Freemen* (Los Angeles: Dove Books, 1998).

17. Shay, *"Here Once the Embattled Farmers Stood,"* 239. Ralph Clark passed away on August 6, 2020. His obituary did not mention the standoff.

CHAPTER 11: TIME TO MAKE SOME LAW

1. State Ex Rel. Olson v. Maxwell, 259 N.W. 2d 621 (ND 1977).

2. In the Interest, of G.H., a Child, 218 N.W. 2d 441 (ND 1974).

3. Ring v. Grand Forks Public School District, 483 F. Supp. 272 (D. N.D. 1980).

4. Unbeknownst to me, in the twelve years since I had graduated from NYU Law School, *Goldberg v. Kelly* had become one of the most important Supreme Court cases in modern times. See David Frum, *How We Got Here: The 70's; the Decade That Brought You Modern Life—for Better or Worse* (New York: Basic Books, 2000), 228–29. Upon retirement, Justice Brennan said that *Goldberg v. Kelly* was the most important ruling of the 1,360 opinions he had authored during his career.

5. *Goldberg*, 397 U.S. 254, at 264 (1970).

6. *Goldberg*, 397 U.S. 254, at 271 (1970).

7. United States v. Kimbell Foods, Inc., 440 U.S. 715 (1979).

8. *Kimbell Foods*, 440 U.S. 715, at 735 (1979).

9. *Goldberg*, 397 U.S. 254, at 264 (1970).

10. See unpublished Memorandum and Order, Hudson v. FmHA, No. GC-79-216-K-0, U.S. District Court, Northern District of Missouri, September 22, 1980, 6–8. See also Hudson v. FmHA, 654 F. 2d 334 (5th Cir. 1981).

11. Decades later, the extent of FmHA's discrimination against Black farmers was demonstrated in the *Pigford v. Glickman* litigation that was followed by the

"Black Farmers Settlement" (also called *Pigford II*). In these cases, the total paid to Black farmers who had shown race discrimination by USDA in these settlements was over $2 billion. See T. Cowan and J. Feder, "The Pigford Cases: USDA Settlement of Discrimination Suits by Black Farmers," *Congressional Research Service*, May 29, 2013, available at crs.gov (RS20430).

CHAPTER 12: EXHAUSTION

1. Associated Press, "Burdick Backs Loan Moratorium," *Bismarck Tribune*, September 29, 1982.

2. "Farm-Lending Agency Attracts Dispute," *Grand Forks Herald*, February 14, 1982.

3. Richard Woodley, "Going Under," *Life*, November 1982.

4. Source: Stan Weston, an employee of FmHA, quoted in an AP story printed in the *Grand Forks Herald*, November 27, 1982.

5. All dialogue is from McCabe hearing transcript, July 21, 1982, held in the District Office, Bismarck, ND.

6. See, e.g., N.D.C.C. 41-09-08 (9-108), Section 1: "[A] description of personal . . . property is sufficient, regardless of whether the description is specific, if the description *reasonably identifies what is described*" (emphasis added).

CHAPTER 13: COMPETENCY OF COUNSEL

1. The reason for the disparate treatment was that some years back, FmHA had been sued by rural housing borrowers from Georgia, and Secretary Bob Bergland, appointed by President Carter, had agreed to follow the law in a formal court settlement. See Vickers v. Bergland, Civ. No. 77-0355 (D. D.C. 1973).

2. My father practiced law in North Dakota for more than fifty years without once representing a for-profit corporation.

3. The analysis I wrote and that was inserted into the reply brief was successful in convincing the court that there was a financial crisis, despite Block's assertion that the agriculture economy was fine. See Judge Flannery's August 29, 1983,

decision in Kjeldahl v. Block, 579 F. Supp. 1130 (D. D.C.), at pages 1135–38. A total of $600 million in emergency loans was eventually released by USDA, but I was never paid.

CHAPTER 14: BITTER HARVEST

1. In 1982, North Dakota was the least likely place in the United States where a murder or other violent crime might occur. Source: disastercenter.com/crime /1982 Rate and Rank of Crime and Imprisonment by US States.html.

2. The phrase "seed cap" is used in North Dakota for the kind of cap called a ballcap elsewhere. The origin of the term is that seed companies gave out these caps with their advertising on them. Of course the caps also carry advertisements for farm machinery, brands of barbed wire, pesticides, and even (today) for presidential candidates, but they are still called seed caps.

3. Interview, Tom Nichols. This woman was one of the participants at the Montana Freemen standoff decades later.

4. James Corcoran, *Bitter Harvest: Gordon Kahl and the Posse Comitatus: Murder in the Heartland* (Fargo: North Dakota Institute for Regional Studies, 2005), 22–26.

5. Ibid., 25.

6. Ibid., 40–48.

7. Ibid., 48–49.

8. Ibid., 49–50.

9. Ibid., 90.

10. Within a few years, a number of North Dakota farmers were inmates at the North Dakota Penitentiary after having followed that advice and being prosecuted for making threats against members of the judiciary.

CHAPTER 15: IF WE EAT, YOU SHALL EAT

1. Sheheke and his wife, Yellow Corn, accompanied Lewis and Clark to Washington, where they met President Jefferson and the elite of Washington, D.C. They were unable to return to their Village until September 22, 1809. See Tracy Potter, *Sheheke: Mandan Indian Diplomat; The Story of White Coyote*

Thomas Jefferson and Lewis and Clark (Helena, MT, and Washburn, ND: Farcountry Press and Fort Mandan Press, 2003), 107–63.

2. Lewis and Clark's journals are replete with references to purchases of food, generally in exchange for metal items used by the Indians for tools (hoes), pots, sewing, weapons (clubs), and other implements.

3. James P. Ronda, *Lewis and Clark Among the Indians* (Lincoln: University of Nebraska Press, 1984), 46.

4. Clay S. Jenkinson, ed., *A Vast and Open Plain: The Writings of the Lewis and Clark Expedition in North Dakota, 1804–1806* (Bismarck: State Historical Society of North Dakota, 2003), 484.

5. Ibid., 417.

6. Ronda, *Lewis and Clark Among the Indians*, 46.

7. Map of United States: "All Farmer Loan Programs Percent Delinquent, Report 616 as of 3-31-83," obtained through discovery in Coleman, Defendants' Exhibit 28.

8. According to the 1980 Census, Burleigh County, where the Folmers lived, was 97.4 percent white. Morton County, where I'd gone to high school, shared a southern border with the Standing Rock Sioux Reservation, but it was still 98.85 percent white. *Statistical Abstract of North Dakota* (Grand Forks: University of North Dakota Press, 1983), 20–21.

9. For more on the history of the Three Affiliated Tribes, readers may wish to explore books such as Roy W. Meyer, *The Village Indians of the Upper Missouri: The Mandans, Hidatsas, and Arikaras* (Lincoln: University of Nebraska Press, 1977); Tracy Potter, *Sheheke: Mandan Indian Diplomat; The Story of White Coyote Thomas Jefferson and Lewis and Clark* (Helena, MT, and Washburn, ND: Farcountry Press and Fort Mandan Press, 2003); Elizabeth Fenn, *Encounters at the Heart of the World: A History of the Mandan People* (New York: Farrar, Straus & Giroux, 2014); and Paul VanDevelder, *Coyote Warrior: One Man, Three Tribes, and the Trial That Forged a Nation* (New York: Little, Brown, 2004). Raymond Cross, the preeminent legal scholar of the MHA nation, wrote "Keeping the American Indian Rancher on the Land: A Socio-Legal Analysis of the Rise and the Demise of American Indian Ranching on the Northern Great Plains," *Washburn Law Journal* 49 (2010), 745–80. Two massive class action

lawsuits redressed failure of the federal government to honor its fiduciary duties as to funds held in Indian Trust Accounts (the "Cobell" litigation) and discrimination by USDA in agricultural loans (the "Keepseagle" litigation).

10. That paper is available among the 1970 papers of Sarah Vogel, in the Sarah Vogel Collection at the North Dakota Archives.

11. The surname Crow's Heart is variously spelled. On Lester and Sharon's affidavit, their surname was spelled "Crows Heart."

12. Fenn, *Encounters at the Heart of the World*, 37–38 and 102–6.

13. *Cattle Queen of Montana* was the last of many movies that Reagan watched while he was president. In this 1954 Western, Reagan played the cowboy hero (he was really a federal undercover agent) who rescues Barbara Stanwyck, the "cattle queen," whose ranch is on homestead land recently taken from the Indians. The dispossessed Indians were being "stirred up" by land speculators who want them to drive the cattle queen away. The movie does have one "good Indian" who is helpful to the whites. See diary entry for January 14, 1989, in *The Reagan Diaries*, ed. Douglas Brinkley (New York: HarperCollins, 2007), 689.

14. Clifford E. Trafzer, ed., *American Indians/American Presidents: A History* (Washington, D.C.: Smithsonian, 2009), 198–99. In December 1988, just before he left office, Reagan gave tribal leaders a twenty-minute audience during which he apologized.

15. He won the election and was elected as the Nonpartisan League floor leader of the House, where he "made a name for himself as a champion of small farmers." Curt Eriksmoen, *Did You Know That?*, vol. 3 ([Fargo, ND]: J & M. Printing, 2009), 87.

16. Robert Vogel left his children boxes of essays, stories, and recollections of his family, including this recollection of Memorial Day in Elbowoods in 1925. Some of the collection is housed at the North Dakota Archives, some at the author's home in Bismarck, North Dakota.

17. Universal Native American citizenship is now codified at 8 USC Section 1401(b). Notwithstanding this law, attempts at voter suppression of Native Americans have continued. Two recent federal voting rights cases by Native Americans against the State of North Dakota—*Brakebill v. Jaeger* and *Spirit Lake Tribe v. Jaeger*—were recently resolved in favor of tribal voters. Information on recent

voter suppression of Indians can be found at the Native American Rights Fund and Campaign Legal Center's websites: narf.org and campaignlegal.org.

18. See, e.g., Trafzer, *American Indians/American Presidents*, chapter 3 ("Dark Days: American Presidents and Native Sovereignty, 1880–1930," by Matthew S. Gilbert).

19. James Wilson, *The Earth Shall Weep: A History of Native America* (New York: Grove Press, 1998), 303–8.

20. Even one of the promised benefits to an Indian of allotment—citizenship and the consequent right to vote—was often illusory. In one case, Standing Rock Sioux Indians who had received allotments still needed to prove they were sufficiently "civilized" to vote in a 1919 county election in North Dakota. Swift v. Leach, 178 N.W. 437, at 438, 43 N.D. 437 (ND 1920).

21. See Trafzer, *American Indians/American Presidents*, chapter 4 ("From Full Citizenship to Self-Determination, 1930–75," by Duane Champagne).

22. Blackorby, *Prairie Populist*, 214–15.

23. All biographical details about Usher Burdick are from Blackorby, *Prairie Populist*.

24. Meyer, *Village Indians of the Upper Missouri*, 106–8.

25. VanDevelder, *Coyote Warrior*, 93.

26. Michael Lawson, *Dammed Indians Revisited: The Continuing History of the Pick-Sloan Plan and the Missouri River Sioux* (Pierre: South Dakota Historical Society Press, 2009), 18.

27. The Standing Rock Sioux (whose tribal lands straddled the border of South Dakota and North Dakota) and several South Dakota tribes were similarly threatened by the Oahe Dam. See Peter Carrels, *Uphill Against Water: The Great Dakota Water War* (Lincoln: University of Nebraska Press, 1999).

28. Senator Watkins is the principal villain in Louise Erdrich's 2020 novel, *The Night Watchman*, which is a fictionalized version of Erdrich's grandfather's fight to save the Turtle Mountain Band of Chippewa Indians from termination in the 1950s, at the same time that Senator Watkins was trying to terminate the tribal status of the Three Affiliated Tribes.

29. Trafzer, *American Indians/American Presidents*, 158–62.

30. Martin Cross is the father of Raymond Cross, the lawyer whose work is featured in *Coyote Warrior*.

31. VanDevelder, *Coyote Warrior*, 116–18. See, e.g., Lawson, *Dammed Indians*, 16–18, for a description of the vision for a Missouri Valley Authority, and its demise.

32. VanDevelder, *Coyote Warrior*, 132.

33. Ibid., 133–34. The violation of treaty rights would not be redressed until passage of the Three Affiliated Tribes Just Compensation Act as part of the Bureau of Reclamation Reform Bill in 1992, with the creation of a perpetual trust fund of $149.2 million, funded, fittingly, by the sale of electricity from Garrison Dam. Kent Conrad, a Democratic-NPL senator from North Dakota, was instrumental in getting the relief that had been omitted in the 1940s. By then, it was recognized that the 1949 law was illegal, as Representative Lemke had so passionately declared upon its adoption. See VanDevelder, *Coyote Warrior*, 238–39.

34. VanDevelder, *Coyote Warrior*, 133.

35. Edward C. Blackorby, *Prairie Rebel: The Public Life of William Lemke* (Lincoln: University of Nebraska Press, 1963), 278.

36. Fenn, *Encounters at the Heart of the World*, 323. A fur trader wrote in 1839 that the smallpox epidemic "very nearly annihilated the whole tribe" (page 328); a federal Indian agent said the upper Missouri country was "one great grave yard" (page 323).

37. The complete list of people displaced by the Garrison Dam flood can be found in VanDevelder, *Coyote Warrior*, 265–72.

38. VanDevelder, *Coyote Warrior*, 288n93.

39. Ibid., 191.

40. Lawson, *Dammed Indians Revisited*, xv.

CHAPTER 16: SPRINGING THE TRAP

1. Our optimism after the *Curry* case faded when USDA persuaded a series of judges that *Curry* was wrongly decided and that because Section 1981a was "permissive" due to use of the word "may," FmHA did not need to implement Section 1981a. These cases included Rowell v. Secretary of Agriculture,

No. 82-181-5 (M. D. Ala., December 6, 1982); Moskiewicz v. Block, No. 82-C-231 (W.D. Wisc., September 7, 1982); and United States v. Hamrick, No. 82-608-3 (So. Car., November 15, 1982). The *Hamrick* decision was reversed on August 2, 1983 (82-1013), by the Fourth Circuit.

2. See, e.g., "Suit Seeks to End 'Suffering,'" *Bismarck Tribune*, March 18, 1983; "Point of Suit Against FmHA Is to End 'Plain Suffering,'" *Grand Forks Herald*, March 17, 1983, B-1; "Suit Asks Leniency for N.D. Farmers," Minneapolis *Star Tribune*, March 16, 1983, 15B.

3. By the end of 1983, forty-seven cases had been filed against FmHA by farmers. See Ronald B. Taylor, "U.S. Foreclosing on Thousands of Farms: Hard Times, Aggressive Reagan Debt Collectors Jolt Homeowners," *Los Angeles Times*, December 25, 1983.

4. Corcoran, *Bitter Harvest*, 111.

5. Letter from Webb/Annear to Ms. Sheila Lieberman, Civil Division, Main Justice, Department of Justice, Washington, D.C. On file with the author, and obtained through a Freedom of Information Act request. The letter was cc'd to Brian Cody, Office of General Counsel, USDA, in Denver, Colorado.

CHAPTER 17: UNITY

1. Because there was no court reporter on the day of the hearing, the dialogue in this scene has been recreated from arguments in the plaintiffs' and defendants' briefs, journalistic accounts of the hearing, and the author's memory.

2. See, e.g., "Farm Loan Moratorium Criticized," *Grand Forks Herald*, February 15, 1983. In a story about USDA's adamant opposition to a bill that would have allowed deferrals, Secretary Block and Undersecretary Frank Naylor claimed that USDA was "using all procedures available to it, including repayment deferrals, to help tens of thousands of those struggling farmers."

3. Map of United States; "All Farmer Loan Programs Percent Delinquent, Report 616 as of 3-31-83," obtained through discovery in Coleman, Defendants' Exhibit 28.

4. See Jerome Johnson, North Dakota State University, Department of Agricultural Economics, "Downward Adjustment in Farmland Values Continued in 1983." Between November 1981 and November 1983, farmland values in North Dakota declined by 7.5 percent (page 1 of report). Further, 40 percent of the farmland

sold in North Dakota during 1983 was due to foreclosure or sale of land to reduce debt (page 6). Report on file with author.

5. OMB, Budget Details, 1983, 280 and 281.

CHAPTER 18: THE DEAD CHICKEN ARGUMENT

1. Harl, *The Farm Debt Crisis of the 1980s*, 21.

2. Ibid., 23.

3. Harl, *Farm Debt Crisis of the 1980s*, 25.

4. Neil Harl, "Agricultural Law: Debtor Credit Relations Symposium Issue, Introduction: A Financial Revolution in Agriculture," *North Dakota Law Review* 60 (1984), 389.

5. Ibid., 389–90.

6. Harl, *Farm Debt Crisis of the 1980s*, 29.

7. Ibid., 39.

8. *Uffda* is a Norwegian word commonly used in North Dakota, roughly equivalent to "Oh, shit," but it can be used in polite company. Even my grandmother occasionally used "uffda" when we misbehaved. *Uffda feda* is another Norwegian phrase, but that one was not to be used in polite company—it is equivalent to the F-bomb.

9. Corcoran, *Bitter Harvest*, 22.

10. Fargo *Forum*, May 12, 1983.

11. In the May 5 order, Judge Van Sickle said, "As to the plaintiffs' arguments regarding the built-in bias of using the state director or other district directors as hearing officers, the court does not have sufficient evidence to conclude that such directors had an active role in the prior decision, and hence does not require any alteration although it will further consider this issue in its order for a permanent injunction." This was not an invitation for further arguments about the use of ALJs, but I felt the phrase "sufficient evidence" was an opening wide enough for me to enter.

12. All the direct quotations from the status conference come from the court transcript, taken at the United States Courthouse, Bismarck, North Dakota, May 23, 1983.

13. FmHA Third Quarter Report on Farmer Program Loans, covering October 1982 to June 1983. On file with author. Despite these stupendous numbers, FmHA had not come close to achieving the goals set out by Stockman: "By the end of 1983, the number of delinquent borrowers in Agriculture Farmers Home Administration (FmHA) programs will be reduced by 70,000, a 20% reduction, through more aggressive collection action and faster resolution of delinquent accounts." Source: FY83 Reagan Budget Proposal (Themes and Management Goals, Debt Collection, 279–80).

CHAPTER 19: THE FRONT STEPS OF THE COURTHOUSE

1. There is no transcript of this hearing; the dialogue is recalled from memory and from the summary of the argument in the later decision of the North Dakota Supreme Court.

2. Lynn Boughey replaced Brian Faller, Judge Van Sickle's clerk who worked on the preliminary injunction order. Typically, federal law clerks are law school graduates with stellar credentials who serve one- or two-year terms as district court clerks before they move up to work as a clerk for a higher court judge, or go to some other legal job. Brian Faller had been offered a position as a clerk for an Eighth Circuit judge.

3. They were Gary and Rosemary Barrett (Iowa), Richard and Betty Harmon (Missouri), Larry and Nancy Robertson (Missouri), and Ross and Maureen Wade (Arkansas). Dale did all the work to find and prepare them.

CHAPTER 20: NOTHING BUT THE TRUTH

1. Richard Woodley, "North Dakota Lawyer Sarah Vogel Fights to Save Farms in the Midwest," *Life*, November 1982, 158.

2. All trial dialogue comes from the *Coleman v. Block* court transcript taken at the United States Courthouse, Bismarck, North Dakota, September 20, 1983.

3. "Judicial notice" is a doctrine whereby a judge can accept as facts certain matters which are known to be true to a veritable certainty by consulting sources of indisputable accuracy, thereby relieving one part of the burden of producing evidence to prove these facts. See Steven H. Gifis, *Barron's Law Dictionary*, 3rd ed. (Hauppauge, NY: Barron's Educational Series, 1991), 259. Examples

would be public laws and public records, the time of sunrise or sunset, or known historic facts. An FmHA regulation would fall squarely within the type of record as to which a court could take "judicial notice."

4. The questioning of Glen Binegar began on September 19. His testimony from the nineteenth and the twentieth has been combined for continuity.

5. 7 CFR 1863.4, "Servicing Delinquent Taxes," says, "If the delinquent tax is not paid and the borrower comes to the office with proceeds for application on the FmHA account secured by the real estate, the county office personnel will endeavor to get the borrower to use the proceeds to pay the delinquent tax." The Folmers' emergency loans were collateralized by both chattel and real estate collateral, so if taxes were delinquent at the time of acceleration, the taxes should have been paid *before* funds were applied to FmHA debts.

6. Affidavit Appendix, pp. B-9 to B-14, at B-10 to B-11. Docket No. 7, filed on March 28, 1983.

7. Many years later, I read about the "Milgram" experiments in which unwitting test subjects were asked by an authority figure to increase the level of electrical shocks to test subjects until the test subject (an actor) appeared to face serious injury or death. Reflecting on the treatment of my clients in the early 1980s, I began to believe that the authoritarian, top-down scheme of control of FmHA (Block and Shuman in Washington, Leet at the state office, and subordinates at district and county offices) played a role in the cruelty of district directors like Binegar and Ottmar. They were cogs in a machine and could not afford to have any sympathy for farmers selected for "elimination." Possibly, Annear was under the same authoritarian pressure emanating from Reagan's Department of Justice and Office of Management and Budget. If so, it was a Milgram experiment with real-life consequences for thousands of farm families like the Folmers.

8. Judge Van Sickle grew up on a small farm near Minot, North Dakota, and obtained a combined college and law degree from the University of Minnesota between 1935 and 1941. In 1941, he enlisted in the Marine Corps, leaving as a combat-hardened captain in 1946. He began practicing law in Minot in 1947 and was elected twice to the North Dakota legislature, in 1957 and 1959. In October 1971, he was nominated by President Nixon to be a United States District Court judge, receiving support from both the Republican and the Democratic–Nonpartisan League senator from North Dakota. He was sworn in in December 1971, without opposition. See Ardell Tharaldson, *Patronage: Histories and Biographies of North Dakota's Federal Judges* (Bismarck: North

Dakota Branch of the Historical Society of the United States Courts in the Eighth Circuit and Northern Lights Press, 2002), 99–114. The Uniform Commercial Code was adopted in every state including North Dakota by the 1960s, and UCC legal issues would often have come up during his years in private practice and as a judge.

CHAPTER 21: WOULDN'T BILL LANGER BE PROUD

1. Decades later, I met Brian Cody, the Office of General Counsel attorney in Denver who was assigned to North Dakota and other Midwestern states. He ruefully told me he'd also celebrated the national injunction when he heard the news. His office was filled with stacks of farmers' FmHA files that reached the ceiling on all available walls. The work he'd need to do to get those cases to U.S. attorneys for foreclosures was beyond his capacity, and he didn't like to do foreclosures. "I was happy for you, and for me!"

2. Ward Sinclair, "FmHA Foreclosures Affected, Class-Action Status Granted to Distressed Farmers," *Washington Post*, November 1, 1983.

3. Ibid.

4. "Farmers Seek FmHA Ruling Clarification," *Grand Forks Herald*, November 3, 1983.

5. Agnes Geelan was North Dakota's first woman mayor and first woman state senator; she was nominated by the NPL to run for Congress in 1948. Eight years later she was endorsed again for Congress, this time by the merged Democratic-NPL Party, which she had helped to create. She was a friend and ally of my grandfather Frank A. Vogel, and she served for many years with my father on the NPL executive committee. The state's foremost expert on the political life and times of William Langer, she wrote *The Dakota Maverick: The Political Life of William Langer*. Agnes died in 1993 at age ninety-seven.

CHAPTER 22: DISCOVERY

1. Every Court of Appeal monitored the length of time cases lingered on the dockets of the district courts and viewed courts with cases that languished for longer than average periods as warranting oversight. By quickly eliminating a number of foreclosures, the clerks knew that their statistics could be improved. Moreover, criminal cases (which were guaranteed a "speedy trial" by the U.S. Constitution)

always had higher precedence on a court's calendar. It's likely that every district court judge and district court clerk who received this packet of decisions from the clerk of court of North Dakota reacted with gratitude and promptly dismissed the cases, with or without motions from the farmers' lawyers.

2. Gail Hand, "GF Attorney Relaxes After FmHA Win," *Grand Forks Herald*, February 19, 1984.

CHAPTER 23: THE BIBLICAL INJUNCTION

1. See Coleman v. Block, docket 113, filed January 30, 1984, "Motion to Show Cause Why Defendants' Temporary Compliance Procedures Should Not Be Cancelled by Court Order," plaintiffs' exhibit A (memo from Shuman), at pages 1–2.

2. Marcia Zarley Taylor, "Lawsuits Buy Time for Some FmHA Borrowers," *Farm Journal*, January 1984, 10.

3. "Pretermination Notice for Farmer Program Borrowers," USDA, December 20, 1983, attached as exhibit to "Motion to Show Cause Why Defendants Temporary Compliance Procedures Should Not Be Cancelled by Court Order," docket 113, *Coleman v. Block.*

4. Associated Press, February 19, 1984, *Bradenton Herald*, A-8. A quarter of a million farmers were in the forty-four states that were part of the national class order, but soon the lawyers for the states that had pending class actions asked leave to join as well, increasing the grand total by thousands more.

5. *Coleman v. Block*, 580 F. Supp. 194 (D. N.D. 1984), at 196.

6. Ibid., 203.

7. 2 Timothy 2:6.

8. *Coleman*, at 203.

9. Ibid., see footnotes 54 and 55 in the *Coleman* decision.

10. *Coleman*, at 201.

11. Ibid., at 200, and footnote 38, citing the trial transcript.

12. Taylor, "Lawsuits Buy Time."

CHAPTER 24: THERE IS ONE BRIGHT SPOT WHERE THE PEOPLE RULE

1. Dr. Neil Harl was one agriculture economist who did see the farm crisis developing, but he was a notable exception. In 1990, Harl published a book titled *The Farm Debt Crisis of the 1980s* in which he said that the agriculture economist community hadn't even recognized that there was an emerging ag crisis until after 1984—by then I'd already won the national permanent Coleman injunction, and the tractorcades of 1978 and 1979 were a distant memory.

2. See, generally, Harl, *Farm Debt Crisis*, which covers the intra–Republican Party process that led up to the adoption of Reagan's 1984 Debt Adjustment Program.

3. See Ibid., 167.

4. Ibid., 243.

5. Ibid., 243.

6. L. Roger Johnson, "The North Dakota Agriculture Mediation Service," *North Dakota Law Review* 70, 296.

7. The amounts before enhancements were Sarah, $78,336.50; Burt, $22,250; Allan, $12,707; Dale, $6,881; and my father, $3,900. Judge Van Sickle awarded an extra 30 percent to me for high risk, and an extra 20 percent for my father. That increased my fee award to $101,837 and my father's to $4,680. We also were to receive $17,278 in reimbursements for costs. *Coleman v. Block*, 589 F. Supp. 1411 (D. N.D. 1984).

8. Premachandra v. Mitts, 753 F.2d 635 (1985) (January 14, 1985).

9. Folmer v. State, 346 N.W.2d 731 (ND 1984).

10. The confiscatory price laws were used many times in negotiations. The Supreme Court issued additional decisions that applied the confiscatory price laws to foreclosures by the Farm Credit System and private lenders. See, e.g., Federal Land Bank v. Lillehaugen, 404 N.W. 2d 452 (ND 1987) and Prudential Ins. Co. v. Butts Farming Ass'n, 406 N.W.2d 662 (ND 1987).

11. The ten states that participated in the *Coleman* case also worked together on many other farm crisis issues. See Humphrey and Haukedahl, "An Attorney General's Role in the Farm Crisis: The Minnesota Experience," *New York University Review of Law & Social Change* 15 (1987), 295–312.

12. Charles W. Calomiris, James Stock, and R. Glenn Hubbard, "The Farm Debt Crisis and Public Policy," Brookings Institution, Brookings Papers on Economic Activity, no. 2, 1986. One of the resources for information on the crisis was Jerry Hansen, of the Center for Rural Affairs.

13. Associated Press, "Actress Taps Cloquet, Rural Roots for Movie," date unknown. On file with author.

14. *Reagan Diaries*, 360.

15. Ibid., 371.

16. Ibid., 271.

17. Harl, *Farm Debt Crisis*, 180.

18. Ibid., 171.

19. Ronald Reagan, Remarks on Signing the Agricultural Credit Act of 1987 Online by Gerhard Peters and John T. Woolley, The American Presidency Project, presidency.ucsb.edu/node/255214.

20. The gameboard was the creation of FLAG's Randi Roth.

EPILOGUE: STRENGTH FROM THE SOIL

1. Bruce M. Van Sickle, "The North Dakota Nine and the Family Farm," *Litigation* 25, no. 4 (Summer 1999), 49.

2. Ibid., 59.

3. David Montgomery, *Growing a Revolution: Bringing Our Soil Back to Life* (New York: W. W. Norton, 2017).

4. Philpott, *Perilous Bounty*, 178 (emphasis added).

INDEX

Note: Page numbers in *italics* refer to illustrations.

A NOTE ON THE AUTHOR

SARAH VOGEL is an attorney and former politician whose career has focused on family farmers and ranchers. Vogel was the first woman in U.S. history to be elected as a state commissioner of agriculture. In 2006, the American Agricultural Law Association awarded her its Distinguished Service Award for contributions to the field of agriculture law, and Willie Nelson honored her at Farm Aid's thirtieth anniversary in 2015 for her service to farmers. An in-demand speaker and a passionate advocate for Native American rights, Vogel lives in Bismarck, North Dakota.

www.sarahmvogel.com